A Sweet,
Separate
Intimacy

A SWEET, SEPARATE INTIMACY

৯৯

Women Writers of the American Frontier, 1800–1922

EDITED BY

Susan Cummins Miller

THE UNIVERSITY OF UTAH PRESS
Salt Lake City

"The Origin of the Robin: An Oral Allegory" and "The Forsaken Brother: A Chippewa Tale" reprinted by permission of Michigan State University Press from the 1997 edition of *Ojibwa Lodge Stories: Life on the Lake Superior Frontier,* edited by Philip P. Mason

Library of Congress Cataloging-in-Publication Data

A sweet separate intimacy : women writers of the American frontier, 1800–1922 / edited by Susan Cummins Miller.
    p. cm.
    Includes bibliographical references and index.
    ISBN 0-87480-637-2 (alk. paper) — ISBN 0-87480-638-0 (pbk. : alk. paper)
    1. Frontier and pioneer life—West (U.S.)—Literary collections. 2. Women pioneers—West (U.S.)—Literary collections. 3. Indians of North America—West (U.S.)—Literary collections. 4. American literature—West (U.S.)
5. American literature—Women authors. 6. West (U.S.)—Literary collections. I. Miller, Susan Cummins, 1949–

PS509.F7 S84 2000
810.8'09287'0978—dc21
                                                                    99-089836

For Jonathan, Jordan, and

Logan whose patience and humor

sustained me

CONTENTS

ACKNOWLEDGMENTS

I WOULD LIKE TO THANK Michigan State University Press for permission to include copyrighted material from the *Literary Voyager; or, Muzzeniegun,* by Henry Rowe Schoolcraft, reprinted as *Ojibwa Lodge Stories: Life on the Lake Superior Frontier,* edited and with an introduction by Philip P. Mason.

I am grateful to staff and volunteers of the following institutions for their help with this project: University of Arizona, Tucson, especially the Special Collections and Reference librarians; Hayden Library, Arizona State University; Tucson–Pima County Public Library; Arizona Historical Society, Tucson; Idaho Historical Society, Boise; Library of Congress, Washington, D.C.; Stanford University Libraries, Palo Alto, California; California Historical Society, San Francisco; Sharlot Hall Museum, Prescott, Arizona; Sosa-Carillo-Frémont House Museum, Tucson; and Mission San Diego de Alcala, San Diego, California.

Friends and family members offered continuous support, suggested writers who might be appropriate for this volume, and led field trips to isolated sites. Steve and Sue Moore took me to Mary Hallock Foote's home site in Boise Canyon and to the Idaho Historical Society. Peter Oberlindacher supplied background information on Foote. Lynda Gibson and Leesa Jacobson suggested Sharlot Mabridth Hall and Isabella Bird. Sean Murphy Stone sent information on Niles, California, and the Miami Valley, Ohio. Candy Rollins Young helped me explore Rose Hartwick Thorpe's neighborhood, the Presidio and Old Town San Diego. Mary Elizabeth Williams loaned an early copy of Elizabeth Bacon Custer's *Following the Guidon.* Justin and Marjorie Miller introduced me to the Southwest Museum; the Ramona Festival in Hemet, California; the California missions; and the back roads of the West. Carole Chapman, librarian at De Anza College, California, did preliminary Internet research on the Cary sisters, Milicent Washburn Shinn, Ina Coolbrith, Frances Dana Gage, and Rose Hartwick Thorpe. Anne and John Chapman facilitated a research trip to Stanford University and created a Writers' Corner at Lake Almanor, California. Jim and Andi Miller introduced me to Powells Bookstore, Portland, Oregon. Patricia Miller aided my research of San Francisco writers. Peggy Miller offered moral support. Susan Armitage and Margaret K. Brady graciously reviewed the manuscript; Armitage also suggested including Hispanic author María Amparo Ruiz de Burton. Susan Emory helped type the manuscript, and Steve Kennedy solved my computer problems.

In particular, I would like to thank my editors, Dawn Marano, Annette Wenda, and Glenda Cotter for their patience, support, and attention to detail; Tom and Mary Judge Ryan, who turned their guesthouse into a writer's refuge; and Jonathan, Jordan, and Logan Matti, who helped with a thousand manuscript crises and who accompanied me on research junkets through the West, beginning at Mary Austin's home in Independence, California, and ending in her country of "lost borders."

A Sweet,
Separate
Intimacy

INTRODUCTION

> The earth is no wanton to give up all her best to every comer, but
> keeps a sweet, separate intimacy for each.
> —Mary Austin, preface to *The Land of Little Rain*

MY TIES TO THE women in this volume run deep. I am a native
Californian, offspring of parents born and reared in the West and
Midwest. As a result, my early reading was steeped in poetry and novels
that captured the western experience: *Little House in the Big Woods,
Ramona, O Pioneers!* and *My Ántonia.* With my family I attended the
Ramona Festival in Hemet; camped by rushing streams, empty Pacific
beaches, and mountain lakes; explored desert canyons undiscovered by
other wanderers. Or so I believed. We lived in a thick-walled old
"California-style" house, reminiscent of Señora Moreno's in *Ramona,*
with a red-tiled patio, arched doorways, deep-set windows, a small orchard, and a woodshed out back. I visited the Southwest Museum, just
down the arroyo, and El Alisal, home of Charles Lummis. There, years
earlier, Lummis and his wife, Eva, hosted parties for western writers, including Mary Austin and Sharlot Mabridth Hall. The publisher of *Out
West,* originally titled *Land of Sunshine,* encouraged the young writers
when their self-confidence flagged. And he employed them. Sharlot
Hall's poem "Out West," written in one creative burst, named Lummis's
magazine and graced the first issue. For a time, Hall was an assistant editor.

Coming from a family of writers, my ear was attuned to poetry recited around the campfire and dinner table, at wakes and marriages. We
had a quote for every occasion. One family member would start a poem.
Others would join in until the lines had run their course and the room
was filled with laughter—or silence, as we savored the moment.
Sometimes we read prose aloud, communing with a West that only my
parents' generation remembered. Yet, on summer mornings spent wandering the back roads and blue highways, we discovered places untouched by the twentieth century. It was the spell of those places that
lured me into a love affair with the earth.

When I turned away from pure science to write fiction set in the region I had explored afoot as a geologist and paleontologist, I looked to women writers of the West for inspiration. Outstanding contemporary writers, such as Leslie Marmon Silko, Barbara Kingsolver, Sharman Apt Russell, and Terry Tempest Williams, have drawn the West into the literary spotlight. But the era from 1800 to 1922, the years of the settlement of the American frontier, seemed to represent a black hole into which women's voices fell without a sound. As Tony Hillerman wrote: "Western movies and a lot of popular fiction give the impression that the West was populated by about eleven women. One was the madam of the boom town's house of ill repute, and the other ten were all demure and wore sunbonnets. Of course the number and variety were greater. In fact, the empty country seemed to attract women who were both remarkably literate and incredibly durable—which should surprise no thoughtful person."[1]

These women left a written record—in poetry, essays, short stories, children's literature, published diaries and letters, journals, and novels—that reveals the opening of the West from a woman's perspective and adds depth to the American literature of the nineteenth and early twentieth centuries. This anthology presents work from a cross section of women writers whose lives were irrevocably affected by the frontier experience and whose writing reflected this change.

The search for authors was a treasure hunt. As I read one book, a footnote or preface would lead to another. Much of the original work resides in special reference collections in libraries and historical museums, or in nineteenth-century anthologies such as those my grandmother left me. But in the last twenty years, renewed interest in the forgotten women writers of the nineteenth century has led to new poetry anthologies and biographies designed to bring the present generation into contact with writers previously overlooked by the mainstream literary establishment. The general-sources section includes these contemporary works.

I struggled with the questions of which authors to include and in what order. Chronological order seemed more logical for the general reader. Narrowing the list of authors proved more problematical. In the end, I selected writers who published only between 1800 and 1922. With few exceptions, these women were well known to their contemporaries. Isabella Bird was English. She did not stay in the West, but captured it for British and American readers. Some women, such as Mary Ann Adams Maverick, Jessie Ann Benton Frémont, Elizabeth Bacon

Custer, Caroline Kirkland, and Carrie Adell Strahorn, wrote of the journey itself. Others, such as Willa Cather, Mary Austin, Alice Corbin Henderson, and Helen Hunt Jackson, permeated their fiction, poetry, and essays with sensory images so strong that readers could smell, hear, and taste the frontier. All published their work. In each case, writing was a way of distilling on paper the stranger-in-a-strange-land experience, the vastness and beauty of the world, and the characters encountered. These women who traveled the rough roads, going where no Anglo-American or European woman had gone before, climbing mountains that Native Americans and newcomers alike gazed upon with awe, felt the import of their journeys. The letter writers and diarists, such as Bird, Kirkland, and Elinore Pruitt Stewart, needed to share the experience with relatives and friends living in comfort somewhere "civilized," in places still considered "back home." They recognized that often it is more difficult to wait for a letter than to act. I believe it was harder for Elizabeth Custer to await word of her husband's fate that early summer of 1876 than it was for George to take his stand at the Little Big Horn. We have her words. She spent the rest of her life trying to salvage her husband's reputation.

These writings reflect a different frontier. They focus as much on the women's experience as on the men of the mountains, mines, and Plains. All of these women were literate. Most were professional writers at a time when women found it difficult to find outlets for their work, and when certain forms of publication were more acceptable for women than others. Because women spent their time and energy raising children, and thus were experts in that field, children's literature, poetry, and hymns were lauded. Because women were "more emotional than men," poetry was considered a reasonable outlet for creativity, especially if the work contained a moral lesson. But in reading these women, I have found them no more passionate or emotional than the men of their time.

Because these women were educated, they represent only a small percentage of the women of the frontier. Theirs is a skewed viewpoint, statistically narrow—a pinhole that focuses the shadow of a solar eclipse on a cardboard box. Several themes recur in their writing: isolation, mystic attachment for the land, death of loved ones, mourning, and frustration when drudgery got in the way of writing. Helen Hunt Jackson turned to writing to cope with the loss of husband and children.

The muse is a jealous partner. Some of these women believed that marriage and a writing life were incompatible. Phoebe Cary, Sharlot Hall, Alice Fletcher, Edith Eaton, and Willa Cather chose the single life.

Mary Austin, Louise Clappe, Elaine Goodale Eastman, Sarah Winnemucca, Ina Coolbrith, and Charlotte Gilman divorced their husbands
(although Gilman later remarried). In a letter to her friend Alice Hewins,
Sharlot Hall wrote: "It is true that the poems you like best express the
feeling we all have of longing for and seeking out the 'Perfect Comrade'—that feeling is part of our growth—it is Growth itself, forcing us
forward into the infinite by making us feel a great lack and emptiness in
the life of the moment. . . . I know now that I was very fortunate in
being born in a wild and unsettled country where I met very few people,
had very few books, and had to realize very early that the 'Perfect
Comrade' was always with me though unseen except by my deepest
self."[2]

Because my own background lay not only in the sciences and literature but also in history and anthropology, I placed these women writers
in a historical context. The "West" was not a static place. The edge of
the frontier migrated westward, like waves crashing against resistant
cliffs, as available land was put to the plow. In 1800, when Jane
Johnston Schoolcraft was born in Sault Ste. Marie, the frontier began at
the Appalachians. Travel east or south took weeks or months. Twenty
years later, when Alice Cary was born in the Miami Valley of western
Ohio, the "West" was just down the road and over the hill. It still took
one to two weeks to travel to New York on poorly maintained wagon
roads. But the vagaries, personalities, challenges, and richness of life on
the newly settled edges of the country imbued their work with the same
sense of place that we find at the end of the century in the works of
Cather, Austin, and Mary Hallock Foote. The land became, in effect, a
character with personality, philosophy, and temperament who changed
clothes with the seasons, became intertwined with the writers' lives, and
grew old with them. And the character of the frontier valleys east of the
Mississippi River was as different from the broad-shouldered Rocky
Mountains and undulating Plains as from the intolerant southwestern
deserts. Thankfully, in the creative voices of these women, we meet these
topographical characters as *they* met them.

What sets these authors apart from other women writers of the era
was that the West was the wellspring of their inspiration. The landscape,
geologically young, was as rough-hewn as the people it bred and fed.
Both land and personalities are represented here. On the Plains, in the
deserts, on the mountainsides, wind-borne dust eroded civilization's
patina; strong light revealed truth. And the constant pressure of living
on the leading edge of an expanding society, while competing with the

local inhabitants for the same ecological niche, bared emotions and behaviors both startling and seductive. In their essays and poetry we hear souls speak most clearly. What those souls tell us is that these women welcomed adventure; felt the beauty of the land, the mystery, the silences; suffered deprivation with humor; and remained open to change. They were survivors.

These women asked, and tried to answer, the eternal questions: Why should one sex or ethnic group or religion be less equal than another, with less protection under the law, with fewer opportunities? How can I understand this frontier with its constant struggle for survival, its separation from kin, its tragedy in a land of promise? Why did my children die? And how do I share these sad, mysterious, quirky, and transcending experiences with others?

The American frontier was not an empty bowl waiting to be filled. The writings of Eastman, Fletcher, and Curtis document Native American stories and chants received from the elder men of the tribes. But cultural traditions muted the voices of both Hispanic and Native American women. To partially balance the perspective, I have included selections from María Amparo Ruiz de Burton ("C. Loyal"), Suzette La Flesche ("Bright Eyes"), Gertrude Bonnin ("Zitkala-Sa"), Jane Johnston Schoolcraft, and Sarah Winnemucca. The reference sections contain additional source works.

I selected the year 1922 as the arbitrary cutoff because in that year Willa Cather finished two novels, *One of Ours* and *The Lost Lady*, both of which lamented the passing of the Old West and the era of the pioneers. One year later Cather won the Pulitzer Prize for *One of Ours*.

This volume is a pastiche designed to give the reader a taste of what women were thinking, feeling, and enduring in a century of transition. Their personalities shine through their words. When I read the larger works from which these were extracted, I felt an instant kinship—as woman/mother/walker of dusty trails—with these adventurers. I wanted to sit with them around a campfire at a bend in the Colorado River, in a cañon at the edge of the Snake River plain, or on a roadhouse porch in the Sierra foothills and listen to their life stories. In this book are bits and pieces of dreams, lives, experiences, and vistas, like squares cut from old cloth and assembled into a crazy quilt of writing styles and forms. I find the vibrant color and variation beautiful. The patchwork design mirrors both the complexity of the chroniclers and the stark lines and angles of the American frontier.

Jane Johnston Schoolcraft

(Bame-wa-wa-ge-zhik-a-quay) ("Rosa," "Leelinau") (Ojibwa)
(1800–1841)

L ONG BEFORE Europeans ventured across the Atlantic, Native American birch-bark canoes plied the Great Lakes corridor, trading in furs and copper. The traditional land of the Ojibwa, or Chippewa, lay across northern Minnesota, Wisconsin, Michigan, southern Canada, and the shores of Lake Superior. As early as 1620, French explorers made contact with the Indians living alongside the rapids of the St. Mary's River that joined Lakes Superior and Huron. The French named the spot Sault de Sainte Marie. At this strategic shipping location, Jesuits established a mission, fur traders built a post and had rendezvous, and French, British, and Americans built successive forts. The Treaty of Paris at the end of the Revolutionary War placed Sault Ste. Marie on the northern edge of the territory claimed by the nascent United States.

In 1800, President John Adams and the United States Congress moved the capital from Philadelphia to Washington, D.C. That year, at Sault Ste. Marie, a daughter was born to John Johnston, a wealthy Irish fur trader, and his Ojibwa wife, Ozha-guscoday-way-quay, the Woman of the Green Valley. The girl's mother named her Bame-wa-wa-ge-zhik-a-quay, or Woman of the Stars Rushing through the Sky. Her father called her Jane. Within Jane Johnston's lifetime, the United States would double in size through the acquisition of the Louisiana and Florida Territories.

When the War of 1812 ended, settlers flooded over the Appalachians, increasing friction between Indians and whites and altering the traditional territories of the various Indian groups. The victorious Americans forced the Ojibwas to cede their lands to the United States. In 1822, the U.S. government sent Henry Rowe Schoolcraft—a geologist, explorer, naturalist, ethnologist, and writer—to serve as Indian agent and intermediary. Schoolcraft had planned to stay a year. Instead, he married Jane Johnston in 1823, fathered three children, and stayed until after her death in 1841.

Jane was a child of two worlds, with a unique perspective during this time of transition. Because there were no schools at Sault Ste. Marie, Jane was educated at home, with her seven brothers and sisters, and in

Ireland. Fluent in English and Chippewa, her mother's language, Jane translated the folklore of her people for Henry Schoolcraft's burgeoning fascination with Native American culture. The Schoolcrafts understood that the clash of cultures on the frontier would inevitably result in the loss of the traditions, lore, music, and history of all the tribes. Theirs was a symbiotic relationship that amassed an invaluable collection of ethnologic information. Henry Schoolcraft's treatise *Algic Researches, Comprising Inquiries Respecting the Mental Characteristics of the North American Indians* (1939), relied heavily on contributions from all of the Johnstons, as well as from their Ojibwa relatives.

In the winter of 1826-1827, while Sault Ste. Marie was snowbound, the Schoolcrafts published a weekly handwritten magazine called the *Literary Voyager; or, Muzzeniegun.* Copies of the magazine circulated through the town, traveled south to Detroit, and east to friends and colleagues interested in Native American studies. In addition to pieces on Ojibwa lore, history, customs, and language, Jane contributed conventional poetry. She wrote under her Ojibwa name, as well as under the pseudonyms "Leelinau" and "Rosa." "Rosa" wrote poetry. "Leelinau" and Bame-wa-wa-ge-zhik-a-quay wrote allegorical Ojibwa tales and legends that Jane learned from her mother. The magazine was so successful that Jane became known from Michigan to England as the "northern Pocahontas." Yet, that winter also saw the death of the Schoolcrafts' firstborn son, William Henry. Although she bore two more children, Jane never completely recovered from the shock of Willy's death.

Jane Johnston Schoolcraft's literary importance is twofold: she served as both writer and conduit for Ojibwa oral history. Her prose reflected the simple, strong style of the oral storyteller, the rhythm heard around Ojibwa hearths during long winter nights. "The Origin of the Robin" and "The Forsaken Brother" reveal the intensity of the Native American relationship with nature, and the abandonment they experienced when separated from their traditional lands. More significantly, these tales captured the voice of Jane's mother—a woman raised in the old ways on an island in western Lake Superior, a woman who never learned to speak English.

_ह_

The Origin of the Robin: An Oral Allegory

SPIRITUAL GIFTS, are sought by the Chippewas through fasting. An old man had an only son, a fine promising lad, who had come to that age which is thought by the Chippewas to be most proper to make the long and final fast, that is to secure through life a guardian spirit, on whom future prosperity or adversity is to depend, and who forms and establishes the character of the faster to great or ignoble deeds.

This old man was ambitious that his son should surpass all others in whatever was deemed most wise and great amongst his tribe. And to fulfil his wishes, he thought it necessary that his son must fast a much longer time than any of those persons known for their great power or wisdom whose fame he envied.

He therefore directed his son to prepare with great ceremony, for the important event. After he had been in the sweating lodge and bath several times, he ordered him to lie down upon a clean mat, in the little lodge expressly prepared for him, telling him, at the same time to bear himself like a man, and that at the expiration of _twelve_ days, he should receive food, and the blessing of his father.

The lad carefully observed this injunction, laying with his face covered with perfect composure, awaiting those happy visitations which were to seal his good or ill fortune. His father visited him every morning regularly to encourage him to perseverance, expatiating at full length on the renown and honor that would attend him through life, if he accomplished the full term prescribed. To these admonitions the boy never answered, but lay without the least sign of unwillingness till the ninth day, when he addressed his father—"My father, my dreams are ominous of evil! May I break my fast now, and at a more propitious time, make a new fast?" The father answered—"My son, you know not what you ask! If you get up now, all your glory will depart. Wait patiently a little longer. You have but three days yet to accomplish what I desire. You know, it is for your own good."

The son assented, and covering himself closer, he lay till the eleventh day, when he repeated his request to his father. The same answer was given him, by the old man, adding, that the next day he would himself prepare his first meal, and bring it to him. The boy remained silent, but lay like a skeleton. No one would have known he was living but by the gentle heaving of his breast.

The next morning the father, elated at having gained his end, prepared a repast for his son, and hastened to set it before him. On coming to the door, he was surprized to hear his son talking to himself. He stooped to listen, and looking through a small aperture, was more astonished when he beheld his son painted with vermillion on his breast, and in the act of finishing his work by laying on the paint as far as his hand could reach on his shoulders, saying at the same time:—"My father has ruined me, as a man; he would not listen to my request; he will now be the loser. I shall be forever happy in my new state, for I have been obedient to my parent; he alone will be the sufferer; for the Spirit is a just one, though not propitious to me. He has shown me pity, and now I must go."

At that moment the old man broke in exclaiming, "My son! my son! do not leave me!" But his son with the quickness of a bird had flown up to the top of the lodge, and perched on the highest pole, a beautiful robin red-breast. He looked down on his father with pity beaming in his eyes, and told him, that he should always be seen happy and contented by the constant cheerfulness and pleasure he would display, that he would still cheer his father by his songs, which would be some consolation to him for the loss of the glory he had expected; and that, although no longer a man, he should ever be the harbinger of peace and joy to the human race.

The Forsaken Brother: A Chippewa Tale

IT WAS A fine summer evening; the sun was scarcely an hour high,—its departing rays beamed through the foliage of the tall, stately elms, that skirted the little green knoll, on which a solitary Indian lodge stood. The deep silence that reigned in this sequested [*sic*] and romantic spot, seemed to most of the inmates of that lonely hut, like the long sleep of death, that was now evidently fast sealing the eyes of the head of this poor family. His low breathing was answered by the sighs of his disconsolate wife and their children. Two of the latter were almost grown up, one was yet a mere child. These were the only human beings near the dying man. The door of the lodge was thrown open to admit the refreshing breeze of the lake, on the banks of which it stood; and as the cool air fanned the head of the poor man, he felt a momentary return of strength, and raising himself a little, he thus addressed his weeping family. "I leave you—thou, who hast been my partner in life, but you will not stay long to suffer in this world. But oh! my children, my poor children! you have just commenced life, and mark me, unkindness, and ingratitude, and every wickedness is in the scene before you. I left my kindred and my tribe, because I found what I have just warned you of. I have contented myself with the company of your mother and yourselves, for many years, and you will find my motives for separating from the haunts of men, were solicitude and anxiety to preserve you from the bad examples you would inevitably have followed. But I shall die content if you, my children promise me, to cherish each other, and on no account to forsake your youngest brother, of him I give you both particular charge." The man became exhausted, and taking a hand of each of his eldest children, he continued—"My daughter! Never forsake your little brother. My son, never forsake your little brother." "Never, never!" they both exclaimed. "Never—never!" repeated the father and expired.

The poor man died happy, because he thought his commands would be obeyed. The sun sank below the trees, and left a golden sky behind, which the family were wont to admire, but no one heeded it now. The lodge that was so still an hour before, was now filled with low and unavailing lamentations. Time wore heavily away—five long moons had passed and the sixth was nearly full, when the mother also died. In her last moments she pressed the fulfilment of their promise to their departed father. They readily renewed their promise, because they were yet free from any selfish motive. The winter passed away, and the beauties of spring cheered the drooping spirits of the bereft little family. The girl, being the eldest, dictated to her brothers, and seemed to feel a tender and sisterly affection for the youngest, who was rather sickly and delicate. The other boy soon showed symptoms of restlessness, and addressed the sister as follows. "My sister, are we always to live as if there were no other human beings in the world. Must I deprive myself the pleasure of associating with my own kind? I shall seek the villages of men; I have determined, and you cannot prevent me." The girl replied, "My brother, I do not say no, to what you desire. We were not prohibited, the society of our fellow mortals, but we were told to cherish each other, and that we should no [do] nothing independent of each other— that neither pleasure nor pain ought ever to separate us, particularly from our helpless brother. If we follow our separate gratifications, it will surely make us forget *him* whom we are alike bound to support." The young man made no answer, but taking his bow and arrows left the lodge, and never returned.

Many moons had come and gone, after the young man's departure, and still the girl administered to the wants of her younger brother. At length, however, she began to be weary of her solitude, and of her charge. Years, which added to her strength and capability of directing the affairs of the household, also brought with them the desire of society, and made her solitude irksome. But in meditating a change of life, she thought only for herself, and cruelly sought to abandon her little brother, as her elder brother had done before.

One day after she had collected all the provisions she had set apart for emergencies, and brought a quantity of wood to the door, she said to her brother. "My brother, you must not stray far from the lodge. I am going to seek our brother: I shall soon be back." Then taking her bundle, she set off, in search of habitations. She soon found them, and was so much taken up with the pleasures and amusements of society, that all affection for her brother was obliterated. She accepted a proposal of marriage, and after that, never more thought of the helpless relative she had abandoned.

In the meantime the elder brother had also married, and settled on the shores of the same lake, which contained the bones of his parents, and the abode of his forsaken brother.

As soon as the little boy had eaten all the food left by his sister, he was obliged to pick berries and dig up roots. Winter came on, and the poor child was exposed to all its rigors. He was obliged to quit the lodge in search of food, without a shelter. Sometimes he passed the night in the clefts of old trees, and ate the refuge meats of the wolves. The latter soon became his only resource, and he became so fearless of these animals, that he would sit close to them whilst they devoured their prey, and the animals themselves seemed to pity his condition, and would always leave something. Thus he lived, as it were, on the bounty of fierce wolves until spring. As soon as the lake was free from ice, he followed his new found friends and companions to the shore. It happened his brother was fishing in his canoe in the lake, a considerable distance out, when he thought he heard the cry of a child, and wondered how any could exist on so bleak a part of the shore. He listened again more attentively, and distinctly heard the cry repeated. He made for shore as quick as possible, and as he approached land, discovered and recognized his little brother, and heard him singing in a plaintive voice—

> *Neesya, neesya, shyegwuh gushuh!*
> *Ween ne myeengunish!*
>   *ne myeengunish!*
> My brother, my brother,
> I am now turning into a Wolf!—
> I am turning into a Wolf.

At the termination of his song, he howled like a Wolf, and the young man was still more astonished when, on getting nearer shore, he perceived his poor brother half turned into that animal. He however, leapt on shore and strove to catch him in his arms, and soothingly said—"My brother, my brother, come to me." But the boy eluded his grasp, and fled, still singing as he fled—"I am turning into a Wolf—I am turning into a wolf," and howling in the intervals.

The elder brother, conscience struck, and feeling his brotherly affection returning with redoubled force, exclaimed in great anguish, "My brother, my brother, come to me." But the nearer he approached the child, the more rapidly his transformation went on, until he changed into a perfect wolf,—still singing and howling, and naming his brother and sister alternately in his song, as he fled into the woods, until his change was complete. At last he said. "I am a wolf," and bounded out of sight.

The young man felt the bitterness of remorse all his days, and the sister, when she heard of the fate of the little boy whom she had so cruelly left, and whom both she and her brother had solemnly promised to foster and protect, wept bitterly; and never ceased to mourn until she died.

Caroline Matilda Stansbury Kirkland

("Mrs. Mary Clavers, an Actual Settler")

(1801–1864)

B Y 1801, New York City had replaced Boston as the most populous city in the United States. Although officially at peace, within four months of Caroline Stansbury's birth, the country would become embroiled in an undeclared war with pirates of the Barbary States of North Africa. In that conflict, which continued for fifteen years, the United States Navy saw its first action along the "Shores of Tripoli."

The United States was growing. The original thirteen states had swelled to sixteen by the additions of Vermont, Kentucky, and Tennessee. The remainder of the land between the Appalachians and the Mississippi River was divided into the Territory Northwest of the Ohio River, the Territory South of the Ohio River, the Mississippi Territory, and the Indiana Territory. Expanding rural populations pushed Native Americans westward, increasing conflict between whites and Indians. In 1825, to solve the "Indian problem," President Monroe proposed to relocate tribes on lands west of the Mississippi River. To further encourage white settlement in the Old Northwest Territory, the government offered land for sale at bargain-basement prices. Speculators flocked to the territory, bought and subdivided large tracts of land, and sold at substantial profit to novice farmers such as Caroline Stansbury Kirkland and her husband.

Caroline Stansbury was the oldest of eleven children in an educationally rich but cash-poor middle-class family. The Stansburys sent their precocious eight-year-old child to study at a Quaker school run by her aunt, Lydia Mott. Possessed of a facile mind and an aptitude for literature and languages, Caroline mastered Latin, French, and German. In her midteens she began teaching at one of Mott's schools in upstate New York. When Stansbury's father died a short time later, her mother moved the family close to Caroline's work, and Caroline contributed to their support. She was teaching in Clinton, New York, when she met William Kirkland, a graduate and tutor at Hamilton College and son of a prominent New England family. Caroline and William became engaged, weathered a two-year separation while he studied in Europe, and were married in 1828. Their relationship was one of equality and joint endeavors. A few months after their marriage, they opened a school in Geneva, New York. That fall, the first of their seven children was born. Only three survived to adulthood.

In 1835, the Kirklands and their three young children moved to Michigan Territory, where they hoped to find the prosperity that had escaped them in New York. Detroit was an old settlement by western standards. In 1701, France had erected a fort on Lake St. Clair, between Lake Erie and Lake Huron, to foster and protect French interests in the Mississippi Valley. England gained possession of Detroit at the end of the French and Indian War (1763). But by the Treaty of Paris (1783), the boundary between the United States and Canada bisected the Great Lakes. It continued eastward to Lake of the Woods, and followed the forty-fifth parallel westward to its intersection—in unexplored territory—with the projected extension of the Mississippi River. Based on this agreement, Detroit became both an American post protecting the border with Canada and a "jumping-off place" for pioneers heading farther west.

William and Caroline Kirkland took positions at the Detroit Female Seminary while they scouted speculative land opportunities in the Michigan Territory west of Detroit. They bought land in Livingston County and helped start a community named Pinckney—the "Montacute" of Caroline's sketches. However, the genteel teachers were unprepared, physically and emotionally, for the rigors of western life. To counteract the isolation and dearth of intellectual stimulation, Caroline wrote letters to her friends in New England describing incidents and characters in Montacute. At her friends' urging, and to supplement their meager income, Caroline offered the sketches for publication. Her first book, *A New Home—Who'll Follow?; or, Glimpses of Western Life by Mrs. Mary Clavers, an Actual Settler* (1839), portrayed a different West than the male-centered heroic and romantic tales offered by novelists such as James Fenimore Cooper. Kirkland, with an unerring eye for detail, highlighted the trials and deprivations faced by the pioneers: muddy roads and bogs, mosquitoes, fatigue, lack of fresh produce and dairy products, land swindlers, exorbitant labor costs, and the difficulty of finding household help. Yet, she ridiculed herself, the unprepared easterner with unrealistic expectations, at the same time she satirized the characters she met. She followed *A New Home* with another collection of sketches, *Forest Life,* in 1842.

Although very popular in the East, the humorously realistic sketches alienated Caroline from her Michigan neighbors. Worse, one financial disaster followed another. The Kirklands gave up on their wilderness experiment in 1843 and returned to New York City. When William drowned in the Hudson River in 1846, Caroline supported the children by teaching and writing, and by editing the *Union Magazine of Literature and Art.*

Caroline never returned to the West. The impact of the eight-year sojourn was so great, however, that she continued to draw upon Michigan experiences throughout her life. When she died from a stroke at age sixty-three, she left behind a body of work that included sketches, stories, articles, letters, editorials, book reviews, and essays. Her revelations encouraged thousands to attempt the westward journey.

Chapter X

> *Mrs. Hardcastle.* I wish we were at home again. I never met so many accidents in so short a journey. Drenched in the mud, overturned in the ditch, jolted to a jelly, and at last to lose our way.
>
> [Oliver Goldsmith,] *She Stoops to Conquer*

AT LENGTH CAME the joyful news that our moveables had arrived in port; and provision was at once made for their transportation to the banks of the Turnip. But many and dire were the vexatious delays, thrust by the cruel Fates between us and the accomplishment of our plans; and it was not till after the lapse of several days that the most needful articles were selected and bestowed in a large wagon which was to pioneer the grand body. In this wagon had been reserved a seat for myself, since I had far too great an affection for my chairs and tables, to omit being present at their debarkation at Montacute, in order to insure their undisturbed possession of the usual complement of legs. And there were the children to be packed this time,—little roley-poley things, whom it would have been in vain to have marked, 'this side up,' like the rest of the baggage.

A convenient space must be contrived for my plants, among which were two or three tall geraniums, and an enormous calla ethiopica. Then D'Orsay [the dog] must be accommodated, of course; and, to crown all, a large basket of live fowls; for we had been told that there were none to be purchased in the vicinity of Montacute. Besides these, there were all our travelling trunks; and an enormous square box crammed with articles which we then, in our greenness, considered indispensable. We have since learned better.

After this enumeration, which yet is only partial, it will not seem strange that the guide and director of our omnibus was to ride

'On horseback after we.'

He acted as a sort of adjutant—galloping forward to spy out the way, or provide accommodations for the troop—pacing close to the wheels to modify our arrangements, to console one of the imps who had bumped his pate, or to give D'Orsay a gentle hint with the riding-whip, when he made demonstrations of mutiny—and occasionally falling behind to pick up a stray handkerchief or parasol.

The roads near Detroit were inexpressibly bad. Many were the chances against our toppling load's preserving its equilibrium. To our inexperience, the risks seemed nothing less than tremendous—but the driver so often reiterated, 'that a'n't nothin',' in reply to our despairing exclamations, and, what was better, so constantly proved his words by passing the most frightful inequalities (Michiganicé, 'sidlings') in safety, that we soon became more confident, and ventured to think of something else besides the ruts and mud-holes.

Our stopping-places after the first day were of the ordinary new country class—the very coarsest accommodations by night and by day, and all at the dearest rate. When every body is buying land, and scarce anybody cultivating it, one must not expect to find living either good or cheap: but, I confess, I was surprised at the dearth of comforts which we observed everywhere. Neither milk, eggs, nor vegetables were to be had, and those who could not live on hard salt ham, stewed dried apples, and bread raised with 'salt risin,' would necessarily run some risk of starvation.

One word as to this and similar modes of making bread, so much practised throughout this country. It is my opinion that the sin of bewitching snow-white flour by means of either of those abominations, 'salt risin,' 'milk emptins,' 'bran east,' or any of their odious compounds, ought to be classed with the turning of grain into whiskey, and both made indictable offences. To those who know of no other means of producing the requisite sponginess in bread than the wholesome hop-yeast of the brewer, I may be allowed to explain the mode to which I have alluded with such hearty reprobation. Here follows the recipe:—

To make milk emptins. Take quantum suf. of good sweet milk—add a teaspoonful of salt, and some water, and set the mixture in a warm place till it ferments, then mix your bread with it; and if you are lucky enough to catch it just in the right moment before the fermentation reaches the putrescent stage, you may make tolerably good rolls, but if you are five minutes too late, you will have to open your doors and windows while your bread is baking.—Verbum sap.

'Salt risin' is made with water slightly salted and fermented like the other; and becomes putrid rather sooner, and 'bran east' is on the same plan. The consequences of letting these mixtures stand too long will become known to those whom it may concern, when they shall travel through the remoter parts of Michigan; so I shall not dwell upon them here—but I offer my counsel to such of my friends as may be removing westward, to bring with them some form of portable yeast (the old fashioned dried cakes which mothers and aunts can furnish, are as good as any)—and also full instructions for perpetuating the same; and to plant hops as soon as they get a corner to plant them in.

'And may they better reck the rede,
Than ever did th' adviser.'

The last two days of our slow journey were agreeably diversified with sudden and heavy showers, and intervals of overpowering sunshine. The weather had all the changefulness of April, with the torrid heat of July. Scarcely would we find shelter from the rain which had drenched us completely—when the sunshine would tempt us forth: and by the time all the outward gear was dried, and matters in readiness for a continuation of our progress, another threatening cloud would drive us back, though it never really rained till we started.

We had taken a newly-opened and somewhat lonely route this time, in deference to the opinion of those who ought to have known better, that this road from having been less travelled, would not be quite so *deep* as the other. As we went farther into the wilderness, the difficulties increased. The road had been but little 'worked,' (the expression in such cases,) and in some parts was almost in a state of nature. Where it wound round the edge of a marsh, where in future times there will be a bridge or drain, the wheels on one side would be on the dry ground, while the others were sinking in the long wet grass of the marsh—and in such places it was impossible to discern inequalities which yet might overturn us in an instant. In one case of this sort, we were obliged to dismount the 'live lumber'—as the man who helped us through phrased it, and let the loaded wagon pass on, while we followed in an empty one which was fortunately at hand—and it was, in my eyes, little short of a miracle that our skilful friend succeeded in piloting safely the top-heavy thing which seemed thrown completely off its centre half a dozen times.

At length we came to a dead stand. Our driver had received special cautions as to a certain *mash* that 'lay between us and our home'—to 'keep to the right'—to 'follow the travel' to a particular point, and then 'turn up stream:' but whether the very minuteness and reiteration of the directions had puzzled him, as is often the case, or whether his good genius had for once forsaken him, I know not. We had passed the deep centre of the miry slough, when, by some unlucky hair's breadth swerving, in went our best horse—our sorrel—our 'Prince,'—the 'off haus,' whose value had been speered three several times since we left Detroit, with magnificent offers of a 'swop!' The noble fellow, unlike the tame beasties that are used to such occurrences, showed his good blood by kicking and plunging, which only made his case more desperate. A few moments more would have left us with a 'single team,' when his master succeeded in cutting the traces with his penknife. Once freed, Prince soon made his way out of the bog-hole and pranced off, far up the green swelling hill which lay before us—out of sight in an instant—and there we sat in the marsh.

There is but one resource in such cases. You must mount your remaining horse, if you have one, and ride on till you find a farmer and one, two, or three pairs of oxen—and all this accomplished, you may generally hope for a release in time.

The interval seemed a *leetle* tedious, I confess. To sit for three mortal hours in an open wagon, under a hot sun, in the midst of a swamp, is not pleasant. The expanse of inky mud which spread around us, was hopeless, as to any attempt at getting ashore. I crept cautiously down the tongue, and tried one or two of the tempting green tufts, which looked as if they *might* afford foothold; but alas! they sank under the slightest pressure. So I was fain to regain my low chair, with its abundant cushions, and lose myself in a book. The children thought it fine fun for a little while, but then they began to want a drink. I never knew children who did not, when there was no water to be had.

There ran through the very midst of all this black pudding, as clear a stream as ever rippled, and the wagon stood almost in it!—but how to get at it? The basket which had contained, when we left the city, a store of cakes and oranges, which the children thought inexhaustible, held now nothing but the napkins, which had enveloped those departed joys, and those napkins, suspended corner-wise, and soaken long and often in the crystal water, served for business and pleasure, till papa came back.

'They're coming! They're coming!' was the cry, and with one word, over went Miss Alice, who had been reaching as far as she could, trying how large a portion of her napkin she could let float in the water.

Oh, the shrieks and the exclamations! how hard papa rode, and how hard mamma scolded! But the little witch got no harm beyond a thorough wetting, and a few streaks of black mud, and felt herself a heroine for the rest of the day.

Chapter XI

Rous'd at his name, up rose the boozy sire,
* * *
In vain, in vain,—the all-composing hour
Resistless falls; the Muse obeys the power.
—*Pope*

THE NIGHT DEWS were falling chill and heavy when we crossed the last log causeway, and saw a dim glimmering in the distance. The children were getting horribly cross and sleepy. The unfortunate anchoring in the black swamp had deranged our plans by about three hours, and when we reached our destined resting-place, which was the log-house where I had been so happy as to make the acquaintance of Miss Irene Ketchum, and her dignified mamma, the family had retired to rest, except Mr Ketchum, who rested without retiring.

The candle, a long twelve I should judge, was standing on the table, and wasting rapidly under the influence of a very long snuff, which reclined upon its side. Upon the same table, and almost touching the tall iron candlestick, was a great moppy head; and this head rested in heavy slumber on the brawny arms of the master of the house.

'Ketchum! Ketchum!' echoed a shrill voice from within the pinned-up sheets in one corner, and I might have thought the woman was setting the dog at us, if I had not recognized the dulcet-treble of the fair Irene from the other bed—'Pa, pa, get up, can't you?'

Thus conjured, the master of the mansion tried to overcome the still potent effects of his evening potations, enough to understand what was the matter, but in vain. He could only exclaim, 'What the devil's got into the women?' and down went the head again.

Mrs. Ketchum had, by this time, exchanged the night for the day cap, and made herself, otherwise, tolerably presentable. She said she had supposed we were not coming, it was so late; (it was just half-past eight,) and then like many other poor souls I have known, tried hard to hide her husband's real difficulty.

'He was *so* tired!' she said.

How long the next hour seemed! A summer day in some company I wot of, would not seem half as tedious. It took all papa's ingenuity, and more than all mamma's patience to amuse the poor children, [till] matters were arranged; but at length the important matter of supper being in some sort concluded, preparations were made for 'retiracy.'

Up the stick ladder we all paced 'slowly and sadly,' Miss Irene preceding us with the remnant of the long twelve, leaving all below in darkness. The aspect of our lodging place was rather portentous. Two bedsteads, which looked as if they might, by no very violent freak of nature, have grown into their present form, a good deal of bark being yet upon them, occupied the end opposite the stairs; and between them was a window, without either glass or shutter—that is to say, politeness aside, a square hole in the house. Three beds spread upon the floor, two chests, and a spinning-wheel, with reel and swifts, completed the plenishing of the room. Two of the beds were already tenanted, as the vibrations of the floor might have told us without the aid of ears, (people snore incredibly after ploughing all day,) and the remainder were at our service. The night air pouring in at the aperture seemed to me likely to bring death on its dewy wings, and when I looked up and saw the stars shining through the crevices in the roof, I thought I might venture to have the wider rent closed, although I had been sensible of some ill resulting from the close quarters at Danforth's. So a quilt, that invaluable resource in the woods, was stuck up before the window, and the unhinged cover of one of the chests was used as a lid for the stairway, for fear the children might fall down. Sheets served to partition off a 'tyring room' round my bed—an expedient frequently resorted to—and so dangerous that it is wonderful so few houses are burnt down in this country. And thus passed my first night in Montacute.

I do not remember experiencing at any time in my life, a sense of more complete uncomfortableness than was my lot, on awakening the next morning. It seemed to arise entirely from my anticipations of the awkward and tedious inconveniences of our temporary sojourn at this place, where every thing was so different from our ideas of comfort, or even decency. But I have since been convinced, that sleeping in an exhausted atmosphere, of which those who slept on the bedsteads felt the effect more sensibly than those who lay on the floor, had no small agency in producing this depression of spirits, so unusual with me.

Be this as it may, my troubles, when the children were to be washed and dressed, became real and tangible enough; for, however philosophical grown people may sometimes be under disagreeables consequent upon a change of habits, children are very epicures, and will put up with nothing that is unpleasant to them, without at least making a noise, which I do detest and dread; though I know mothers ought to 'get used to such things.' I have heard that eels get accustomed to being skinned, but I doubt the fact.

That morning was the first and the last time I ever attempted to carry through the ordinary nursery routine, in a log hut, without a servant, and with a skillet for a wash-basin.

The little things did get dressed after awhile, however, and were safely escorted down the stick ladder, and it was really a pleasure to see them careering round the house, rioting in their freedom, and to hear now and then a merry laugh, awakening the echoes. Children are the true *bijouterie* of the woods and wilds. How weary would my last three years have been, without the cares and troubles they have brought me!

Our breakfast, of undistinguishable green tea, milk-rising bread, and salt ham, did not consume much time, and most fortunately we here found milk for the children, who of course made out sumptuously. It was the first time since we left Detroit, that we had been able to procure more than a small allowance for the tea.

My first care was to inquire where I might be able to procure a domestic, for I saw plainly I must not expect any aid from Miss Irene or her younger sister, who were just such 'captive-princess' looking damsels as Miss Martineau mentions having seen at a country inn somewhere on her tour.[3]

'Well, I do n't know,' said Mrs. Ketchum, in reply to my questions; 'there was a young lady here yesterday that was saying she did n't know but she'd live out a spell till she'd bought her a new dress.'

'Oh! But I wish to get a girl who will remain with me; I should not like to change often.'

Mrs. Ketchum smiled rather scornfully at this, and said there were not many girls about here that cared to live out long at a time.

My spirits fell at this view of the matter. Some of my dear theorizing friends in the civilized world had dissuaded me most earnestly from bringing a maid with me.

'She would always be discontented and anxious to return; and you'll find plenty of good farmers' daughters ready to live with you for the sake of earning a little money.'

Good souls! how little did they know of Michigan! I have since that day seen the interior of many a wretched dwelling, with almost literally nothing in it but a bed, a chest, and a table; children ragged to the last degree, and potatoes the only fare; but never yet saw I one where the daughter was willing to own herself obliged to live out at service. She would 'hire out' long enough to buy some article of dress perhaps, or 'because our folks have been sick, and want a little money to pay the doctor,' or for some such special reason; but never as a regular calling, or with an acknowledgment of inferior station.

This state of things appalled me at first; but I have learned a better philosophy since. I find no difficulty now in getting such aid as I require, and but little in retaining it as long as I wish, though there is always a desire of making an occasional display of independence. Since living with one for wages is considered by common consent a favor, I take it as a favor; and, this point once conceded, all goes well. Perhaps I have been peculiarly fortunate; but certainly with one or two exceptions, I have little or nothing to complain of on this essential point of domestic comfort.

To be sure, I had one damsel who crammed herself almost to suffocation with sweetmeats and other things which she esteemed very nice; and ate up her own pies and cake, to the exclusion of those for whom they were intended; who would put her head in at a door, with—'*Miss* Clavers, did you holler! I thought I *heered* a yell.'

And another who was highly offended, because room was not made for her at table with guests from the city, and that her company was not requested for tea visits. And this latter high-born damsel sent in from the kitchen a circumstantial account *in writing*, of the instances wherein she considered herself aggrieved; well written it was, too, and expressed with much *naïveté,* and abundant respect. I answered it in the way which 'turneth away wrath.' Yet it was not long before this fiery spirit was aroused again, and I was forced to part with my country belle. But these instances are not very tremendous even to the city habits I brought with me; and I cannot say I regret having been obliged to relinquish what was, after all, rather a silly sort of pride. But bless me! how I get before my story! I viewed the matter very differently when I was at Ketchum's. My philosophy was of slow growth.

On reflection, it was thought best not to add another sleeper to the loft, and I concluded to wait on myself and the children while we remained at Ketchum's, which we hoped would be but for a day or two. I can only say, I contrived to *simplify* the matter very much, when I had no one to depend on but myself. The children had dirty faces, and aprons which would have effected their total exclusion from genteel society, more than half the time; and I was happy to encourage the closest intimacy between them and the calves and chickens, in order to gain some peace within doors. Mrs. Ketchum certainly had her own troubles during our sojourn under her leaky roof; for the two races commingled not without loud and long effervescence, threatening at times nothing short of a Kilkenny-cat battle, ending in mutual extermination.

My office, on these occasions, was an humble imitation of the plan of the celestials in ancient times; to snatch away the combatant in whom I was most interested, and then to secrete him for a while, using as a desert island one of the beds in the loft, where the unfortunate had to dree a weary penance, and generally come down quite tame.

Frances Dana Barker Gage

("Aunt Fanny")
(1808–1884)

FRANCES DANA GAGE was born in Marietta, Ohio, the year Congress enacted a law forbidding future slave importation and penalizing those merchants caught trafficking in slaves. It was five years after Ohio had been admitted to the Union, three years before the first steamboat plied the Ohio River, and four years before the United States engaged in a second war with Britain—the War of 1812. Although the power of eastern Native American tribes such as the Miami, the Wyandot, the Shawnee, and the Delaware had diminished, anti-Indian fervor was high. The violent clashes between cultures remained fresh in the memories of both civilizations. It would be thirty-four years before the last Ohio tribe forfeited its land to white settlers.

Ohio, the first state carved from national domain land at the edge of the American frontier, was a microcosm of territorial expansion. Maps depict a hodgepodge of different land-allotment surveys that ultimately resulted in the standardized six-mile-square grid system applied throughout the West. The Ohio River, the southern boundary of the state, was the westward extension of the Mason-Dixon line, the division between slaveholding and nonslaveholding states. Towns along the river became stops on the Underground Railroad, refuges for slaves who followed "the drinking gourd" northward. Gage's parents, Joseph and Elizabeth Dana Barker, were among those who aided escaping blacks.

Splinter religious movements, such as the Shakers and the Fourierists, settled the river valleys, secure behind the wall of the Appalachians to the east, Great Lakes to the north, Ohio River to the south, and endless wilderness to the west. They sought to build utopias in isolation. But the frontier extended so quickly that their communities became pockets within the broader framework of settlement. Yet, these groups had a profound effect on the political and social lives of those born in Ohio in the early years of settlement and statehood. Their beliefs in tolerance, individual freedom, the evils of slavery, the sanctity of the body, and the basic equality of the sexes made Ohio fertile ground for the social-rights movements of the nineteenth century. And because Ohio was situated on one of the main fluvial thoroughfares of the frontier, the flow of ideas from West to East accompanied the exchange of goods.

Gage was a poet, journalist, editor, novelist, children's writer, and activist for the temperance, woman's rights, and abolitionist movements. Her poems contain ironic humor, while pointing out the inequities inherent in a system that restricts the freedom of women and people of color. She was a keen observer: "Reminiscences of Sojourner Truth" provides a compelling picture of a former slave, mother of thirteen, bearer of physical and emotional scars. Because Truth was illiterate, posterity relies largely on Gage's description of Truth's first major speech. Although Gage's "Reminiscences" was not published until 1866, fifteen years after the Akron conference, the article cemented Truth's place in history. Scholars may debate the veracity of Gage's use of generalized idiomatic language, but they cannot debate the descriptive power of the scene Gage documents.

Gage herself was a natural orator, a commanding presence. She was elected president of the first Ohio Women's Constitutional Conference. Her poetry opened that convention and many that followed. Her speech evoked the pioneer experience, the carving from the landscape of a new civilization. An idealist, she was neither strident nor divisive. In *her* utopia, freedom and educational opportunities would be guaranteed to all; alcoholism and abuse would be eradicated. She worked to make that happen, first in Ohio, then in St. Louis, where she was a minority voice in a slaveholding state. Her abolitionist views alienated her Missouri neighbors, who torched her home more than once. To curb her voice, local newspapers refused to print her articles and letters. However, like Sojourner Truth, she refused to be silenced.

Although Gage had little formal schooling, she worked as a writer throughout her life, contributing articles, poetry, and stories to newspapers and magazines, including *St. Nicholas.* After the Civil War, Gage wrote several novels, the most popular of which was *Elsie Magoon,* a contrived and moralistic temperance tale set on the Ohio frontier. But contained within the novel is the journalistic piece excerpted here, a sentimental reminiscence of her childhood along the Muskingum River, and a tribute to the early settlers, including her parents.

Gage has been a footnote in the struggle for individual freedom because she moved west, away from the locus of the three social movements that defined her life and belief system. In addition, Gage downplayed her own role in order to emphasize the efforts of others. She remained on the fringes, an observer who saw the connections between people and their responsibilities toward society. She recognized the inherent goodness in mankind. Her simple philosophy held that power and alcohol corrupted that goodness. The concept was logical, but threatening to the status quo.

For more than a century, we have used Gage's writing to view characters and conditions in the nineteenth century. But it is a two-way mirror that allows us to know Gage as well—and to determine how much, or how little, has changed in the last century and a half.

Address to Woman's Rights Convention, Akron, Ohio, May 28, 1851

I AM AT A LOSS, kind friends, to know whether to return you thanks, or not, for the honor conferred upon me. And when I tell you that I have never in my life attended a regular business meeting, and am entirely inexperienced in the forms and ceremonies of a deliberative body, you will not be surprised that I do not feel remarkably grateful for the position. For though you have conferred an honor upon me, I very much fear I shall not be able to reflect it back. I will try.

When our forefathers left the old and beaten paths of New England, and struck out for themselves in a new and unexplored country, they went forth with a slow and cautious step, but with firm and resolute hearts. The land of their fathers had become too small for their children. Its soil answered not their wants. The parents shook their heads and said, with doubtful and foreboding faces: "Stand still, stay at home. This has sufficed for us; we have lived and enjoyed ourselves here. True, our mountains are high and our soil is rugged and cold; but you won't find a better; change, and trial, and toil, will meet you at every step. Stay, tarry with us, and go not forth to the wilderness."

But the children answered: "Let us go; this land has sufficed for you, but the one beyond the mountains is better. We know there is trial, toil, and danger; but for the sake of our children, and our children's children, we are willing to meet all." They went forth, and pitched their tents in the wilderness. An herculean task was before them; the rich and fertile soil was shadowed by a mighty forest, and giant trees were to be felled. The Indians roamed the wild, wide hunting-grounds, and claimed them as their own. They must be met and subdued. The savage beasts howled defiance from every hill-top, and in every glen. They must be destroyed. Did the hearts of our fathers fail? No; they entered upon their new life, their new world, with a strong faith and a mighty will. For they saw in the prospection a great and incalculable good. It was not the work of an hour, nor of a day; not of weeks or months, but of long struggling, toiling, painful years. If they failed at one point, they took hold at another. If their paths through the wilderness were at first crooked, rough, and dangerous, by little and little they improved them. The forest faded away, the savage disappeared, the wild beasts were destroyed, and the hopes and prophetic visions of their far-seeing powers in the new and untried country, were more than realized.

Permit me to draw a comparison between the situation of our forefathers in the wilderness, without even so much as a bridle-path through its dark depths, and our present position. The old land of moral, social, and political privilege, seems too narrow for our wants; its soil answers not to our growing, and we feel that we see clearly a better country that we might inhabit. But there are mountains of established law and custom to overcome; a wilderness of prejudice to be subdued; a powerful foe of selfishness and self-interest to overthrow; wild beasts of pride, envy, malice, and hate to destroy. But for the sake of our children and our children's children, we have entered upon the work, hoping and praying that we may be guided by wisdom, sustained by love, and led and cheered by the earnest hope of doing good.

I shall enter into no labored argument to prove that woman does not occupy the position in society to which her capacity justly entitles her. The rights of mankind emanate from their natural wants and emotions. Are not the natural wants and emotions of humanity common to, and shared equally by, both sexes? Does man hunger and thirst, suffer cold and heat more than woman? Does he love and hate, hope and fear, joy and sorrow more than woman? Does his heart thrill with a deeper pleasure in doing good? Can his soul writhe in more bitter agony under the consciousness of evil or wrong? Is the sunshine more glorious, the air more quiet, the sounds of harmony more soothing, the perfume of flowers more exquisite, or forms of beauty more soul-satisfying to his senses, than to hers? To all these interrogatories every one will answer, No!

Where then did man get the authority that he now claims over one-half of humanity? From what power the vested right to place woman— his partner, his companion, his helpmeet in life—in an inferior position? Came it from nature? Nature made woman his superior when she made her his mother; his equal when she fitted her to hold the sacred position of wife. Does he draw his authority from God, from the language of holy writ? No! For it says that "Male and female created he *them,* and gave *them* dominion." Does he claim it under law of the land? Did woman meet with him in council and voluntarily give up all her claim to be her own law-maker? Or did the majesty of might place this power in his hands?—the power of the strong over the weak makes man the master! Yes, there, and there only, does he gain his authority.

In the dark ages of the past, when ignorance, superstition, and bigotry held rule in the world, might made the law. But the undertone, the still small voice of Justice, Love, and Mercy, have ever been heard, pleading the cause of humanity, pleading for truth and right; and their low, soft tones of harmony have softened the lion heart of might, and, little by little, he has yielded as the centuries rolled on; and man, as well as woman, has been the gainer by every concession. We will ask him to yield still; to allow the voice of woman to be heard; to let her take the position which her wants and emotions seem to require; to let her enjoy her natural rights. Do not answer that woman's position is now all her natural wants and emotions require. Our meeting here together this day proves the contrary; proves that we have aspirations that are not met. Will it be answered that we are factious, discontented spirits, striving to disturb the public order, and tear up the old fastness of society? So it was said of Jesus Christ and His followers, when they taught peace on earth and good-will to men. So it was said of our forefathers in the great struggle for freedom. So it has been said of every reformer that has ever started out the car of progress on a new and untried track.

We fear not man as an enemy. He is our friend, our brother. Let woman speak for herself, and she will be heard. Let her claim with a calm and determined, yet loving spirit, her place, and it will be given her. I pour out no harsh invectives against the present order of things— against our fathers, husbands, and brothers; they do as they have been taught; they feel as society bids them; they act as the law requires. Woman must act for herself.

Oh, if all women could be impressed with the importance of their own action, and with one united voice, speak out in their own behalf, in behalf of humanity, they could create a revolution without armies, without bloodshed, that would do more to ameliorate the condition of mankind, to purify, elevate, ennoble humanity, than all that has been done by reformers in the last century.

Reminiscences by Frances D. Gage: Sojourner Truth

THE LEADERS OF the movement trembled on seeing a tall, gaunt black woman in a gray dress and white turban, surmounted with an uncouth sun-bonnet, march deliberately into the church, walk with the air of a queen up the aisle, and take her seat upon the pulpit steps. A buzz of disapprobation was heard all over the house, and there fell on the listening ear, "An abolition affair!" "Woman's rights and niggers!" "I told you so!" "Go it, darkey!"

I chanced on that occasion to wear my first laurels in public life as president of the meeting. At my request order was restored, and the business of the Convention went on. Morning, afternoon, and evening exercises came and went. Through all these sessions old Sojourner, quiet and reticent as the "Lybian Statue," sat crouched against the wall on the corner of the pulpit stairs, her sun-bonnet shading her eyes, her elbows on her knees, her chin resting upon her broad, hard palms. At intermission she was busy selling the "Life of Sojourner Truth," a narrative of her own strange and adventurous life. Again and again, timorous and trembling ones came to me and said, with earnestness, "Don't let her speak, Mrs. Gage, it will ruin us. Every newspaper in the land will have our cause mixed up with abolition and niggers, and we shall be utterly denounced." My only answer was, "We shall see when the time comes."

The second day the work waxed warm. Methodist, Baptist, Episcopal, Presbyterian, and Universalist ministers came in to hear and discuss the resolutions presented. One claimed superior rights and privileges for man, on the ground of "superior intellect"; another, because of the "manhood of Christ; if God had desired the equality of woman, He would have given some token of His will through the birth, life, and death of the Saviour." Another gave us a theological view of the "sin of our first mother."

There were very few women in those days who dared to "speak in meeting"; and the august teachers of the people were seemingly getting the better of us, while the boys in the galleries, and the sneerers among the pews, were hugely enjoying the discomfiture, as they supposed, of the "strong-minded." Some of the tender-skinned friends were on the point of losing dignity, and the atmosphere betokened a storm. When,

35

slowly from her seat in the corner rose Sojourner Truth, who, till now, had scarcely lifted her head. "Don't let her speak!" gasped half a dozen in my ear. She moved slowly and solemnly to the front, laid her old bonnet at her feet, and turned her great speaking eyes to me. There was a hissing sound of disapprobation above and below. I rose and announced "Sojourner Truth," and begged the audience to keep silence for a few moments.

The tumult subsided at once, and every eye was fixed on this almost Amazon form, which stood nearly six feet high, head erect, and eyes piercing the upper air like one in a dream. At her first word there was a profound hush. She spoke in deep tones, which, though not loud, reached every ear in the house, and away through the throng at the doors and windows.

"Wall, chilern, whar dar is so much racket dar must be somethin' out o' kilter. I tink dat 'twixt de niggers of de Souf and de womin at de Norf, all talkin' 'bout rights, de white men will be in a fix pretty soon. But what's all dis here talkin' 'bout?

"Dat man ober dar say dat womin needs to be helped into carriages and lifted ober ditches, and to hab de best place everywhar. Nobody eber helps me into carriages, or ober mud-puddles, or gibs me any best place!" And raising herself to her full height, and her voice to a pitch like rolling thunder, she asked, "And a'n't I a woman? Look at me! Look at my arm." (and she bared her right arm to the shoulder, showing her tremendous muscular power). I have ploughed, and planted, and gathered into barns, and no man could head me! And a'n't I a woman? I could work as much and eat as much as a man—when I could get it—and bear de lash as well! And a'n't I a woman? I have borne thirteen chilern, and seen 'em mos' all sold off to slavery, and when I cried out with my mother's grief, none but Jesus heard me! And a'n't I a woman?

"Den dey talks 'bout dis ting in de head; what dis dey call it?" ("Intellect," whispered some one near.) "Dat's it, honey. What's dat got to do wid womin's rights or nigger's rights? If my cup won't hold but a pint, and yourn holds a quart, wouldn't ye be mean not to let me have my little half-measure full?" And she pointed her significant finger, and sent a keen glance at the minister who had made the argument. The cheering was long and loud.

"Den dat little man in black dar, he say women can't have as much rights as men, 'cause Christ wan't a woman! Whar did your Christ come from?" Rolling thunder couldn't have stilled that crowd, as did those deep, wonderful tones, as she stood there with outstretched arms and eyes of fire. Railing her voice still louder, she repeated, "Whar did your Christ come from? From God and a woman! Man had nothin' to do wid Him." Oh, what a rebuke that was to that little man.

Turning again to another objector, she took up the defense of Mother Eve. I can not follow her through it all. It was pointed, and witty, and solemn; eliciting at almost every sentence deafening applause; and she ended by asserting: "If de fust woman God ever made was strong enough to turn de world upside down all alone, dese women togedder (and she glanced her eye over the platform) ought to be able to turn it back, and get it right side up again! And now dey is asking to do it, de men better let 'em." Long-continued cheering greeted this. "'Bleeged to ye for hearin' on me, and now ole Sojourner han't got nothin' more to say."

Amid roars of applause, she returned to her corner, leaving more than one of us with streaming eyes, and hearts beating with gratitude. She had taken us up in her strong arms and carried us safely over the slough of difficulty turning the whole tide in our favor. I have never in my life seen anything like the magical influence that subdued the mobbish spirit of the day, and turned the sneers and jeers of an excited crowd into notes of respect and admiration. Hundreds rushed up to shake hands with her, and congratulate the glorious old mother, and bid her God-speed on her mission of "testifyin' agin concerning the wickedness of this 'ere people."

Chapter XXI

The First Steamboat on the Waters of the Muskingum

IT HAPPENED TO be my good fortune, ladies and gentlemen, to be training "young ideas how to shoot," in the beautiful little town of Marietta,
in the year 1820. Marietta, you all know, is located at the junction of the
Muskingum River with the La Belle Riviére, of the old French settlers,
or, in plain English, the beautiful river Ohio, and is famous for two
things. First, as being a place of mounds, covert-ways, dykes, ditches,
squares, and embankments, or, as familiarly called, "ancient works and
fortifications," supposed to have been made by a people far more cultivated than the Indians who roamed the forest, when the oldest civilized
inhabitant first pitched his tent in the beautiful valley.

Secondly, it was famed as being the first point upon which the Ohio
Company landed, after leaving Pittsburg, or old Fort du Quesne, at the
head-waters of navigation; and consequently, the first settlement of Ohio
was made at this same town.

To me it was famous in another regard; that the early inhabitants, unlike most Western town-makers, had been too sensible to crowd themselves uncomfortably; and had in laying out theirs, provided a good
common, wide streets, preserved their "ancient works," and left each
landholder a lot large enough for a garden and door-yard. This liberality
of land is often a matter of wonder to travellers among us; but I suppose
our grandsires had not then dreamed of a half-acre lot west of the
Alleghanies ever being worth half a million; or that they should live to
see cities and towns strewn in grandeur and wealth, to the very slopes of
the Rocky Mountains.

Ah, it was a delightful winter, that! Every day brought to me new
treasures of history from the early times of this interesting people. I lingered many a day in their beautiful cemetery, where slept the last earthly
remains of their leader, old General Rufus Putnam, who brought his gallant band so bravely through the wilderness, and stood steadfastly by
them through the varied and sore trials of border life.

There, too, at the foot of a great mound, reared by the hands of a lost race, slept old Commodore Abraham Whipple, who, as his epitaph tells us, fired the first gun of the Revolution; and performed the still bolder feat of taking the first ship, or barge, down the waters of the Ohio and Mississippi into the Gulf of Mexico; a daring deed in those days, when the Indian hunting-grounds lay nearly the entire distance on either side.

Many a winter evening sped away, almost unheeded, as I listened to the tales of old Judge Cutler, of the valiant deeds of those valiant men, of their nobleness and courage; of the heroism of the women, their un-shaken faith and hope through the seven years' war, and their garrison life; tales of the hunt, and chase, and victory; of the savage treachery and bloody massacre; of their losses and crosses, their hunger and toil, and their triumph at last, when they arose more than conquerors, from the conflict of years.

There, too, I heard the tale of the Fairy Isle, where Blennerhasset and his beautiful wife made their Eden home, ere a wild ambition swept over it, and left it all blackness and ruin.

These stories became to me as household words. . . . From the Alleghanies to the buffalo-beats of Nebraska, every native-born Western man and woman owes these old settlers a debt of gratitude and love, for teaching the world how strong and brave the human heart can be.

But the one great topic of interest at the time of my residence among the people, was the new steamboat building at the river-side, which was the first experiment of the kind ever tried there. Its builder was Capt. John Greene, born on the banks of the Muskingum, who had long fol-lowed its waters as a keel-boatman. The name of the trim little craft was the *Rufus Putnam,* after the memorable founder of this new world.

Many were the prophecies of failure. The "old fogies" of that day were as genuine antiques, as the same class of fossils of the present day; and shook their heads as ominously over any innovations upon the old order. But for all their glowering looks and dark sayings, Capt. Greene kept on the even tenor of his way, and accomplished his work. As the crowning feat of his temerity, he advertised that the "Rufus Putnam" would make a trip to Zanesville, in the month of March, and take, free of charge, any of the old settlers on the banks of the river. People did not so easily leave home then as now; and when the time came there were no more to accept the kind invitation, than could be accommodated on a craft of less than one hundred and fifty tons.

A steamboat upon the winding waters of the Muskingum? It was impossible! The man was crazed! He would run his prow into the crooked banks, he would stave her on a snag, get aground on the bars, or blow up, as had the "Washington," a few years before!

But Capt. G—— was not to be turned from his purpose by all their croaking. He had walked the crooked stream for years, with his shoulder to the setting pole, and stood with his hand upon the helm through storm and dangers. He knew it thoroughly, and he had no fears. So when the spring winds came, softening the icy chains, and setting the brooks and rills free; bringing down the gentle showers, and swelling the buds of the buckeye and red-bud, and the Muskingum rose half-banks to welcome his enterprise,—he announced the day and hour of his departure.

The fires in the sugar camps were not yet extinguished, nor had the swallows and bluebirds been wooed back to their old haunts, by the green boughs of the willows; though here and there a blue violet was peeping to see if the icicles were all gone, and wild anemonies in sunny nooks whispered of the "good time coming."

On the day fixed, a loud-mouthed cannon, posted upon her prow, told the people for miles around that the "Putnam" was on her way, and would call at their doors and take a breathing-spell, while they tied on cloaks and bonnets, and got ready to join the jovial party. . . .

In a long bend of the river, six miles above Marietta, called "Rainbow," by the old pioneers, from its resemblance to an arch; on the inner side of the curve, and hidden in the beautiful vale which it hugged in its embrace, were located several families of old settlers, who had lived through the trials and dangers of the Indian war, and who, as soon as the peace was declared, and the garrison opened its doors, had gone forth with their families, and settled on their farms in this beautiful area, surrounded by high hills, and bordered by the stream.

"Shall we go?" asked "uncle W——," as the loud report of the cannon came booming through the hills; but the smoke rolled up from his sugar camp, and the plough stood in the furrow, and he turned to his husbandry and smiled,—he could not be tempted away.

"Shall we go?" asked Frank of his father, a brave old veteran of the Revolution, who had lost one limb in battle, but was "worth as much as a well man yet." It was he, old Capt. Jonathan Devol, who built the first floating-mill on the waters of Muskingum, that gave bread to the settlers. As the "Putnam" poured out its salute before his door, and the band played the "Star-Spangled Banner," he hobbled out upon his cane, and bowed low his venerable head to the gallant Captain of the proud craft. The wind stretched out to their full size and length the stars and stripes that floated from her prow, and waved their recognition to the salute of the old soldier.

"Let us go," said Israel Putnam, a lineal descendant of the venerable Pomfret hero,—"let us go, Helen;" and in a moment they were flying in the light canoe to the steamer's side, while the cannon again sent out its signal.

"Shall we go?" asked the young Russells; but the careful father and prudent mother shook their heads; how could they decide which of the half-dozen beautiful girls, or industrious boys, should leave the farm and its labors. On went the boat. The loud salute was fired before a brick mansion. Hats were flung high, and handkerchiefs waved, and the boat passed on. Now they were at the semi-circle that enclosed the farm of Col. Joseph Barker, the beautiful spot which the English novelist, Murray, has called Mooshanna.

"Shall we go?" asked the daughters, with beating hearts, as they looked down, from their home on the bluff, at the flying steamer.

But the old Colonel shook his head, as if not stirred by the excitement which called others from their homes to line the banks and wave their cheers to the flying stranger.

"Pho, pho!" said he, "can't you see it from here? I have seen it at Marietta; it's nothing but a steamboat!"

And he hummed his tune, and worked away with a drawing-knife at a hoop for the rain-barrel. But what troubled his eyes just then?

"Plague take the dust!" he exclaimed, as he drew out his bandana from the pocket of his home-made, brown, hunting-shirt. He wiped his eyes again and again; the dust would not away. Ah! it was the dust and cobwebs of time that troubled him; of old memories, of early hardships, of dangers, toils and death; of friends long gone, linked to the present by every success and every triumph.

His heart was full—full to the brim, of those old stirring times; and, welling up they ran over at his eyes. Memories of days when he was young, when the hair upon his brow was not silvered; when he roamed the dense forest, rifle in hand, and peered cautiously for the savage foe behind every tree and fallen log; when the panther lay crouched in the path, and the rattlesnake coiled itself by the wayside, and the wild wolf howled nightly upon the hills; of the days when friends and brothers went out at morn, and returned not at nightfall; when sickness and sorrow came with heavy steps, and there were none to help; when the fire swept away the toil of years, and the hopes of days to come.

But the danger had passed; the savage and the wild beast were subdued. Friends, neighbors, children, peace, prosperity and abundance had come as the reward of past perils. It was no wonder that his eyes filled with tears, and his heart beat a loud response to the spirit-stirring notes of "Hail Columbia," as they came floating over his wide meadows. He tried to keep cool under it all; but the glittering blade made tremulous motions in his hands.

Boom! went the cannon, as the steamer shot by the line that separated his field from his neighbor. On, on went the boat, circling round the bend, while he whittled away at his hoop, unwilling, like many other old men, to own, even to himself, that nature was struggling for utterance in his soul; unwilling to let her speak aloud in the language of joy and triumph.

The girls had sped away to the river-bank, and the mother stood gazing from the window; there were memories tugging at her heart-strings, too, as Capt. Green[e], who was an old friend, passed the spot where the settler's cabin had stood at first; where the tall pear-tree pointed to the sky, and the great elm spread its mighty arms over an acre of soil,— where he had often moored his keel-boat, and built his camp-fire, in years long gone,—and ordered another salute in memory of those days.

The Colonel could stand no more; his horse was out in an instant; and though no Bucephalus, he knew his master's will and did it. The Colonel mounted, the enthusiasm of boyhood and the vigor of manhood seemed burning in his veins, hurling the cool gravity of age from its seat; and, grasping the reins, down the hill and across the valley he dashed, and met the gallant Captain at the upper end of the bend. The old man raised himself in his stirrups, lifted his hat on high, and gave one loud, long *huzza* that went echoing through the hills far above the din of wheels or roar of the spouting stream, and was followed almost instantly by a blast from the old cannon which made the very tree-tops tremble. The band struck up "Yankee Doodle," and gave the gray-haired pioneer a hearty cheer. On flew the boat, on flew "old grey,"— but it was in vain; the new power subdued the old,—and with a bow and another wave of his hat, the proud old farmer went back to his thoughts and his work. . . .

The first eight miles up the Muskingum is a fair sample of the entire journey. People rushed to the banks for miles away, to see the mighty wonder of the age. Many had never heard of a steamboat, for newspapers did not travel the world as now; and fear and terror took fast hold upon such, when they first heard the report of the great gun.

It was not the Fourth of July, nor the Twenty-Second of February,—why then should guns be fired? Timid ones were sure that the "British were coming again;" others, who heard the roar of steam, ran to their neighbors for prayers; the day of judgment might be at hand. One old lady, who had heard of the fabulous sea-serpent, fled to the hills with her grandchildren, lest, like Jonah, they should be swallowed alive. An old salt suggested that a whale had lost his way, and was floundering and spouting up the fresh water of the Muskingum.

All this excitement may seem strange to those who see daily the magnificent boats of the present gliding quietly by their doors. They can have no conception of the noisy, puffing crafts of forty years ago, which often heralded themselves from a distance of four or five miles, with every revolution of the wheel; and the curiosity and wonder they created could not be equalled now, were we to see a long line of rail-cars flying by steam through the air. Less a wonder would such a phenomenon be to us, than was the "Rufus Putnam" to a majority of the settlers on the banks of the *beautiful Muskingum* in the year of our Lord 1820. . . .

Sarah Margaret Fuller Ossoli
(1810–1850)

E ARLY IN THE nineteenth century, while New Englanders were dealing with the effects of intermittent trade embargoes with Britain and France and the impressment of American seamen by British vessels, white westerners faced a consolidation of tribes under the Shawnee chief, Tecumseh, and his brother, Tenskwatawa, "the Prophet." Tecumseh envisioned a confederation of tribes that jointly held, tilled, and hunted land separate from white men. Although Tecumseh wished to avoid war with white Americans, he planned for the eventuality by stockpiling guns and ammunition obtained from the British in Canada. The U.S. government, fearful that an Indian empire in the West would restrict the available arable land, took the initiative. In 1811, while Tecumseh was traveling in the South, William Henry Harrison engaged the Prophet and a large force of braves at Tippecanoe, Indiana. Neither side could claim decisive victory. A year later, Tecumseh sided with the British in the War of 1812. When he died at the Battle of the Thames in 1813, his dream of a confederacy died with him.

Over the next thirty years, other Indian leaders attempted to unite regional tribes to resist the westward expansion of the whites and the concomitant ceding of tribal lands to the American government. One major leader in conflicts along the upper Mississippi Valley was Black Hawk, mentioned by Fuller in her *Summer on the Lakes, in 1843*. Black Hawk led an armed uprising of Sauk and Fox Indians in Wisconsin Territory and Illinois in 1832. The resistance failed. By the time Margaret Fuller went on her western tour of the Great Lakes, the region was largely "pacified."

Fuller, for a time the most influential woman writer in America, was born in Cambridgeport, Massachusetts. The eldest child of a Harvard-educated lawyer-politician, young Margaret's formal education began at six. She spent her childhood learning Latin, French, Greek, English grammar, and Italian under her father's tutelage. She read the classics instead of playing, wrote letters in French, and recited in the evenings. Joyful moments came from forays into the garden with her mother and brothers, but times of rest were rare. When she began her autobiography at thirty, five years after her father's death from cholera, Margaret wrote of her resentment at being deprived of a normal childhood. Yet, through "Miranda," a pseudonymous character in *Woman in the Nineteenth Century,* Fuller espouses the form of upbringing she received.

At fourteen, Fuller was sent to boarding school for a year to learn the social graces. It was a painful time, exacerbated by her inability to relate intellectually with her classmates, her feelings of superiority, and, perversely, her need to be accepted and loved. In *Summer on the Lakes, in 1843,* Fuller describes this time, but attributes the events to a fictional character, Mariana.

After her father's death, Fuller taught in Boston and Rhode Island in order to support her family. In Boston, she led women's discussion groups that focused on history and literature. She studied and debated transcendental philosophy with Ralph Waldo Emerson, impressing him with her intellect, knowledge, and writing ability. She taught herself German, and published translations of Goethe and other philosophical German works, book reviews, and essays, most of them in the *Dial,* a transcendentalist publication.

The death of her father postponed Fuller's dream to travel in Europe. In 1843, however, she traveled with friends through the Great Lakes. Her single trip west was a woman scholar's journey, one in which she interpreted the western experience for the eastern literary establishment. Fuller described the western scene, but interspersed autobiographical episodes, poetry based on classical themes, discourses on morality and German mysticism, condescending observations on the poverty and slovenliness of the common settler and the Indian, and a marked preference for abodes that more closely mimicked the New England farms of her acquaintance. At the same time, however, she noted the unavailing drudgery of the woman settler's situation, the unparalleled beauty of the prairies, the intimidation of mountainless vistas, and the mystery and richness of an Eden that was being destroyed by the ax and plow. Sensory images both excited and repelled her. She came away with a deeper appreciation of the costs to women who were courageous enough to venture west. That insight added depth to Fuller's greatest work, *Woman in the Nineteenth Century,* published in 1845.

Summer on the Lakes, in 1843, led Horace Greeley to offer Fuller the position of literary editor of the *New York Tribune.* In 1846, Fuller went to Europe as a paid correspondent for the *Tribune.* While in Italy she met, and presumably married, Giovanni Angelo Ossoli, who was deeply involved in the Italian Revolution of 1848. Fuller, in eyewitness dispatches to the *Tribune,* covered the establishment of the short-lived Republic, as well as its subsequent overthrow by Austria and France.

In the summer of 1850, Fuller, Ossoli, and their young son, Angelo, sailed for the United States. Their ship foundered and sank off Fire Island, New York. There were no survivors. Neither Fuller's body nor her unpublished manuscripts were found. But her earlier writing served as a foundation for the woman's rights movement that blossomed in the latter half of the nineteenth century.

Chapter III

[June 1843]

IN THE AFTERNOON of this day we reached the Rock river, in whose neighborhood we proposed to make some stay, and crossed at Dixon's ferry.

This beautiful stream flows full and wide over a bed of rocks, traversing a distance of near two hundred miles, to reach the Mississippi. Great part of the country along its banks is the finest region of Illinois, and the scene of some of the latest romance of Indian warfare. To these beautiful regions Black Hawk returned with his band "to pass the summer," when he drew upon himself the warfare in which he was finally vanquished. No wonder he could not resist the longing, unwise though its indulgence might be, to return in summer to this home of beauty.

Of Illinois, in general, it has often been remarked that it bears the character of country which has been inhabited by a nation skilled like the English in all the ornamental arts of life, especially in landscape gardening. That the villas and castles seem to have been burnt, the enclosures taken down, but the velvet lawns, the flower gardens, the stately parks, scattered at graceful intervals by the decorous hand of art, the frequent deer, and the peaceful herd of cattle that make picture of the plain, all suggest more of the masterly mind of man, than the prodigal, but careless, motherly love of nature. Especially is this true of the Rock river country. The river flows sometimes through these parks and lawns, then betwixt high bluffs, whose grassy ridges are covered with fine trees, or broken with crumbling stone, that easily assumes the forms of buttress, arch and clustered columns. Along the face of such crumbling rocks, swallows' nests are clustered, thick as cities, and eagles and deer do not disdain their summits. One morning, out in the boat along the base of these rocks, it was amusing, and affecting too, to see these swallows put their heads out to look at us. There was something very hospitable about it, as if man had never shown himself a tyrant near them. What a morning that was! Every sight is worth twice as much by the early morning light. We borrow something of the spirit of the hour to look upon them.

The first place where we stopped was one of singular beauty, a beauty

of soft, luxuriant wildness. It was on the bend of the river, a place chosen by an Irish gentleman. . . .

There was a peculiar charm in coming here, where the choice of location, and the unobtrusive good taste of all the arrangements, showed
such intelligent appreciation of the spirit of the scene, after seeing so
many dwellings of the new settlers, which showed plainly that they had
no thought beyond satisfying the grossest material wants. Sometimes
they looked attractive, the little brown houses, the natural architecture
of the country, in the edge of the timber. But almost always when you
came near, the slovenliness of the dwelling and the rude way in which
objects around it were treated, when so little care would have presented
a charming whole, were very repulsive. Seeing the traces of the Indians,
who chose the most beautiful sites for their dwellings, and whose habits
do not break in on that aspect of nature under which they were born, we
feel as if they were the rightful lords of a beauty they forbore to deform.
But most of these settlers do not see it at all; it breathes, it speaks in vain
to those who are rushing into its sphere. Their progress is Gothic, not
Roman, and their mode of cultivation will, in the course of twenty, perhaps ten, years, obliterate the natural expression of the country. . . .

Leaving this place, we proceeded a day's journey along the beautiful
stream, to a little town named Oregon. We called at a cabin, from whose
door looked out one of those faces which, once seen, are never forgotten; young, yet touched with many traces of feeling, not only possible,
but endured; spirited, too, like the gleam of a finely tempered blade. It
was a face that suggested a history, and many histories, but whose scene
would have been in courts and camps. At this moment their circles are
dull for want of that life which is waning unexcited in this solitary recess.

The master of the house proposed to show us a "short cut," by which
we might, to especial advantage, pursue our journey. This proved to be
almost perpendicular down a hill, studded with young trees and stumps.
From these he proposed, with a hospitality of service worthy an
Oriental, to free our wheels whenever they should get entangled, also, to
be himself the drag, to prevent our too rapid descent. Such generosity
deserved trust; however, we women could not be persuaded to render it.
We got out and admired, from afar, the process. Left by our guide—and
prop! we found ourselves in a wide field, where, by playful quips and
turns, an endless "creek," seemed to divert itself with our attempts to
cross it. Failing in this, the next best was to whirl down a steep bank,

which feat our charioteer performed with an air not unlike that of Rhesus, had he but been as suitably furnished with chariot and steeds!

At last, after wasting some two or three hours on the "short cut," we got out by following an Indian trail,—Black Hawk's! How fair the scene through which it led! How could they let themselves be conquered, with such a country to fight for! . . .

Passing through one of the fine, park-like woods, almost clear from underbrush and carpeted with thick grasses and flowers, we met, (for it was Sunday,) a little congregation just returning from their service, which had been performed in a rude house in its midst. It had a sweet and peaceful air, as if such words and thoughts were very dear to them. The parents had with them all their little children; but we saw no old people; that charm was wanting, which exists in such scenes in older settlements, of seeing the silver bent in reverence beside the flaxen head.

At Oregon, the beauty of the scene was of even a more sumptuous character than at our former "stopping place." Here swelled the river in its boldest course, interspersed by halcyon isles on which nature had lavished all her prodigality in tree, vine, and flower, banked by noble bluffs, three hundred feet high, their sharp ridges as exquisitely definite as the edge of a shell; their summits adorned with those same beautiful trees, and with buttresses of rich rock, crested with old hemlocks, which wore a touching and antique grace amid the softer and more luxuriant vegetation. Lofty natural mounds rose amidst the rest, with the same lovely and sweeping outline, showing everywhere the plastic power of water,— water, mother of beauty, which, by its sweet and eager flow, had left such lineaments as human genius never dreamt of.

Not far from the river was a high crag, called the Pine Rock, which looks out, as our guide observed, like a helmet above the brow of the country. It seems as if the water left here and there a vestige of forms and materials that preceded its course, just to set off its new and richer designs.

The aspect of this country was to me enchanting, beyond any I have ever seen, from its fullness of expression, its bold and impassioned sweetness. Here the flood of emotion has passed over and marked everywhere its course by a smile. The fragments of rock touch it with a wildness and liberality which give just the needed relief. I should never be tired here, though I have elsewhere seen country of more secret and alluring charms, better calculated to stimulate and suggest. Here the eye and heart are filled.

How happy the Indians must have been here! It is not long since they were driven away, and the ground, above and below, is full of their traces.

"The earth is full of men."

You have only to turn up the sod to find arrowheads and Indian pottery. On an island, belonging to our host, and nearly opposite his house, they loved to stay, and, no doubt, enjoyed its lavish beauty as much as the myriad wild pigeons that now haunt its flower-filled shades. Here are still the marks of their tomahawks, the troughs in which they prepared their corn, their caches.

A little way down the river is the site of an ancient Indian village, with its regularly arranged mounds. As usual, they had chosen with the finest taste. It was one of those soft shadowy afternoons when we went there, when nature seems ready to weep, not from grief, but from an overfull heart. Two prattling, lovely little girls, and an African boy, with glittering eye and ready grin, made our party gay; but all were still as we entered their little inlet and trod those flowery paths. They may blacken Indian life as they will, talk of its dirt, its brutality, I will ever believe that the men who chose that dwelling-place were able to feel emotions of noble happiness as they returned to it, and so were the women that received them. Neither were the children sad or dull, who lived so familiarly with the deer and birds, and swam that clear wave in the shadow of the Seven Sisters. . . .

The sixth July we left this beautiful place. It was one of those rich days of bright sunlight, varied by the purple shadows of large sweeping clouds. Many a backward look we cast, and left the heart behind.

Our journey to-day was no less delightful than before, still all new, boundless, limitless. Kinmont says, that limits are sacred; that the Greeks were in the right to worship a god of limits. I say, that what is limitless is alone divine, that there was neither wall nor road in Eden, that those who walked there lost and found their way just as we did, and that all the gain from the Fall was that we had a wagon to ride in. I do not think, either, that even the horses doubted whether this last was any advantage.

Everywhere the rattlesnake-weed grows in profusion. The antidote survives the bane. Soon the coarser plantain, the "white man's footstep," shall take its place. We saw also the compass plant, and the western tea plant. Of some of the brightest flowers an Indian girl afterwards told me the medicinal virtues. I doubt not those students of the soil knew a use to every fair emblem, on which we could only look to admire its hues and shape.

After noon we were ferried by a girl, (unfortunately not of the most picturesque appearance) across the Kishwaukie, the most graceful stream, and on whose bosom rested many full-blown water-lilies, twice as large as any of ours. I was told that, *en revanche,* they were scentless, but I still regret that I could not get at one of them to try.

Query, did the lilied fragrance which, in the miraculous times, accompanied visions of saints and angels, proceed from water or garden lilies?

Kishwaukie is, according to tradition, the scene of a famous battle, and its many grassy mounds contain the bones of the valiant. On these waved thickly the mysterious purple flower, of which I have spoken before. I think it springs from the blood of the Indians, as the hyacinth did from that of Apollo's darling.

The ladies of our host's family at Oregon, when they first went there, after all the pains and plagues of building and settling, found their first pastime in opening one of these mounds, in which they found, I think, three of the departed, seated in the Indian fashion.

One of these same ladies, as she was making bread one winter morning, saw from the window a deer directly before the house. She ran out, with her hands covered with dough, calling the others, and they caught him bodily before he had time to escape.

Here (at Kishwaukie) we received a visit from a ragged and barefoot, but bright-eyed gentleman, who seemed to be the intellectual loafer, the walking Will's coffeehouse of the place. He told us many charming snake stories; among others, of himself having seen seventeen young ones reënter the mother snake, on the intrusion of a visiter.

This night we reached Belvidere, a flourishing town in Boon county, where was the tomb, now despoiled, of Big Thunder. In this later day we felt happy to find a really good hotel. From this place, by two days of very leisurely and devious journeying, we reached Chicago, and thus ended a journey, which one at least of the party might have wished unending. . . .

> *Farewell, ye soft and sumptuous solitudes!*
> *Ye fairy distances, ye lordly woods,*
> *Haunted by paths like those that Poussin knew,*
> *When after his all gazers eyes he drew;*
> *I go,—and if I never more may steep*

An eager heart in your enchantments deep,
Yet ever to itself that heart may say,
Be not exacting; thou hast lived one day;
Hast looked on that which matches with thy mood,
Impassioned sweetness of full being's flood,
Where nothing checked the bold yet gentle wave,
Where nought repelled the lavish love that gave.
A tender blessing lingers o'er the scene,
Like some young mother's thought, fond, yet serene,
And through its life new-born our lives have been.
Once more farewell,—a sad, a sweet farewell;
And, if I never must behold you more,
In other worlds I will not cease to tell
The rosary I here have numbered o'er;
And bright-haired Hope will lend a gladdened ear,
And Love will free him from the grasp of Fear,
And Gorgon critics, while the tale they hear,
Shall dew their stony glances with a tear,
If I but catch one echo from your spell;—
And so farewell,—a grateful, sad farewell!

Mary Ann Adams Maverick
(1818–1898)

FROM THE DAY of Mary Adams's marriage in 1836, her history was tied to that of Texas.

Adams's husband, Samuel Augustus Maverick, was a Yale graduate, lawyer, land speculator, and politician. Originally from South Carolina, he had left Alabama for Texas in 1834. It was the era of Sam Houston and Stephen Austin, the Bowie brothers and Davy Crockett. Texas was still a province of Mexico, where Santa Anna was president. In 1835, the North American settlers had seceded from Mexico and set up a provisional government in Austin. When Samuel Maverick traveled to San Antonio de Bexar, he was arrested by the Mexican army and tried for treason. He escaped, and helped lead the Texas army in the battle to evict the Mexican garrison and retake San Antonio. On February 22, 1836, while Maverick was in Austin signing the Declaration of Independence of the Republic of Texas, Santa Anna laid siege to the Alamo. The fortress of San Antonio, which was held by less than two hundred Texans, fell on March 6, 1836. Six weeks later, on the banks of the San Jacinto River, Maverick helped Sam Houston rout the Mexican army and capture Santa Anna. The United States refused to annex Texas, but recognized the Lone Star Republic the next year.

In the summer of 1836, with peace ensured in Texas, Samuel Maverick went back to Tuscaloosa to marry Mary Ann Adams. Seventeen months later, the Mavericks, their baby son, Mary's brother, and a retinue of ten slaves set foot in Texas. She was nineteen. In the next sixty years she would bear ten children, and bury five. Through it all, she recorded their history in pocket journals and letters.

A gentlewoman, born and raised on an Alabama plantation, Mary Maverick carried west her southern prejudices. She disparaged Native Americans. She both patronized and praised her Mexican neighbors. She brought slaves to Texas to work in the house and fields. Yet, her book documents their heroism and loyalty. They, too, were among the earliest American settlers in Texas, eventually working their own plots of land donated by the Mavericks. They, too, sank deep roots into the Texas soil, fought for the land, and died there.

In 1845, the United States annexed the Lone Star Republic as the twenty-eighth state. Texas entered the Union as a slaveholding state because slaves were needed to develop and work the cotton fields, the major cash crop. During the Civil War, slavery linked Texas with the Confederacy. Four of the Mavericks' sons donned gray uniforms. All survived the war.

Mary Maverick wrote only one book, an unsophisticated autobiography based on her journals. First published with her son in 1896, *Memoirs* was edited and republished by her son and granddaughter after Maverick's death. As a woman's record of the early days in eastern Texas, the book is historically valuable. Maverick describes their life in San Antonio, in a homestead on the Colorado River, and on a ranch at Decrows Point on Matagorda Bay. Mary and Samuel survived Indian raids, wars with Mexico, and financial disasters. Cholera, typhoid, smallpox, scarlatina, yellow fever, dysentery, malaria, and food poisoning swept through the population. In 1842, Samuel was again captured while defending San Antonio from attack by the Mexican army. He was released in Mexico City seven months later, after marching twelve hundred miles. In his absence, Mary developed and managed their property on the Colorado River in Texas. On the day of his release, their second daughter was born. Samuel did not meet her until she was five weeks old.

In matter-of-fact language, Mary Maverick described captivity experiences of white women and children taken by Indians, offbeat western characters such as Dr. Weideman, and the dangers inherent in everyday activities. Friends drowned while crossing streams or boating offshore; Indians lay in wait for berry pickers and surveying parties. Maverick recognized that she and her family were making history. In an effort to preserve the memory of the children who died, and so future generations would understand the Mavericks' contribution to the formation of a state, she recorded events as they unfolded. She was not concerned that her viewpoint was biased. Perhaps her story is more valuable because of its honest presentation.

Chapter VII

Doctor Weideman

LATE IN THE afternoon of the Indian fight, of the 19th, I visited Mrs. Higginbotham's, as I have before stated. While I was there, Dr. Weideman came up to her grated front window, and placed a severed Indian head upon the sill. The good doctor bowed courteously and saying, "With your permission, Madam," disappeared. Soon after he returned with another bloody head, when he explained to us that he had viewed all the dead Indians, and selected these two heads, male and female, for the skulls, and also had selected two entire bodies, male and female, to preserve as specimen skeletons. He said: "I have been long exceedingly anxious to secure such specimens—and now, ladies, I must hurry and get a cart to take them to my house," and off he hurried all begimed with dirt and blood, (having been with his good horse one of the foremost in pursuit.) Now he was exulting for the cause of science in his "magnificent specimens" and before it was quite dark, he came with his cart and its frightful load, took his two heads and disappeared. His house was the old Chaves place, on the side of Acequia Street, (now Main Avenue,) north of Main Plaza. Dr. Weideman, a Russian, was a very learned man of perhaps thirty-five years of age, was a surgeon and M.D., spoke many living tongues and had travelled very extensively. In former years, he had buried a lovely young wife and son, and becoming restless, had sought and secured employment under the Russian Government. In fact the Emperor of Russia had sent him to Texas to find and report anything and everything, vegetable and animal grown in Texas—and he had selected a worthy man, for Dr. Weideman was a devotee to science. He grew enthusiastic over our Western Texas and her climate and constantly accompanied the "Minute Men" on their expeditions and numerous surveying parties.

Dr. Weideman took the Indian heads and bodies to his home as I have mentioned, and put them into a large soap boiler on the bank of the "esequia," or ditch, which ran in front of his premises. During the night of the 20th he emptied the boiler, containing water and flesh from the bones, into the ditch. Now this ditch furnished the drinking water generally for the town. The river and the San Pedro Creek, it was understood, were for bathing and washing purposes, but a city ordinance prohibited, with heavy fines, the throwing of any dirt or filth into the ditch—for it was highly necessary and proper to keep the drinking water pure.

On the 21st, it dawned upon the dwellers upon the banks of the ditch that the doctor had defiled their drinking water. There arose a great hue and cry and all the people crowded to the mayor's office—the men talked in loud and excited tones, the women shrieked and cried—they rolled up their eyes in horror, they vomited, and many thought they were poisoned and must die. Dr. Weideman was arrested and brought to trial, he was overwhelmed with abuse, he was called "diabolo," "demonio[,]" "sin verguenza," etc., etc. He took it quite calmly, told the poor creatures they would not be hurt—that the Indian poison had all run off with the water long before day—paid his fine and went off laughing.

The doctor had a Mexican servant who had been pretty good, and lived with him two years—but Jose would steal—and one day he stole the doctor's watch, a valuable gold timepiece. Dr. Weideman after inquiring and waiting several weeks in vain, determined to have his watch, if he had to use magic to get it. He had several Mexican men servants, for he kept horses, wild animals, snakes and birds and also cultivated a fine garden—with wild flowers, etc., he satisfied himself that Jose was the thief. He invited several gentlemen to come to his house a certain evening about full of the moon, and he told his servants that would summon the spirits to point out the thief. When the appointed time came, he caused a fire to be built on the flat dirt roof of his house, over which he placed a pot filled with liquids. Hither he brought his company and the servants. He was dressed in a curious robe or gown covered with weird figures, and a tall wonderful cap rested on his head. In his hand he held a twisted stick with which he stirred the liquid in the pot, uttering the while words in an unknown tongue. He was very solemn and occasionally he would turn around slowly and gaze upward into space. Finally he told all present that he would put out the fire, and cool the liquid, and then each person in turn should dip his hand in, and the thief's hand would turn black. Each one advanced in due order and submitted his hand to the test, and after each experiment the doctor would stir and mutter and turn around again. Jose waited until the very last, he came up quite unwillingly, and when he withdrew his hand from the pot it was black. Jose was terribly frightened, he fell upon his knees and acknowledged the theft then and there and begged for mercy. The Doctor got his watch back and did not discharge Jose, who never after stole again.

The Mexicans when they saw the doctor on the streets would cross themselves, and avoid him—they said he was leagued with the devil; he claimed that the spirits of the Indians, whose bodies he had dissected, were under his enchantment and that he could make them tell him anything. He set his skeleton Indians up in his garden, in his summer house, and dared anybody to steal on his premises. It is needless to say, everything he had was sacred from theft.

Dr. Weideman was very good to the sick and wounded. He would not take pay for his services, and saved many lives by his skill and attention. He was universally liked and respected by the Americans. In 1843 or '44 he was drowned in attempting to cross Peach Creek, near Gonzales when the water was very high—his horse and himself and one other man were carried down by the rapid current and drowned, whilst the others of the party barely escaped.

During the summer of this year, 1840, Colonel Henry Karnes[4] upon returning from Houston when yellow fever was prevailing there, was taken down with yellow fever. The Colonel and Dr. Weideman were great friends, and the Doctor hardly left his room till he was out of danger. Karnes thought though his business required him in Houston, and contrary to the doctor's advice, he started back before he was strong enough. He travelled stretched out in a light wagon—took a relapse after the first day and came back to his friends. But his case was now hopeless, and he died from his great imprudence, and the good doctor put on the deepest mourning for his friend. Colonel Karnes was a short, thick-set man with bright red hair. While he was uneducated, he was modest, generous and devoted to his friends. He was brave and untiring and a terror to the Indians. They called him "Capitan Colorado" (Red Captain) and spoke of him as "Muy Wapo" (very brave). Four or five years before he died, he was taken prisoner by the Comanches, and the squaws so greatly admired his hair of "fire" that they felt it and washed it to see if it would fade; and, when the color held fast, they would not be satisfied until each had a lock.

Louise Amelia Knapp Smith Clappe
("Dame Shirley")
(1819–1906)

L OUISE CLAPPE was born and died in New Jersey. In between, she taught school in Amherst, Massachusetts, married and divorced a surgeon named Fayette Clapp, accompanied him to the California gold fields, became a writer, taught high school and evening classes in San Francisco, and spoke to eastern audiences about life in the West. She is famous today because of her realistic portrayal of life in California boomtowns during the gold rush.

In the winter of 1848, James W. Marshall discovered gold while building Johann Augustus Sutter's sawmill on the American River in California's San Joaquin Valley. Newspaper reports, confirmed later that year by President Polk, sparked the first of a series of gold rushes that enticed adventurers, land speculators, settlers, and merchants to attempt the perilous journey west. Newlyweds Louise and Fayette Clapp were among them (Louise later added an e to the end of "Clapp").

When Louise Smith's father, a teacher, died in 1832, followed by her mother in 1837, the seven children were separated. Louise and her younger sister Mary Jane (Molly) became wards of an Amherst attorney and received boarding-school educations. While on vacation in 1839, she met Alexander Hill Everett, a diplomat and editor twenty years her senior. They corresponded for eight years, until she rejected Everett in favor of Clapp. It was Everett who suggested that Louise take up the pen.

When Louise married Fayette Clapp, a medical student five years her junior, he took a leave of absence from school and they headed by ship for California. Fayette anticipated striking it rich by opening a practice in the gold fields. However, his poor health, her nervous headaches, and snowbound Sierra winters kept them in San Francisco for more than a year. Finally, in 1851, Fayette felt well enough to journey to Rich Bar, on the North Fork of the Feather River. Louise spent the spring at Marysville, California, waiting for Fayette to collect her. And while she waited, she wrote letters to her sister Molly and pseudonymous poems and letters that she published in the Marysville paper. The letters to

Molly continued when Louise reached the gold fields, but they were not published until 1854–1855, after the Clappes returned to San Francisco.

The letters' value lies in the fact that they were not written for publication. They are the private correspondence of a private person describing a foreign lifestyle for an easterner. Details mattered—details of place, of people, of mining operations, even of geology. Although the spelling of the mineralogical names is archaic, the minerals are correctly identified. Clappe took pains to learn as much as she could about every aspect of the crude life and cohabitants of the mining towns. She was both appalled and fascinated by the brutality of the area, the mob justice, the whippings, the elaborate furnishings, the menus of feasts, the abodes, the flora, and the characters. She did not close her eyes or sterilize the scene for Molly's benefit.

Only later, after returning to San Francisco and separating from Fayette, did Louise share her adventures with the public. That she was able to publish "California, in 1851: A Trip into the Mines"—letters sent east two to three years before—implies that she kept copies. Louise recognized the value of her writing. So did her contemporaries in San Francisco, including Bret Harte. But when he was accused of plagiarizing her material for his short stories, Clappe defended him.

Despite Clappe's independent and forthright spirit, she differed from many of her contemporaries by publicly denouncing the woman's rights movement. At the same time the "Shirley Letters" were being carried in the *Pioneer*, Clappe published an essay titled "The Equality of the Sexes." In prose that contained none of the wit and unstudied charm of the "Letters," Clappe attacked the strident representatives of "Bloomerism," and argued for continuation of traditional, gender-based societal roles and occupations.

The Clappes divorced in 1857. After a long teaching career in San Francisco, Louise returned to the East Coast. When she died in 1906, letters from Alexander Hill Everett were among her few possessions. Her correspondence to him has never been recovered.

California, in 1851. Letter Third. A Trip into the Mines

Rich Bar, East Branch of the North Fork of Feather River, September 20, 1851

I INTEND TO-DAY, dear M., to be as disagreeably statistical and as praise-worthily matter-of-factish as the most dogged utilitarian could desire. I shall give you a full, true and particular account of the discovery, rise and progress of this place, with a religious adherence to *dates,* which will rather astonish your unmathematical mind. But let me first describe the spot, as it looked to my wondering and unaccustomed eyes. Remember, I had never seen a mining district before; and had just left San Francisco, amid whose flashy-looking shops and showy houses the most of my time had been spent, since my arrival into the Golden State. Of course, to me, the *coup d'œuil* of Rich Bar was charmingly fresh and original. Imagine a tiny valley, about eight hundred yards in length and, perhaps, thirty in width, (it was measured for my especial information,) apparently hemmed in by lofty hills, almost perpendicular, draperied to their very summits with beautiful fir trees; the blue-bosomed "Plumas," or Feather River I suppose I must call it, undulating along their base, and you have as good an idea as I can give you of the *locale* of "Barra Rica," as the Spaniards so prettily term it.

In almost any of the numerous books written upon California, no doubt you will be able to find a most scientific description of the origin of these "Bars." I must acknowledge, with shame, that my ideas on the subject are distressingly vague. I could never appreciate the poetry or the humor, of making one's wrists ache by knocking to pieces gloomy look-ing stones, or in dirtying one's fingers by analysing soils, in a vain at-tempt to fathom the osteology, or anatomy of our beloved earth; though my heart is thrillingly alive to the faintest shade of color, and the infinite variety of styles in which she delights to robe her ever-changeful and ever-beautiful *surface.* In my unscientific mind the *formations* are with-out form and void; and you might as well talk Chinese to me, as to em-broider your conversation with the terms "horn-blende," "mica," "lime-stone," "slate," "granite" and "quartz," in a hopeless attempt to enlighten me as to their merits. The dutiful diligence with which I attended course after course of lectures on Geology by America's greatest illustrator of that subject, arose rather from my affectionate reverence for our beloved Dr. H., and the fascinating charm which his glorious mind throws round every subject which it condescends to illuminate, than to any interest in the dry science itself. It is, therefore, with a most humiliating consciousness of my geological deficiencies, that I offer you the only explanation which I have been able to obtain from those most learned in such matters here. I gather from their remarks, that these bars are formed by deposits of earth, rolling down from the mountains, crowding the river aside and occupying a portion of its deserted bed. If my definition is unsatisfactory, I can but refer you to some of the aforesaid works upon California.

Through the middle of Rich Bar runs the street, thickly planted with about forty tenements; among which figure round tents, square tents, plank hovels, log cabins, &c,—the residences, varying in elegance and convenience from the palatial splendor of "The Empire," down to a "local habitation," formed of pine boughs, and covered with old calico shirts.

To-day I visited the "Office;" the only one on the river. I had heard so much about it from others, as well as from F., that I really *did* expect something extra.[5] When I entered this imposing place, the shock to my optic nerves was so great that I sank, helplessly, upon one of the benches which ran, divan-like, the whole length (ten feet!) of the building, and laughed till I cried. There was, of course, no floor; a rude nondescript in one corner, on which was ranged the medical library, consisting of half a dozen volumes, did duty as a table. The shelves, which looked like sticks snatched hastily from the wood-pile and nailed up without the least alteration, contained quite a respectable array of medicines. The white canvas window stared everybody in the face, with the interesting information painted on it, in perfect grenadiers of capitals, that this was Dr.——'s office.

At my loud laugh, (which, it must be confessed, was noisy enough to give the whole street assurance of the presence of a woman,) F. looked shocked, and his partner looked prussic acid. To him, (the partner, I mean, he hadn't been out of the mines for years)—the "Office" was a thing sacred and set apart for an almost admiring worship. It was a beautiful, architectural ideal, embodied in pine shingles and cotton cloth. Here, he literally "lived, and moved, and had his being," his bed and his board. With an admiration of the fine arts, truly praiseworthy, he had fondly decorated the walls thereof with sundry pictures from Godey, Graham and Sartain's Magazines, among which, fashion plates with imaginary monsters, sporting miraculous waists, impossible wrists and fabulous feet, largely predominated.

During my call at the office, I was introduced to one of the *finders* of Rich Bar—a young Georgian, who afterwards gave me a full description of all the facts connected with its discovery. This unfortunate had not spoken to a woman for two years; and in the elation of his heart at the joyful event, he rushed out and invested capital in some excellent champaign [*sic*], which I, on Willie's principle of "doing in Turkey as the Turkies do," assisted the company in drinking to the honor of my own arrival. I mention this, as an instance, that nothing can be done in California without the sanctifying influence of the *spirit;* and it generally appears in a much more "questionable shape" than that of sparkling wine. Mr. H. informed me, that on the twentieth of July, 1850, it was rumored at Nelson's Creek—a mining station situated at the Middle Fork of the Feather River, about eighty miles from Marysville—that one of those vague "Somebodies"—a near relation of the "They Says"—had discovered mines of a remarkable richness in a north-easterly direction, and about forty miles from the first-mentioned place. Anxious and immediate search was made for "Somebody," but, as our western brethren say, he "wasn't thar!" But his absence could not deter the miners when once the golden rumor had been set afloat. A large company packed up their goods and chattels, generally consisting of a pair of blankets, a frying-pan, some flour, salt pork, brandy, pick-axe and shovel, and started for the new Dorado. They "traveled, and traveled, and traveled," as we used to say in the fairy stories, for nearly a week in every possible direction, when one evening, weary and discouraged, about one hundred of the party found themselves at the top of that famous hill, which figures so largely in my letters, whence the river can be distinctly seen. Half of the number concluded to descend the mountain that night, the remainder stopping on the summit until the next morning. On arriving at Rich Bar, part of the adventurers camped there, but many went a few miles further down the river. The next morning two men turned over a large stone, beneath which they found quite a sizable piece of gold. They washed a small pan-full of the dirt, and obtained from it two hundred and fifty-six dollars. Encouraged by this success, they commenced staking off the legal amount of ground allowed to each person for mining purposes; and, the remainder of the party having descended the hill, before night the entire bar was "claimed." In a fortnight from that time, the two men who found the first bit of gold had each taken out six thousand dollars. Two others took out thirty-three pounds of gold in eight hours; which is the best day's work that has been done on this branch of the river; the largest amount ever taken from one pan-full of dirt was fifteen hundred dollars. In little more than a week after its discovery, five hundred men had settled upon the bar for the summer.—Such is the wonderful alacrity with which a mining town is built. Soon after was discovered on the same side of the river—about half a mile apart, and at nearly the same distance from this place—the two bars, "Smith" and "Indian," both very rich; also another, lying across the river, just opposite Indian, called "Missouri Bar." There are several more, all within a few miles of here, called "Frenchman's," "Taylor's," "Brown's," "The Junction," "Wyandott" and "Muggin's." But they are at present of little importance as mining stations.

Those who worked in these mines during the fall of 1850 were extremely fortunate; but, alas! the Monte fiend ruined hundreds! Shall I tell you the fate of two of the most successful of these gold hunters? From poor men, they found themselves at the end of a few weeks, absolutely rich. Elated with their good fortune, seized with a mania for Monte, in less than a year, these unfortunates,—so lately respectable and intelligent, became a pair of drunken gamblers. One of them at this present writing, works for five dollars a day and boards himself out of that; the other actually suffers for the necessaries of life,—a too common result of scenes in the mines.

There were but few that dared to remain in the mountains during the winter for fear of being buried in the snow; of which at that time they had a most vague idea. I have been told that in these sheltered valleys it seldom falls to the depth of more than a foot, and disappears almost invariably within a day or two. Perhaps there were three hundred that concluded to stay; of which number, two-thirds stopped on Smith's Bar, as the labor of mining there is much easier than it is here. Contrary to the general expectation, the weather was delightful until about the middle of March; it then commenced storming, and continued to snow and rain incessantly for nearly three weeks. Supposing that the rainy season had passed, hundreds had arrived on the river during the previous month. The snow, which fell several feet in depth on the mountains, rendered the trail impassable and entirely stopped the pack trains; provisions soon became scarce, and the sufferings of these unhappy men were, indeed, extreme. Some adventurous spirits, with true Yankee hardihood, forced their way through the snow to the Frenchman's ranch, and packed flour *on their backs,* for more than forty miles! The first meal that arrived sold for three dollars a pound. Many subsisted for days on nothing but barley, which is kept here to feed the pack-mules on. One unhappy individual who could not obtain even a little barley, for love or money, and had eaten nothing for three days, forced his way out to the Spanish rancho fourteen miles distant, and in less than an hour after his arrival, had devoured *twenty-seven* biscuit and a corresponding quantity of other eatables, and, of course, drinkables to match. Don't let this account alarm you. There is no danger of another famine here. They tell me that there is hardly a building in the place that has not food enough in it to last its occupants for the next two years; besides, there are two or three well-filled groceries in town.

Alice Cary
(1820–1871)

Phoebe Cary
(1824–1871)

Accoring to biographer Mary Clemmer Ames, the Cary family traveled by wagon and flatboat from New Hampshire to the Old Northwest Territory in 1802. Christopher Cary, a veteran of the Revolutionary War and his son, Robert, settled in the Miami Valley of western Ohio, just north of Cincinnati and Fort Washington. A year after the Carys arrived, Fort Washington was abandoned as Ohio joined the Union—the first state to be formed from national domain land at the edge of the American frontier. Cincinnati became the hub of commerce along the Ohio River, with a population of nearly ten thousand by 1820. That year, Robert and Elizabeth Jessup Cary gave birth to their fourth child, Alice, at the family farm near the village of Mount Healthy. The farm and village provided the settings, plots, and characters for Alice's *Clovernook; or, Recollections of Our Neighborhood in the West* (1852), and for much of the Cary sisters' verse.

The year 1820 also coincided with the Missouri Compromise. In order to maintain a balance in Congress between slaveholding and non-slaveholding states, Maine was admitted to the Union as a free state, Missouri as a slave state. In future, new states formed from the Louisiana Territory north of 36°30' would be nonslaveholding. People throughout the nation took sides on an issue that would eventually lead to civil war. Because the Carys were Universalists, and because their farm lay north of the Ohio River in territory where slavery was banned by the Northwest Ordinance of 1787, their sympathies lay with abolition.

Phoebe, the sixth of nine Cary children, was born in 1824, at the end of the frontier period in Ohio. Because Alice and Phoebe were needed to work at home, they had little formal schooling. There were few books in the house, but the family subscribed to a Universalist newspaper in Cincinnati. The *Trumpet* published Alice's first poem when she was eighteen, about the same time her younger sister Phoebe published her first poem in the *Boston Globe*.

In 1835, consumption, or tuberculosis, claimed Elizabeth Cary, Alice and Phoebe's mother. Two years earlier, Alice's favorite sisters, Rhoda and Lucy, had died of the same disease. Alice took over the running of the household for her father, a poorly educated, reticent farmer. It is clear from Alice's sketches, especially "My Grandfather," that she felt unnoticed and unaccepted, an onlooker observing the family from outside the charmed circle. But she noted and retained details of family and village life that enriched her short prose work and elevated it above other women's writing of the era.

From the edge of the frontier, both Alice and Phoebe continued to publish their poetry in religious and secular periodicals. Eventually, in 1849, their inclusion in an anthology of female poets drew favorable attention from Edgar Allen Poe, and increased demand for their work. They published their first volume of poetry in 1850. That same year Alice, after being rejected by a suitor, moved to New York. Phoebe joined her six months later, and the two supported themselves by writing. They earned enough to buy a home on East Twentieth Street, where they hosted a popular literary salon each Sunday evening. In 1868, Sorosis, a women's literary society, grew out of their informal salon. Alice Cary was the first president. Sorosis later evolved into the Association for the Advancement of Women.

Although she considered herself a poet, Alice also wrote children's stories, novels, western sketches, and short stories. Her best work, *Clovernook* and *Clovernook, Second Series* (1853), has a dark realism imbued with supernaturalism. The narrator is both within and without the framework of the story, consciously observing characters that diverge from stereotypical frontier types. They behave in unexpected ways, at least for that time and place: parents are distant and unloving, and they play favorites; children die, unmourned by anyone but the narrator. Alice Cary was bold enough to portray the western woman as complex, mysterious, and capable of strong passion and great emotional distance.

Phoebe Cary turned down marriage proposals, choosing to physically and emotionally support her workaholic sister. Phoebe's poetry reflected the accepted themes of the times: romance and tragedy, morality and Christianity, human rights, woman's rights, and remembrances of her childhood in the country. But she also displayed her witty, irreverent sense of humor by publishing parodies. She boldly took on Shakespeare, Longfellow, Oliver Goldsmith, Poe, Wordsworth, and others, for which she was chastised by later biographers (see, for example, *The Poems of*

Alice and Phoebe Cary). "Granny's House," from *Poems and Parodies* (1854), is a parody of Tennyson's "Locksley Hall." In addition to writing, Phoebe worked in 1870 as assistant editor of the *Republic*, a woman's rights newspaper in New York City.

When Alice developed tuberculosis, Phoebe cared for her until Alice died in 1871. Phoebe died six months later. Their work continues to be anthologized today.

An Order for a Picture

Oh, good painter, tell me true,
Has your hand the cunning to draw
Shapes of things that you never saw?
Aye? Well, here is an order for you.

Woods and corn fields, a little brown,—
The picture must not be over-bright,—
Yet all in the golden and gracious light
Of a cloud, when the summer sun is down.
Alway and alway, night and morn,
Woods upon woods, with fields of corn
Lying between them, not quite sere,
And not in the full, thick, leafy bloom,
When the wind can hardly find breathing-room
Under their tassels,— cattle near,
Biting shorter the short green grass,
And a hedge of sumach and sassafras,
With bluebirds twittering all around,—
(Ah, good painter, you can't paint sound!)
These, and the house where I was born,
Low and little, and black and old,
With children, many as it can hold,
All the windows, open wide,—
Heads and shoulders clear outside,
And fair young faces all ablush:
Perhaps you may have seen, some day,
Roses crowding the self-same way,
Out of a wilding, wayside bush.

Listen closer. When you have done
With woods and corn fields and grazing herds,
A lady, the loveliest ever the sun
Looked down upon you must paint for me:
Oh, if I only could make you see

The clear blue eyes, the tender smile,
The sovereign sweetness, the gentle grace,
The woman's soul, and the angel's face
That are beaming on me all the while,
I need not speak these foolish words:
Yet one word tells you all I would say,—
She is my mother: you will agree
That all the rest may be thrown away.

Two little urchins at her knee
You must paint, sir: one like me,—
The other with a clearer brow,
And the light of his adventurous eyes
Flashing with boldest enterprise:
At ten years old he went to sea,—
God knoweth if he be living now,—
He sailed in the good ship *Commodore,*
Nobody ever crossed her track
To bring us news, and she never came back.
Ah, it is twenty long years and more
Since that old ship went out of the bay
With my great-hearted brother on her deck:
I watched him till he shrank to a speck,
And his face was toward me all the way.
Bright his hair was, a golden brown,
The time we stood at our mother's knee:
That beauteous head, if it did go down,
Carried sunshine into the sea!

Out in the fields one summer night
We were together, half afraid
Of the corn-leaves' rustling, and of the shade
Of the high hills, stretching so still and far,—
Loitering till after the low little light
Of the candle shone through the open door,
And over the hay-stack's pointed top,
All of a tremble and steady to drop,
The first half-hour, the great yellow star,
That we, with staring, ignorant eyes,
Had often and often watched to see

Propped and held in its place in the skies
By the fork of a tall red mulberry-tree,
Which close in the edge of our flax-field grew,—
Dead at the top,—just one branch full
Of leaves, notched round, and lined with wool,
From which it tenderly shook the dew
Over our heads, when we came to play
In its hand-breadth of shadow day after day.
Afraid to go home, sir; for one of us bore
A nest full of speckled and thin-shelled eggs,—
The other, a bird, held fast by the legs,
Not so big as a straw of wheat:
The berries we gave her she would n't eat,
But cried and cried, till we held her bill,
So slim and shining, to keep her still.

At last we stood at our mother's knee.
Do you think, sir, if you try,
You can paint the look of a lie?
If you can, pray have the grace
To put it solely in the face
Of the urchin that is likest me:
I think 't was solely mine, indeed:
But that's no matter,—paint it so;
The eyes of our mother—(take good heed)—
Looking not on the nestful of eggs,
Nor the fluttering bird, held so fast by the legs,
But straight through our faces down to our lies,
And, oh, with such injured, reproachful surprise!
I felt my heart bleed where that glance went, as though
A sharp blade struck through it.

                              You, sir, know
That you on the canvas are to repeat
Things that are fairest, things most sweet,—
Woods and corn fields and mulberry-tree,—
The mother,—the lads with their bird, at her knee:
But, oh, that look of reproachful woe!
High as the heavens your name I'll shout,
If you paint me the picture, and leave that out.

ॐ

My Grandfather

CHANGE IS THE order of nature; the old makes way for the new; over the perished growth of the last year brighten the blossoms of this. What changes are to be counted, even in a little noiseless life like mine! How many graves have grown green; how many locks have grown gray; how many, lately young, and strong in hope and courage, are faltering and fainting; how many hands that reached eagerly for the roses are drawn back bleeding and full of thorns; and saddest of all, how many hearts are broken! I remember when I had no sad memory, when I first made room in my bosom for the consciousness of death. How—like striking out from a wilderness of dew-wet blossoms where the shimmer of the light is lovely as the wings of a thousand bees, into an open plain where the clear day strips things to their natural truth—we go from young visions to the realities of life!

I remember the twilight, as though it were yesterday—gray, and dim, and cold, for it was late in October, when the shadow first came over my heart, that no subsequent sunshine has ever swept entirely away. From the window of our cottage home streamed a column of light, in which I sat stringing the red berries of the brier-rose.

I had heard of death, but regarded it only with that vague apprehension which I felt for the demons and witches that gather poison herbs under the new moon, in fairy forests, or strangle harmless travellers with wands of the willow, or with vines of the wild grape or ivy. I did not much like to think about them, and yet I felt safe from their influence.

There might be people, somewhere, that would die some time; I didn't know, but it would not be myself, or any one I knew. They were so well and so strong, so full of joyous hopes, how could their feet falter, and their eyes grow dim. And their fainting hands lay away their work, and fold themselves together! No, no—it was not a thing to be believed.

Drifts of sunshine from that season of blissful ignorance often come back, as lightly

> As the winds of the May-time flow,
> And lift up the shadows brightly
> As the daffodil lifts the snow—

the shadows that have gathered with the years! It is pleasant to have them thus swept off—to find myself a child again—the crown of pale pain and sorrow that presses heavily now, unfelt, and the graves that lie lonesomely along my way, covered up with flowers—to feel my mother's dark locks falling on my cheek, as she teaches me the lesson or the prayer—to see my father, now a sorrowful old man whose hair has thinned and whitened almost to the limit of three score years and ten, fresh and vigorous, strong for the race—and to see myself a little child, happy with a new hat and a pink ribbon, or even with the string of brier-buds that I called coral. Now I tie it about my neck, and now around my forehead, and now twist it among my hair, as I have somewhere read great ladies do their pearls. The winds are blowing the last yellow leaves from the cherry tree—I know not why, but it makes me sad. I draw closer to the light of the window, and slyly peep within: all is quiet and cheerful; the logs on the heath are ablaze; my father is mending a bridle-rein, which "Traveller," the favorite riding horse, snapt in two yesterday, when frightened at the elephant that (covered with a great white cloth) went by to be exhibited at the coming show,—my mother is hemming a ruffle, perhaps for me to wear to school next quarter—my brother is reading a newspaper, I know not what, but I see, on one side, the picture of a bear: let me listen—and flattening my cheek against the pane, I catch his words distinctly, for he reads loud and very clearly—it is an improbable story of a wild man who has recently been discovered in the woods of some far-away island—he seems to have been there a long time, for his nails are grown like claws, and his hair, in rough and matted strings, hangs to his knees; he makes a noise like something between the howl of a beast and a human cry, and, when pursued, runs with a nimbleness and swiftness that baffle the pursuers, though mounted on the fleetest of steeds, urged through brake and bush to their utmost speed. When first seen, he was sitting on the ground and cracking nuts with his teeth; his arms are corded with sinews that make it probable his strength is sufficient to strangle a dozen men; and yet on seeing human beings, he runs into the thick woods, lifting such a hideous scream, the while, as make his discoverers clasp their hands to their ears. It is suggested that this is not a solitary individual, become wild by isolation, but that a race exists, many of which are perhaps larger and of more terrible aspects; but whether they have any intelligible language, and whether they live in caverns of rocks or in trunks of hollow trees, remains for discovery by some future and more daring explorers.

My brother puts down the paper and looks at the picture of the bear.

"I would not read such foolish stories," says my father, as he holds the bridle up to the light, to see that it is neatly mended; my mother breaks the thread which gathers the ruffle; she is gentle and loving, and does not like to hear even implied reproof, but she says nothing; little Harry, who is playing on the floor, upsets his block-house, and my father, clapping his hands together, exclaims, "This is the house that Jack built!" and adds, patting Harry on the head, "Where is my little boy? this is not he, this is a little carpenter; you must make your houses stronger, little carpenter!" But Harry insists that he is the veritable little Harry, and no carpenter, and hides his tearful eyes in the lap of my mother, who assures him that he is her own little boy, and soothes his childish grief by buttoning on his neck the ruffle she has just completed; and off he scampers again, building a new house, the roof of which he makes very steep, and calls it grandfather's house, at which all laugh heartily.

While listening to the story of the wild man I am half afraid, but now, as the joyous laughter rings out, I am ashamed of my fears, and skipping forth, I sit down on a green ridge which cuts the door-yard diagonally, and where, I am told, there was once a fence. Did the rose-bushes and lilacs and flags that are in the garden, ever grow here? I think—no, it must have been a long while ago, if indeed the fence were ever here, for I can't conceive the possibility of such change, and then I fall to arranging my string of brier-buds into letters that will spell some name, now my own, and now that of some one I love. A dull strip of cloud, from which the hues of pink and red and gold have but lately faded out, hangs low in the west; below is a long reach of withering woods—the gray sprays of the beech clinging thickly still, and the gorgeous maples shooting up here and there like sparks of fire among the darkly magnificent oaks and silvery columned sycamores—the gray and murmurous twilight gives way to darker shadows and a deeper hush.

I hear, far away, the beating of quick hoof-strokes on the pavement; the horseman, I think to myself, is just coming down the hill through the thick woods beyond the bridge. I listen close, and presently a hollow rumbling sound indicates that I was right; and now I hear the strokes more faintly—he is climbing the hill that slopes directly away from me; but now again I hear distinctly—he has almost reached the hollow below me—the hollow that in summer is starry with dandelions and now is full of brown nettles and withered weeds—he will presently have passed—where can he be going, and what is his errand? I will rise up and watch. The cloud passes from the face of the moon, and the light streams full and broad on the horseman—he tightens his rein, and looks eagerly toward the house—surely I know him, the long red curls, streaming down his neck, and the straw hat, are not to be mistaken—it is Oliver Hillhouse, the miller, whom my grandfather, who lives in the steep-roofed house, has employed three years—longer than I can remember! He calls to me, and I laughingly bound forward, with an exclamation of delight, and put my arms about the slender neck of his horse, that is champing the bit and pawing the pavement, and I say, "Why do you not come in?"

He smiles, but there is something ominous in his smile, as he hands me a folded paper, saying, "Give this to your mother"; and, gathering up his reins, he rides hurriedly forward. In a moment I am in the house, for my errand, "Here, mother, is a paper which Oliver Hillhouse gave me for you." Her hand trembles as she receives it, and waiting timidly near, I watch her as she reads; the tears come, and without speaking a word she hands it to my father.

That night there came upon my soul the shadow of an awful fear; sorrowful moans and plaints disturbed my dreams that have never since been wholly forgot. How cold and spectral-like the moonlight streamed across my pillow; how dismal the chirping of the cricket in the hearth; and how more than dismal the winds among the naked boughs that creaked against my window. For the first time in my life I could not sleep, and I longed for the light of morning. At last it came, whitening up the East, and the stars faded away, and there came a flush of crimson and purple fire, which was presently pushed aside by the golden disk of the sun. Daylight without, but within there was thick darkness still.

I kept close about my mother, for in her presence I felt a shelter and protection that I found no where else.

"Be a good girl till I come back," she said, stooping and kissing my forehead; "mother is going away to-day, your poor grandfather is very sick."

"Let me go too," I said, clinging close to her hand. We were soon ready; little Harry pouted his lips and reached out his hands, and my father gave him his pocket-knife to play with; and the wind blowing the yellow curls over his eyes and forehead, he stood on the porch looking eagerly while my mother turned to see him again and again. We had before us a walk of perhaps two miles—northwardly along the turnpike nearly a mile, next, striking into a grass-grown road that crossed it, in an easternly direction nearly another mile, and then turning northwardly again, a narrow land bordered on each side by old and decaying cherry-trees, led us to the house, ancient fashioned, with high steep gables, narrow windows, and low, heavy chimneys of stone. In the rear was an old mill, with a plank sloping from the door-sill to the ground, by way of step, and a square open window in the gable, through which, with ropes and pulleys, the grain was drawn up.

This mill was an especial object of terror to me, and it was only when my aunt Carry led me by the hand, and the cheerful smile of Oliver Hillhouse lighted up the dusky interior, that I could be persuaded to enter it. In truth, it was a lonesome sort of place, with dark lofts and curious binns, and ladders leading from place to place; and there were cats creeping stealthily along the beams in wait for mice or swallows, if, as sometimes happened, the clay nest should be loosened from the rafter, and the whole tumble ruinously down. I used to wonder that aunt Carry was not afraid in the old place, with its eternal rumble, and its great dusty wheel moving slowly round and round, beneath the steady tread of the two sober horses that never gained a hair's breadth for their pains; but on the contrary, she seemed to like the mill, and never failed to show me through all its intricacies, on my visits. I have unravelled the mystery now, or rather, from the recollections I still retain, have apprehended what must have been clear to older eyes at the time.

A forest of oak and walnut stretched along this extremity of the farm, and on either side of the improvements (as the house and barn and mill were called) shot out two dark forks, completely cutting off the view, save toward the unfrequented road to the south, which was traversed mostly by persons coming to the mill, for my grandfather made the flour for all the neighborhood round about, besides making corn-meal for Johnny-cakes, and "chops" for the cows.

He was an old man now, with a tall, athletic frame, slightly bent, thin locks white as the snow, and deep blue eyes full of fire and intelligence, and after long years of uninterrupted health and useful labor, he was suddenly stricken down, with no prospect of recovery.

"I hope he is better," said my mother, hearing the rumbling of the mill-wheel. She might have known my grandfather would permit no interruption of the usual business on account of his illness—the neighbors, he said, could not do without bread because he was sick, nor need they all be idle, waiting for him to die. When the time drew near, he would call them to take his farewell and his blessing, but till then let them sew and spin, and do all things just as usual, so they would please him best. He was a stern man—even his kindness was uncompromising and unbending, and I remember of his making toward me no manifestation of fondness, such as grandchildren usually receive, save once, when he gave me a bright red apple, without speaking a word till my timid thanks brought out his "Save your thanks for something better." The apple gave me no pleasure, and I even slipt into the mill to escape from his cold forbidding presence.

Nevertheless, he was a good man, strictly honest, and upright in all his dealings, and respected, almost reverenced, by everybody. I remember once, when young Winters, the tenant of Deacon Granger's farm, who paid a great deal too much for his ground, as I have heard my father say, came to mill with some withered wheat, my grandfather filled up the sacks out of his own flour, while Tommy was in the house at dinner. That was a good deed, but Tommy Winters never suspected how his wheat happened to turn out so well.

As we drew near the house, it seemed to me more lonesome and desolate than it ever looked before. I wished I had staid at home with little Harry. So eagerly I noted every thing, that I remember to this day, that near a trough of water, in the lane, stood a little surly looking cow, of a red color, and with a white line running along her back. I had gone with aunt Carry often when she went to milk her, but to-day she seemed not to have been milked. Near her was a black and white heifer, with sharp short horns, and a square board tied over her eyes; two horses, one of them gray, and the other sorrel, with a short tail, were reaching their long necks into the garden, and browsing from the currant bushes. As we approached they trotted forward a little, and one of them, half playfully, half angrily, bit the other on the shoulder, after which they returned quietly to their cropping of the bushes, heedless of the voice that from across the field was calling to them.

A flock of turkeys were sunning themselves about the door, for no one came to scare them away; some were black, and some speckled, some with heads erect and tails spread, and some nibbling the grass; and with a gabbling noise, and a staid and dignified march, they made way for us. The smoke arose from the chimney in blue, graceful curls, and drifted away to the woods; the dead morning-glory vines had partly fallen from the windows, but the hands that tended them were grown careless, and they were suffered to remain blackened and void of beauty, as they were. Under these, the white curtain was partly put aside, and my grandmother, with the speckled handkerchief pinned across her bosom, and her pale face, a shade paler than usual, was looking out, and seeing us she came forth, and in answer to my mother's look of inquiry, shook her head, and silently led the way in. The room we entered had some home-made carpet, about the size of a large table-cloth, spread in the middle of the floor, the remainder of which was scoured very white; the ceiling was of walnut wood, and the side walls were white-washed—a table, an old-fashioned desk, and some wooden chairs, comprised the furniture. On one of the chairs was a leather cushion; this was set to one side, my grandmother neither offering it to my mother, nor sitting in it herself, while, by way of composing herself, I suppose, she took off the black ribbon with which her cap was trimmed. This was a more simple process than the reader may fancy, the trimming, consisting merely of a ribbon, always black, which she tied around her head after the cap was on, forming a bow and two ends just above the forehead. Aunt Carry, who was of what is termed an even disposition, received us with her usual cheerful demeanor, and then, re-seating herself comfortably near the fire, resumed her work, the netting of some white fringe.

I liked aunt Carry, for that she always took especial pains to entertain me, showing me her patchwork, taking me with her to the cow-yard and dairy, and also to the mill, though in this last I fear she was a little selfish; however, that made no difference to me at the time, and I have always been sincerely grateful to her: children know more, and want more, and feel more, than people are apt to imagine.

On this occasion she called me to her, and tried to teach me the mysteries of her netting, telling me I must get my father to buy me a little bureau, and then I could net fringe and make a nice cover for it. For a little time I thought I could, and arranged in my mind where it should be placed, and what should be put into it, and even went so far as to inquire how much fringe she thought would be necessary. I never attained to much proficiency in the netting of fringe, nor did I ever get the little bureau, and now it is quite reasonable to suppose I never shall.

Presently my father and mother were shown into an adjoining room, the interior of which I felt an irrepressible desire to see, and by stealth I obtained a glimpse of it before the door closed behind them. There was a dull brown and yellow carpet on the floor, and near the bed, on which was a blue and white coverlid, stood a high-backed wooden chair, over which hung a towel, and on the bottom of which stood a pitcher, of an unique pattern. I know not how I saw this, but I did, and perfectly remember it, notwithstanding my attention was in a moment completely absorbed by the sick man's face, which was turned towards the opening door, pale, livid, and ghastly. I trembled and was transfixed; the rings beneath the eyes, which had always been deeply marked, were now almost black, and the blue eyes within looked glassy and cold, and terrible. The expression of agony on the lips (for his disease was one of a most painful nature) gave place to a sort of smile, and the hand, twisted among the gray locks, was withdrawn and extended to welcome my parents, as the door closed. That was a fearful moment; I was near the dark steep edges of the grave; I felt, for the first time, that I was mortal too, and I was afraid.

Aunt Carry put away her work, and taking from a nail in the window-frame a brown muslin sun-bonnet, which seemed to me of half a yard in depth, she tied it on my head, and then clapt her hands as she looked into my face, saying, "bo-peep!" at which I half laughed and half cried, and making provision for herself in grandmother's bonnet, which hung on the opposite side of the window, and was similar to mine, except that it was perhaps a little larger, she took my hand and we proceeded to the mill. Oliver, who was very busy on our entrance, came forward, as aunt Carry said, by way of introduction, "A little visiter I've brought you," and arranged a seat on a bag of meal for us, and taking off his straw hat, pushed the red curls from his low white forehead, and looked bewildered and anxious.

"It's quite warm for the season," said aunt Carry, by way of breaking silence, I suppose. The young man said "yes," abstractedly, and then asked if the rumble of the mill were not a disturbance to the sick room, to which aunt Carry answered, "No, my father says it is his music."

"A good old man," said Oliver, "he will not hear it much longer," and then, even more sadly, "every thing will be changed." Aunt Carry was silent, and he added, "I have been here a long time, and it will make me very sorry to go away, especially when such trouble is about you all."

"Oh, Oliver," said aunt Carry, "you don't mean to go away?" "I see no alternative," he replied; "I shall have nothing to do; if I had gone a year ago it would have been better." "Why?" asked aunt Carry; but I think she understood why, and Oliver did not answer directly, but said, "Almost the last thing your father said to me was, that you should never marry any who had not a house and twenty acres of land; if he has not, he will exact that promise of you, and I cannot ask you not to make it, nor would you refuse him if I did; I might have owned that long ago, but for my sister (she had lost her reason) and my lame brother, whom I must educate to be a schoolmaster, because he never can work, and my blind mother; but God forgive me! I must not and do not complain; you will forget me, before long, Carry, and some body who is richer and better, will be to you all I once hoped to be, and perhaps more."

I did not understand the meaning of the conversation at the time, but

I felt out of place some way, and so, going to another part of the mill, I watched the sifting of the flour through the snowy bolter, listening to the rumbling of the wheel. When I looked around I perceived that Oliver had taken my place on the meal-bag, and that he had put his arm around the waist of aunt Carry in a way I did not much like.

Great sorrow, like a storm, sweeps us aside from ordinary feelings, and we give our hearts into kindly hands—so cold and hollow and meaningless seem the formulæ of the world. They had probably never spoken of love before, and now talked of it as calmly as they would have talked of any thing else; but they felt that hope was hopeless; at best, any union was deferred, perhaps, for long years; the future was full of uncertainties. At last their tones became very low, so low I could not hear what they said; but I saw that they looked very sorrowful, and that aunt Carry's hand lay in that of Oliver as though he were her brother.

"Why don't the flour come through?" I said, for the sifting had become thinner and lighter, and at length quite ceased. Oliver smiled, faintly, as he arose, and saying, "This will never buy the child a frock," poured a sack of wheat into the hopper, so that it nearly run over. Seeing no child but myself, I supposed he meant to buy me a new frock, and at once resolved to put it in my little bureau, if he did.

"We have bothered Mr. Hillhouse long enough," said aunt Carry, taking my hand, "and will go to the house, shall we not?"

I wondered why she said "Mr. Hillhouse." For I had never heard her say so before; and Oliver seemed to wonder, too, for he said reproachfully, laying particular stress on his own name, "You don't bother Mr. Hillhouse, I am sure, but I must not insist on your remaining if you wish to go."

"I don't want you to insist on my staying," said aunt Carry, "if you don't want to, and I see you don't," and lifting me out to the sloping plank, that bent beneath us, we descended.

"Carry," called a voice behind us; but she neither answered nor looked back, but seemed to feel a sudden and expressive fondness for me, took me up in her arms, though I was almost too heavy for her to lift, and kissing me over and over, said I was light as a feather, at which she laughed as though neither sorrowful nor lacking for employment.

This little passage I could never precisely explain, aside from the ground that "the course of true love never did run smooth." Half an hour after we returned to the house, Oliver presented himself at the door, saying, "Miss Caroline, shall I trouble you for a cup, to get a drink of water?" Carry accompanied him to the well, where they lingered some time, and when she returned her face was sunshiny and cheerful as usual.

The day went slowly by, dinner was prepared, and removed, scarcely tasted; aunt Carry wrought at her fringe, and grandmother moved softly about, preparing teas and cordials.

Towards sunset the sick man became easy, and expressed a wish that the door of his chamber might be opened, that he might watch our occupations and hear our talk. It was done accordingly, and he was left alone. My mother smiled, saying she hoped he might yet get well, but my father shook his head mournfully, and answered, "He wishes to go without our knowledge." He made amplest provision for his family always, and I believe had a kind nature, but he manifested no little fondnesses, nor did he wish caresses for himself. Contrary to the general tenor of his character, was a love of quiet jests, that remained to the last. Once, as Carry gave him some drink, he said, "You know my wishes about your future, I expect you to be mindful."

I stole to the door of his room in the hope that he would say something to me, but he did not, and I went nearer, close to the bed, and timidly took his hand in mine; how damp and cold it felt! Yet he spoke not, and climbing upon the chair, I put back his thin locks, and kissed his forehead. "Child, you trouble me," he said, and these were the last words he ever spoke to me.

The sun sunk lower and lower, throwing a beam of light through the little window, quite across the carpet, and now it reached the sick man's room, climbed over the bed and up the wall; he turned his face away, and seemed to watch its glimmer upon the ceiling. The atmosphere grew dense and dusky, but without clouds, and the orange light changed to a dull lurid red, and the dying and dead leaves dropt silently to the ground, for there was no wind, and the fowls flew into the trees, and the gray moths came from beneath the bushes and fluttered in the waning light. From the hollow tree by the mill came the bat wheeling and flitting blindly about, and once or twice its wings struck the window of the sick man's chamber. The last sunlight faded off at length, and the rumbling of the mill-wheel was still: he had fallen asleep in listening to its music.

The next day came the funeral. What a desolate time it was! All down the lane were wagons and carriages and horses, for every body that knew my grandfather would pay him the last honors he could receive in the world. "We can do him no further good," they said, "but it seemed right that we should come." Close by the gate waited the little brown wagon to bear the coffin to the grave, the wagon in which he was used to ride while living. The heads of the horses were drooping, and I thought they looked consciously sad.

The day was mild, and the doors and windows of the old house stood all open, so that the people without could hear the words of the preacher. I remember nothing he said; I remember of hearing my mother sob, and of seeing my grandmother with her face buried in her hands, and of seeing aunt Carry sitting erect, her face pale but tearless, and Oliver near her, with his hands folded across his breast save once or twice, when he lifted them to brush away tears.

I did not cry, save from a frightened and strange feeling, but kept wishing that we were not so near the dead, and that it were another day. I tried to push the reality away with thoughts of pleasant things—in vain I remember the hymn, and the very air in which it was sung.

> "Ye fearful souls fresh courage take,
> The clouds ye so much dread,
> Are big with mercy, and shall break
> In blessings on your head.
> Blind unbelief is sure to err,
> And scan his works in vain;
> God is his own interpreter,
> And he will make it plain."

Near the door blue flagstones were laid, bordered with a row of shrubberies and trees, with lilacs, and roses, and pears, and peach-trees, which my grandfather had planted long ago, and here, in the open air, the coffin was placed, and white cloth removed, and folded over the lid. I remember how it shook and trembled as the gust came moaning from the woods, and died off over the next hill, and that two or three withered leaves fell on the face of the dead, which Oliver gently removed, and brushed aside a yellow-winged butterfly that hovered near.

The friends hung over the unsmiling corpse till they were led weeping and one by one away; the hand of some one rested for a moment on the forehead, and then the white cloth was replaced, and the lid screwed down. The coffin was placed in the brown wagon, with a sheet folded about it, and the long train moved slowly to the burial-ground woods, where the words "dust to dust" were followed by the rattling of the earth, and the sunset light fell there a moment, and the dead leaves blew across the smoothly shapen mound.

When the will was read, Oliver found himself heir to a fortune—the mill and homestead and half the farm—provided he married Carry, which he must have done, for though I do not remember the wedding, I have had an aunt Caroline Hillhouse almost as long as I can remember. The lunatic sister was sent to an asylum, where she sung songs about a faithless lover till death took her up and opened her eyes in heaven. The mother was brought home, and she and my grandmother lived at their ease, and sat in the corner, and told stories of ghosts, and witches, and marriages, and deaths, for long years. Peace to their memories! for they have both gone home; and the lame brother is teaching school, in his leisure playing the flute, and reading Shakspeare—all the book he reads.

Years have come and swept me away from my childhood, from its innocence and blessed unconsciousness of the dark, but often comes back the memory of its first sorrow!

Death is less terrible to me now.

Our Homestead

Our old brown homestead reared its walls,
From the way-side dust aloof,
Where the apple-boughs could almost cast
Their fruitage on its roof:
And the cherry-tree so near it grew,
That when awake I've lain,
In the lonesome nights, I've heard the limbs,
As they creaked against the pane:
And those orchard trees, O those orchard trees!
I 've seen my little brothers rocked
In their tops by the summer breeze.

The sweet-brier under the window-sill,
Which the early birds made glad,
And the damask rose by the garden fence,
Were all the flowers we had.
I 've looked at many a flower since then,
Exotics rich and rare,
That to other eyes were lovelier,
But not to me so fair;
For those roses bright, O those roses bright!
I have twined them in my sister's locks,
That are hid in the dust from sight!

We had a well, a deep old well,
Where the spring was never dry,
And the cool drops down from the mossy stones
Were falling constantly:
And there never was water half so sweet
As that in my little cup,
Drawn up to the curb by the rude old sweep,
That my father's hand set up;
And that deep old well, O that deep old well!

I remember yet the plashing sound
Of the bucket as it fell.

Our homestead had an ample hearth,
Where at night we loved to meet;
There my mother's voice was always kind,
And her smile was always sweet;
And there I've sat on my father's knee,
And watched his thoughtful brow,
With my childish hand in his raven hair,—
That hair is silver now!
But that broad hearth's light, O that broad hearth's light!
And my father's look, and my mother's smile,—
They are in my heart to-night!

Homes for All (Plea for the Homeless)

Columbia, fairest nation of the world,
Sitting in queenly beauty in the west,
With all thy banners around about thee furled,
Nursing the cherub Peace upon thy breast;
Ever did daughter of a kingly line
Look on a lovelier heritage than thine!

Thou hast deep forests stretching far away,
The giant growth of the long centuries,
From whose dim shadows to the light of day
Come forth the mighty rivers toward the seas,
To walk like happy lovers, hand in hand,
Down through the green vales of our pleasant land.

Thou hast broad prairies, where the lovely flowers
Blossom and perish with the changing year;
Where harvests wave not through the summer hours,
Nor with the autumn ripen in the ear;
And beautiful lakes that toss their milky spray
Where the strong ship hath never cleaved its way.

And yet with all thy broad and fertile land,
Where hands sow not, nor gather in the grain,
Thy children come and round about thee stand,
Asking the blessing of a home in vain,—
Still lingering, but with feet that long to press
Through the green windings of the wilderness.

In populous cities do men live and die,
That never breathe the pure and liberal air;
Down where the damp and desolate rice-swamps lie,
Wearying the ear of Heaven with constant prayer,
Are souls that never yet have learned to raise
Under God's equal sky the psalm of praise.

Turn not, Columbia! from their pleading eyes;
Give to thy sons that ask of thee a home;
So shall they gather round thee, not with sighs,
But as young children to their mother come;
And brightly to the centuries shall go down
The glory that thou wearest like a crown.

"The Barefoot Boy"

Ah! "Barefoot Boy!" you have led me back
O'er the waste of years profound,
To the still, sweet spots, which memory
Hath kept as haunted ground.
You have led me back to the western hills,
Where I played through the summer hours;
And called my little playmate up
To stand among the flowers.

We are hand in hand in the fields again,
We are treading through the dew!
And not the poet's "barefoot boy,"
Nor him the artist drew,

Is half so brave and bold and good,
Though bright their colors glow,
As the darling playmate that I had
And lost, so long ago!

I touch the spring-time's tender grass,
I find the daisy buds;
I feel the shadows deep and cool,
In the heart of the summer woods;
I see the ripened autumn nuts,
Like thick hail strew the earth;
I catch the fall of the winter snow,
And the glow of the cheerful hearth!

But alas! my playmate, loved and lost,
My heart is full of tears,
For the dead and buried hopes, that are more
Than our dead and buried years:
And I cannot see the poet's rhymes,
Nor the lines the artist drew,
But only the boy that held my hand,
And led my feet through the dew!

❧

Granny's House

Comrades, leave me here a little, while as yet 't is early morn,
Leave me here, and when you want me, sound upon the dinner-horn.
'T is the place, and all about it, as of old, the rat and mouse
Very loudly squeak and nibble, running over Granny's house;—
Granny's house, with all its cupboards, and its rooms as neat as wax,
And its chairs of wood unpainted, where the old cats rubbed their backs,
Many a night from yonder garret window, ere I went to rest,
Did I see the cows and horses come in slowly from the west;
Many a night I saw the chickens, flying upward through the trees,
Roosting on the sleety branches, when I thought their feet would freeze;
Here about the garden wandered, nourishing a youth sublime
With the beans, and sweet potatoes, and the melons which were prime;

When the pumpkin-vines behind me with their precious fruit reposed,
When I clung about the pear-tree, for the promise that it closed,
When I dipt into the dinner far as human eye could see,
Saw the vision of the pie, and all the dessert that would be.
In the spring a fuller crimson comes upon the robin's breast;
In the spring the noisy pullet gets herself another nest;
In the spring a livelier spirit makes the ladies' tongues more glib;
In the spring a young boy's fancy lightly hatches up a fib.
Then her cheek was plump and fatter than should be for one so old,
And she eyed my every motion, with a mute intent to scold.
And I said, My worthy Granny, now I speak the truth to thee,—
Better believe it,—I have eaten all the apples from one tree.
On her kindling cheek and forehead came a color and a light,
As I have seen the rosy red flashing in the northern night;
And she turned,—her fist was shaken at the coolness of the lie;
She was mad, and I could see it, by the snapping of her eye,
Saying I have hid my feelings, fearing they should do thee wrong,—
Saying, "I shall whip you, Sammy, whipping, I shall go it strong!"
She took me up and turned me pretty roughly, when she'd done,
And every time she shook me, I tried to jerk and run;
She took off my little coat, and struck again with all her might,
And before another minute I was free and out of sight.
Many a morning, just to tease her, did I tell her stories yet,
Though her whisper made me tingle, when she told me what I'd get;
Many an evening did I see her where the willow sprouts grew thick,
And I rushed away from Granny at the touching of her stick.
O my Granny, old and ugly, O my Granny's hateful deeds,
O the empty, empty garret, O the garden gone to weeds,
Crosser than all fancy fathoms, crosser than all songs have sung,
I was puppet to your threat, and servile to your shrewish tongue,
Is it well to wish thee happy, having seen thy whip decline
On a boy with lower shoulders, and a narrower back, than mine?
Hark, my merry comrades call me, sounding on the dinner-horn,—
They to whom my Granny's whippings were a target for their scorn;
Shall it not be scorn to me to harp on such a mouldered string?
I am shamed through all my nature to have loved the mean old thing;
Weakness to be wroth with weakness! woman's pleasure, woman's spite,
Nature made them quicker motions, a considerable sight.
Woman is the lesser man, and all thy whippings matched with mine
Are as moonlight unto sunlight, and as water unto wine.

Here at least when I was little, something. O, for some retreat
Deep in yonder crowded city where my life began to beat,
Where one winter fell my father, slipping off a keg of lard;
I was left a trampled orphan, and my case was pretty hard,
Or to burst all links of habit, and to wander far and fleet,
On from farm-house unto farm-house till I found my Uncle Pete,
Larger sheds and barns, and newer, and a better neighborhood,
Greater breadth of field and woodland, and an orchard just as good.
Never comes my Granny, never cuts her willow switches there;
Boys are safe at Uncle Peter's, I'll bet you what you dare.
Hangs the heavy fruited pear-tree: you may eat just what you like;
'T is a sort of little Eden, about two miles off the pike.
There, methinks, would be enjoyment, more than being quite so near
To the place where even in manhood I almost shake with fear.
There the passions, cramped no longer, shall have scope and breathing space.
I will 'scape that savage woman, she shall never rear my race;
Iron-jointed, supple-sinewed, they shall dive and they shall run;
She has caught me like a wild goat, but she shall not catch my son.
He shall whistle to the dog, and get the books from off the shelf,
Not, with blinded eyesight, cutting ugly whips to whip himself.
Fool again, the dream of fancy! no, I don't believe it 's bliss,
But I'm certain Uncle Peter's is a better place than this.
Let them herd with narrow foreheads, vacant of all glorious gains,
Like the horses in the stables, like the sheep that crop the lanes;
Let them mate with dirty cousins,—what to me were style or rank,
I the heir of twenty acres, and some money in the bank?
Not in vain the distance beckons, forward let us urge our load,
Let our cart-wheels spin till sundown, ringing down the grooves of road;
Through the white dust of the turnpike she can't see to give us chase:
Better seven years at uncle's, than fourteen at Granny's place.
O, I see the blessed promise of my spirit hath not set!
If we once get in the wagon, we will circumvent her yet.
Howsoever these things be, a long farewell to Granny's farm:
Not for me she'll cut the willows, not at me she'll shake her arm.
Comes a vapor from the margin, blackening over heath and holt,
Cramming all the blast before it,—guess it holds a thunderbolt:
Wish 't would fall on Granny's house, with rain, or hail, or fire, or snow,
Let me get my horses started Uncle Peteward, and I'll go.

Jessie Ann Benton Frémont
(1824–1902)

IN TUCSON, the Frémont Museum occupies an old one-story adobe on the grounds of the Community Center. In similar fashion, the name "Frémont" is attached to towns, streets, mountain peaks, and rivers across the West. The explorer behind the name was John Charles Frémont, "the Pathmarker." His fame resulted as much from the writing talent and drive of his wife, Jessie Benton Frémont, as from his exploits, brilliant and controversial though they were. Jessie helped him write summaries of his expeditions, popular works of the mid-nineteenth century. And when he repeatedly fell from grace, she strove to resurrect his fame in print.

Jessie Ann Benton, the second child of Sen. Thomas Hart Benton, a Jacksonian Democrat from Missouri, was named for her pioneering paternal grandfather. During her childhood, Jessie became a seasoned traveler, splitting her time between the Benton home in St. Louis, their residence in Washington, D.C., and her maternal grandfather's Virginia estate, Cherry Grove. She was her father's confidante, student, researcher, sometime secretary, and lifelong supporter. Like him she believed in the concept of "Manifest Destiny": that America was destined to occupy the continent from Atlantic to Pacific, despite the fact that Mexico owned the majority of the West. Like him she worked, albeit behind the scenes, to make that concept a reality.

Jessie met John Charles Frémont when she was fifteen. The attraction was instantaneous and mutual. Over her parents' objections, the headstrong Jessie eloped with Frémont in 1841. Six months later, in 1842, John embarked on the first of three major expeditions with the U.S. Topographical Survey. He explored a route to Oregon, mapped South Pass, and planted a flag atop the Wind River Mountains. When he returned six months later, Jessie helped him write the summary report, which was published by Congress.

John Frémont's second expedition (1843–1844) explored and named the Great Basin. His third (1845–1846) followed a southern route from the Arkansas, Rio Grande, and Colorado Rivers to the Sierra Nevada. After crossing the mountains, he traveled up the coast to Monterey, California, where Gen. José Castro commanded the Mexican garrison.

There, four months before the United States attacked Mexico, Frémont erected a flag on Gavilan Peak. When Castro threatened to forcibly evict the small American force, Frémont moved north to Oregon. But after President Polk declared war on May 13, 1846, Frémont joined a group of settlers in Sonoma who established the Republic of California (in what was known as the Bear-Flag Revolt). Frémont became the short-lived republic's first director. After Frémont worked with Brig. Gen. Stephen Watts Kearny and Commo. Robert Stockton to conquer California, the United States received title to the territory under the Treaty of Guadalupe Hidalgo in 1848. But Frémont's refusal to obey Kearny's orders in California led to a court-martial. Although President Polk later remitted the guilty verdict, Frémont resigned his commission. He set off on a disastrous, privately funded fourth expedition in the winter of 1848–1849, hoping to discover a railroad route across the Rockies. He lost his equipment and ten men before reaching California.

While her husband adventured in the West, Jessie remained in the East. But in 1849, with her husband in disgrace, Jessie headed with their six-year-old daughter, Lily, for a new life in California. There, gold mining made them wealthy. Two more children were born. In 1851, John served as U.S. senator from California, which led them back to the East.

In 1856, John ran for president on the new Republican Party ticket, but was defeated by James Buchanan. During the Civil War, John served first as head of the Department of the West, centered in St. Louis, and later in western Virginia. But he was always out of step with his commanding officers, including President Lincoln. In 1863, Jessie penned *The Story of the Guard* in an attempt to rescue her husband's reputation.

After the war, John lost their wealth in a series of bad investments and railroad promotions. The Frémonts retreated to rural New York, yet continued to live above their means. Jessie began writing travel pieces and personal sketches to supplement their income. Her popular articles were eventually collected in a series of books. *A Year of American Travel* (1878) described her trip with Lily from St. Louis to New Orleans, across the Isthmus of Panama, and by ship to San Diego and Monterey in 1849. *Souvenirs of My Time* (1887) included reminiscences of those early California days. And *Far West Sketches* (1890), her most famous and best-written work, captured life in the Sierra foothills during the gold rush.

But Jessie's writing could not earn enough to keep the family afloat. They sold their home and possessions, and rented a series of houses and apartments. As their situation became more destitute, Jessie arranged to have John appointed territorial governor in Arizona. In 1878, Jessie again threw herself into the role of a politician's wife. But John Frémont was not a popular governor. While in Prescott and Tucson, he spent more time searching for investment opportunities than governing. He resigned in 1881, and they returned to New York, where Jessie collaborated with John on his *Memoirs of My Life* (1887). It did not sell.

For health reasons, the Frémonts moved to Los Angeles. In 1890, John died while on a business trip to New York. Jessie's women friends and supporters raised enough money to buy a home for her and Lily. Jessie lived there until her death at seventy-eight. Her ashes were interred next to John at a spot overlooking the Hudson River.

IF WHEN LOOKING back to Saint Louis I feel its fresh life, cheerful move-ment and ample outlook in refreshing contrast to the metes and bounds and endeavors to repeat past phases of life of the East, how can I tell all that name, "California," represents? If our East has a life of yesterday, and the West of to-day, then here to-morrow *had* come. . . .

To me it was the Land of Promise and gladness. Getting to San Francisco in the windy weather of June [1849], a bad cough was added to the hurt to the lungs left by my Panama illness, and I was taken to the softer air of Monterey. I met there a young officer, thin to gauntness, and not considered more likely to live than myself. To that exquisite pine and sea air we each owe new life. As it chanced, we did not meet again until the end of our late war when General Sherman and myself, talking over those Monterey days, thought we had been of some use for people given up as "consumptive."

I had gone up the coast fearing the news I might meet of Mr. Frémont's winter journey overland. Its cruel sufferings when he was midway, I learned at Panama, but kept on my way refusing to give up even in my own mind to the doubts almost every one had of his getting through.

At the first California port, San Diego, we met the news that he *had* arrived and hurried on to San Francisco. . . .

It is presumption to put that comprehensive name [California] to this fragmentary brief paper, when the space given me would not answer for a mere index of the many delightful pictures memory brings up; episodes illustrating character under new and trying conditions with results chiefly good—even under the test of sudden and great success. . . .

Even in '49 when we were pretty much in the conditions of ship-wrecked people where each one becomes a law to himself, the element of good decidedly prevailed. And California does not owe her beautiful harvests of grain and wine and fruits to fitful use of energies. To be sure the climate makes unbroken energetic health. A young friend who had grown up in the interior, said very fairly when in Washington: "It is very easy to kept Lent here on shad and terrapin, but on salt-fish it *is* a penance." Winters below zero with pneumonia attached, and ninety de-grees and sun-strokes for summer, allow no such vitality as is the rule in "that fair land of flowers." Exertion is a penance half the time here.

I wish I could tell you of my lovely camping-out travel for months; of my visits by the way to the ranches of the native Californians and their genuine hospitality and their good housekeeping; their immense fami-lies—fourteen, twenty, even twenty-six children, among whom sickness was unknown, and the wonderful grandmothers—all were proofs of the fine climate. One of these grandmothers, a Madame Castro, over eighty when I saw her, remains to me a type of this patriarchal and contented people as they were until we brought among them our American unrest and turmoil.

She wished to thank me in person for "Don Flémon's" protection of all women during the military movements in taking the country; she was old, so she sent me word, but would come to see me in Monterey if sure of finding me there.

I had the only carriage in the country—built in New Jersey for me and shipped out months before, so that I found my transportation ready. . . .

It was my Pullman car, for in it I could sleep by night, and go com-fortably wherever wheels could go. The California women travelled but little and that on horseback, or in the slow heavy creaking *carreta*, a low wagon-body without a spring, with solid wood wheels, and drawn by oxen. I would not let the old lady be jolted in that way for me and went willingly enough to her.

The want of undergrowth, the beautiful grasses and wild flowers and the fine trees made all the coast-country look like parks, and the framing of landscape for the family picture was good when we reached the group waiting us in front of the long low house.

There was fashion, even here. It was "de modo" to wear on fine oc-casions a full petticoat of scarlet broadcloth with points of green silk, stitched beautifully point upward, as a border around the bottom. Over this a gown of the dull-toned damasked Chinese satin. Madame Castro wore the obligatory English scarlet cloth petticoat and her gown of olive satin was pulled through the pocket holes either side, making a good watteau effect. A small crape [*sic*] shawl of many soft colors was crossed over the breast and the ends trimly tucked back. Sunburned and natu-rally dark, she had still much of the rich color of the young women near her. Her brilliant black eyes were large and steady, and the thick white hair made a puff as it was turned back from the face and coiled in a large plait at the neck. Children, grandchildren and great-grandchildren were around her, assembled to do me honor—coming forward, as she named each, with smiles that showed their beautiful white teeth—as fine almost in the venerable mother of all as in the Murillo girls. Her dignity of welcome, and the good she invoked for me in return for the care they had had from Mr. Frémont was sincere and impressive. And so beautifully free from self-consciousness!

She, and all the native people, were erect and of free firm movement. You could see that neither in mind or body had they known depressing influences.

I do not like to remember how we changed all that. A carefully drawn treaty had guarded their rights, but this proved of no avail.

They could not answer the searchers of titles . . . for these were only a peaceful people, with herds and flocks and fruits and vines.

The men lived much on horseback and had excitement and pleasure in theirs and their neighbors' cattle interests. Dancing and abundant but temperate feasting brought together the families, and though I saw this only in its dying phase, it was even then "enjoyment"—not as a phrase but as a fact.

The roomy long one-story houses with shaded courtyard and large high-walled garden made the boundary of the women's lives. Here they overlooked diligently their Indian servant girls—baptized and "Christians"—who were good at fine sewing and in cooking food which was savory and wholesome. We could turn into any rancho and find this same contented orderly abundant home living; whatever they had was offered without explanations or efforts at varying. No end of fancy needlework decorated their wearing and house-linen. They were amused that I should admire it so much; like their good cookery it was the survival of Spanish convent-training coming down to them in household tradition and therefore only matter-of-course.

All that is only a memory to them as to me. It was so strangely peaceful and contented I like to tell of it. . . .

The heat, which becomes intense in these inland valleys, had made me ill and I came down, rather suddenly, from our mining place in the mountains to San Francisco and sea-air, getting a start of twelve miles by leaving home in the late afternoon and resting for the night at Murray's—a comfortable inn on the Merced river. The good bridge there, and Osborne's ferry on the Touolumné, and their two good inns, decided the route. Having our own travelling resources we chose our own hours. We had a pair of horses which made the eighty miles in two days, getting through in time for the afternoon boat from Stockton, where they rested until the return. In cool weather they had several times made it in one day, but that was necessity, and the man who always drove them knew how to spare a horse and was fond of these two. "Coachman" I cannot call him. He was a spare, wiry Tennessee Indian with enough colored blood to have been a slave; he had freed himself— sharply, I fancy.

For years he had been the most noted hunter, of grizzly bear especially, in all those mountains; a silent solitary man, who chose to stay with us. He loved money, but money alone could not buy his services. He was a "lucky" (persevering) miner and had lived to himself; but he had a thorough alleigance [sic] to Mr. Frémont, and when we went up there, gave to my youngest boy, a child of three years, all the unused tenderness of an embittered nature.

He was a character; known and feared—no man ever "fooled-round" Isaac, and as he was absolutely sober and not quarrelsome (though swift and deadly in retaliation), he made all the guard I needed.

Soon after we left Murray's in the cool gray morning, we met a "prairie schooner" with its twelve-in-hand mule team, and halted for Isaac to ask about the water in the Touolumné, a mountain river with sudden rises that scared me when the current made the open ferry-boat sway dangerously off from the rope.

They warned us we could not rest there the afternoon and night as was our custom. Mrs. Osborne herself had left because of diphtheria there, "bad." That meant no rest for the horses.

Isaac never talked or exclaimed, but he knew how to act.

As carefully as possible he worked the faithful horses, but the heat and deep hot dust were hard on them. And if they gave out there was not a house or tree or water for stretches of ten and twenty miles.

Isaac was alarmed too for me, and grieved for the little boy, who was as patient and reasonable as he was miserable. I did almost give out, but when you must you not only *must* but you *do*. One of the horses began to suffer; they could not know, poor things, why we hurried past the big barns and the cool shade of the noble oaks at Osborne's. When night fell [it was] still a long pull to Stockton, and Prince's back was a limp straight line with hanging head and stumbling feet.

Suddenly Isaac turned to me: "Now, don't you say nothing—I'm going to take you *thar,* to the Ten-mile House. Prince can't go any further."

This Ten-mile House we always gave a wide berth to in our journeyings—you could drive where you pleased on those flat treeless plains, and we were best pleased not to pass through that place; a "wagon-stand" with its corral and barns and smithy on one side of the road, and on the other a tavern, whose owner was a sinner as well as a publican if report was true; and the nearness to Stockton made it, a roughish resort.

This was about as bad as the diphtheria at Osborne's; but having recognized what must be done Isaac admitted no weak side-issues.

The moon was up and curious wagoners came forward—incredulous—as they recognized the carriage. A brief explanation from Isaac made them into active helpers about the horses, while Isaac leading, I and the child followed him up the path of the enclosure to the porch of the tavern where sat an enormously large old man who roared at us as we neared—asking, Who was it? What did we want that time o' night?

Recognizing Isaac, he moderated, but broke out afresh at my name—he wanted no (very blank) black republicans coming into *his* house—he wouldn't have any fine madam there anyhow.

The given-out horse—the child—the sick woman—"No! *no!* NO!"

"Go round the other side of the porch," directed Isaac, "where you can't hear him. He can't come after you—he can't git about without help—and nobody's going to help him *this time.*"

There was a little two-pronged oil-lamp flaring away in the window behind him, and by its light I saw Isaac's thin features, all twitching with passion. But he controlled himself, and said only that he must see what could be done for the horse, and could I just wait on the porch?

"Well, but don't you be long about it! I won't have 'em here!"

"*C'est Croque—mitaine mamman?*" (the nursery-French for ogres and terrible creatures). The little man had eyed it all as a show, and until now had not spoken.

I told him we must both keep very still, and we moved off as far as the porch permitted; to be met by a trembling haggard woman with such a *very* young baby, who was listening in fear and begged me with tears to get away.

Another roar:

"See! Here—YOU! You can set in the parlor—come out o' that fog."

Venturing near enough to thank him, I asked to stay outside. The young locust trees were in bloom, and filling the night air with a dear remembered home fragrance—"Let me stay by the locust trees. They reminded me of home and my father," I said, nearly crying; I was so tired and it was all so unexpected and miserable.

"Where's your home? Who's your father? What's his name?"

I answered: "Saint Louis"—"and Senator Benton."

"WHAT! Senator Benton? Tom Benton?"

And being satisfied of this, with a roar louder than any yet, he cried out for one and another until several men were about him; all was changed now—he could not enough shew his good will. His outcry had brought Isaac from the sick horse, and to him and to all he commanded attention to me: "You, Ike, you go round to the kitchen—there's a woman thar, a pore-good-for-nothing-sickly-thing with more children 'an she can handle and she's got another—I had to take the lot along with her husband and now he can't cook, he's down with the chills. Have that woman up, Ike, and make her wait on the madam.

"Tom Benton's daughter! Lord! how I did fight for him them Bank times in Mizoury," etc., etc., etc.,—"and there's young chickens and eggs—git the lady a supper."

While to another was given the order for "wine," and lo! bottles of various kinds (for *me!* a water-drinker by training and preference).

He meant it so well that, with the aid of my handkerchief, I managed to empty a glass of an explosive compound he named "champagne" without risking any of it within my mouth. I do not wonder that the loud cries, the queer surroundings, his big bloated form made the child think him an "ogre;" but he was now intent on hospitality and inter-mingled his broken recollections of my father, and election work, with sudden vociferations for more attentions to me. He had himself brought along in his great chair to the end of the porch where the locust blossoms looked like a snowfall in the moonlight. "Them locusses, I planted 'em to remind me of old Mizoury," and before long he was talking to me almost gently; he thought he had dropsy, and found a sort of comfort when I reminded him of General [Andrew] Jackson's long sufferings and death from the same disease. "That's so! I know that's true! Well, well, what's good enough for Andy Jackson's good enough for me."

He had not heard of my father's death. He could not realize so much will and strength and accumulated power, gone.

"What am I?" he kept saying. "I'm nothin' to nobody. Nobody minds me now I can't git round—they pretend they don't hear me call and I git mad. Well—I *am* glad to have Tom Benton's daughter in my house before I die."

He was in pain though, and had to be carried off, telling me to stay as long as I had a mind to—"jist you take all you want. Rest that horse," etc., etc., etc.

But very, very early that horse was on duty, and we crept into Stockton where a hot bath and a good sleep left no trace of our misadventures. Only to the poor "ogre" as to myself, a memory of the good influences of the locust blossoms.

Helen Maria Fiske Hunt Jackson

("H. H.," "Marah," "Saxe Holm")
(1830–1885)

HELEN FISKE and Emily Dickinson were born two months apart in Amherst, Massachusetts, where Nathan Fiske was a professor at Amherst University. Although Helen and Emily played together as youngsters, their schooling and later lives took far different courses. Helen's parents both died of tuberculosis when she was in her teens. She and her younger sister, Ann, lived in a series of guardians' houses and boarding schools until Helen married Edward Bissell Hunt, brother of the governor of New York.

Edward Hunt was a graduate of West Point, a brilliant engineer, inventor, and theoretical mathematician who published in several fields. They had two boys. The first died in infancy, the second, Rennie, at nine—only eighteen months after Hunt died in an accident while inspecting a torpedo prototype.

To deal with her grief and loneliness, Helen turned to poetry. The "sorrow" poems were published in the *Nation* and the *New York Evening Post* in 1865 under the pen name "Marah." The *Post* also published her first prose piece on Bethlehem, New Hampshire, which she signed "H. H." Deciding to pursue a literary career, she moved to Newport, Rhode Island, an artists' colony. There, Thomas Wentworth Higginson, the man who published Emily Dickinson's poetry after her death, served as Helen's mentor and agent. Her travel essays and poetry were well received, as were short stories published under the pseudonym "Saxe Holm," children's stories and articles, and book reviews. Eventually, her poetry, short stories, and essays were popular enough to be collected and published in book form. By the time Helen moved to Colorado for her health in 1873, she was a nationally known and respected writer, albeit an anonymous one.

Moving to Colorado Springs changed Helen's life. She met William Sharpless Jackson, a railroad executive and banker, who took her on drives into the mountains. Helen had not planned to remarry, but Sharpless, six years her junior, repeatedly proposed. Helen finally accepted, with the proviso that she continue her writing career. They married in 1875, in a Quaker ceremony at her sister's home. However,

Helen's demanding writing schedule and Jackson's railroad trips left them little time together. Gradually, they began to lead separate lives. By 1879, Helen was ready for a new challenge. It came in the form of a crusade in support of the Ponca Indians.

While in Boston to visit relatives, Helen attended a reception for the Ponca chief, Standing Bear, and his Omaha translators: Frank La Flesche; his sister, Susette (Bright Eyes); and Thomas Tibbles, a newspaperman who spearheaded the movement to rescue the Poncas. For Helen, who had previously avoided involvement in human-rights movements, it was an epiphany. She energetically pursued the Ponca case for restoration of their tribal lands, and helped them raise money for food and clothing. She wrote articles in the newspapers, contacted the secretary of the interior, and researched the Ponca problem at the Astor Library in New York. Her research documented innumerable instances of injustice to Indian tribes in the first hundred years of the United States. She was both the lightning rod for the cause and the link between the disparate personalities involved in the fight, including Sarah Winnemucca, Susette La Flesche, and Alice Fletcher.

William Jackson became concerned that Helen's views on Indian rights and broken treaties would antagonize the people of their adopted state. But she refused to be swayed. Early in 1881, *A Century of Dishonor: A Sketch of the United States Government's Dealings with Some of the Indian Tribes* hit the bookstores. Helen sent a copy to each member of Congress, visited them personally, and was rewarded by a favorable resolution. It was only the beginning of her crusade.

In the next four years, Helen continued to work on the "Indian question." She shifted her focus to California after touring and describing the California missions and the Indian tribes who were being systematically deprived of their land. The government hired her to investigate the problem more fully, and she coauthored the *Report on the Conditions and Needs of Mission Indians* with Abbott Kinney. It made her no more popular in California than her previous book had made her in Colorado. To garner popular support for remedying the Indian situation, she set out to write a novel. The plot came to her in a flash one morning. She worked nonstop on the book for the next four months.

Ramona, published in 1884, is the work most closely associated with Helen Hunt Jackson. The southern California setting, the exotic and strong protagonist, and the romance of the Spanish heritage enthralled America. The tragedy with a falsely happy ending drew thousands of tourists to California, pilgrims who searched for the locales described in the book and the trails taken by the lovers, Ramona and Alessandro. Characteristically, Helen was dismayed that sympathy for the Indians was lost in the public's appreciation of the love story.

Throughout Helen Hunt Jackson's writing career, she corresponded with Emily Dickinson. Jackson was Emily's sounding board, one of her strongest links with the world outside Amherst, and perhaps the only person in America who recognized the genius of Dickinson's poetry. The regard and respect was mutual between the activist and the recluse. Jackson encouraged Emily to publish; she refused, although she included poems in many of her letters. In the summer of 1885, when Helen died of cancer in San Francisco, one strong strut in Dickinson's life collapsed. Nine months later, and a continent away, Emily Dickinson died.

In the following years, others took up the Indian cause. Ramona's name—affixed to town, convent, festival, and theater—seeped into the very texture of southern California life. The book joined the permanent reading list of California schoolchildren. Although Jackson's poetry and nonfiction deserve study and attention today, through fiction she effected change and gained regional immortality.

In keeping with her wishes, Helen Hunt Jackson was buried on the slopes of Cheyenne Mountain. But so many of her readers came to visit her grave that she was reinterred in Colorado Springs six years later.

Cheyenne Mountain

By easy slope to west as if it had
No thought, when first its soaring was begun,
Except to look devoutly to the sun,
It rises and has risen, until glad,
With light as with a garment, it is clad.
Each dawn, before the tardy plains have won
One ray; and after day has long been done
For us, the light doth cling reluctant, sad
To leave its brow.
               Beloved mountain, I
Thy worshipper as thou the sun's, each morn
My dawn, before the dawn, receive from thee;
And think, as thy rose-tinted peaks I see
That thou wert great when Homer was not born.
And ere thou change all human song shall die.

. . . IN THE WESTERN suburbs of Los Angeles is a low adobe house, built after the ancient style, on three sides of a square, surrounded by orchards, vineyards, and orange groves, and looking out on an old-fashioned garden, in which southernwood, rue, lavender, mint, marigolds, and gillyflowers hold their own bravely, growing in straight and angular beds among the newer splendors of verbenas, roses, carnations, and geraniums. On two sides of the house runs a broad porch, where stand rows of geraniums and chrysanthemums growing in odd-shaped earthen pots. Here may often be seen a beautiful young Mexican woman, flitting about among the plants, or sporting with a superb St. Bernard dog. Her clear olive skin, soft brown eyes, delicate sensitive nostrils, and broad smiling mouth, are all of the Spanish madonna type; and when her low brow is bound, as is often her wont, by turban folds of soft brown or green gauze, her face becomes a picture indeed. She is the young wife of a gray-headed Mexican señor, of whom—by his own most gracious permission—I shall speak by his familiar name, Don Antonio. Whoever has the fortune to pass as a friend across the threshold of this house, finds himself transported, as by a miracle, into the life of a half century ago. The rooms are ornamented with fans, shells, feather and wax flowers, pictures, saints' images, old laces and stuffs, in the quaint gay Mexican fashion. On the day when I first saw them, they were brilliant with bloom. In every one of the deep window-seats stood a cone of bright flowers, its base made by large white datura blossoms, their creamy whorls all turned outward, making a superb decoration. I went for but a few moments' call. I staid [sic] three hours, and left, carrying with me bewildering treasures of pictures of the olden time.

Don Antonio speaks little English; but the señora knows just enough of the language to make her use of it delicious, as she translates for her husband. It is an entrancing sight to watch his dark, weather-beaten face, full of lightning changes as he pours out torrents of his nervous, eloquent Spanish speech; watching his wife intently, hearkening to each word she uses, sometimes interrupting her urgently with "No, no; that is not it"; for he well understands the tongue he cannot or will not use for himself. He is sixty-five years of age, but he is young: the best waltzer in Los Angeles to-day; his eye keen, his blood fiery quick; his memory like a burning-glass bringing into sharp light and focus a half century as if it were a yesterday. Full of sentiment, of an intense and poetic nature, he looks back to the lost empire of his race and people on the California shores with a sorrow far too proud for any antagonisms or complaints. He recognizes the inexorableness of the laws under whose workings his nation is slowly, surely giving place to one more representative of the age. Intellectually he is in sympathy with progress, with reform, with civilization at its utmost; he would not have had them stayed, or changed, because his people could not keep up, and were not ready. But his heart is none the less saddened and lonely.

This is probably the position and point of view of most cultivated Mexican men of his age. The suffering involved in it is inevitable. It is part of the great, unreckoned price which must always be paid for the gain the world gets, when the young and strong supersede the old and weak.

A sunny little south-east corner room in Don Antonio's house is full of the relics of the time when he and his father were foremost representatives of ideas and progress in the City of Angels, and taught the first school that was kept in the place. This was nearly a half century ago. On the walls of the room still hang maps and charts which they used; and carefully preserved, with the tender reverence of which only poetic natures are capable, are still to be seen there the old atlases, primers, catechisms, grammars, reading-books, which meant toil and trouble to the merry, ignorant children of the merry and ignorant people of that time.

The leathern covers of the books are thin and frayed by long handling; the edges of the leaves worn down as if mice had gnawed them: tattered, loose, hanging by yellow threads, they look far older than they are, and bear vivid record of the days when books were so rare and precious that each book did doubled and redoubled duty, passing from hand to hand and house to house. It was on the old Lancaster system that Los Angeles set out in educating its children; and here are still preserved the formal and elaborate instructions for teachers and schools on that plan; also volumes of Spain's laws for military judges in 1781, and a quaint old volume called "Secrets of Agriculture, Fields and Pastures," written by a Catholic father in 1617, reprinted in 1781, and held of great value in its day as a sure guide to success with crops. Accompanying it was a chart, a perpetual circle, by which might be foretold, with certainty, what years would be barren and what ones fruitful.

Almanacs, histories, arithmetics, dating back to 1750, drawing-books, multiplication-tables, music, and bundles of records of the branding of cattle at the San Gabriel Mission, are among the curiosities of this room. The music of the first quadrilles ever danced in Mexico is here: a ragged pamphlet, which, no doubt, went gleeful rounds in the City of the Angels for many a year. It is a merry music, simple in melody, but with an especial quality of light-heartedness, suiting the people who danced to it.

There are also in the little room many relics of a more substantial sort than tattered papers and books: a branding-iron and a pair of handcuffs from the San Gabriel Mission; curiously decorated clubs and sticks used by the Indians in their games; boxes of silver rings and balls made for decorations of bridles and on leggings and knee-breeches. The place of honor in the room is given, as well it might be, to a small cannon, the first cannon brought into California. It was made in 1717, and was brought by Father Junipero Sierra to San Diego in 1769. Afterward it was given to the San Gabriel Mission, but it still bears its old name, "San Diego." It is an odd little arm, only about two feet long, and requiring but six ounces of powder. Its swivel is made with a rest to set firm in the ground. It has taken many long journeys on the backs of mules, having been in great requisition in the early mission days for the firing of salutes at festivals and feasts.

Don Antonio was but a lad when his father's family removed from the city of Mexico to California. They came in one of the many unfortunate colonies sent out by the Mexican Government, during the first years of the secularization period, having had a toilsome and suffering two months, going in wagons from Mexico to San Blas, then a tedious and uncomfortable voyage of several weeks from San Blas to Monterey, where they arrived only to find themselves deceived and disappointed in every particular, and surrounded by hostilities, plots, and dangers on all sides. So great was the antagonism to them that it was at times difficult for a colonist to obtain food from a Californian. They were arrested on false pretenses, thrown into prison, shipped off like convicts from place to place, with no one to protect them or plead their cause. Revolution succeeded upon revolution, and it was a most unhappy period for all re-fined and cultivated persons who had joined the colony enterprises. Young men of education and breeding were glad to earn their daily bread by any menial labor that offered. Don Antonio and several of his young friends, who had all studied medicine together, spent the greater part of a year in making shingles. The one hope and aim of most of them was to earn money enough to get back to Mexico. Don Antonio, however, seems to have had more versatility and capacity than his friends, for he never lost courage; and it was owing to him that at last his whole family gathered in Los Angeles and established a home there. This was in 1836. There were then only about eight hundred people in the pueblo, and the customs, superstitions, and ignorances of the earliest days still held sway. The missions were still rich and powerful, though the confusions and conflicts of their ruin had begun. At this time, the young Antonio, being quick at accounts and naturally ingenious at all sorts of mechanical crafts, found profit as well as pleasure in journeying from mission to mission, sometimes spending two or three months in one place, keeping books, or repairing silver and gold ornaments.

The blow-pipe which he made for himself at that time his wife exhibits now with affectionate pride, and there are few things she enjoys better than translating, to an eager listener, his graphic stories of the incidents and adventures of that portion of his life.

While he was at the San Antonio Mission, a strange thing happened. It is a good illustration of the stintless hospitality of those old missions, that staying there at the time were a notorious gambler and a celebrated juggler who had come out in the colony from Mexico. The juggler threatened to turn the gambler into a crow; the gambler, after watching his tricks for a short time, became frightened, and asked young Antonio, in serious good faith, if he did not believe the juggler had made a league with the devil. A few nights afterward, at midnight, a terrible noise was heard in the gambler's room. He was found in convulsions, foaming at the mouth, and crying:

"Oh, father! father! I have got the devil inside of me! Take him away."

The priest dragged him into the chapel, showered him with holy water, and exorcised the devil, first making the gambler promise to leave off his gambling forever. All the rest of the night the rescued sinner spent in the chapel, praying and weeping. In the morning, he announced his intention of becoming a priest, and began his studies at once. These he faithfully pursued for a year, leading all the while a life of great devotion. At the end of that time, preparations were made for his ordination at San José. The day was set, the hour came: he was in the sacristy, had put on the sacred vestments, and was just going toward the church door, when he fell to the floor, dead. Soon after this juggler was banished from the country, trouble and disaster having everywhere followed on his presence.

On the first breaking out of hostilities between California and the United States, Don Antonio took command of a company of Los Angeles volunteers, to repel the intruders. By this time he had attained a prominent position in the affairs of the pueblo; had been alcalde and, under Governor Michel[t]orena, inspector of public works. It was like the fighting of children, the impetuous attempts that heterogeneous little bands of Californians, here and there, made to hold their country. They were plucky from first to last, for they were everywhere at a disadvantage, and fought on, quite in the dark as to what Mexico meant to do about them—whether she might not any morning deliver them over to the enemy. Of all Don Antonio's graphic narratives of the olden time, none is more interesting than those which describe his adventures during the days of this contest. On one of the first approaches made by the Americans to Los Angeles, he went out with his little haphazard company of men and boys to meet them. He had but one cannon, a small one, tied by ropes on a cart axle. He had but one small keg of powder which was good for anything; all the rest was bad, would merely go off "pouf, pouf," the señora said, and the ball would pop down near the mouth of the cannon. With this bad powder he fired his first shots. The Americans laughed; this is child's play, they said, and pushed on closer. Then came a good shot, with the good powder, tearing into their ranks and knocking them right and left; another, and another. "Then the Americans began to think, these are no pouf balls; and when a few more were killed, they ran away and left their flag behind them. And if they had only known it, the Californians had only one more charge left of the good powder, and the next minute it would have been the Californians that would have had to run away themselves," merrily laughed the señora as she told the tale.

This captured flag, with important papers, were intrusted to Don Antonio to carry to the Mexican head-quarters at Sonora. He set off with an escort of soldiers, his horse decked with silver trappings, his sword, pistols—all of the finest: a proud beginning of a journey destined to end in a different fashion. It was in winter time; cold rains were falling; by night he was drenched to the skin, and stopped at a friendly Indian's tent to change his clothes. Hardly had he got them off when the sound of horses' hoofs was heard. The Indian flung himself down, put his ear to the ground, and exclaimed, "Americanos! Americanos!" Almost in the same second they were at the tent's door. As they halted, Don Antonio, clad only in his drawers and stockings, crawled out at the back of the tent, and creeping on all fours reached a tree up which he climbed, and sat safe hidden in the darkness among its branches listening, while his pursuers cross-questioned the Indians, and at last rode away with his horse. Luckily, he had carried into the tent the precious papers and the captured flag: these he intrusted to an Indian to take to Sonora, it being evidently of no use for him to try to cross the country thus closely pursued by his enemies. All night he lay hidden; the next day he walked twelve miles across the mountains to an Indian village where he hoped to get a horse. It was dark when he reached it. Cautiously he opened the door of the hut of one whom he knew well. The Indian was preparing poisoned arrows: fixing one on the string and aiming at the door, he called out, angrily, "Who is there?"

"It is I, Antonio."

"Don't make a sound," whispered the Indian, throwing down his arrow, springing to the door, coming out and closing it softly. He then proceeded to tell him that the Americans had offered a reward for his head, and that some of the Indians in the rancheria were ready to betray or kill him. While they were yet talking, again came the sound of the Americans' horses' hoofs galloping in the distance. This time there seemed no escape. Suddenly Don Antonio, throwing himself on his stomach, wriggled into a cactus patch near by. Only one who has seen California cactus thickets can realize the desperateness of this act. But it succeeded. The Indian threw over the cactus plants an old blanket and some refuse stalks and reeds; and there once more, within hearing of all his baffled pursuers said, the hunted man lay, safe, thanks to Indian friendship. The crafty Indian assented to all the Americans proposed, said that Don Antonio would be sure to be caught in a few days, advised them to search in a certain rancheria which he described, a few miles off, and in an opposite direction from the way in which he intended to guide Don Antonio. As soon as the Americans had gone, he bound up Antonio's feet in strips of raw hide, gave him a blanket and an old tattered hat, the best his stores afforded, and then led him by a long and difficult trail to a spot high up in the mountains where the old women of the band were gathering acorns. By the time they reached this place, blood was trickling from Antonio's feet and legs, and he was well-nigh fainting with fatigue and excitement. Tears rolled down the old women's cheeks when they saw him. Some of them had been servants in his father's house and loved him. One brought gruel; another bathed his feet; others ran in search of healing leaves of different sorts. Bruising these in a stone mortar, they rubbed him from head to foot with the wet fiber. All his pain and weariness vanished as by magic. His wounds healed, and in a day he was ready to set off for home. There was but one pony in the old women's camp. This was old, vicious, blind of one eye, and with one ear cropped short; but it looked to Don Antonio far more beautiful than the gay steed on which he had ridden away from Los Angeles three days before. There was one pair of ragged shoes of enormous size among the old women's possessions. These were strapped on his feet by leathern thongs, and a bit of old sheepskin was tied around the pony's body. Thus accoutered and mounted, shivering in his drawers under his single blanket, the captain and flag-bearer turned his face homeward. At the first friend's house he reached he stopped and begged for food. Some dried meat was given to him, and a stool on the porch offered to him. It was the house of a dear friend, and the friend's sister was his sweetheart. As he sat there eating his meat the women eyed him curiously. One said to the other, "How much he looks like Antonio!"

At last the sweetheart, coming nearer, asked him if he were "any relation of Don Antonio?"

"No," he said. Just at that moment his friend rode up, gave one glance at the pitiful beggar sitting on his porch, shouted his name, dashed toward him, and seized him in his arms. Then was a great laughing and half weeping, for it had been rumored that he had been taken prisoner by the Americans.

From this friend he received a welcome gift of a pair of trousers, many inches too short for his legs. At the next house his friend was as much too tall, and his second pair of gift trousers had to be rolled up in thick folds around his ankles.

Finally, he reached Los Angeles in safety. Halting in a grove outside the town, he waited till twilight before entering. Having disguised himself in the rags which he had worn from the Indian village, he rode boldly up to the porch of his father's house, and in an impudent tone called for brandy. The terrified women began to scream; but his youngest sister, fixing one piercing glance on his face, laughed out gladly, and cried:

"You can't fool me; you are Antonio."

Sitting in the little corner room, looking out, through the open door on the gay garden and breathing its spring air, gay even in midwinter, and as spicy then as the gardens of other lands are in June, I spent many an afternoon listening to such tales as this. Sunset always came long before its time, it seemed, on these days.

Occasionally, at the last moment, Don Antonio would take up his guitar, and, in a voice still sympathetic and full of melody, sing an old

Spanish love song, brought to his mind by thus living over the events of his youth. Never, however, in his most ardent youth, could his eyes have gazed on his fairest sweetheart's face with a look of greater devotion than that with which they now rest on the noble, expressive countenance of his wife, as he sings the ancient and tender strains. Of one of them I once won from her, amid laughs and blushes, a few words of translation:

> *"Let us hear the sweet echo*
> *Of your sweet voice that charms me.*
> *The one that truly loves you,*
> *He says he wishes to love;*
> *That the one who with ardent love adores you,*
> *Will sacrifice himself for you.*
> *Do not deprive me,*
> *Owner of me,*
> *Of that sweet echo*
> *Of your sweet voice that charms me."*

Near the western end of Don Antonio's porch is an orange tree, on which were hanging at this time twenty-five hundred oranges, ripe and golden among the glossy leaves. Under this tree my carriage always waited for me. The señora never allowed me to depart without bringing to me, in the carriage, farewell gifts of flowers and fruit; clusters of grapes, dried and fresh; great boughs full of oranges, more than I could lift. As I drove away, thus, my lap filled with bloom and golden fruit, canopies of golden fruit over my head, I said to myself often: "Fables are prophesies. The Hesperides have come true."

Chapter II

THE SEÑORA MORENO'S house was one of the best specimens to be
found in California of the representative house of the half barbaric, half
elegant, wholly generous and free-handed life led there by Mexican men
and women of degree in the early part of this century, under the rule of
the Spanish and Mexican viceroys, when the laws of the Indies were still
the law of the land, and its old name "New Spain," was an ever-present
link and stimulus to the warmest memories and deepest patriotisms of
its people.

It was a picturesque life, with more of sentiment and gayety in it,
more also that was truly dramatic, more romance, than will ever be seen
again on those sunny shores. The aroma of it all lingers there still; industries and inventions have not yet slain it; it will last out its century,—
in fact, it can never be quite lost, so long as there is left standing one
such house as the Señora Moreno's.

When the house was built, General Moreno owned all the land within
a radius of forty miles,—forty miles westward, down the valley to the
sea; forty miles eastward, into the San Fernando Mountains; and good
forty miles more or less along the coast. The boundaries were not very
strictly defined; there was no occasion, in those happy days, to reckon
land by inches. It might be asked, perhaps, just how General Moreno
owned all this land, and the question might not be easy to answer. It was
not and could not be answered to the satisfaction of the United States
Land Commission, which, after the surrender of California, undertook
to sift and adjust Mexican land-titles; and that was the way it had come
about that the Señora Moreno now called herself a poor woman. Tract
after tract, her lands had been taken away from her; it looked for a time
as if nothing would be left. Every one of the claims based on deeds of gift
from Governor Pio Pico, her husband's most intimate friend, was disal-
lowed. They all went by the board in one batch, and took away from the
Señora in a day the greater part of her best pasture-lands. They were
lands which had belonged to the Bonaventura Mission, and lay along
the coast at the mouth of the valley down which the little stream which
ran past her house went to the sea; and it had been a great pride and delight to the Señora, when she was young, to ride that forty miles by her
husband's side, all the way on their own lands, straight from their house

to their own strip of shore. No wonder she believed the Americans thieves, and spoke of them always as hounds. The people of the United States have never in the least realized that the taking possession of California was not only a conquering of Mexico, but a conquering of California as well; that the real bitterness of the surrender was not so much to the empire which gave up the country, as to the country itself which was given up. Provinces passed back and forth in that way, helpless in the hands of great powers, have all the ignominy and humiliation of defeat, with none of the dignities or compensations of the transaction.

Mexico saved much by her treaty, spite of having to acknowledge herself beaten; but California lost all. Words cannot tell the sting of such a transfer. It is a marvel that a Mexican remained in the country; probably none did, except those who were absolutely forced to it.

Luckily for the Señora Moreno, her title to the lands midway in the valley was better than those lying to the east and the west, which had once belonged to the missions of San Fernando and Bonaventura; and after all the claims, counter-claims, petitions, appeals, and adjudications were ended, she still was left in undisputed possession of what would have been thought by any new-comer into the country to be a handsome estate, but which seemed to the despoiled and indignant Señora a pitiful fragment of one. Moreover, she declared that she should never feel secure of a foot of even this. Any day, she said, the United States Government might send out a new Land Commission to examine the decrees of the first, and revoke such as they saw fit. Once a thief, always a thief. Nobody need feel himself safe under American rule. There was no knowing what might happen any day; and year by year the lines of sadness, resentment, anxiety, and antagonism deepened on the Señora's fast aging face.

It gave her unspeakable satisfaction, when the Commissioners, laying out a road down the valley, ran it at the back of her house instead of past the front. "It is well," she said. "Let their travel be where it belongs, behind our kitchens; and no one have sight of the front doors of our houses, except friends who have come to visit us." Her enjoyment of this never flagged. Whenever she saw, passing the place, wagons or carriages belonging to the hated Americans, it gave her a distinct thrill of pleasure to think that the house turned its back on them. She would like always to be able to do the same herself; but whatever she, by policy or in business, might be forced to do, the old house, at any rate, would always keep the attitude of contempt,—its face turned away.

One other pleasure she provided herself with, soon after this road

was opened,—a pleasure in which religious devotion and race antagonism were so closely blended that it would have puzzled the subtlest of
priests to decide whether her act were a sin or a virtue. She caused to be
set up, upon every one of the soft rounded hills which made the beautiful rolling sides of that part of the valley, a large wooden cross; not a hill
in sight of her house left without the sacred emblem of her faith. "That
the heretics may know, when they go by, that they are on the estate of a
good Catholic," she said, "and that the faithful may be reminded to
pray. There have been miracles of conversion wrought on the most hardened by a sudden sight of the Blessed Cross."

There they stood, summer and winter, rain and shine, the silent,
solemn, outstretched arms, and became landmarks to many a guideless
traveller who had been told that his way would be by the first turn to the
left or the right, after passing the last one of the Señora Moreno's
crosses, which he couldn't miss seeing. And who shall say that it did not
often happen that the crosses bore a sudden message to some idle heart
journeying by, and thus justified the pious half of the Señora's impulse?
Certain it is, that many a good Catholic halted and crossed himself when
he first beheld them, in the lonely places, standing out in sudden relief
against the blue sky; and if he said a swift short prayer at the sight, was
he not so much the better?

The house was of adobe, low, with a wide veranda on the three sides
of the inner court, and a still broader one across the entire front, which
looked to the south. These verandas, especially those on the inner court,
were supplementary rooms to the house. The greater part of the family
life went on in them. Nobody stayed inside the walls, except when it was
necessary. All the kitchen work, except the actual cooking, was done
here, in front of the kitchen doors and windows. Babies slept, were
washed, sat in the dirt, and played, on the veranda. The women said
their prayers, took their naps, and wove their lace there. Old Juanita
shelled her beans there, and threw the pods down on the tile floor; till towards night they were sometimes piled up high around her, like the corn-
husks at a husking. The herdsmen and shepherds smoked there, lounged
there, trained their dogs there; there the young made love, and the old
dozed; the benches, which ran the entire length of the walls, were worn
into hollows, and shone like satin; the tiled floors also were broken and
sunk in places, making little wells, which filled up in times of hard rains,
and were then an invaluable addition to the children's resources for
amusement, and also to the comfort of the dogs, cats, and fowls, who
picked about among them, taking sips from each.

The arched veranda along the front was a delightsome place. It must have been eighty feet long, at least, for the doors of five large rooms opened on it. The two westernmost rooms had been added on, and made four steps higher than the others; which gave to that end of the veranda the look of a balcony, or loggia. Here the Señora kept her flowers; great red water-jars, hand-made by the Indians of San Luis Obispo Mission, stood in close rows against the walls, and in them were always growing fine geraniums, carnations, and yellow-flowered musk. The Señora's passion for musk she had inherited from her mother. It was so strong that she sometimes wondered at it; and one day, as she sat with Father Salvierderra in the veranda, she picked a handful of the blossoms, and giving them to him, said, "I do not know why it is, but it seems to me if I were dead I could be brought to life by the smell of musk."

"It is in your blood, Señora," the old monk replied. "When I was last in your father's house in Seville, your mother sent for me to her room, and under her window was a stone balcony full of growing musk, which so filled the room with its odor that I was like to faint. But she said it cured her of diseases, and without it she fell ill. You were a baby then."

"Yes," cried the Señora, "but I recollect that balcony. I recollect being lifted up to a window, and looking down into a bed of blooming yellow flowers; but I did not know what they were. How strange!"

"No. Not strange, daughter," replied Father Salvierderra. "It would have been stranger if you had not acquired the taste, thus drawing it in with the mother's milk. It would behoove mothers to remember this far more than they do."

Besides the geraniums and carnations and musk in the red jars, there were many sorts of climbing vines,—some coming from the ground, and twining around the pillars of the veranda; some growing in great bowls, swung by cords from the roof of the veranda, or set on shelves against the walls. These bowls were of gray stone, hollowed and polished, shining smooth inside and out. They also had been made by the Indians, nobody knew how many ages ago, scooped and polished by the patient creatures, with only stones for tools.

Among these vines, singing from morning till night, hung the Señora's canaries and finches, half a dozen of each, all of different generations, raised by the Señora. She was never without a young bird-family on hand; and all the way from Bonaventura to Monterey, it was thought a piece of good luck to come into possession of a canary or finch of Señora Moreno's raising.

Between the veranda and the river meadows, out on which it looked,

all was garden, orange grove, and almond orchard; the orange grove always green, never without snowy bloom or golden fruit; the garden
never without flowers, summer or winter; and the almond orchard, in
early spring, a fluttering canopy of pink and white petals, which, seen
from the hills on the opposite side of the river, looked as if rosy sunrise
clouds had fallen, and become tangled in the tree-tops. On either hand
stretched away other orchards,—peach, apricot, pear, apple, pomegran-
ate; and beyond these, vineyards. Nothing was to be seen but verdure or
bloom or fruit, at whatever time of year you sat on the Señora's south
veranda.

A wide straight walk shaded by a trellis so knotted and twisted with
grapevines that little was to be seen of the trellis wood-work, led straight
down from the veranda steps, through the middle of the garden, to a little brook at the foot of it. Across this brook, in the shade of a dozen
gnarled old willow-trees, were set the broad flat stone washboards on
which was done all the family washing. No long dawdling, and no running away from the work on the part of the maids, thus close to the eye
of the Señora at the upper end of the garden; and if they had known how
picturesque they looked there, kneeling on the grass, lifting the dripping
linen out of the water, rubbing it back and forth on the stones, sousing
it, wringing it, splashing the clear water in each other's faces, they would
have been content to stay at the washing day in and day out, for there
was always somebody to look on from above. Hardly a day passed that
the Señora had not visitors. She was still a person of note; her house the
natural resting-place for all who journeyed through the valley; and whoever came, spent all of his time, when not eating, sleeping, or walking
over the place, sitting with the Señora on the sunny veranda. Few days in
winter were cold enough, and in summer the day must be hot indeed to
drive the Señora and her friends indoors. There stood on the veranda
three carved oaken chairs, and a carved bench, also of oak, which had
been brought to the Señora for safe keeping by the faithful old sacristan
of San Luis Rey, at the time of the occupation of that Mission by the
United States troops, soon after the conquest of California. Aghast at the
sacrilegious acts of the soldiers, who were quartered in the very church
itself, and amused themselves by making targets of the eyes and noses of
the saints' statues, the sacristan, stealthily, day by day and night after
night, bore out of the church all that he dared to remove, burying some
articles in cottonwood copses, hiding others in his own poor little hovel,
until he had wagon-loads of sacred treasures. Then, still more stealthily,
he carried them, a few at a time, concealed in the bottom of a cart, under

a load of hay or of brush, to the house of the Señora, who felt herself deeply honored by his confidence, and received everything as a sacred trust, to be given back into the hands of the Church again, whenever the Missions should be restored, of which at that time all Catholics had good hope. And so it had come about that no bedroom in the Señora's house was without a picture or a statue of a saint or of the Madonna; and some had two; and in the little chapel in the garden the altar was surrounded by a really imposing row of holy and apostolic figures, which had looked down on the splendid ceremonies of the San Luis Rey Mission, in Father Peyri's time, no more benignly than they now did on the humbler worship of the Señora's family in its diminished estate. That one had lost an eye, another an arm, that the once brilliant colors of the drapery were now faded and shabby, only enhanced the tender reverence with which the Señora knelt before them, her eyes filling with indignant tears at thought of the heretic hands which had wrought such defilement. Even the crumbling wreaths which had been placed on some of these statues' heads at the time of the last ceremonial at which they had figured in the Mission, had been brought away with them by the devout sacristan, and the Señora had replaced each one, holding it only a degree less sacred than the statue itself.

This chapel was dearer to the Señora than her house. It had been built by the General in the second year of their married life. In it her four children had been christened, and from it all but one, her handsome Felipe, had been buried while they were yet infants. In the General's time, while the estate was at its best, and hundreds of Indians living within its borders, there was many a Sunday when the scene to be witnessed there was like the scenes at the Missions,—the chapel full of kneeling men and women; those who could not find room inside kneeling on the garden walks outside; Father Salvierderra, in gorgeous vestments, coming, at close of the services, slowly down the aisle, the close-packed rows of worshippers parting to right and left to let him through, all looking up eagerly for his blessing, women giving him offerings of fruit or flowers, and holding up their babies that he might lay his hands on their heads. No one but Father Salvierderra had ever officiated in the Moreno chapel, or heard the confession of a Moreno. He was a Franciscan, one of the few now left in the country; so revered and beloved by all who had come under his influence, that they would wait long months without the offices of the Church, rather than confess their sins or confide their perplexities to any one else. From this deep-seated attachment on the part of the Indians and the older Mexican families in the country to the

Franciscan Order, there had grown up, not unnaturally, some jealously of them in the minds of the later-come secular priests, and the position of the few monks left was not wholly a pleasant one. It had even been rumored that they were to be forbidden to continue longer their practice of going up and down the country, ministering everywhere; were to be compelled to restrict their labors to their own colleges at Santa Barbara and Santa Inez. When something to this effect was one day said in the Señora Moreno's presence, two scarlet spots sprang on her cheeks, and before she bethought herself, she exclaimed, "That day, I burn down my chapel!"

Luckily, nobody but Felipe heard the rash threat, and his exclamation of unbounded astonishment recalled the Señora to herself.

"I spoke rashly, my son," she said. "The Church is to be obeyed always; but the Franciscan Fathers are responsible to no one but the Superior of their own order; and there is no one in this land who has the authority to forbid their journeying and ministering to whoever desires their offices. As for these Catalan priests who are coming in here, I cannot abide them. No Catalan but has bad blood in his veins!"

There was every reason in the world why the Señora should be thus warmly attached to the Franciscan Order. From her earliest recollections the gray gown and cowl had been familiar to her eyes, and had represented the things which she was taught to hold most sacred and dear. Father Salvierderra himself had come from Mexico to Monterey in the same ship which had brought her father to be the commandante of the Santa Barbara Presidio; and her best-beloved uncle, her father's eldest brother, was at that time the Superior of the Santa Barbara Mission. The sentiment and romance of her youth were almost equally divided between the gayeties, excitements, adornments of the life at the Presidio, and the ceremonies and devotions of the life at the Mission. She was famed as the most beautiful girl in the country. Men of the army, men of the navy, and men of the Church, alike adored her. Her name was a toast from Monterey to San Diego. When at last she was wooed and won by Felipe Moreno, one of the most distinguished of the Mexican generals, her wedding ceremonies were the most splendid ever seen in the country. ... She was then just twenty. A close observer would have seen even then, underneath the joyous smile, the laughing eye, the merry voice, a look thoughtful, tender, earnest, at times enthusiastic. This look was the reflection of those qualities in her, then hardly aroused, which made her, as years developed her character and stormy fates thickened around her life, the unflinching comrade of her soldier husband, the passionate adherent of the Church. Through wars, insurrections, revolutions, downfalls, Spanish, Mexican, civil, ecclesiastical, her standpoint, her poise, remained the same. She simply grew more and more proudly, passionately, a Spaniard and a Moreno; more and more stanchly and fierily a Catholic, and a lover of the Franciscans.

Isabella Lucy Bird Bishop
(1831–1904)

WHILE AMERICAN WRITERS such as Helen Hunt Jackson, Margaret Fuller, and Frances Gage were taking the grand tour of Europe in the nineteenth century—and describing the sights, sounds, customs, and mores in articles and books—European writers such as Charles Dickens, Harriet Martineau, and Isabella Bird were doing the same for armchair English adventurers.

On May 10, 1869, the Union Pacific Railroad met the Central Pacific at Promontory Point, Utah. It was only the first stage in the great railroad boom in the West. Other rail lines soon crossed the country north and south of the first transcontinental rail line. Trains carried settlers, goods, supplies, and tourists west, while timber, ore, produce, meat, and grain went east. Towns blossomed beside the rails, providing food and services to a population on the move. In 1873, this rapid western expansion, coupled with overspeculation by eastern and western financiers, triggered a panic that temporarily closed Wall Street and led to a depression. That same year, British writer and explorer Isabella Bird traversed the United States and recorded her observations of American life in the industrial age.

Isabella Bird was born in Yorkshire, England, the daughter of a clergyman. Early religious training combined with a sturdy constitution and adventurous nature provided fertile ground for missionary zeal. Although Bird did not travel to convert, she carefully noted the needs of the people in the countries she visited. She was an organizer rather than a field operative—the advance guard gathering information for those who would come later. Unlike other women writers, she traveled alone, relying on instinct, fate, and Providence to protect and guide her. Along the way, she described her adventures in letters to her younger sister, Henrietta. Bird's observations of Canada, the United States, China, Korea, Malaysia, Japan, India, Tibet, Persia, and the Sandwich Islands (now Hawaii) were published in periodicals and books, and garnered her a place among England's premier explorers.

By 1873, the veteran traveler had visited North America four times and had published *The Englishwoman in America* (1856). After spending six months in the Sandwich Islands, Bird crossed the Wild West on her way home to England. Starting out by ferry in San Francisco, she continued by train across the Sierra Nevada to Lake Tahoe and on to Colorado, where she spent the fall and early winter. Wearing a "Hawaiian riding costume," Bird explored the Rocky Mountains by buggy, wagon, horseback, and foot. Along the way she met the English emigrant "Mountain Jim" Nugent. In this dissolute, one-eyed trapper, Bird found a poetic, adventurous soul to match her own. Mountain Jim guided her through the Estes Park region, and prodded and hauled her up Long's Peak. But his solicitous conduct proved a temporary lapse. The next year, Mountain Jim was shot and killed.

Bird married John Bishop in 1881. He died in 1886. She did not re-marry, but renewed her solo travels and writing until her death at seventy-three.

Bird's letters of her American trip were first published in *Leisure Hours*. In 1879, they were collected and published as *A Lady's Life in the Rocky Mountains*. Her terrain descriptions and observations of American life are as fresh today as they were more than a century ago.

Letter VII

Estes Park, Colorado, *October.*

As THIS ACCOUNT of the ascent of Long's Peak could not be written at the time, I am much disinclined to write it, especially as no sort of description within my powers could enable another to realize the glorious sublimity, the majestic solitude, and the unspeakable awfulness and fascination of the scenes in which I spent Monday, Tuesday, and Wednesday.

Long's Peak, 14,700 feet high, blocks up one end of Estes Park, and dwarfs all the surrounding mountains. From it on this side rise, snowborn, the bright St. Vrain, and the Big and Little Thompson. By sunlight or moonlight its splintered grey crest is the one object which, in spite of wapiti and bighorn, skunk and grizzly, unfailingly arrests the eyes. From it come all storms of snow and wind, and the forked lightnings play round its head like a glory. It is one of the noblest of mountains, but in one's imagination it grows to be much more than a mountain. It becomes invested with a personality. In its caverns and abysses one comes to fancy that it generates and chains the strong winds, to let them loose in its fury. The thunder becomes its voice, and the lightnings do it homage. Other summits blush under the morning kiss of the sun, and turn pale the next moment; but it detains the first sunlight and holds it round its head for an hour at least, till it pleases to change from rozy red to deep blue; and the sunset, as if spell-bound, lingers latest on its crest. The soft winds which hardly rustle the pine needles down here are raging rudely up there round its motionless summit. The mark of fire is upon it; and though it has passed into a grim repose, it tells of fire and upheaval as truly, though not as eloquently, as the living volcanoes of Hawaii. Here under its shadow one learns how naturally nature worship, and the propitiation of the forces of nature, arose in minds which had no better light.

Long's Peak, "the American Matterhorn," as some call it, was ascended five years ago for the first time. I thought I should like to attempt it, but up to Monday, when Evans left for Denver, cold water was thrown upon the project. It was too late in the season, the winds were likely to be strong, etc.; but just before leaving, Evans said that the weather was looking more settled, and if I did not get farther than the timberline it would be worth going. Soon after he left, "Mountain Jim" came in, and he would go up as guide, and the two youths who rode here with me from Longmount and I caught at the proposal. Mrs. Edwards at once baked bread for three days, steaks were cut from the steer which hangs up conveniently, and tea, sugar, and butter were benevolently added. Our picnic was not to be a luxurious or "well-found" one, for, in order to avoid the expense of a pack mule, we limited our luggage to what our saddle horses could carry. Behind my saddle I carried three pair of camping blankets and a quilt, which reached to my shoulders. My own boots were so much worn that it was painful to walk, even about the park, in them, so Evans had lent me a pair of his hunting boots, which hung to the horn of my saddle. The horses of the two young men were equally loaded, for we had to prepare for many degrees of frost. "Jim" was a shocking figure; he had on an old pair of high boots, with a baggy pair of old trousers made of deer hide, held on by an old scarf tucked into them; a leather shirt, with three or four ragged unbuttoned waistcoats over it; an old smashed wideawake, from under which his tawny, neglected ringlets hung; and with his one eye, his one long spur, his knife in his belt, his revolver in his waistcoat pocket, his saddle covered with an old beaver skin, from which the paws hung down; his camping blankets behind him, his rifle laid across the saddle in front of him, and his axe, canteen, and other gear hanging to the horn, he was as awful-looking a ruffian as one could see. By way of contrast, he rode a small Arab mare, of exquisite beauty, skittish, high spirited, gentle, but altogether too light for him, and he fretted her incessantly to make her display herself.

Heavily loaded as all our horses were, "Jim" started over the half-mile of level grass at a hard gallop, and then throwing his mare on her haunches, pulled up alongside of me, and with a grace of manner which soon made me forget his appearance, entered into a conversation which lasted for more than three hours, in spite of the manifold checks of fording streams, single file, abrupt ascents and descents, and other incidents of mountain travel. The ride was one series of glories and surprises, of "park" and glade, of lake and stream, of mountains on mountains, cul-minating in the rent pinnacles of Long's Peak, which looked yet grander and ghastlier as we crossed an attendant mountain 11,000 feet high. The slanting sun added fresh beauty every hour. There were dark pines against a lemon sky, grey peaks reddening and etherealizing, gorges of deep and infinite blue, floods of golden glory pouring through canyons of enormous depth, an atmosphere of absolute purity, an occasional foreground of cotton-wood and aspen flaunting in red and gold to in-tensify the blue gloom of the pines, the trickle and murmur of streams fringed with icicles, the strange *sough* of gusts moving among the pine tops—sights and sounds not of the lower earth, but of the solitary, beast-haunted, frozen upper altitudes. From the dry, buff grass of Estes Park we turned off up a trail on the side of a pine-hung gorge, up a steep pine-clothed hill, down to a small valley, rich in fine, sun-cured hay about eighteen inches high, and enclosed by high mountains whose deepest hollow contains a lily-covered lake, fitly named "The Lake of the Lilies." Ah, how magical its beauty was, as it slept in silence, while *there* the dark pines were mirrored motionless in its pale gold, and *here* the great white lily cups and dark green leaves rested on amethyst-colored water!

From this we ascended into the purple gloom of great pine forests which clothe the skirts of the mountains up to a height of about 11,000 feet, and from their chill and solitary depths we had glimpses of golden atmosphere and rose-lit summits, not of "the land very far off," but of the land nearer now in all its grandeur, gaining in sublimity by near-ness—glimpses, too, through a broken vista of purple gorges, of the il-limitable Plains lying idealised in the late sunlight, their baked, brown expanse transfigured into the likeness of a sunset sea rolling infinitely in waves of misty gold.

We rode upwards through the gloom on a steep trail blazed through the forest, all my intellect concentrated on avoiding being dragged off my horse by impending branches, or having the blankets badly torn, as those of my companions were, by sharp dead limbs, between which there was hardly room to pass—the horses breathless, and requiring to stop every few yards, though their riders, except myself, were afoot. The gloom of the dense, ancient, silent forest is to me awe inspiring. On such an evening it is soundless, except for the branches creaking in the soft wind, the frequent snap of decayed timber, and a murmur in the pine tops as of a not distant waterfall, all tending to produce *eeriness* and a sadness "hardly akin to pain." There no lumberer's axe has ever rung.

The trees die when they have attained their prime, and stand there, dead and bare, till the fierce mountain winds lay them prostrate. The pines grew smaller and more sparse as we ascended, and the last stragglers wore a tortured, warring look. The timber line was passed, but yet a little higher a slope of mountain meadow dipped to the south-west towards a bright stream trickling under ice and icicles, and there a grove of the beautiful silver spruce marked our camping ground. The trees were in miniature but so exquisitely arranged that one might well ask what artist's hand had planted them, scattering them here, clumping them there, and training their slim spires towards heaven. Hereafter, when I call up memories of the glorious, the view from this camping ground will come up. Looking east, gorges opened to the distant Plains, then fading into purple grey. Mountains with pine-clothed skirts rose in ranges, or, solitary, uplifted their grey summits, while close behind, but nearly 3,000 feet above us, towered the bald white crest of Long's Peak, its huge precipices red with the light of a sun long lost to our eyes. Close to us, in the caverned side of the Peak, was snow that, owing to its position, is eternal. Soon the afterglow came on, and before it faded a big half-moon hung out of the heavens, shining through the silver blue foliage of the pines on the frigid background of snow, and turning the whole into fairyland. The "photo" which accompanies this letter is by a courageous Denver artist who attempted the ascent just before I arrived, but, after camping out at the timber line for a week, was foiled by the perpetual storms, and was driven down again, leaving some very valuable apparatus about 3,000 feet from the summit.

Unsaddling and picketing the horses securely, making the beds of pine shoots, and dragging up logs for fuel, warmed us all. "Jim" built up a great fire, and before long we were all sitting around it at supper. It didn't matter much that we had to drink our tea out of the battered meat tins in which it was boiled, and eat strips of beef reeking with pine smoke without plates or forks.

"Treat Jim as a gentleman and you'll find him one," I had been told; and though his manner was certainly bolder and freer than that of gentlemen generally, no imaginary fault could be found. He was very agreeable as a man of culture as well as a child of nature; the desperado was altogether out of sight. He was very courteous and even kind to me, which was fortunate, as the young men had little idea of showing even ordinary civilities. That night I made the acquaintance of his dog "Ring," said to be the best hunting dog in Colorado, with the body and legs of a collie, but a head approaching that of a mastiff, a noble face with a wistful human expression, and the most truthful eyes I ever saw in an animal. His master loves him if he loves anything, but in his savage moods ill-treats him. "Ring's" devotion never swerves, and his truthful eyes are rarely taken off his master's face. He is almost human in his intelligence, and, unless he is told to do so, he never takes notice of any one but "Jim." In a tone as if speaking to a human being, his master, pointing to me, said, "Ring, go to that lady, and don't leave her again to-night." "Ring" at once came to me, looked into my face, laid his head on my shoulder, and then lay down beside me with his head on my lap, but never taking his eyes from "Jim's" face.

The long shadows of the pines lay upon the frosted grass, an aurora leaped fitfully, and the moonlight, though intensely bright, was pale beside the red, leaping flames of our pine logs and their red glow on our gear, ourselves, and Ring's truthful face. One of the young men sang a Latin student's song and two Negro melodies; the other "Sweet Spirit, hear my Prayer." "Jim" sang one of Moore's melodies in a singular falsetto, and all together sang, "The Star-spangled Banner" and "The Red, White, and Blue." Then "Jim" recited a very clever poem of his own composition, and told some fearful Indian stories. A group of small silver spruces away from the fire was my sleeping place. The artist who had been up there had so woven and interlaced their lower branches as to form a bower, affording at once shelter from the wind and a most agreeable privacy. It was thickly strewn with young pine shoots, and these, when covered with a blanket, with an inverted saddle for a pillow, made a luxurious bed. The mercury at 9 P.M. was 12° below the freezing point. "Jim," after a last look at the horses, made a huge fire, and stretched himself out beside it, but "Ring" lay at my back to keep me warm. I could not sleep, but the night passed rapidly. I was anxious about the ascent, for gusts of ominous sound swept through the pines at intervals. Then wild animals howled, and "Ring" was perturbed in spirit about them. Then it was strange to see the notorious desperado, a red-handed man, sleeping as quietly as innocence sleeps. But, above all, it was exciting to lie there, with no better shelter than a bower of pines, on a mountain 11,000 feet high, in the very heart of the Rocky Range, under twelve degrees of frost, hearing sounds of wolves, with shivering stars looking through the fragrant canopy, with arrowy pines for bed-posts, and for a night lamp the red flames of a camp-fire.

Day dawned long before the sun rose, pure and lemon colored. The rest were looking after the horses, when one of the students came running to tell me that I must come farther down the slope, for "Jim" said he had never seen such a sunrise. From the chill, grey Peak above, from the everlasting snows, from the silvered pines, down through mountain ranges with their depths of Tyrian purple, we looked to where the Plains lay cold, in blue-grey, like a morning sea against a far horizon. Suddenly, as a dazzling streak at first, but enlarging rapidly into a dazzling sphere, the sun wheeled above the grey line, a light and glory as when it was first created. "Jim" involuntarily and reverently uncovered his head, and exclaimed, "I believe there is a God!" I felt as if, Parsee-like, I must worship. The grey of the Plains changed to purple, the sky was all one rose-red flush, on which vermilion cloud-streaks rested; the ghastly peaks gleamed like rubies, the earth and heavens were new created. Surely "the Most High dwelleth not in temples made with hands!" For a full hour those Plains simulated the ocean, down to whose limitless expanse of purple, cliff, rocks, and promontories swept down.

By seven we had finished breakfast, and passed into the ghastlier solitudes above, I riding as far as what, rightly or wrongly, are called the "Lava Beds," an expanse of large and small boulders, with snow in their crevices. It was very cold; some water which we crossed was frozen hard enough to bear the horse. "Jim" had advised me against taking any wraps, and my thin Hawaiian riding dress, only fit for the tropics, was penetrated by the keen air. The rarefied atmosphere soon began to oppress our breathing, and I found that Evan's boots were so large that I had no foothold. Fortunately, before the real difficulty of the ascent began, we found, under a rock, a pair of small overshoes, probably left by the Hayden exploring expedition, which just lasted for the day. As we were leaping from rock to rock, "Jim" said, "I was thinking in the night about your traveling alone, and wondering where you carried your Derringer, for I could see no signs of it." On my telling him that I traveled unarmed, he could hardly believe it, and adjured me to get a revolver at once.

On arriving at the "Notch" (a literal gate of the rock), we found ourselves absolutely on the knifelike ridge or backbone of Long's Peak, only a few feet wide, covered with colossal boulders and fragments, and on the other side shelving in one precipitous, snow-patched sweep of 3,000 feet to a picturesque hollow, containing a lake of pure green water. Other lakes, hidden among dense pine woods, were farther off, while close above us rose the Peak, which, for about 500 feet, is a smooth, gaunt, inaccessible-looking pile of granite. Passing through the "Notch," we looked along the nearly inaccessible side of the Peak, composed of boulders and *débris* of all shapes and sizes, through which appeared broad, smooth ribs of reddish-colored granite, looking as if they upheld the towering rock mass above. I usually dislike bird's-eye and panoramic views, but, though from a mountain, this was not one. Serrated ridges, not much lower than that on which we stood, rose, one beyond another, far as that pure atmosphere could carry the vision, broken into awful chasms deep with ice and snow, rising into pinnacles piercing the heavenly blue with their cold, barren grey, on, on for ever, till the most distant range upbore unsullied snow alone. There were fair lakes mirroring the dark pine woods, canyons dark and blue-black with unbroken expanses of pines, snow-slashed pinnacles, wintry heights frowning upon lovely parks, watered and wooded, lying in the lap of summer; North Park floating off into the blue distance, Middle Park closed till another season, the sunny slopes of Estes Park, and winding down among the mountains the snowy ridge of the Divide, whose bright waters seek both the Atlantic and Pacific Oceans. There, far below, links of diamonds showed where the Grand River takes its rise to seek the mysterious Colorado, with its still unsolved enigma, and lose itself in the waters of the Pacific; and nearer the snow-born Thompson bursts forth from the ice to begin its journey to the Gulf of Mexico. Nature, rioting in her grandest mood, exclaimed with voices of grandeur, solitude, sublimity, beauty, and infinity, "Lord, what is man, that Thou art mindful of him? or the son of man, that Thou visitest him?" Never-to-be-forgotten glories they were, burnt in upon my memory by six succeeding hours of terror.

You know I have no head and no ankles, and never ought to dream of mountaineering; and had I known that the ascent was a real mountaineering feat I should not have felt the slightest ambition to perform it. As it is, I am only humiliated by my success, for "Jim" dragged me up, like a bale of goods, by sheer force of muscle. At the "Notch" the real business of the ascent began. Two thousand feet of solid rock towered above us, four thousand feet of broken rock shelved precipitously below; smooth granite ribs, with barely foothold, stood out here and there; melted snow refrozen several times, presented a more serious obstacle; many of the rocks were loose, and tumbled down when touched. To me it was a time of extreme terror. I was roped to "Jim," but it was of no use; my feet were paralyzed and slipped on the bare rock, and he said it was useless to try to go that way, and we retraced our steps. I wanted to return to the "Notch," knowing that my incompetence would detain the party, and one of the young men said almost plainly that a woman was a dangerous encumbrance, but the trapper replied shortly that if it were not to take a lady up he would not go up at all. He went on to explore, and reported that further progress on the correct line of ascent was blocked by ice; and then for two hours we descended, lowering ourselves by our hands from rock to rock along a boulder-strewn sweep of 4,000 feet, patched with ice and snow, and perilous from rolling stones. My fatigue, giddiness, and pain from bruised ankles, and arms half pulled out of their sockets, were so great that I should never have gone halfway had not "Jim," *nolens volens,* dragged me along with a patience and skill, and withal a determination that I should ascend the Peak, which never failed. After descending about 2,000 feet to avoid the ice, we got into a deep ravine with inaccessible sides, partly filled with ice and snow and partly with large and small fragments of rock, which were constantly giving away, rendering the footing very insecure. That part to me was two hours of painful and unwilling submission to the inevitable; of trembling, slipping, straining, of smooth ice appearing when it was least expected, and of weak entreaties to be left behind while the others went on. "Jim" always said that there was no danger, that there was only a short bad bit ahead, and that I should go up even if he carried me!

Slipping, faltering, gasping from the exhausting toil in the rarefied air, with throbbing hearts and panting lungs, we reached the top of the gorge and squeezed ourselves between two gigantic fragments of rock by a passage called the "Dog's Lift," when I climbed on the shoulders of one man and then was hauled up. This introduced us by an abrupt turn round the south-west angle of the Peak to a narrow shelf of considerable length, rugged, uneven, and so overhung by the cliff in some places that it is necessary to crouch to pass at all. Above, the Peak looks nearly vertical for 400 feet; and below, the most tremendous precipice I have ever seen descends in one unbroken fall. This is usually considered the most dangerous part of the ascent, but it does not seem so to me, for such foothold as there is is secure, and one fancies that it is possible to hold on with the hands. But there, and on the final, and, to my thinking, the worst part of the climb, one slip, and a breathing, thinking, human being would lie 3,000 feet below, a shapeless, bloody heap! "Ring" refused to traverse the Ledge, and remained at the "Lift" howling piteously.

From thence the view is more magnificent even than that from the "Notch." At the foot of the precipice below us lay a lovely lake, wood embosomed, from or near which the bright St. Vrain and other streams take their rise. I thought how their clear cold waters, growing turbid in the affluent flats, would heat under the tropic sun, and eventually form part of that great ocean river which renders our far-off islands habitable by impinging on their shores. Snowy ranges, one behind the other, extended to the distant horizon, folding in their wintry embrace the beauties of Middle Park. Pike's Peak, more than one hundred miles off, lifted that vast but shapeless summit which is the landmark of southern Colorado. There were snow patches, snow slashes, snow abysses, snow forlorn and soiled looking, snow pure and dazzling, snow glistening above the purple robe of pine worn by all the mountains; while away to the east, in limitless breadth, stretched the green-grey of the endless Plains. Giants everywhere reared their splintered crests. From thence, with a single sweep, the eye takes in a distance of 300 miles—that distance to the west, north, and south being made up of mountains ten, eleven, twelve, and thirteen thousand feet in height, dominated by Long's Peak, Gray's Peak, and Pike's Peak, all nearly the height of Mont Blanc! On the Plains we traced the rivers by their fringe of cotton-woods to the distant Platte, and between us and them lay glories of mountain, canyon, and lake, sleeping in depths of blue and purple most ravishing to the eye.

As we crept from the ledge round a horn of rock I beheld what made me perfectly sick and dizzy to look at—the terminal Peak itself—a smooth, cracked face or wall of pink granite, as nearly perpendicular as anything could well be up which it was possible to climb, well deserving the name of the "American Matterhorn."[6]

Scaling, not climbing, is the correct term for this last ascent. It took one hour to accomplish 500 feet, pausing for breath every minute or two. The only foothold was in narrow cracks or on minute projections on the granite. To get a toe in these cracks, or here and there on a scarcely obvious projection, while crawling on hands and knees, all the while tortured with thirst and gasping and struggling for breath, this was the climb; but at last the Peak was won. A grand, well-defined mountain top it is, a nearly level acre of boulders, with precipitous sides all round, the one we came up being the only accessible one.

It was not possible to remain long. One of the young men was seriously alarmed by bleeding from the lungs and the intense dryness of the day and the rarefication of the air, at a height of nearly 15,000 feet, made respiration very painful. There is always water on the Peak, but it was frozen as hard as a rock and the sucking of ice and snow increases thirst. We all suffered severely from the want of water, and the gasping for breath made our mouths and tongues so dry that articulation was difficult, and the speech of all unnatural.

From the summit were seen in unrivalled combination all the views which had rejoiced our eyes during the ascent. It was something at last to stand upon the storm-rent crown of this lonely sentinel of the Rocky Range, on one of the mightiest of the vertebrae of the backbone of the North American continent, and to see the waters start for both oceans. Uplifted above love and hate and storms of passion, calm amidst the eternal silences, fanned by zephyrs and bathed in living blue, peace rested for that one bright day on the Peak, as if it were some region

"Where falls not rain, or hail, or any snow,
    Or ever wind blows loudly."

We placed our names, with the date of ascent, in a tin within a crevice, and descended to the Ledge, sitting on the smooth granite, getting our feet into cracks and against projections, and letting ourselves down by our hands, "Jim" going before me, so that I might steady my feet against his powerful shoulders. I was no longer giddy, and faced the precipice of 3,500 feet without a shiver. Repassing the Ledge and Lift, we accomplished the descent through 1,500 feet of ice and snow, with many falls and bruises, but not worse mishap, and there separated, the young men taking the steepest but most direct way to the "Notch," with the intention of getting ready for the march home, and "Jim" and I taking what he thought the safer route for me—a descent over boulders for 2,000 feet, and then a tremendous ascent to the "Notch." I had various falls, and once hung by my frock, which caught on a rock, and "Jim" severed it with his hunting knife, upon which I fell into a crevice full of soft snow. We were driven lower down the mountains than he had intended by impassable tracts of ice, and the ascent was tremendous. For the last 200 feet the boulders were of enormous size, and the steepness fearful. Sometimes I drew myself up on my hands and knees, sometimes crawled; sometimes "Jim" pulled me up by my arms or a lariat, and sometimes I stood on his shoulders, or he made steps for me of his feet and hands, but at six we stood on the "Notch" in the splendor of the sinking sun, all color deepening, all peaks glorifying, all shadows purpling, all peril past.

"Jim" had parted with his *brusquerie* when we parted from the students, and was gentle and considerate beyond anything, though I knew that he must be grievously disappointed, both in my courage and strength. Water was an object of earnest desire. My tongue rattled in my mouth, and I could hardly articulate. It is good for one's sympathies to have for once a severe experience of thirst. Truly, there was

> "Water, water, everywhere,
> But not a drop to drink."

Three times its apparent gleam deceived even the mountaineer's practiced eye, but we found only a foot of "glare ice." At last, in a deep hole, he succeeded in breaking the ice, and by putting one's arm far down one could scoop up a little water in one's hand, but it was tormentingly insufficient. With great difficulty and much assistance I recrossed the "Lava Beds," was carried to the horse and lifted upon him, and when we reached the camping ground I was lifted off him, and laid on the ground wrapped up in blankets, a humiliating termination of a great exploit. The horses were saddled, and the young men were all ready to start, but "Jim" quietly said, "Now, gentlemen, I want a good night's rest, and we shan't stir from here to-night." I believe they were really glad to have it so, as one of them was quite "finished." I retired to my arbor, wrapped myself in a roll of blankets, and was soon asleep.

When I woke, the moon was high shining through the silvery branches, whitening the bald Peak above, and glittering on the great abyss of snow behind, and pine logs were blazing like a bonfire in the cold still air. My feet were so icy cold that I could not sleep again, and getting some blankets to sit in, and making a roll of them for my back, I sat for two hours by the camp-fire. It was weird and gloriously beautiful. The students were asleep not far off in their blankets with their feet towards the fire. "Ring" lay on one side of me with his fine head on my arm, and his master sat smoking, with the fire lighting up the handsome side of his face, and except for the tones of our voices, and an occasional crackle and splutter as a pine knot blazed up, there was no sound on the mountain side. The beloved stars of my far-off home were overhead, the Plough and Pole Star, with their steady light; the glittering Pleiades, looking larger than I ever saw them, and "Orion's studded belt" shining gloriously. Once only some wild animals prowled near the camp, when "Ring," with one bound, disappeared from my side; and the horses, which were picketed by the stream, broke their lariats, stampeded, and came rushing wildly towards the fire, and it was fully half an hour before they were caught and quiet was restored. "Jim," or Mr. Nugent, as I always scrupulously called him, told stories of his early youth, and of a great sorrow which had led him to embark on a lawless and desperate life. His voice trembled, and tears rolled down his cheek. Was it semi-conscious acting, I wondered, or was his dark soul really stirred to its depths by the silence, the beauty, and the memories of youth?

We reached Estes Park at noon of the following day. A more successful ascent of the Peak was never made, and I would not now exchange my memories of its perfect beauty and extraordinary sublimity for any other experience of mountaineering in any part of the world. Yesterday snow fell on the summit, and it will be inaccessible for eight months to come.

María Amparo Ruiz de Burton
("C. Loyal")
(1832–1895)

IN BAJA AND Alta California a unique rancho system replaced the old mission-centered agricultural system after Mexico achieved independence from Spain in 1821. The ranchos were tracts of land granted in return for loyal services to the Mexican government. The focus of this pastoral life was the raising of cattle for hides that were shipped to tanneries outside California. Richard Henry Dana's *Two Years before the Mast* (1840) recorded one trip around Cape Horn to collect and transport California hides. Local Indians worked the ranchos, much as European serfs had in feudal times.

During the Mexican War of 1846–1848, American troops occupied Baja California in addition to Alta California and portions of mainland Mexico. In Baja, Californios who accepted American citizenship, such as María Amparo Ruiz, were transported north to Monterey after the Treaty of Guadalupe Hidalgo ended hostilities. The treaty returned Baja California to Mexico, confirmed American ownership of Texas, and added Alta California, Nevada, Utah, and parts of New Mexico, Arizona, Wyoming, and Colorado to the United States. The new international border separated the Ruiz family from their landholdings around Ensenada, south of San Diego. During her lifetime, María Amparo Ruiz de Burton watched the breakdown of the old rancho system, as settlers drawn by the hospitable climate of California and the gold rush of 1849 challenged Mexican and Spanish land grants in court, or simply occupied the land.

María Amparo Ruiz, born in Loreto, Baja California Sur, was related to many of the famous old California families, including the Castros (see Jessie Ann Benton Frémont's *Souvenirs of My Time*). One grandfather was a former governor of Baja California; a great-uncle commanded the Presidio at San Diego. But when the Americans, commanded by West Point graduate Capt. Henry S. Burton, took Baja in the summer of 1847, María's traditional Mexican world changed radically. She was just fifteen. A year later, she sailed with other refugees to Monterey, California. There, in 1849, María Amparo Ruiz married Henry Burton.

The Burtons remained in California until Henry was transferred east just prior to the Civil War. He survived the war, but died in 1869, leaving María with two children. She returned to the Jamul Ranch, east of San Diego, which her husband had purchased before the war. But squatters had reduced the size of Pio Pico's old rancho. María struggled to support her children by ranching, farming, writing, and even mining. She never regained the relative wealth and status of her youth.

Ruiz de Burton wrote two romance novels, both anonymously, after her husband's death. In *Who Would Have Thought It?* (1872), an aristocratic Mexican girl is rescued from Apache captors, transported to the Northeast, and pitted against avaricious abolitionists. *The Squatter and the Don*, self-published in 1885, publicizes the plight of the Californios in the wake of the Mexican War. It is a bold exposé of events that affected Ruiz de Burton, her friends, and relatives during a time of major transition in California's history, a time when most Hispanic women, hampered by tradition, refrained from expressing their views in print.

Chapter III

Pre-Empting under the Law

"ALL ABOARD for San Diego!" shouted a voice from a wagon, as it rumbled past Darrell, who walked leisurely with a satchel in his hand, swinging it unconsciously, lost in thought. He looked up and saw that the wagon whence the voice came carried ten or twelve men, sitting on trunks and packages and carpet-bags. These men Mathews and Gasbang had presented to him, saying that they were settlers already residing at the Alamar rancho, and others who were going down to take up claims, at the same time that he would locate his. Darrell looked at his future neighbors with feelings of anything but pleasure. The broad, vulgar face of Gasbang, with its square jaws, gray beard, closely clipped, but never shaved, his compressed, thin, bloodless lips, his small, pale, restless eyes and flat nose, Darrell soon recognized, though the wagon was going rapidly. Mathews' visage was equally noticeable for its ugliness, though of a different type; for his face was long and shaved; his nose was pinched and peaked and red; his cheeks were flabby; and his long, oily, dusty, hair dragged over his neck in matted, meshy locks, while a constant frown settled on his brow. As he was broad-shouldered and rather tall, his face seemed made for some other man much weaker than himself. His face looked mean and discontented, while his body seemed strong and self-reliant.

The wagon had arrived and gone away, and the men had walked aboard the boat, when Darrell, still swinging his satchel abstractedly, stood on the wharf looking at the steamer as if not quite resolved to go. He felt no sympathy, no liking, for any of those men with whom he was now associated.

It was different to have Gasbang as his hired man, as before, but now he was not under orders, and was much older. Years, moreover, had not improved his low nature. Darrell had no higher opinion of the others. He was sure these were not the sort of people whom his wife would like to have for neighbors. He felt self-accused and irresolute. A shout from Gasbang, who was observing him from the steamer's deck, made Darrell look up quickly, ashamed of having betrayed his irresolution. "I can return immediately, if things don't suit me," he thought, walking towards the gang-plank.

"Come on. Your luggage is all aboard, I took care of it," Gasbang said, coming to meet him. He snatched Darrell's satchel, in friendly obsequiousness, to carry it for him. "Come along; you'll be left," said he, and Darrell followed him, half-disgusted at his vulgar officiousness. "I got your berth for you. The steamer is so crowded, that men have to be crammed into rooms by the bunch, so you and I and Mathews must room together."

"That is all right," said Darrell, with a shiver of disgust, and went to take a seat on deck where he could be alone.

The bustle and hurry of getting off was over at last, and the steamer was furrowing her way through the spacious bay of San Francisco towards the Golden Gate. Groups of passengers stood here and there, admiring the beautiful harbor and its surrounding country. Darrell sat alone, fixing his gaze upon the receding verdure of Alameda County. Above that green, undulating line of diminishing hills, which seemed to fly from him, Darrell could see plainly one face, one form, beautiful to him as none other could be, the face and form of his wife, his beloved Mary. This was the first time he had ever left her for any longer time than a two days' absence, since they were married. Now he might be absent several months, for if he decided to locate in San Diego County, he would first build a house before he sent for his family. He would first send for Clarence—his eldest son—and then, when a comfortable home was prepared, the family would come.

The voyage down the coast was made safely. Darrell had managed to keep away from his fellow-travelers, to think of home unmolested.

It was a bright morning of January, 1872, when he stood far forward, watching the course of the steamer Orizaba, as she made her way around Point Loma, then between Ballast Point and the sandy peninsula, and passing by La Playa, came in sight of San Diego city.

"Here we are," said John Gasbang; "how do you like the looks of our little city, Mr. Darrell?"

"Very well; it is larger than I supposed, and the site of it seems very pleasant."

"Pleasant! I should say it was. A perfect slope, sir, as gentle and regular as if made to order. The best drained city in the world, sir, when we put in sewers. Too poor for that, yet, sir, but we are coming to it, sir, growing, growing, sir."

"When we get the railroad," added Mathews, with a mouth full of tobacco, spitting profusely on the deck.

"Exactly, and we'll soon have that. Our news from Washington is very encouraging. Tom Scott will visit us this summer," Gasbang said.

"I like a town with plenty of trees," said Darrell, with his gaze fixed on the approaching panorama, thinking that his wife would be pleased with the place, she being so fond of trees. "I had no idea you had so many trees about you. Many are small, yet, but all seem healthy."

"And health-giving trees, they are, too. Most of them are eucalyptus and pepper trees, the healthiest in the world. You never hear of any malarial fevers in San Diego, sir, never. Our perfect climate, the fine sloping ground of our town site, our eucalyptus trees, sea breezes and mountain air, make San Diego a most healthy little city," said Gasbang.

"That is an excellent recommendation, as life is not worth having without health," Darrell observed.

"We have it here," Hughes said. "A man has to be very imprudent not to keep well in our climate, sir. All we want now is a little stimulus of business prosperity, and the railroad is sure to bring us that. Then San Diego will be the best place on the coast for a residence."

The loud report of a cannon, close by, made Darrell jump and look around quickly, not knowing what that explosion could mean.

"That is our visiting card to the people of San Diego, to announce our coming," said the captain, laughingly. "I am sorry it startled you."

"That is nothing. I didn't know I had nerves. I believe that is what women call it. I was not expecting such a military salute," Darrell said.

"O yes, we always give it. The San Diego people are very military. At least, I should say the settlers on Señor Alamar's rancho are, as I hear they practice rifle shooting there all the time," the captain said, looking at Mathews and Gasbang.

"That is a shot at us," Gasbang answered, laughing.

"But it is a blank cartridge, meant not to hurt," the captain replied.

"The rifle practice is in dark nights," said a young Spaniard, who had been listening at what was said by the others.

"Or in the daytime, if the cattle deserve it," Mathews said.

"That is very creditable and brave, to shoot tame cows," the Spaniard rejoined.

"Perhaps you had better come and try it," Mathews returned.

"Thank you. It is the mischievous brutes I would like to shoot, not the good, useful cattle;" so saying, the Spaniard walked away, followed by the scowls of the settlers.

"That is impudence for you," Gasbang exclaimed.

"Those greasers ain't half crushed yet. We have to tame them like they do their mustangs, or shoot them, as we shoot their cattle," said Mathews.

"O, no. No such violent means are necessary. All we have to do is to take their lands, and finish their cattle," said Hughes, sneeringly, looking at Darrell for approval. But he did not get it. Darrell did not care for the Spanish population of California, but he did not approve of shooting cattle in the way which the foregoing conversation indicated. To do this, was useless cruelty and useless waste of valuable property, no matter to whom it might belong. To destroy it was a loss to the State. It was folly.

"Why must cattle be shot? Can't they be kept off, away from your crops without shooting them?" he asked.

"Not always. At first, that is, for the first three years after we located our claims," Gasbang said; "we had to shoot them all the time. Now the Don has sold a good many, or sent them to the mountains; so that few have been killed."

"I suppose fencing would be too expensive."

"Phew! It would be ruinous, impossible," Mathews said.

"Mr. Mechlin is the only one who has attempted to put up any fences," Romeo said, who had been listening in silence.

"He did so, because he is an old hypocrite," Mathews said.

"Because his daughter Lizzie is going to marry Gabriel Alamar, and of course, they have to be on friendly terms," said Hughes.

"That ain't the reason. He fenced a hundred acres the first year, and he never sows outside, so that he's not at all troubled by the Don's cattle," said Romeo.

"But Gabriel is going to marry Lizzie all the same, and the two families are as thick as can be. Old Mechlin has gone back on us. I wish he would go away," Mathews said.

"Why should he go? He paid a very good price for his farm, and has made many improvements," said Romeo.

"Who did he buy from?" asked Darrell.

"From me. I sold him that claim, and took up another a mile up the valley," said Mathews.

"And a good bargain it was, too," Romeo observed.

Mathews gave him a black look, but made no answer.

The steamer had now reached the wharf. The deck was filled with passengers and their baggage ready for shore. Pittikin, with wife and daughters blonde and freckled, and Hughes, with his wife and daughters dark and gypsy-looking, were all there, ready for their drive to Alamar.

There were several wagons, light and heavy, waiting to convey the newly-arrived and their luggage to the Alamar rancho. Darrell, having his choice of conveyances, preferred to go in a light wagon with Romeo Hancock, but Gasbang and Mathews joined him. Miller and Hager had come to meet their prodigal sons, who had been in San Francisco for several months, when they had permission to remain only a few weeks. But they had fallen into Peter Roper's company, and that individual had represented the fascinations of whiskey most alluringly to them, advising them to have a good time now that they had the opportunity. They yielded to the tempter, and now had returned home like repentant prodigals.

In a few hours Darrell was driving by Don Mariano Alamar's house, a one-story mansion on a low hill, with a broad piazza in front, and in the interior a court formed by two wings, and a row of rooms variously occupied at its back. That the house was commodious, Darrell could see. There was a flower garden in front. At the back there were several *"corrales"* for cattle and horses. At the foot of the hill, on the left, there was an orchard, and some grain fields enclosed with good fences.

Darrell took notice of all these particulars. He also noticed that there were females on the front piazza. He was taken to see the best unoccupied lands to make his selection. He ran his practiced eye over the valley from the highest point on the hill. He then came to the next bench; he stopped there, also, and finally came to the broad slope of the foot-hills.

"I think I'll locate here," said he, "if no one else has already filed a claim to this land."

This he said to his fellow-settlers, all being present, addressing all.

"I am sure I have no objection," said Hughes.

"Nor I, neither," said Gasbang. "What do you say, Pittikin and Mathews? Do you know *if* this land is located, or who done it?"

Mathews shook his head in the negative, and kept on chewing his tobacco in silence.

Pittikin said, "I reckon nobody is located here, and if they *done it,* why don't they leave stakes? They leave no stakes, no notice to settlers; they can't make any row if somebody else takes the land."

"Well, I want to respect everybody's right; so I want you all to bear witness, that I found no stakes or notices of anybody. I don't want to jump anybody's claim; I want a fair deal. I shall locate two claims here— one in my own name and one for my oldest son, Clarence," said Darrell.

"You'll take 320 acres?" asked Hughes.

"Yes, 320 acres,—according to law," replied Darrell.

"All right. Let us measure them now," said Gasbang. "We have time to mark the limits and put the corner stakes. I have a cord here in my wagon, which is a chain's length. That will do the business."

"That will do temporarily, I suppose; but I'll have the two claims properly surveyed afterwards according to law," Darrell said.

"Of course, you will. We all know you will do the fair thing by everybody, and follow the law strictly," said Hughes. In which opinion all concurred.

"Have you all made your selections?" Darrell asked Hughes.

"Yes; Pittikin and I will locate near Hancock. We like that valley; it is further off, but better soil," said Hughes. "My oldest boy will put a claim near me, and Miller's two boys have staked theirs also. I think we'll like that location better."

"I am glad you like it. I think this is good enough soil for me," Darrell said.

"It is good enough for anybody. The whole rancho is all good soil. Let us put the stakes now," said Gasbang; and assisted by Mathews, Romeo Hancock and Sumner Pittikin, Darrell proceeded by making a rough guess to measure 320 acres (more or less), and put the corner stakes.

"This is what I call business," said Gasbang, carrying cheerfully one end of the rope used for measurement; "and all inside of the law. That is the beauty of it—all perfectly lawful."

And so it was.

The stakes having been placed, Darrell felt satisfied. Next day he would have the claim properly filed, and in due time a surveyor would measure them. All would be done "according to law" and in this easy way more land was taken from its legitimate owner.

This certainly was a more simple way of appropriating the property of *"the conquered"* than in the days of Alaric or Hannibal.

There would have been bloodshed then. Now tears only flowed; silent tears of helpless discouragement; of a presentiment of impending desolation.

Sadly Doña Josefa and her daughters had witnessed from the half-closed shutters of their bedroom windows Mr. Darrell's performance, and fully anticipated serious trouble therefrom.

Don Mariano Alamar, Gabriel and Victoriano—his two sons—had also silently witnessed Mr. Darrell's *lawful* appropriation of their own property. Gabriel was pale and calm. Victoriano was biting his lips, and his face was flushed.

"The government has for sale hundreds of millions of acres, but yet these men must come and take my land, as if there was no other," said Don Mariano, sadly.

"And as we pay the taxes on the land that they will cultivate, our taxes will double next year," Gabriel added.

"Undoubtedly. That climax to injustice has been the most fatal of all the hardships imposed upon us. George could not believe me when I told him that we (the land-owners) have to pay the taxes on the land culti-vated by the pre-emptors, and upon all the improvements they make and enjoy. When he at last understood that such unfair laws did exist, he was amazed, but understood then why the settlers wished to prolong litiga-tion, since it is *the natives'* who must bear the burden of taxation, while the titles are in the courts, and thus the pre-emptors hold the land free."

"I wish we were squatters," Victoriano remarked.

"During litigation, yes; but there have been cases where honest men have, in good faith, taken lands as squatters, and after all, had to give them up. No, I don't blame the squatters; they are at times like our-selves, victims of a wrong legislation, which unintentionally cuts both ways. They were set loose upon us, but a law without equity recoils upon them more cruelly. Then we are all sufferers, all victims of a defec-tive legislation and subverted moral principles."

Alice Cunningham Fletcher
(1838–1923)

A MONG THOSE WHO ventured west after the Louisiana Purchase in
1803 were scientists and topographical engineers driven to navigate, observe, measure, map, categorize, quantify, and describe the bounty of the frontier. What began with the Jefferson-sanctioned journey of Lewis and Clark in 1804-1806 continued through the nineteenth century and into the twentieth. Spurred to find routes across the wilderness for trappers, wagons, and railroads, to determine the mineral potential of the country, and to provide topographic maps for the military, men such as Henry Rowe Schoolcraft, Fielding Meek, Joseph Ives, William Emory, John Wesley Powell, George Wheeler, Ferdinand Hayden, and Clarence King fought to fill in the blank slate of the unexplored territory beyond the Mississippi River. Interest in the land was followed by interest in contemporary and extinct aboriginal peoples. While surveying the Green-Colorado River system and the Rocky Mountain region, geologist and naturalist John Wesley Powell began studying Native American languages and customs. In 1879, he founded and served as first director of the U.S. Bureau of Ethnology, a position he held even while directing the U.S. Geological Survey, founded the same year. Establishment of the bureau reflected the growing passion of the American people for knowledge about the original inhabitants of the continent. From this demand for answers a science was born. Alice Fletcher became one of ethnology's first American practitioners.

Alice Fletcher, the child of a consumptive father and his second wife, was born in Cuba, where her parents had sought refuge from the New York winter. Thomas Fletcher died before his daughter's second birthday. Ten years later, her mother remarried. Fletcher biographer Joan Mark speculates that Alice was required to flee either abuse or great restrictions at the hands of her stepfather. A wealthy friend, Claudius Conant, rescued Fletcher by employing her as governess until she was in her thirties, and then paying enough salary for her to rent rooms in New York.

Because Alice destroyed the records of her first forty years, we have little knowledge of her schooling. But Alice Fletcher was well educated. More important, she developed a love of learning that promoted independent research. When she left the Conants, she became involved with Sorosis, the women's club that the Cary sisters helped form in 1868. Out of Sorosis grew the Association for the Advancement of Women five years later. From both groups, Alice Fletcher gained organizational experience, speaking skills, and enough self-confidence to launch herself on the lecture circuit after Conant died in 1877.

When audiences expressed interest in archaeological and ethnological topics during her lectures, Fletcher began a course of self-study. Her lectures on American prehistory were so popular that Frederick Ward Putnam invited her to study with him at Harvard's Peabody Museum of American Archaeology and Ethnology. She continued that association throughout her life, receiving the Thaw Fellowship for ethnological study in 1891. The fellowship, the first for a woman at Harvard, helped support Fletcher throughout her career.

What pulled Fletcher west to study tribes firsthand, a radical concept for a woman in the nineteenth century? The catalysts were Susette "Bright Eyes" La Flesche and her half brother, Francis; Standing Bear; and Thomas Tibbles. Like Helen Hunt Jackson, Alice Fletcher heard Susette La Flesche interpret for Ponca chief Standing Bear during a lecture tour of the East in 1879. It was an epiphany for Fletcher. Within two years, she had convinced Susette, now married to Tibbles, to help her begin studying the Omaha. In the fall of 1881, Alice Fletcher set out to do fieldwork among the Plains Indians. Her guides were Bright Eyes and Tibbles.

Shortly after Fletcher took up residence among the Omaha, Chief Joseph Iron-Eye La Flesche asked her to intercede with the government on behalf of the tribe. Joseph was convinced that the only way the Omaha could remain in Nebraska was if they gained title to their lands. Controversy over this issue split the tribe, with Susette La Flesche Tibbles and her husband leading the opposing faction. But ultimately Fletcher was successful: the congressional act of August 7, 1882, secured land in severalty for the Omaha tribe. Fletcher made the allotments, becoming renowned—and at times denigrated—for her impartiality. She also created a system of small loans to help Native Americans buy land and build houses. When Congress passed the Dawes General Allotment or Severalty Act of February 1887, Alice Fletcher was appointed as special agent in charge of land allotments on the Winnebago and Nez Perce reservations. The job taxed her health and her patience.

Fletcher had no ties in New York and Boston except professional ones. In the West, among the Omaha, however, Fletcher developed both professional and emotional attachments. Francis La Flesche, nearly twenty years her junior, became Fletcher's interpreter, coauthor, and companion. They worked together, published together, and shared a home in Washington, D.C. Theirs was a complex relationship—more than mother-son, yet never a marriage. To maintain decorum, they were forced to live and travel with a chaperon. In 1888 and for eighteen years thereafter, that person was photographer Jane Gay, who kept a diary of their time together. Competition between Gay and Francis La Flesche for Fletcher's attention finally broke up the trio.

Alice Fletcher is remembered not only for her extensive research and publications on Native American history and culture, but also for being the driving force behind the creation of the School of American Archaeology. She chose the old Governor's Palace in Santa Fe for the school's headquarters and Edgar L. Hewett as the director. Fletcher ignored the controversy engendered in the eastern archaeological community by both decisions. She relished her annual visits to archaeological excavations in New Mexico, during which she fell in love with southwestern landscape and culture. Although she continued to reside in the East, her heart lay in the West. When Fletcher died at eighty-five, her cremated remains were interred in Santa Fe.

Politics and "Pipe-Dancing"

AMONG THE PECULIARITIES of the fellowship pipes is the absence of the bowl, thus indicating their typical character. It is also noteworthy that all the articles used in their construction are connected with myths and symbols of the sun, earth, thunder, and fire, bringing together many emblems used in ancient religious rites over a wide area of country and among Indians of diverse linguistic stock.

Literally, there are no ancient or original pipes, but through the ritual the fashion of them has been kept intact for generations. They are said to be "older than the flat-stemmed, red-stone official tribal pipes," and the Indians state, in proof of this assertion, the latter can be "used by the chiefs alone," while these (the wa-wan pipes) "are for all the people." This statement is particularly interesting when it is remembered that the chiefs derive their authority from the people, who are the primary power. "So great is the affection and respect we feel for these pipes," said an Omaha, "that were we to see them imitated in corn-husk we would show them honor." This is a strong testimony to their symbolic character. The stem is of ash, the opening through it is made with fire, and must be perfect; if in former days a man had presented one of these pipes, and the breath could not pass freely through it, the sacrilege would have cost him his life. Seven spans of the thumb and forefinger constitute the standard of length for the stem. Seven red streamers—four of painted buckskin, and three of dyed hair, the latter tied on by cord made of the white hair from the breast of the rabbit—are fastened along the stem, which is painted green. Near the mouthpiece is placed the head of the large woodpecker, the bill opened and turned back upon the head, exposing the inner side, which is painted green. A bunch of owl-feathers is bound on near the middle of the stem, and the bowl-end is covered with the head, neck, and breast of the mallard duck, the four buckskin streamers holding it in place. Last of all, the fan-shaped arrangement of eagle-feathers depends from the stem, the buckskin thong which holds them being tipped with downy feathers of the eagle.

The number seven is repeated in many ways: seven kinds of articles are used in making the pipes; there are seven ceremonial movements, and seven parts in the ceremony. The number occurs so often that it seems as though its use could not have been accidental. The green paint on the stem is symbolic of the verdant, fruitful earth and the clear sky. The red streamers tell of the rising sun sending its beams up to the zenith. The rabbit and woodpecker are connected with myths of the sun. The owl and the duck are related to the destructive and conserving forces in nature. The eagle is the fierce bird of battle, and allied to the thunder and fire. The downy feathers floating from the ends of the thongs indicate the falling away of the immature when the eagle in its power and strength rises from its nest to go forth on its mission of war or peace. The pipe having the seven white eagle-feathers is spoken of as the masculine, and the dark-feathered pipe as the feminine. The crotched stick upon which they rest is colored red for the east. Upon the gourds and tobacco-pouch is painted in green a circle with four equidistant lines starting from it; the circle symbolizing the horizon-line, the space within the sky, the lines standing for the four quarters or winds. The gourds are spoken of as the eggs, and when not used are slipped under the eagle-feathers when the pipes are at ceremonial rest. The braided sweet-grass attached to the pouch lends its savor when the giver of a horse lights with it his pipe, filled from the tobacco in the pouch. The downy feather tied in the hair of the pipe-bearers and dancers links them to the eagle and its symbols.

The ritual of the pipes and the meaning of the ceremonies are given the host over the head of the little child called Hun-ga. This word means "the ancient one, the one who goes before, the leader." It is the name of the gens having charge of the two sacred tents containing the sacred pole and the white buffalo-skin, and it is also the designation of one half of the tribal circle. The word has a meaning that refers to the earliest time or knowledge, and the child is chosen to represent innocence and docility; its head is covered with down like the young eagle; the brilliant red paint on its face denotes the rays of the rising sun; the black lines indicate the shadows or experiences of life, which finally end in death. This symbolic painting is put on the face of a dead member of the Hun-ga gens, and is indicative of the entrance of the man into another life.

Along the stem of the pipe a straight groove is cut, and the incision colored red. This is explained over the head of the Hun-ga as follows: "My son, you have bestowed on me many gifts, but they will soon be gone. That which I am about to give to you will remain with you forever, if you will to keep it. The words which I am about to give you are worth more than many gifts; if you hold to them your way in life shall be as the groove in this pipe-stem, which signifies the straight path toward peace and happiness."

The tie formed by the pipes brings amity and help as between father and son. It is a tie that unites men and their families who have no kinship bond; and while it is not tribal in its direct effect, it weaves members of different communities together, and produces results that become tribal in their influence. The pipes are prized by ambitious men, as they afford opportunities for making gifts which can be counted as wa-thin´ae-thae; while the poor and unfortunate hold them in high regard, as through them they are often fed, clothed, and rendered comfortable.

In the passing away of old customs the younger generations are losing the knowledge of the details of these ceremonies. But few know even that there is a ritual belonging to these pipes, and it is doubtful if there lives an Omaha to-day who has received it fully. While the esoteric portion of the ceremonies is thus lost, there yet remains a general understanding of the symbolism, and this, with the beauty of the songs, lingers with reverent affection in the memory of those who have shared in the wa-wan.

Eight years ago some of the leading Omahas agreed to exhibit to me the ceremonies connected with these pipes, and to place a set of them in my keeping. The act was so unusual that a word of explanation seems to be demanded.

While living with the tribe, and studying their life and history, I grew to know the fervor with which the people loved their land, and to see that over each fireside hung a shadow that would not lift—the fear of compulsory removal to the Indian Territory, such as their kindred, the Ponkas, had suffered a few years before. The sorrow and the helplessness of the people moved me deeply; closing my scientific note-books, I passed months in gathering statistics of the work they had done on their little homes and farms, and, armed with these, entered Washington to plead their cause. As a result, an act of Congress gave them patents of their lands in severalty, and for the two years following I was busy carrying out the provisions of that act. This work done, and the great gift of peace and security being with the people, the leaders opened to me the meaning and beauty of these pipes, and permitted me to carry them forth on a new mission, and one that may help to interpret the Indian to the white man, and to reveal a kinship in aspirations, beneath strangely differing external conditions—a kinship often unrecognized, indeed hardly guessed at, by either race through the medium of superstition, prejudice, and cruelty.

"The fierce birds on the pipes and the wildcat never lose their prey, but these animals here give their unfailing power to bring good feelings, and gifts for the poor. The pipes can subdue the anger of the worst man and make him at peace with his enemy," said an Omaha one day. His friend, who stood looking at the pipes, as they hung on the walls of my room, remarked:

"My grandfather knew the ritual; he would take the pipes and pray by them, and his prayers were always heard. This is hard to believe, but it is true. Some of the songs in the ritual ask for fair weather, and when sung the sun shines. This too is strange, but it is true. When we see the streamers on the pipes we think of the dawn; the day is coming, light and peace are coming, and with them good hearts, and gifts, and help to the poor."

Said another man: "My father knew all these things; I know but little, but I think about what I know. I know the green circle and the four lines are for all the earth and the four winds that fill the sky; peace and good will fill the earth and the sky by these pipes. All things bear their part; the birds, the animals, the trees, the earth, and men share in them; the pipes are of God."

The occasion on which I saw the ceremonies exemplified was that of my first meeting with the people out of my room, where a painful and dangerous illness had kept me for many months. The feast I had prepared for that night would serve about one hundred; but as I watched the crowds pouring into the great earth lodge, my housewifely spirit took alarm; I felt sure the food could not be made to go around. Turning to the former head chief at my side, I asked if the entrance could not be closed to prevent the disaster that was pending. "No," he replied; "they can come: the pipes are free to all. Do not fear for the food; the servers will understand." So I rested in faith, for nothing short of a miracle, I was sure, could provide enough for the two hundred and more men, women, and children who gathered to witness the ceremonies.

Soon I heard faintly the song of approach; it grew more and more distinct, and at last came with full choral volume as the bearers moved slowly through the long passage into the lodge, where the blazing fire in the center caught the colors of the waving pipes as of the eagle descending. From the first sound of the music until the pipes were laid at rest, silence fell on the assembly; a decorous pause followed the close of the ritual songs, and then the merry chatter was resumed.

Half a dozen women gathered at the fire, but no one entered the space between it and the pipes, and preparation for the feast began. As the occasion was informal, women did the cooking. The picturesqueness of the scene was full of charm; the leaping flames of the wood-fire glinted on the ornaments, and sent dancing shadows all about the lodge, bringing into relief the rich hues of the faces, the glossy hair, sparkling eyes, and white teeth that laughter revealed. Happiness pervaded the place as women rolled out the dough on boards resting partly on the lap, partly on the ground; children chased in and out about their elders, while the pots bubbled on the fire, the piles of round cakes of fried bread grew taller and taller, and the coffee sent out savory puffs of steam. By and by the food was ready, then two or three of the men made grave speeches referring to the affection felt toward the pipes, but "sadness lay at their hearts because of the informality of the present ceremonies, which they had consented to perform for good reasons, and in no spirit of disrespect." The wood was piled on the fire, and the flames leaped high, lighting up the black ribbed dome of the lodge until it shone like polished ebony. Then the pipe-bearers arose, and exemplified with ritual songs the raising of the pipes and their movement around the lodge, facing the people, and waving over them the blessing of peace and fellowship as they sat closely grouped against the wall. The firelight revealed the brilliant hues, the wing-like shadows followed like a phantom bird, the men and women caught up the refrain, and a wave of song enveloped the pipes as they passed in joyful solemnity about the lodge.

When the pipes were laid at rest, an Indian friend, who, having lost a promising son, had been in retirement for two years, took this occasion, as a delicate tribute of friendship to me, to lay aside his mourning and to return to the festivities of his friends. Stepping into the space between the pipes and the fire, he said:

"Shall the pipes of our fathers pass unheeded about the fire, and our hearts lie cold!"

Then in a few words he gave a horse to a man who had recently met with a sorrow like his own great grief, and presented a number of articles of clothing and food to poor and aged people.

A former chief arose, and in a stirring speech thanked the giver, bidding him welcome once more among the people; then with praises of the pipes he exhorted the young men to lead lives honorable in peace and industry. Meanwhile an old man had passed out of the lodge, and we heard his voice ringing through the night air as he sang the generous deed of my friend.

Then another man advanced in front of the pipes, leading his four-year old son. The man and boy were both in the dress of the white man. He had long been living and working on his farm, in every way committed to our mode of life, which added to the pathos of his act.

"The pipes," he said, "were the care of my fathers. My son is born into their rights. Now we do not often see them." Tears filled his eyes, and with breaking voice he added, "I want my boy to touch the pipes of my fathers." And, taking a little stick that the child held in his hand, the father threw it into my lap. It was the gift of a pony, which I at once presented to the pipes, that its value might be used to feed the hungry.

Tribal Life among the Omahas

FROM ONE OF the so-called "cities" of the upper Missouri, armed only with so much governmental indorsement as would insure me courteous assistance from officers stationed at posts on the frontier, and the respectful recognition of reservation officials, I set out upon my journey into the Indian country. It was years ago, but, except for the personal milestones down the vista, it would seem to me as distant as a dream. For I behold fields of waving grain where then was unbroken prairie, the glistening track of the locomotive where the buffalo trail broke through the sod, and thriving towns, the ambitious spires of which rise incisive above the sky-line, where then was only the Indian home, as unobtrusive and as harmonious with nature as the nest of the bird; and I hear the "busy hum of men," the tones of many people speaking many tongues, where then silence was broken only by the cry of the coyote, the wings of the locust, or the waves of the wind on the wide sea of the tall prairie-grass.

It was in a stout covered wagon drawn by a pair of well-conditioned mules, and packed in with boxes, bundles, tin cans, blankets, and all the paraphernalia of a camper who takes his life in his own hand and depends only upon his own providence as he goes out into an unknown land for an unknown time, cutting off all communications with any base of supplies behind him. But this is not the place to recite my many adventures as I toiled on over what was in my early school days the Great American Desert, leaving behind even the most intrepid pioneer, crossing the very fringe of civilization, until at last I came out upon the boundless prairie, where no plow had ever turned a furrow, and the grass reached to the top of my wagon. This, and nothing more: not the glimmer of water anywhere; not a cloud in the white sky to temper with a shadow the intense glare of the August sun; not a landmark to help the eye to measure distance; and silence, save for the rustle of the yellow grass and the muffled tread of the mules in the rich, black loam. There was no touch of familiarity in the scene, no association of song or story; only a vague impression that a race had passed over and left no trace. I could find nothing to connect myself with nature so unaltered by man; there was nothing here on my own plane of life; and thus, alone and self-centered, a sense of loneliness began to oppress me, when a sound fell upon my ear—a strange sound, but with a human tone in it. It trembled through the air with more penetration than volume, rising and falling in weird cadences. Out over the rolling prairie I saw on one of the billowy hills, sharply defined above the horizon, an Indian on horseback; his head was erect, and his statuesque body was one with the pony that with drooping head ambled along in its own unconscious independence.

The easy figure, the wayward song, the solitary man in the vastness of incontaminate nature, the apparent content of him, the absence of all concern with time, of all knowledge of the teeming life out of which I had come, and which was even now surging toward him, threatening to engulf his race, touched a new thought-center and awoke a new interest. Old prejudices, old opinions, were all behind me; I had crossed the line, another race had welcomed me with a song, and casting the old standards aside, I began the study of the Indian in his own home, by his side, from his own standpoint.

In the years which have passed since then I have never ceased to strive patiently for more knowledge of the Indian. I have gone back with him into the dim past, have shared with him the changing present, have tried to forecast his future, have alternately hoped and despaired for him, pressed always by the desire which is sure to arise in those who succeed in catching a glimpse of his real character—the intense desire to "do something" for his betterment; his protection, if you will. In these papers I can give only bits of the knowledge gained, only hints of the complexities of details which make up the "simple life" of the race we are so rapidly supplanting on this continent.

I have lived with the Indian in his homes. Sometimes it was the "wickiup," a mere cluster of branches twisted together; sometimes a framework covered with mats made of rushes, or, as in the forest tribes, with the bark of the elm-tree. These bark houses are still found among the Winnebagos, and they are not unlike a section of the long house of the Iroquois.

Indian dwellings are generally communal. In the long house each family has a section and a fireplace of its own. West of the Rocky Mountains the long house was built by setting up three poles in a triangle, tying their tops together. Several of these groups were placed in a line, and over all mats were laid. Within each triangle of poles dwelt a family, having its separate fire; six, eight, or ten fires were often seen in perspective down the middle of the long dwelling. On the Pacific coast the communal houses were, and are, large square structures of logs, having, in some tribes, carved posts within and totem-poles without. There are compartments along the side walls in which each family sets up its own hearthstone. Families living in single habitations gratify their communal feelings by huddling their huts together, sometimes connecting them by mats stretched between, forming a wind-break or shade. In the observance of religious ceremonies there is a reversion to primitive customs, and the long communal tent is still erected and used on such occasions.

The most elaborate structure used for a dwelling by the tribes of the West was the earth lodge. The outline—a circle with an oblong projection toward the east—was carefully measured and traced on the ground, the sod cut from within the figure, and the earth well tramped by the feet of the builders. The framework was of poles, and the dome-shaped roof of closely laid poles was supported by large posts, five or more in number, set in a circle a little back of the central fireplace. Outside the wall of poles great bundles of the coarse prairie-grass were laid, and over all a double layer of sods, so that when completed the wall was nearly two feet thick at the bottom, and sloped gently to the line where it joined the roof, which was also very thick. To frame it well about the central opening required considerable skill. The exterior resembles a mound more than a swelling. The grass creeps upon it, and over it the birds drop seeds, from which flowers grow, so that it is completely covered with verdure and bloom, except at the top, where the blackened sod tells of the heat and smoke of the fire below. It is difficult to avoid the idea of intimacy with nature that these abodes convey. They suggest no occupation or disturbing possession of man, and but for the waving line of smoke they would not be noticed by the inexperienced eye. It seems as though Mother Earth had lifted her flowery robe and taken her children under it. The ground plan of the earth lodge is common to structures from the Arctic Ocean to the Gulf of Mexico. When I passed through the long passageway of an Eskimo dwelling to the semi-subterranean room, with its domed roof and central opening for light and smoke, I was reminded of the earth lodge of the Indians. Students of the Southwestern tribes have pointed out the resemblance between the ground outline of the Navajo *hogan* and that of the primitive lava *pueblo,* and how the form of the present pueblos has been evolved by bringing together a number of these round dwellings within a rectangular area. But the *estufa,* where all the religious rites and ceremonies are performed, even in the modern pueblo still preserves the ancient circular shape. So the Indians of the North, who now live in tents, when they assemble to observe certain sacred rites draw the outline of the earth lodge upon the ground, and remove the sod, laying bare the fresh earth, upon which they drop offerings of tobacco, sweet grass, or the down of birds. It is a well known law that ancient forms which have pertained to the practical necessities of life in a forgotten age are preserved in religious ceremonies by symbols which in time become overlaid with mythical meanings.

The Indian's love of outdoor life makes even a wickiup too confined for constant habitation, so everywhere one sees an open shelter from the sun, a simple framework of poles thatched with boughs. These are sometimes isolated, and sometimes project like a portico from the bark or mat house. Here the people eat, work, have their social chats, receive visitors, and in warm weather sleep undisturbed by fear of marauders.

Few habitations are more picturesque than Indian tents, whether grouped on the prairie, half buried amid the tall grass and brilliant flowers, or clustered under the trees. Frequently the outside of the tent is decorated with a brilliant symbolical device representing some power of earth or air a vision of which has appeared to the head of the family in his fastings and vigils.

Pleasing as the tents are day by day, with the waving shadows of the grass or the broad flecks of sunlight from between the branches of the trees upon their white sides, which shade into a dull brown at the tops, where the skin-covering is discolored by the smoke ascending in lazy, blue columns, the true time to enjoy the beauty of an Indian camp is at night. Then the tents are illuminated by a central fire, and are all aglow under the stars, the silhouettes of the inmates creating an animated shadow world. Here one catches the picture of a group of children watching an elder twisting his fingers to form a fox chasing a rabbit on the tent wall (perhaps some one is telling a myth about the little fellow, for suddenly the shadow rabbit sits up, waving his ears as though he had outwitted his pursuer); yonder a woman is lifting the pestle, pounding corn in the great wooden mortar; near by are some young girls with their heads together, whispering secrets; old men recline on one elbow, smoking; and over there a young man is bidding the baby boy dance; while the sound of song and friendly chatter fills the air. The picture is of a life simple and contented within itself.

The sweat lodge, which is almost universal among Indian tribes, is built, when possible, on the margin of a stream, and is practically a small tight tent or lodge. When the people take a bath in the steam rising from water sprinkled upon heated stones, they generally sing religious songs; and no ceremony is entered upon by the "mystery men" without first passing through this semi-religious act of purification, for danger and disease are believed to be averted by its agency.

On every journey that I made with the Indians I was surprised afresh by the ease with which the home traveled; for, except when the family lived in an earth lodge, everything was packed up and taken along. If any were so fortunate as to possess a surplus supply of food or clothing, they would store it in a cache, which they might either conceal or leave undisguised. The cache was dug in a dry place, sometimes lined with poles, but often left with no wall but the hard soil. The goods were covered with skins, the earth was thrown over, and the place marked with piles of stones. Meat, corn, clothing, and other personal property were kept for months in this manner, and no one disturbed the hidden store.

Many a time, while the morning stars were still shining, I have watched the mother dismantle the tent-poles, wrench them out of their earth sockets, and lash them two on a side, to a meek pony that had outlived his skittish days, and was now to be trusted with the little ones, who would ride in a comfortable nest made of the folded tent-cover fastened between the trailing poles. Before ponies were obtainable, dogs were the burden-bearers, and in some remote places they are still used. Great were the snarls and quarrels incident to a dog-train. Often an irritable fellow would find himself on his back, or caught by his poles, so that he became frantic with impotent rage. When fording a stream, the children and the puppies were carried over on the backs of women; the dogs and ponies had to plunge for themselves.

The tribes living on the larger rivers used boats of various constructions. The circular skin boat, made by stretching a rawhide over a framework of withes, was to be found on the Missouri, and curiously resembled those in use centuries ago on the Euphrates. Fairly heavy loads could be transported in these primitive vessels, and they were commonly used by the early traders.

Indian journeyings were not the mere wanderings of a homeless people, but had always a purpose and an objective point in view. Aside from war expeditions, offensive or defensive, there were hunting and fishing excursions, which took place as regularly as the seasons came round. But the Indian always came back to his home, his strong attachment to which we have been forced to recognize in the perils of those ejectments we have from time to time undertaken in the interests of our own race, although the incursions of a stranger enemy, or the exigencies of food-supply, sometimes forced a tribe to change its location in search of safety or subsistence.

Indians, contrary to widely received opinions, are of a social nature, and fond of paying friendly visits, the etiquette of which would make a chapter of itself. Not much attention is given to the order of their going while in the dust of travel, but when arrived within a short distance of their destination a halt is called, the ponies are relieved of their burdens, the rawhide packs are opened, and gala dresses and fine ornaments come to light. The two young men selected to be the bearers of gifts of tobacco deck themselves for their mission and ride on in advance. A surprise party is not in the Indian's list of amusements; he takes his enemy unawares, but not his friend. The young men return with messages of welcome; sometimes members of the family to be visited come with them personally to conduct the party. Meanwhile all have been busy prinking: brushing and braiding their locks, painting their faces, and donning their best gear, the wide prairie their dressing-room, their mirrors each other's eyes. When the visiting party is again *en route,* there is not a man or woman who is not gorgeous with color and the glitter of shell or feather finery. Even the children have daubs of fresh paint on their plump, little cheeks, while the dudes are wonderful to behold, resplendent in necklaces, embroidered leggings, and shirts, and with ornaments innumerable braided into their scalp-locks. The visit over, the Indians go back to their homes pleased and contented, happy if they find, as may not always be the case, that the enemy have not been at work in their absence. . . .

Ina Donna Coolbrith

(Josephine Donna Smith)

(1841–1928)

NATIVE AMERICANS, African Americans, and Hispanics were not the only groups to suffer persecution, violent confrontation, and disenfranchisement in the West. Mormon pioneers experienced a similar fate.

In 1831, in an exodus reminiscent of the Puritan emigration to New England more than two hundred years before, Joseph Smith led the Mormon faithful from New York to the frontier. Smith first settled in Kirtland, Ohio. But anti-Mormon sentiment triggered by Smith's presidential aspirations and the collapse of his bank divided the Kirtland group and forced Smith and some of his followers to join others on the fringes of settled territory. Smith's younger brother, Don Carlos Smith, and his wife, Agnes, were among those who trekked to Missouri. There they encountered similar bigotry. Joseph and his brother Hyrum were incarcerated. Neighbors burned Mormon houses and drove them from the state.

In the winter of 1839, Don Carlos, Agnes, and their two small girls moved northeast, buying and settling land around Commerce (renamed Nauvoo), Illinois. Joseph and Hyrum followed. Nauvoo grew quickly, reinforced by converts from Europe and the eastern United States. The influx upset the balance of power within the state. Mormon self-sufficiency coupled with isolationist tendencies antagonized neighboring communities. In 1844, the Mormon community itself became divided over the question of polygamy, a tenet divinely revealed to Smith the year before. Joseph and Hyrum Smith quelled the rebellion and limited the Nauvoo press. But the dissidents sought help from the Illinois government. Faced with charges of plural marriages and restricting the free rights of the citizenry, the Smith brothers surrendered. A mob murdered them in the summer of 1844. Leadership of the Mormons passed to Brigham Young.

Brigham Young and the Mormon elders, again faced with a volatile situation, sought land outside the boundaries of the United States. They turned west toward the Great Basin desert, a land of sand and alkali lakes and searing heat. The bulwark of the Rocky Mountains protected the territory. Although claimed by Mexico, there were no settlements that far north, and Mexico welcomed a buffer against the expanding United States. The only potential conflicts were sporadic meetings with nomadic Indian tribes. Early in 1846, the Mormons began their final journey through "Indian Country," blazing the Mormon Trail along the North Platte River, over South Pass and the Wasatch Range, to the valley of the Great Salt Lake. They reached their "Land of Deseret" on July 24, 1847—almost exactly three years after the Smith brothers' murder. Nine months later, Mexico ceded the land to the United States at the end of the Mexican War. There was no place else to go. The Mormons stayed and prospered in the new Utah Territory.

Not all Mormons elected to accompany Young to Utah. One who did not was Agnes Coolbrith Smith, the widow of Don Carlos. Her husband, a printer by trade, had died in Nauvoo a few months after his third daughter, Josephine "Ina" Donna, was born. Five years later, as the majority of the Mormons began their journey west, Agnes Smith married William Pickett, a lawyer and newspaperman from St. Louis. She and her two surviving children, Agnes and Ina, moved to St. Louis. From that point on, Agnes and the girls kept their Mormon ties a secret.

In 1851, when Ina was ten, the family started for California by wagon train, following the Overland Trail through Independence, St. Joseph, Fort Laramie and South Pass, Sublette Cutoff to Hudspeth's Cutoff, Humboldt River through Carson Sink to the Truckee River. Jim Beckwourth guided them across the Sierra Nevada on a route he discovered. California would be Ina's home for the rest of her life.

Ina Coolbrith published her first poetry at fifteen, in the *Los Angeles Star*. Her early poetry, typical of the age and her youth, included sentimental verses about love and death. At seventeen, she married ironmonger and minstrel Robert Carsley, an abusively jealous man. The marriage produced one child, but lasted less than four years. The child, mentioned in two of Coolbrith's poems, died before Coolbrith moved north.

In 1862, Ina chose to start a new life in San Francisco, the literary hub of the West. Her mother, stepfather, and twin brothers moved with her. She adopted her mother's maiden name, found a job teaching elementary school, and published her poetry and prose, most often in the *Californian* and its successor, the *Overland Monthly*. Through her writing she met Bret Harte, Charles Warren Stoddard, Joaquin Miller, and the rest of the San Francisco literati. They gathered in her drawing room; they asked for editorial advice. Eventually, Coolbrith, Harte, and Stoddard became known as the "Golden Gate Trinity." When Joaquin

Miller left for England in 1881, Coolbrith sent with him a bay wreath and her poem "With a Wreath of Laurel" to lay on Lord Byron's grave.

Needing additional income to support her orphaned niece and nephew as well as poet Joaquin Miller's daughter, Coolbrith began working for the Oakland Public Library in 1874. Later, she was librarian for the Mercantile Library and the Bohemian Club in San Francisco. She composed "California" for the first graduating class at the University of California at Berkeley. The state legislature named her the first poet laureate of California in 1915.

Coolbrith's poetry reflects strong mood swings. Sunny paeans to nature follow dark musings on loss, the unfairness of life, and the difficulties of a monetarily insecure single woman, lacking status in society and forced to compose her verse in moments snatched from job and household duties. Despite these obstacles, Coolbrith published numerous poems, many of which were collected in *A Perfect Day, and Other Poems* (1881), *The Singer of the Sea* (1894), *Songs from the Golden Gate* (1895), and *Wings of Sunset* (1929).

In 1906, Coolbrith's house was destroyed in the San Francisco earthquake. Such was her literary status that California writers, including Mary Austin, Gertrude Atherton, Jack London, Charles Warren Stoddard, and Mary Hallock Foote, contributed stories to the *Spinners' Book of Fiction* to help defray expenses.

Only after Coolbrith's death at eighty-six did relatives reveal her early years and links to the Church of Jesus Christ of Latter-day Saints. In 1932, a mountain overlooking Beckwourth's pass was renamed Mount Ina Coolbrith to honor the first white child to cross it. And in San Francisco, on a sandstone crag near her former residence, lies tiny Coolbrith Park. From its poet's corner on rare sunny mornings one can look north across the Bay to Angel Island and Sausalito.

California

Commencement Poem, Written for the University of California,
July 1871

Was it the sigh and shiver of the leaves?
Was it the murmur of the meadow brook,
That in and out the reeds and water-weeds
Slipped silverly, and on their tremulous keys
Uttered her many melodies? Or voice
Of the far sea, red with the sunset gold,
That sang within her shining shores, and sang
Within the Gate, that in the sunset shone
A gate of fire against the outer world?

For ever as I turned the magic page
Of that old song the old, blind singer sang
Unto the world, when it and song were young—
The ripple of the reeds, or odorous,
Soft sigh of leaves, or voice of the far sea—
A mystical, low murmur, tremulous
Upon the wind, came in with musk of rose,
The salt breath of the waves, and far, faint smell
Of laurel up the slopes of Tamalpais. . . .

"Am I less fair, am I less fair than these,
Daughters of far-off seas?
Daughters of far-off shores—bleak, over-blown
With foam of fretful tides, with wail and moan
Of waves, that toss wild hands, that clasp and beat
Wild, desolate hands above the lonely sands,
Printed no more with pressure of their feet:
That chase no more the light feet flying swift
Up golden sands, nor lift
Foam fingers white unto their garment hem,
And flowing hair of them.

"For these are dead: the fair, great queens are dead!
The long hair's gold a dust the wind bloweth
Wherever it may list;
The curvéd lips, that kissed
Heroes and kings of men, a dust that breath,
Nor speech, nor laughter, ever quickeneth;
And all the glory sped
From the large, marvelous eyes, the light whereof
Wrought wonder in their hearts—desire, and love!
And wrought not any good:
But strife, and curses of the gods, and flood,
And fire and battle-death!
Am I less fair, less fair,
Because that my hands bear
Neither a sword, nor any flaming brand
To blacken and make desolate my land,
But on my brows are leaves of olive boughs,
And in mine arms a dove!

"Sea-born and goddess, blossom of the foam,
Pale Aphrodite, shadowy as a mist
Not any sun hath kissed!
Tawny of limb *I* roam,
The dusks of forests dark within my hair;
The far Yosemite,
For garment and for covering of me,
Wove the white foam and mist,
The amber and the rose and amethyst
Of her wild fountains, shaken loose in air.
And I am of the hills and of the sea:
Strong with the strength of my great hills, and calm
With calm of the fair sea, whose billowy gold
Girdles the land whose queen and love I am!
Lo! Am I less than thou,
That with a sound of lyres, and harp-playing,
Not any voice doth sing
The beauty of mine eyelids and my brow?
Nor hymn in all my fair and gracious ways,
And lengths of golden days,
The measure and the music of my praise?

"Ah, what indeed is this
Old land beyond the seas, that ye should miss
For her the grace and majesty of mine?
Are not the fruit and vine
Fair on my hills, and in my vales the rose?
The palm-tree and pine
Strike hands together under the same skies
In every wind that blows.
What clearer heavens can shine
Above the land whereon the shadow lies
Of her dead glory, and her slaughtered kings,
And lost, evanished gods?
Upon my fresh green sods
No king has walked to curse and desolate:
But in the valleys Freedom sits and sings,
And on the heights above;
Upon her brows the leaves of olive boughs,
And in her arms a dove;
And the great hills are pure, undesecrate,
White with their snows untrod,
And mighty with the presence of their God!

"Hearken, how many years
I sat alone, I sat alone and heard
Only the silence stirred
By wind and leaf, by clash of grassy spears,
And singing bird that called to singing bird.
Heard but the savage tongue
Of my brown savage children, that among
The hills and valleys chased the buck and doe,
And round the wigwam fires
Chanted wild songs of their wild savage sires,
And danced their wild, weird dances to and fro,
And wrought their beaded robes of buffalo.
Day following upon day,
Saw but the panther crouched upon the limb,
Smooth serpents, swift and slim,
Slip through the reeds and grasses, and the bear
Crush through his tangled lair
Of chapparal, upon the startled prey!

"Listen, how I have seen
Flash of strange fires in gorge and black ravine;
Heard the sharp clang of steel, that came to drain
The mountain's golden vein—
And laughed and sang, and sang and laughed again,
Because that 'now,' I said, 'I shall be known!
I shall not sit alone;
But reach my hands unto my sister lands!
And they? Will they not turn
Old, wondering dim eyes to me, and yearn—
Aye, they will yearn, in sooth,
To my glad beauty, and my glad fresh youth!'

"What matters though the morn
Redden upon my singing fields of corn!
What matters though the wind's unresting feet
Ripple the gold of wheat,
And my vales run with wine,
And on these hills of mine
The orchard boughs droop heavy with ripe fruit?
When with nor sound of lute
Nor lyre, doth any singer chant and sing
Me, in my life's fair spring:
The matin song of me in my young day?
But all my lays and legends fade away
From lake and mountain to the farther hem
Of sea, and there be none to gather them.

"Lo! I have waited long!
How longer yet must my strung harp be dumb,
Ere its great master come?
Till the fair singer comes to wake the strong,
Rapt chords of it unto the new, glad song!
Him a diviner speech
My song-birds wait to teach:
The secrets of the field
My blossoms will not yield
To other hands than his;
And, lingering for this,
My laurels lend the glory of their boughs

To crown no narrower brows.
For on his lips must wisdom sit with youth;
And in his eyes, and on the lids thereof,
The light of a great love—
And on his forehead, truth!" . . .

Was it the wind, or the soft sigh of leaves,
Or sound of singing waters? Lo, I looked,
And saw the silvery ripples of the brook,
The fruit upon the hills, the waving trees,
And mellow fields of harvest; saw the Gate
Burn in the sunset: the thin thread of mist
Creep white across the Saucelito hills;
Till the day darkened down the ocean rim,
The sunset purple slipped from Tamalpais,
And bay and sky were bright with sudden stars!

ℭℛ

In the Grand Cañon

The strongholds these of those strange, mighty gods
Who walked the earth before man's feeble race,
And, passing hence to their unknown abodes
In farther worlds, left here their awful trace.
Turrets, and battlements, and toppling towers,
That spurn the torrent foaming at their base,
And pierce the clouds, uplifting into space.
No sound is here, save where the river pours
Its ice-born flood, or when the tempests sweep
In rush of battle, and the lightnings leap
In thunder to the cliffs; no wing outspread
Above these walls, lone and untenanted
By man or beast,—but where the eagle soars
Above the crags,—and by the gates they guard,
Huge, and as motionless, on either hand,
The rock-hewn sentinels in silence stand,
Through the long centuries keeping watch and ward.
Up from the sheer abysses that we tread,
Wherein pale shadow holds her mystic sway,

And night yields never wholly to the day,
To where, in narrowing light far overhead,
Arch capping arch and peak to peak is wed,
We gaze, and veil our eyes in silent awe,
As when Jehovah's form the prophet saw.

❧

With a Wreath of Laurel

O winds, that ripple the long grass!
O winds, that kiss the jeweled sea!
Grow still and lingering as you pass
About this laurel tree.

Great Shasta knew you in the cloud
That turbans his white brow; the sweet,
Cool rivers; and the woods that bowed
Before your pinions fleet.

With meadow scents your breath is rife;
With red-wood odors, and with pine:
Now pause and thrill with twofold life,
Each spicy leaf I twine.

The laurel grows upon the hill
That looks across the western sea.
O winds, within the boughs be still,
O sun, shine tenderly,

And birds, sing soft about your nests:
I twine a wreath for other lands;
A grave! Nor wife nor child has blest
With touch of loving hands.

Where eyes are closed, divine and young,
Dusked in a night no morn may break,
And hushed the poet lips that sung,
The songs none else may wake:

Unfelt the venomed arrow-thrust,
Unheard the lips that hiss disgrace,
While the sad heart is dust, and dust
The beautiful, sad face!

For him I pluck the laurel crown!
It ripened in the western breeze,
Where Saucelito's hills look down
Upon the golden seas;

And sunlight lingered in its leaves
From dawn, until the scarce dimmed sky
Changed to the light of stars; and waves
Sang to it constantly.

I weave, and strive to weave a tone,
A touch, that, somehow, when it lies
Upon his sacred dust, alone,
Beneath the English skies,

The sunshine of the arch it knew,
The calm that wrapt its native hill,
The love that wreathed its glossy hue,
May breathe around it still!

Listening Back

There are no comrade-roses at my window,
No green things in the lane;
Upon the roof no sibilant soft patter,
The lullaby of rain;
Without is silence and within is silence,
Till silence grows a pain.

Within is silence and without is silence,
The snow is on the sill,

In snow the window framed, instead of roses,
And snow is very still. . . .
I wonder is it singing in the grasses,
The rain—upon my Hill?

Elizabeth Clift Bacon Custer

(1842–1933)

IN 1860, with the United States enmeshed in civil war, territorial expansion came to a virtual halt. For five years men skirmished at crossroads, fought pitched battles in forests and cornfields, starved in prisoner-of-war camps. The country lost two hundred thousand men. But the Civil War also produced heroes such as West Point graduate George Armstrong Custer, one of the youngest major generals in the country's short history. In 1864, "Libbie" Bacon of Monroe, Michigan, linked her fate to his.

Elizabeth Bacon Custer's maternal grandparents had traveled to Michigan in a covered wagon. Her father, Judge Daniel Bacon, had walked there from New England. Of the Bacons' four children, only Elizabeth survived childhood. She was twelve when her mother died. Subsequently, Elizabeth remained cheerful and composed in her father's presence. She released her grief in the diaries she kept throughout her childhood.

After they married, Libbie accompanied "Autie" on all his campaigns, beginning with the Virginia front during the last year of the Civil War, through Texas, Kansas, and the Dakota Territory. They lived in tents or government housing. They traveled by wagon or horseback. They experienced fires, floods, earthquakes, epidemics, poisonous animals, and isolation. While apart, they wrote each other long detailed letters that Libbie saved and incorporated into *"Boots and Saddles," Tenting on the Plains,* and *Following the Guidon.* Her writing paints a portrait of a class-conscious, prejudiced, pampered army officer's wife. The books are revisionist history, because Elizabeth Custer consciously left out the negative aspects of her husband's personality and military history. But her willingness to share the intimate details of their life together offset the negative press resulting from military investigations into the causes of "Custer's Last Stand." In effect, she worked hard to create the Custer myth.

Elizabeth Custer was a natural and prolific writer. In addition to books, she published magazine articles and children's stories, such as "The Kid," in order to support herself after her husband's death.

Libbie and Autie had no children, and she did not remarry. Although the nadir of her life occurred when she was thirty-four, she lived—and wrote—another fifty-seven years.

Chapter XV

[Fort Riley, Kansas]

IT WAS A GREAT change for us from the bustle and excitement of the cavalry, as they prepared for the expedition, to the dull routine of an infantry garrison that replaced the dashing troopers. It was intensely quiet, and we missed the clatter of the horses' hoofs, the click of the currycomb, which had come from the stables at the morning and evening grooming of the animals, the voices of the officers drilling the recruits, the constant passing and repassing of mounted men in front of our quarters; above all, the enlivening trumpet-calls ringing out all day, and we rebelled at the drum and bugle that seemed so tame in contrast. There were no more long rides for me, for Custis Lee [Elizabeth Custer's horse] was taken out at my request, as I feared no one would give him proper care at the post. Even the little chapel where the officers' voices had added their music to the chants, was now nearly deserted. The chaplain was an interesting man, and the General and most of the garrison had attended the services during the winter. Only three women were left to respond, and, as we had all been reared in other churches, we quaked a good deal, for fear our responses would not come in the right place. . . .

We had not been long alone, when a great danger threatened us. The level plateau about our post, and the valley along the river near us, were covered with dry prairie grass, which grows thickly and is matted down into close clumps. It was discovered, one day, that a narrow thread of fire was creeping on in our direction, scorching these tufts into shrivelled brown patches that were ominously smoking when first seen. As I begin to write of what followed, I find it difficult; for even those living in Western States and Territories regard descriptions of prairie-fires as exaggerated, and are apt to look upon their own as the extreme to which they ever attain. I have seen the mild type, and know that a horseman rides through such quiet conflagrations in safety. The trains on some of our Western roads pass harmless through belts of country when the flames are about them; there is no impending peril, because the winds are moderate. When a tiny flame is discovered in Kansas or other States, where the wind blows a hurricane so much of the time, there is not a moment to lose. Although we saw what was hardly more than a suspicion of smoke, and the slender, sinuous, red tongue along the ground, we women had read enough of the fires in Kansas to know that the small blaze meant that our lives were in jeopardy. Most of us were then unacquainted with those precautions which the experienced Plains-man takes, and, indeed, we had no ranchmen near to set us the example of caution that the frontiersman so soon learns. We should have had furrows ploughed around the entire post in double lines, a certain distance apart, to check the approach of fire. There was no time to fight the foe with a like weapon, by burning over a portion of the grass between the advancing blaze and our post. The smoke rose higher and higher beyond us, and curling, creeping fire began to ascend into waves of flame with alarming rapidity, and in an incredibly short time we were overshadowed with a dark pall of smoke.

The Plains were then new to us. It is impossible to appreciate their vastness at first. The very idea was hard to realize, that from where we lived we looked on an uninterrupted horizon. We felt it must be the spot where some one first said, "The sky fits close down all around." It fills the soul with wonder and awe to look upon the vastness of that sea of land for the first time. As the sky became lurid, and the blaze swept on toward us, surging to and fro in waving lines as it approached nearer and nearer, it seemed that the end of the world, when all shall be rolled together as a scroll, had really come. The whole earth appeared to be on fire. The sky was a sombre canopy above us, on which flashes of brilliant light suddenly appeared as the flames rose, fanned by a fresh gust of wind. There were no screams nor cries, simply silent terror and shiverings of horror, as we women huddled together to watch the remorseless fiend advancing with what appeared to be inevitable annihilation of the only shelter we had. . . . The river was half a mile away, and our feet could not fly fast enough to reach the water before the enemy would be upon us. There was no such thing as a fire-engine. The Government then had not even provided the storehouses and quarters with the Babcock Extinguisher. We were absolutely powerless, and could only fix our fascinated gaze on the approaching foe.

In the midst of this appalling scene, we were startled anew by a roar and shout from the soldiers' barracks. Some one had, at last, presence of mind to marshal the men into line, and, assuming the commanding tone that ensures action and obedience in emergencies, gave imperative orders. Every one—citizen employees, soldiers and officers—seized gunny sacks, blankets, poles, anything available that came in their way, and raced wildly beyond the post into the midst of the blazing grass. Forming a cordon, they beat and lashed the flames with the blankets, so twisted as to deal powerful blows. It was a frenzied fight. The soldiers yelled, swore and leaped frantically upon beds of blazing grass, condensing a lifetime of riotous energy into these perilous moments. . . .

No sooner had the flames been stamped out of one portion of the plain, than the whole body of men were obliged to rush off in another direction and begin the thrashing and tramping anew. It seemed to us that there was no such thing as conquering anything so insidious. But the wind, that had been the cause of danger, saved us at last. That very wind which we had reviled all winter for its doleful howlings around our quarters and down the chimneys; that self-same wind that had infuriated us by blowing our hats off when we went out to walk, or impeded our steps by twisting our skirts into hopeless folds about our ankles—was now to be our savior. Suddenly veering, as is its fashion in Kansas, it swept the long tongues of flame over the bluffs beyond us, where the lonely coyote and its mate were driven into their lair. By this vagary of the element, that is never anywhere more variable than in Kansas, our quarters, our few possessions, and no doubt our lives, were saved. With faces begrimed and blistered, their clothes black with soot and smoke, their hands burnt and numb from violent effort, the soldiers and citizen employees dragged their exhausted bodies back to garrison, and dropped down anywhere to rest.

The tinge of green that had begun to appear was now gone, and the charred, smoke-stained earth spread as far as we could see, making more desolate the arid, treeless country upon which we looked. It was indeed a blackened and dismal desert that encircled us, and we knew that we were deprived of the delight of the tender green of early spring, which carpets the Plains for a brief time before the sun parches and turns to russet and brown the turf of our Western prairies. . . .

We soon found that we had reached a country where the weather could show more remarkable and sudden phases in a given time than any portion of the United States. The cultivation of the ground, planting of trees, and such causes, have materially modified some of the extraordinary exhibitions that we witnessed when Kansas was supposed to be the great American desert. With all the surprises that the elements furnished, there was one that we would gladly have been spared. One quiet day I heard a great rumbling in the direction of the plateau where we had ridden so much, as if many prairie-schooners, heavily laden, were being spirited away by the stampede of mules. Next, our house began to rock, the bell to ring, and the pictures to vibrate on the wall. The mystery was solved when we ran to the gallery, and found the garrison rushing out of barracks and quarters. Women and children ran to the parade-ground, all hatless, some half-dressed. Everybody stared at every one else, turned pale, and gasped with fright. It was an earthquake, sufficiently serious to shake our stone quarters and overturn the lighter articles, while farther down the gulley the great stove at the sutler's store was tumbled over and the side of the building broken in by the shock. There was a deep fissure in the side of the bank, and the waters of the Big Blue were so agitated that the bed of the river twelve feet deep was plainly visible.

The usual session of the "Did-you-evers" took place, and resolutions were drawn up—not committed to paper, however—giving the opinion of women on Kansas as a place of residence. We had gone through prairie-fire, pestilence, mutiny, a river freshet, and finally, an earthquake: enough exciting events to have been scattered through a life-time were crowded into a few weeks. Yet in these conclaves, when we sought sympathy and courage from one another, there was never a suggestion of returning to a well-regulated climate.

Chapter XXIX

Our Life's Last Chapter

OUR WOMEN'S HEARTS fell when the fiat went forth that there was to be a summer campaign, with probably actual fighting with Indians.

Sitting Bull refused to make a treaty with the Government, and would not come in to live on a reservation. Besides his constant attacks on the white settlers, driving back even the most adventurous, he was incessantly invading and stealing from the land assigned to the peaceable Crows. They appealed for help to the Government that had promised to shield them.

The preparations for the expedition were completed before my husband returned from the East, whither he had been ordered. The troops had been sent out of barracks into a camp that was established a short distance down the valley. As soon as the general returned we left home and went into camp.

The morning for the start came only too soon. My husband was to take Sister Margaret and me out for the first day's march, so I rode beside him out of camp. The column that followed seemed unending. The grass was not then suitable for grazing, and as the route of travel was through a barren country, immense quantities of forage had to be transported. The wagons themselves seemed to stretch out interminably. There were pack-mules, the ponies already laden, and cavalry, artillery, and infantry followed, the cavalry being in advance of all. The number of men, citizens, employés, Indian scouts, and soldiers was about twelve hundred. There were nearly seventeen hundred animals in all.

As we rode at the head of the column, we were the first to enter the confines of the garrison. About the Indian quarters, which we were obliged to pass, stood the squaws, the old men, and the children singing, or rather moaning, a minor tune that has been uttered on the going out of Indian warriors since time immemorial. Some of the squaws crouched on the ground, too burdened with their trouble to hold up their heads; others restrained the restless children who, discerning their fathers, sought to follow them.

The Indian scouts themselves beat their drums and kept up their peculiar monotonous tune, which is weird and melancholy beyond description. Their war-song is misnamed when called music. It is more of a lament or a dirge than an inspiration to activity. This intoning they kept up for miles along the road. After we had passed the Indian quarters we came near Laundress Row, and there my heart entirely failed me. The wives and children of the soldiers lined the road. Mothers, with streaming eyes, held their little ones out at arm's-length for one last look at the departing father. The toddlers among the children, unnoticed by their elders, had made a mimic column of their own. With their handkerchiefs tied to sticks in lieu of flags, and beating old tin pans for drums, they strode lustily back and forth in imitation of the advancing soldiers. They were fortunately too young to realize why the mothers wailed out their farewells. . . .

From the hour of breaking camp, before the sun was up, a mist had enveloped everything. Soon the bright sun began to penetrate this veil and dispel the haze, and a scene of wonder and beauty appeared. The cavalry and infantry in the order named, the scouts, pack-mules, and artillery, and behind all the long line of white-covered wagons, made a column altogether some two miles in length. As the sun broke through the mist a mirage appeared, which took up about half of the line of cavalry, and thenceforth for a little distance it marched, equally plain to the sight on the earth and in the sky.

The future of the heroic band, whose days were even then numbered, seemed to be revealed, and already there seemed a premonition in the supernatural translation as their forms were reflected from the opaque mist of the early dawn.

The sun, mounting higher and higher as we advanced, took every little bit of burnished steel on the arms and equipments along the line of horsemen, and turned them into glittering flashes of radiating light. The yellow, indicative of cavalry, outlined the accoutrements, the trappings of the saddle, and sometimes a narrow thread of that effective tint followed the outlines even up to the head-stall of the bridle. At every bend of the road, as the column wound its way round and round the low hills, my husband glanced back to admire his men, and could not refrain from constantly calling my attention to their grand appearance. . . .

The general could scarcely restrain his recurring joy at being again with his regiment, from which he had feared he might be separated by being detained on other duty. His buoyant spirits at the prospect of the activity and field-life that he so loved made him like a boy. He had made every plan to have me join him later on, when they should have reached the Yellowstone. . . .

We made our camp the first night on a small river a few miles beyond the post. There the paymaster made his disbursements, in order that the debts of the soldiers might be liquidated with the sutler.

In the morning the farewell was said, and the paymaster took sister and me back to the post.

With my husband's departure my last happy days in garrison were ended, as a premonition of disaster that I had never known before weighed me down. I could not shake off the baleful influence of depressing thoughts. . . .

The first steamer that returned from the Yellowstone brought letters from my husband, with the permission, for which I had longed unutterably, to join him by the next boat. The Indians had fired into the steamer when it had passed under the high bluffs in the gorges of the river. I counted the hours until the second steamer was ready. They were obliged, after loading, to cover the pilot-house and other vulnerable portions of the upper deck with sheet-iron to repel attacks. Then sand-bags were placed around the guards as protection, and other precautions taken for the safety of those on board. All these delays and preparations made me inexpressibly impatient, and it seemed as if the time would never come for the steamer to depart.

Meanwhile our own post was constantly surrounded by hostiles, and the outer pickets were continually subjected to attacks. It was no unusual sound to hear the long-roll calling out the infantry before dawn to defend the garrison. We saw the faces of the officers blanch, brave as they were, when the savages grew so bold as to make a day-time sortie upon our outer guards. A picture of one day of our life in those disconsolate times is fixed indelibly in my memory.

On Sunday afternoon, the 25th of June, our little group of saddened women, borne down with one common weight of anxiety, sought solace in gathering together in our house. We tried to find some slight surcease from trouble in the old hymns; some of them dated back to our childhood's days, when our mothers rocked us to sleep to their soothing strains. I remember the grief with which one fair young wife threw herself on the carpet and pillowed her head in the lap of a tender friend. Another sat dejected at the piano and struck soft chords that melted into the notes of the voices. All were absorbed in the same thoughts, and their eyes were filled with far-away visions and longings. Indescribable yearning for the absent, and untold terror for their safety, engrossed each heart. The words of the hymn,

> "E'en though a cross it be,
> Nearer, my God, to thee,"

came forth with almost a sob from every throat.

At that very hour the fears that our tortured minds had portrayed in imagination were realities, and the souls of those we thought upon were ascending to meet their Maker.

On the 5th of July—for it took that time for the news to come—the sun rose on a beautiful world, but with its earliest beams came the first knell of disaster. A steamer came down the river bearing the wounded from the battle of the Little Big Horn, of Sunday, June 25th. This battle wrecked the lives of twenty-six women at Fort Lincoln, and orphaned children of officers and soldiers joined their cry to that of their bereaved mothers.

From that time the life went out of the hearts of the "women who weep," and God asked them to walk on alone and in the shadow.

Sarah Winnemucca Hopkins

(So-mit-tone, Thocmetony) (Paiute)
(1844?–1891)

LIKE SUSETTE LA FLESCHE, Zitkala-Sa, and Edith Eaton, Sarah Winnemucca was torn between the white and the nonwhite cultures. Of
Northern Paiute ancestry, Winnemucca married three white men, but
found happiness with none. She campaigned for the Paiute cause, but
her education, mostly informal homeschooling, set her apart from other
members of her tribe. Her mother, older sister, and younger brother died
at the hands of white settlers, yet Winnemucca worked boldly within the
system to achieve lasting peace and adequate territory for her people.
Her weapons were words, both spoken and written.

When Thocmetony, or Shell-flower, was born, the homeland of the
Northern Paiutes, a Shoshoni-speaking conglomerate of hunters and
gatherers, encompassed northwestern Utah Territory and adjoining
parts of California, southern Oregon, and southwestern Idaho. The
region's forbidding landscape is crowned with old volcanic rocks and
even older sedimentary rocks. Streams arise in the sagebrush- and piñon-
dotted ranges, and disappear in alkali sinks. Emigrants feared this stretch
between the easy water and grass of the Plains and northern Rockies and
the Sierra Nevada of California. For the most part, they left this land to
the Paiutes and related tribes—until, in 1859, gold and silver were discovered on Mount Davidson in the Washoe Mountains.

The Comstock Lode, the richest deposit in the United States, drew
miners and speculators to Virginia City from east and west of the Sierra
Nevada. Farmers and ranchers followed, suppliers for the burgeoning
population. Lawyers, doctors, and writers came, including young
Samuel Clemens, who wrote for the Virginia City newspaper, and later
described the setting and characters in *Roughing It* (1872). Within two
years of the discovery of gold, Nevada achieved territorial status. Three
years later, it was admitted to the Union. Its capital, Carson City, was in
Paiute country. But by 1864, the Paiutes had been pushed onto the most
inhospitable pieces of land—land that was too hot, too arid, too infertile
to till or ranch. And Sarah Winnemucca, as a child and young woman,
suffered through the transition.

Both Sarah's grandfather, Captain Truckee, who had guided emigrants across the Sierra Nevada, and her father, Old Chief Winnemucca, a guide for John Frémont, anticipated the future and advocated peaceable relations with the whites. Sarah and her sister, Elma, boarded with white families and learned to read and write English. In her autobiography, *Life among the Piutes: Their Wrongs and Claims,* Sarah states that they also attended a convent school in San Jose until the prejudice of white parents forced them to leave. Racial slurs and public vendettas dogged Sarah throughout her life.

Although Sarah's family attempted to assimilate into the white world, other Paiutes fiercely resisted white encroachment. The Paiute war of 1860, fought the year following the Comstock Lode discovery, resulted in the confinement of Paiutes to the Pyramid Lake Reservation. In succeeding years, competing Paiute bands murdered each other along with isolated ranchers and miners. Whites massacred Indian villages, decimating the native population. In 1865, Sarah's mother, brother, and sister died during, or as a result of, the Mud Lake Massacre. Sarah, emotionally scarred, decided that survival for the remainder of her family and her tribe would be ensured only through working with and for the government.

Sarah Winnemucca scouted for the army. She warned local officers of impending Paiute and Bannock attacks. She wrote letters revealing depredation by the Indian agents. The Paiutes were forced from Nevada to Oregon to Washington and finally back to Nevada, where there was not enough arable land to sustain the tribe. Finally, in 1879, the same year that Bright Eyes La Flesche launched her public career, Sarah joined the lecture circuit. Success and notoriety followed. She made powerful friends along the East Coast. Because of her attacks on governmental policies, she also made powerful enemies who reviled her in the press.

In December 1881, to counteract the bad press and to effect change, Helen Hunt Jackson included one of Winnemucca's letters in *A Century of Dishonor.* Several months later, Winnemucca published "The Pah-Utes" in the *Californian.* Mary Tyler Mann published Sarah's autobiography in 1883. Using the proceeds from that book, and with the help of Mann's sister, Elizabeth Peabody, Sarah started an Indian school in Lovelock, Nevada. It lasted four years, eventually succumbing to lack of sufficient monetary support. Part of the problem was Sarah's consumptive third husband, Lewis Hopkins, a compulsive gambler.

After a six-year marriage, much of it spent separately, Hopkins died in 1887. It was too late for Sarah to regain her reputation and, with it, support for her school. In addition, the Dawes Act, passed in 1887 and supported by Winnemucca, forced all Indian children to be educated in English-language, white-operated schools. Defeated, Sarah went to live with her sister, Elma, who had married a white man and was living at Henry's Lake, Idaho. Sarah died there in 1891, at age forty-seven.

Sarah Winnemucca's writing is not elegant prose. It is, however, a firsthand account of the lifestyle, traditions, customs, and folklore of a society caught between two worlds. Whites who studied the Indians, such as Alice Fletcher, could not help but bring with them the prejudices that attended development in white society. Winnemucca's writing, although subjected to editorial censorship by well-intended whites, presents a viewpoint without patronizing overtones. It also presents the viewpoint of a segment of society—minority women—that was largely overlooked in the nineteenth century. If some of Winnemucca's "facts" are incorrect, that is less relevant than the attitude and feelings of an Indian woman whose family was slaughtered, whose land was taken, and whose heritage was destroyed.

ᘓ

Letter from Sarah Winnemucca, an Educated Pah-Ute Woman

To Major H. Douglas, U.S. Army:

SIR,—I learn from the commanding officer at this post that you desire full information in regard to the Indians around this place, with a view, if possible, of bettering their condition by sending them on the Truckee River Reservation. All the Indians from here to Carson City belong to the Pah-Ute tribe. My father, whose name is Winnemucca, is the head chief of the whole tribe; but he is now getting too old, and has not energy enough to command, nor to impress on their minds the necessity of their being sent on the reservation. In fact, I think he is entirely opposed to it. He, myself, and most of the Humboldt and Queen's River Indians were on the Truckee Reservation at one time; but if we had stayed there it would be only to starve. I think that if they had received what they were entitled to from the agents, they would never have left them. So far as their knowledge of agriculture extends, they are quite ignorant, as they have never had the opportunity of learning; but I think, if proper pains were taken, that they would willingly make the effort to maintain themselves by their own labor, providing they could be made to believe that the products were their own, for their own use and comfort. It is needless for me to enter into details as to how we were treated on the reservation while there. It is enough to say that we were confined to the reserve, and had to live on what fish we might be able to catch in the river. If this is the kind of civilization awaiting us on the reserves, God grant that we may never be compelled to go on one, as it is much preferable to live in the mountains and drag out an existence in our native manner. So far as living is concerned, the Indians at all military posts get enough to eat and considerable cast-off clothing.

But how long is this to continue? What is the object of the Government in regard to Indians? Is it enough that we are at peace? Remove all the Indians from the military posts and place them on reservations such as the Truckee and Walker River Reservations (as they were conducted), and it will require a greater military force stationed round to keep them within the limits than it now does to keep them in subjection. On the other hand, if the Indians have any guarantee that they can secure a permanent home on their own native soil, and that our white neighbors can be kept from encroaching on our rights, after having a reasonable share of ground allotted to us as our own, and giving us the required advantages of learning, I warrant that the savage (as he is called to-day) will be a thrifty and law-abiding member of the community fifteen or twenty years hence.

Sir, if at any future time you should require information regarding the Indians here, I will be happy to furnish the same if I can.

Sarah Winnemucca
Camp McDermitt, Nevada, April 4th, 1870

ॐ

The Pah-Utes

OUR HOME IS AT the sink of Humboldt River, by the Carson Mountains. My father and I were both born there, about four miles from the railroad. My Indian name is So-mit-tone, meaning Shell-flower. I was educated at the St. Mary's Convent in San Jose.

On our mountains there are many pine trees. We gather the nuts for the winter. This was our principal food, which our women commenced to gather about the middle of August. Our men used to hunt, and after that, our women go into the valleys to gather different kinds of seeds. The men go to fish along the Humboldt and Truckee rivers. They dry game of all kinds, and lay it up for the winter. Later in the fall the men hunt rabbits. The furs are afterwards woven into blankets, called rabbits'-fur blankets. In the winter they all get together to locate their lodges, and all their supplies are collected and put into one place. They remain there about six months, having merry-making, eating and drinking, and getting married; and they give themselves up to great enjoyment until the spring opens. Then they go to the fishing-grounds; and when the roots begin to grow, the women dig them up. The name of this root in Indian is called *yak-bah,* and tastes like carrots. They boil them, like potatoes, and use them in soups, and also dry them. Another root is called *camas* root—a little root that looks like chestnuts; and *kouse* root, which tastes a little like hard bread. In early days, when white people came among us, they used to eat our food, and compare it with theirs. The same toil was gone through with every year, to lay up the winter supplies; and in these days they always seemed to have plenty of food, and plenty of furs to keep them warm in the winter time.

Now you must not suppose that my people are weak or uncourageous. They are not what you call "slouches." There are the Utes and the Pah-Utes. We helped the Bannacks and the Umatillas in the war, because we were kindred of theirs. They are our cousins; therefore we helped them. Now you say, Why did they make war? I will tell you: Your white men are too greedy. They had a little prairie, called the Camas Prairie, about fifty miles long by twenty wide. They wanted it because it supplied them with roots, and prevented them from starving. The white man wanted it, because the roots were good for his cattle, and could make milk and beef and hides and tallow; so he tried to rob them of these lands. They did not like this, and because he despised them, and would give them no redress, they killed him. But the cattle alone were not the cause of this war. The agents were worse than the cattle: what the cattle left the agents took. The agents buy their places for so much, and mean to make their money out of the poor Indians.

During my great-grandfather's time there was a tribe of Indians lived in our country, called Side-okah, which means man-eaters, or cannibals. They were not very large in numbers. They used to seek to kill us; and when they caught us they would have a grand feast. In this way they lived for a number of years, until my people made war with them. Then we had war, and they fought too, but they did not kill many of us. They fought with bows and arrows, just the same as we did. They seemed to fear nothing, would even sport with and catch the arrows directed to them, which flew past. They could jump up and catch the arrows as they would pass over their heads, showing great agility. We fought them for a long time, until their number was quite small. They used to trap us, by digging pit-falls in the ground and wells in the paths. We were so afraid of them that we used to crawl at night; and sometimes our people would fall into these places after dark. When we had fought them some time, they saw that we were getting the best of them. Then they made canoes out of the tule grasses, and floated out on the Humboldt Lake; and they lived on the lake for a short time, but had to leave it again for the land. We kept pushing them out; then they went into a great cave. They did not remain there long, on account of lack of water. They then went into the *tule* marshes, but my people surrounded the *tules,* and set them on fire, and when they saw they were getting killed, they ran back into the cave. There they remained, and my people watched them when they would come out to get water, and then kill them. Then, to make quick work of it, they went to work packing wood, and piled it up in front of the mouth of the cave, they pulled it inside, and of course the cave was very soon filled; and then they set fire to the outside. In that way my people killed all these cannibals, smothered in the cave. Then we owned all their land, which was called the Side-okahs' land by other Indians, and it lay along the Humboldt River in Nevada.

After the Side-okahs were exterminated we lived peaceably, now and then only having a little fight with other tribes—no tribes being allowed to settle among us. If they came on very important business they could stay a while: or if they came for a visit, they would be entertained by feasts and plays and dancing: amusing them all the time they were with us. They always brought presents to our chiefs, and they gave them presents to take back; but they were never allowed to settle with us or marry with us, each tribe maintaining its own individuality very pronounced; every nation speaking a different language.

Our language is not a written one, but oral; neither have we any signs to convey information to distant parties—only verbal messages sent by our warriors traveling on foot; as they could go over rough ground, rocks, and places that ponies could not, and they could endure more. If our relations were sick at a distance we would signal to the others by a fire on the highest top of the mountain. Three times during the night in the same place is a signal for sickness. For moving, our signal would be several fires all in a row, in the same direction we were to move. Fires of that description were peaceable ones; but we had, also, war-signals of fire. In olden times, the way we used to make fire was with two sticks both made of sage brush. One had a hole in the middle, and was about six inches long by two or three in diameter. This was laid down on dried grass, rotten wood, and such materials. Another stick was sharpened at the end like a top. This was put into the hole, and rubbed between the hands, causing a friction which ignited the materials, and we had a fire. We never had flint, nor knew its uses until the white man came to us. Signal fires for war are made in the day-time. A man takes a torch longer than his arm, made of sage brush bark, lighted at the end. He runs towards our encampment, and warns us that the enemy is coming, by making quick fires as he comes towards us, lighting the sage brush as he comes. Then when he gets in sight of the camp he halloos, gives a warwhoop, and runs three times round the encampment and halts in front of the chief's lodge. The warriors by this time are all ready to fight the enemy with their quivers and arrows. He then relates what he saw at a distance. In those early times we always had scouts and spies out, so that we would not be surprised by our enemies.

The traditions of our people are handed down from father to son. The chief is considered to be the most learned, and the leader of the tribe. The doctor, however, is thought to have more inspiration. He is supposed to be in communion with spirits; and we call him "doctor," as you white people call your medicine-man; and the word is not taken from the English language, as may be supposed, but purely Indian. We do not call him a medicine-man, because he does not dose us, as your doctors do, and therefore we call him "doctor." He cures the sick by the laying on of hands, and prayers and incantations and heavenly songs. He infuses new life into the patient, and performs most wonderful feats of skill in his practice. It is one of the most solemn ceremonies of our tribe. He clothes himself in the skins of young, innocent animals, such as the fawn; and decorates himself with the plumage of harmless birds, such as the dove and humming-bird and little birds of the forest—no such things as hawks' feathers, eagles', or birds of prey. His clothing is emblematic of innocence. If he cannot cure the sick person, he tells him that the spirits of his relations hover around and await his departure. Then they pray and sing around his death-bed, and wait for the spirit to take its flight; and then, after the spirit leaves the body, they make merry, because he is beyond care, and they suppose in heaven. They believe there is only joy in that place; that sorrow is before and not after death; that when the soul departs, it goes to peace and happiness, and leaves all its misery behind.

The warrior is the reverse of the doctor. The warrior wears eagles' feathers during the battle. He wears the claws of an eagle around his neck and head. The eagle is our national bird; the Americans taking that emblematic notion from the Indians in the early days of their nation. Some braves that have ridden in the battle front, and have only been engaged once or twice, wear the claws of a grizzly bear, to show they have been in battle; the same as the medal that was given to my brother Natchez for saving three men's lives, showing his bravery.

I will now speak about the chief. His rank is inherited from father to son, the oldest son being the chief by law. If he is dead, the one next to him becomes chief; or, if there are no sons, the next male relative; but never a woman. The custom of having more wives than one arose from the capture of other tribes during war. If the women were pretty, the chief claimed them—but only one wife. The first married is claimed as legal and head of the rest, and is acknowledged in public as the chief's wife. The others are not called wives, but merely assistants—*pe-nut-to-no-dequa*, in Indian. The heirs of the first wife, and she herself, take precedence over the others. The chief, as also the head of every family, is supposed to teach his children the traditions of the tribe. At times of leisure in the evening, and at twilight, these traditions are related around the camp-fires to eager listeners. No note of time is taken, and no record of ages is known. Once in a while, when the spirit moves the chief, he arises and speaks in a loud voice to his people. At these times, all work must cease. If a woman is cooking a meal, it must be left undone. All fold their hands, incline their heads, and listen to what he has to say; and then, when he is through, they go on again with their work, as left before he commenced to speak. Before every event, the chief gets up first in the morning, and the people are warned to get ready. If it is for a fishing excursion, he tells them to get ready—all that are to go. The old women and children stay behind in the lodges, while the young married women and daughters accompany their relations, to carry the game which is caught by the braves.

These excursions sometimes last ten days, the people remain wherever night overtakes them. When through, they return to their lodges, having great rejoicing; and divide their game with the poor and aged and sick—no payment ever being required for such attention. Their belief is to have what they can enjoy on earth, and share it with each other, as they cannot carry anything out of this world. When they die possessed of horses and other goods, their wearing apparel is given to the poor, and some portion of it is buried with them. Horses are generally killed, for they think the dead man will not have any further use for them; and this is considered the last token of honor and respect that can be shown on this earth to the memory of the dead. The way that my people mourn for their dead is by cutting their hair close to their heads, and laying it on the body of the dead to decorate it. The hair of his wife and that of his children, braided and ornamented with beads, is laid upon the dead man's breast; and if the wife refuses to part with her hair to thus honor her husband, she becomes the object of pity and scorn, laughed at, spit upon, and abused by the whole tribe. Thus they seldom refuse to part with their hair. The doctor also contributes ornaments from his person, and is not allowed to doctor any other sick person for some time, until he again gets into favor by some prophecy or inspiration supposed to come from the spirits. These are old traditions. Nowadays he knows his value. He will not attend a patient unless he is paid, as white folks pay their doctors. Thus we follow your customs as our association grows with you. Our doctor now charges a fee of five dollars, or as the case may be, as white folks do.

Indian girls are not allowed to mingle freely with the braves; never go out walking or riding with them; nor have they anything to say to each other. Even in courting the same strictness is observed. A young brave takes a notion to marry a young girl, but cannot do so until he has been declined. The woman removes from the rest of the family to a small wickeup, or lodge, where she remains one month by herself, abstaining from flesh, and living only on seeds or berries. She must be very industrious during that time, going out every morning at daybreak to gather wood and logs, which she arrays in five different piles. This labor is repeated at noon and at sundown. Every five days she is acknowledged by the other women and men to be a young lady ready to marry, and at these times the wood is set on fire, she jumping over the piles while they are burning. Eating, drinking, and dancing are indulged in every fifth day. Then at the end of the month she returns to her father, casting away all her old clothing, and appearing before her parents in new robes made of buckskin.

The ceremony of courtship is as follows: The brave seeks the place where the Indian maiden is at rest. If she discovers him, she gets up and goes away. He never follows her, but comes again the following night, and so on indefinitely. Then when her parents give consent to their marriage, she is given a feast, at which he is invited to partake. At no other time is he allowed to eat with the family. The ceremony of marriage is very simple. The lady passes the brave some food in a dish. He takes it and sets it down; then they are considered man and wife. They remove to a lodge by themselves if able; if not, they remain in their father's lodge. When the first child is born, they go by themselves and work for others, remaining that way one month. They do not eat meat of any kind during this period, and bathe every five days. After that they return to their old home again. Deformed children among this people are almost unknown.

Cooking is performed in willow baskets woven so tight as to hold water. Seeds are ground between two stones. A fire is built, and small stones are thrown into it. When hot, these are dropped into the basket that contains the water, causing it to boil, when the meal is stirred in, and hot rocks continually thrown in until the mush is cooked. Meat for stews and soup is cooked in the same manner. In early times meat was generally eaten this way, and the use of salt was not known until after the advent of the white man.

Virtue was a quality whose absence was punished by death—either by burning alive or stoning to death. My people are not so severe in these later days. The ceremony of marriage is not so strictly carried out as in olden times. They take a woman now without much ado, as white people do, and leave them oftener than of old. One of the latest evidences of civilization is divorce—an indulgence taken advantage of to abandon an old wife and secure a young one. They argue that it is better for them to do so than to leave their young women for the temptation of the white man.

In 1867 I was interpreter for my people; but even then they had nothing. The game has been all killed, except a few rabbits. The pine trees have all been destroyed, so that we can get no more nuts. The cattle have trampled out the grass in our little valleys, and we can dig no more roots. If the white people leave us, to go over the mountains to California, as some people tell us, we must go over the mountains with them too, or else starve. If we cannot get wild game, we must take tame game, like cows or steers; the same as the white people would do if they had nothing to eat, and nothing to feed their wives and little ones with.

When we were shivering and starving, the soldiers were our best friends. They gave us their cast-off clothing, and they gave us rations. When I left the convent and went back among my people, it was funny to see the men and women dressed in soldiers' overcoats and pants. They thought it was the grandest kind of dress. Then the agent promised us provisions and clothes for the winter; but he lied. He knew he lied when he said it. That winter our children were shivering, while he was amassing money by selling the things which the government voted for us. This is how your civilization treats us. Are we to be blamed for thinking that you care for us like the snake in the grass? When I carried the dispatches for the soldiers, they promised Sarah money. Did she ever get it? or did she get any thanks for doing this? None: nobody said "thank you" to poor Sarah. I was greatly deceived when I came to San Francisco to get money and help for my starving people. I thought my own people would help. I call the Methodists my own people. They preached and they prayed, but they did nothing else for my poor, hungry, shivering people. I know something about sermons myself, and can preach a better sermon than any of their ministers. The soldiers are much better than the ministers. The Indian is like my white brother, Emperor Norton: he likes epaulets.

Once the Indians possessed all this beautiful country; now they have none. Then they lived happily, and prayed to the Great Spirit. But the white man came, with his cursed whisky and selfishness and greed, and drove out the poor Indian, because he was more numerous and better armed and knew more knowledge. I see very well that all my race will die out. In a few short years there will be none left—no, not one Indian in the whole of America. I dare say the white man is better in some respects; but he is a bigger rascal, too. He steals and lies more than an Indian does. I hope some other race will come and drive him out, and kill him, like he has done to us. Then I will say the Great Spirit is just, and that it is all right.

Martha Dunham Summerhayes

(1846–1911)

B EFORE EUROPEANS AND Americans arrived, a succession of Native
American cultures occupied a site where three intermittent rivers
come together at the foot of the Santa Catalina Mountains in southern
Arizona. Seventeen hundred years ago, the Hohokam constructed a village of stone and adobe. When the Hohokam disappeared, the Tohono
O'odham, Pimas, and Apaches harvested mesquite beans, saguaro fruit,
and prickly pear *tunas* and *nopalitos*, and Mexican ranchers ran cattle in
the rich riparian habitat. At this spot in 1873, in order to put distance
between U.S. soldiers and the saloons and cribs of Tucson, the army established Camp Lowell, headquarters for the Fifth Cavalry. Six years
later, at the height of the Apache wars, the camp became Fort Lowell.
When Martha Summerhayes arrived with her officer husband and two
children in 1886, nothing but cactus and creosote, palo verde and
mesquite surrounded the fort. To escape the desert heat, families slept
outside amid the nocturnal rustlings of pack rats, Colorado River toads,
snakes, arachnids, coyotes, and the occasional wandering bull.

The Apaches had been placed on reservations a short time before the
Summerhayeses arrived in Arizona. The reservation lifestyle, however,
was anathema to the traditional Apache. Worse, Indian agents siphoned
off much of the rations. Periodically, groups would leave the reservations to hunt or join relatives across the Mexican border. Supplies were
stolen from American and Mexican settlers residing along the escape
corridors, especially the San Pedro Valley south of Tucson. Sometimes
the settlers were killed, sometimes not. The army tracked down the
bands and returned them to the reservation. It was hazardous work for
hunter and hunted alike. Geronimo's band of Chiricahua Apaches, the
last and most famous of the renegade bands, was not subdued until late
summer 1886, while Martha was at Fort Lowell. Shortly thereafter,
Martha and her husband, Jack, left Arizona for the last time.

Martha Dunham was raised on Nantucket Island in "a town half
Quaker, half Puritan." In order to learn to speak and read German, she
spent time in Prussia, where she fell in love with the glitter of military
uniforms. When she returned home, she married 2d Lt. John "Jack"
Summerhayes, a Civil War veteran. She accompanied him west in 1874.

After a few months at Fort Russell at Cheyenne, Wyoming Territory, Jack was transferred to Fort Apache, Arizona Territory, where the army was engaged in the Apache wars. Young Martha, raised within sight and smell of the sea, followed Jack to a dry, desolate, fear-inspiring land that took its toll on her physical and emotional health.

Although the transcontinental railroad had been completed in 1869, five years later it had not yet reached Arizona. Access to this part of the Southwest was either overland via stage or wagon or by ship from Los Angeles or San Francisco, around Baja California, to the Colorado River. In the days before dams and irrigation reduced flow on the Colorado, steamships plied the river as far north as Fort Mojave. On her first trip to Arizona, Martha Summerhayes went by train to San Francisco, ocean steamer to Port Isabel at the mouth of the Colorado, side-wheeler to Fort Mojave, and army ambulance to Fort Apache. There during the winter, her first child was born. Inexperienced and unable to find help, she and her son became ill. A transfer to Ehrenberg, on the shores of the Colorado, did not help. Martha and her son survived the summer and winter, but her health was so poor that she returned to Nantucket. It was in the East that she discovered how much the western experience had already changed her. She returned to Jack, to the army, and to the West. She remained there, except for trips east to visit her family and to have her second child, until Jack was transferred to the East Coast.

The Summerhayeses' postings read like a roster of the Old West: Forts Mojave, Whipple, Verde, Apache, McDowell, Lowell, and Yuma, Arizona; Forts Halleck and McDermitt, Nevada; Angel Island, California; Fort Niobrara, Nebraska; Santa Fe, New Mexico; and Fort Sam Houston, Texas. But before she could find the beauty of the southwestern desert, Martha had to come to grips with sandstorms, tripledigit heat, rotting meat, centipedes, tarantulas, ants, rattlesnakes, thirst, and watching soldiers die of heat prostration. Her sense of humor and remarkable adaptability saved her.

Martha allowed people into her life, talked to them, learned from them. Although patronizing toward the Indians, she nonetheless interacted with them as individuals, and recognized personal character and beauty: Apache chief Diablo's dancing eyes and handsome face and Old Chief Winnemucca's dress and bearing. If Jack had not disapproved, Martha would have adopted Hispanic dress, more comfortable in the wilting heat of Ehrenberg. As it was, she enjoyed frijoles and tortillas, bathed naked in the muddy Colorado each morning, took siestas in the afternoon, and learned to speak Spanish.

Santa Fe, with its perfect climate, ancient Spanish heritage and architecture, and its surrounding Indian pueblos, was her favorite post. She felt that the mysterious city and culture embraced her when they arrived in 1889. It showed just how much she had changed after fifteen years in the West.

Like Mary Adams Maverick, Martha Summerhayes produced only one book, intended both for her children and for publication. She wrote *Vanished Arizona: Recollections of My Army Life* approximately thirty years after her introduction to the desert Southwest, when her memories had had an opportunity to age. Whereas Elizabeth Bacon Custer wrote of army life from the standpoint of a general's wife, Martha Summerhayes wrote from the standpoint of a lieutenant's wife adapting to the most isolated western outposts. There are striking differences between the military experiences of the two "camp followers." Because of its realistic depiction of western landscape, culture, and characters in the last quarter of the nineteenth century, *Vanished Arizona* is considered a regional classic.

Martha's eye for detail and her honesty draw us into her good-natured portrayals of army life. In the end, it is both a love story, as Lawrence Clark Powell points out, and a record of one woman's transformation. "The desert was new to me then. . . . I did not see much to admire in the desolate waste lands through which we were travelling," she says at the end of chapter 7. "I did not dream of the power of the desert, nor that I should ever long to see it again. But as I write, the longing possesses me, and the pictures then indelibly printed upon my mind, long forgotten amidst the scenes and events of a half a lifetime, unfold themselves like a panorama before my vision and call me to come back, to look upon them once more."

Today, only a few weathered adobe walls and a museum remind us of army life at Fort Lowell more than a century ago. But across the valley, starkly white against the surrounding desert, stands Mission San Xavier del Bac, the "Dove of the Desert"—almost unchanged after two hundred years.

Chapter XXIV

Up the Valley of the Gila

THE DECEMBER SUN was shining brightly down, as only the Arizona sun can shine at high noon in winter, when we crossed the Colorado on the primitive ferry-boat drawn by ropes, clambered up into the great thorough-brace wagon (or ambulance) with its dusty white canvas covers all rolled up at the sides, said good-bye to our kind hosts of Fort Yuma, and started, rattling along the sandy main street of Yuma City, for old Camp MacDowell.

Our big blue army wagon, which had been provided for my boxes and trunks, rumbling along behind us, empty except for the camp equipage.

But it all seemed so good to me: I was happy to see the soldiers again, the drivers and teamsters, and even the sleek Government mules. The old blue uniforms made my heart glad. Every sound was familiar, even the rattling of the harness with its ivory rings and the harsh sound of the heavy brakes reinforced with old leather soles.

Even the country looked attractive, smiling under the December sun. I wondered if I had really grown to love the desert. I had read somewhere that people did. But I was not paying much attention in those days to the analysis of my feelings. I did not stop to question the subtle fascination which I felt steal over me as we rolled along the smooth hard roads that followed the windings of the Gila River. I was back again in the army; I had cast my lot with a soldier, and where he was, was home to me.

In Nantucket, no one thought much about the army. The uniform of the regulars was never seen there. The profession of arms was scarcely known or heard of. Few people manifested any interest in the life of the Far West. I had, while there, felt out of touch with my oldest friends. Only my darling old uncle, a brave old whaling captain, had said: "Mattie, I am much interested in all you have written us about Arizona; come right down below and show me on the dining-room map just where you went."

Gladly I followed him down the stairs, and he took his pencil out and began to trace. After he had crossed the Mississippi, there did not seem to be anything but blank country, and I could not find Arizona, and it was written in large letters across the entire half of this antique map, "Unexplored."

"True enough," he laughed. "I must buy me a new map."

But he drew his pencil around Cape Horn and up the Pacific coast, and I described to him the voyages I had made on the old "Newbern," and his face was aglow with memories.

"Yes," he said, "in 1826, we put into San Francisco harbor and sent our boats up to San José for water and we took goats from some of those islands, too. Oh! I know the *coast* well enough. We were on our way to the Ar'tic Ocean then, after right whales."

But, as a rule, people there seemed to have little interest in the army and it had made me feel as one apart.

Gila City was our first camp; not exactly a city, to be sure, at that time, whatever it may be now. We were greeted by the sight of a few old adobe houses, and the usual saloon. I had ceased, however, to dwell upon such trifles as names. Even "Filibuster," the name of our next camp, elicited no remark from me.

The weather was fine beyond description. Each day, at noon, we got out of the ambulance, and sat down on the warm white sand, by a little clump of mesquite, and ate our luncheon. Coveys of quail flew up and we shot them, thereby insuring a good supper.

The mules trotted along contentedly on the smooth white road, which followed the south bank of the Gila River. Myriads of lizards ran out and looked at us. "Hello, here you are again," they seemed to say.

The Gila Valley in December was quite a different thing from the Mojave desert in September; and although there was not much to see, in that low, flat country, yet we three were joyous and happy.

Good health again was mine, the travelling was ideal, there were no discomforts, and I experienced no terrors in this part of Arizona.

Each morning, when the tent was struck, and I sat on the camp-stool by the little heap of ashes, which was all that remained of what had been so pleasant a home for an afternoon and a night, a little lonesome feeling crept over me, at the thought of leaving the place. So strong is the instinct and love of home in some people, that the little tendrils shoot out in a day and weave themselves around a spot which has given them shelter. Such as those are not born to be nomads.

Camps were made at Stanwix, Oatman's Flat, and Gila Bend. There we left the river, which makes a mighty loop at this point, and struck across the plains to Maricopa Wells. The last day's march took us across the Gila River, over the Maricopa desert, and brought us to the Salt River. We forded it at sundown, rested our animals a half hour or so, and drove through the MacDowell cañon in the dark of the evening, nine miles more to the post. A day's march of forty-five miles. (A relay of mules had been sent to meet us at the Salt River, but by some oversight, we had missed it.)

Jack had told me of the curious *cholla* cactus, which is said to nod at the approach of human beings, and to deposit its barbed needles at their feet. Also I had heard stories of this deep, dark cañon and things that had happened there.

Fort MacDowell was in Maricopa County, Arizona, on the Verde River, seventy miles or so south of Camp Verde; the roving bands of Indians, escaping from Camp Apache and the San Carlos reservation, which lay far to the east and southeast, often found secure hiding places in the fastnesses of the Superstition Mountains and other ranges, which lay between old Camp MacDowell and these reservations.

Hence, a company of cavalry and one of infantry were stationed at Camp MacDowell, and the officers and men of this small command were kept busy, scouting, and driving the renegades from out of this part of the country back to their reservations. It was by no means an idle post, as I found after I got there; the life at Camp MacDowell meant hard work, exposure and fatigue for this small body of men.

As we wound our way through this deep, dark cañon, after crossing the Salt River, I remembered the things I had heard, of ambush and murder. Our animals were too tired to go out of a walk, the night fell in black shadows down between those high mountain walls, the *chollas,* which are a pale sage-green color in the day-time, took on a ghastly hue. They were dotted here and there along the road, and on the steep mountain-sides. They grew nearly as tall as a man, and on each branch were great excrescences which looked like people's heads, in the vague light which fell upon them.

They nodded to us, and it made me shudder; they seemed to be something human.

The soldiers were not partial to MacDowell cañon; they knew too much about the place; and we all breathed a sigh of relief when we emerged from this dark uncanny road and saw the lights of the post, lying low, long, flat, around a square.

Chapter XXIX

Changing Station

IT WAS THE CUSTOM to change the stations of the different companies of a regiment about every two years. So the autumn of '82 found us on the way to Fort Halleck, a post in Nevada, but differing vastly from the desolate MacDermit station. Fort Halleck was only thirteen miles south of the Overland Railroad, and lay near a spur of the Humboldt range. There were miles of sage-brush between the railroad and the post, but the mountains which rose abruptly five thousand feet on the far side, made a magnificent background for the officers' quarters, which lay nestled at the bottom of the foot-hills.

"Oh! what a lovely post!" I cried, as we drove in.

Major Sanford of the First Cavalry, with Captain Carr and Lieutenant Oscar Brown, received us. "Dear me," I thought, "if the First Cavalry is made up of such gallant men as these, the old Eighth Infantry will have to look out for its laurels."

Mrs. Sanford and Mrs. Carr gave us a great welcome and vied with each other in providing for our comfort, and we were soon established.

It was so good to see the gay yellow of the cavalry again! Now I rode, to my heart's content, and it was good to be alive; to see the cavalry drill, and to ride through the cañons, gorgeous in their flaming autumn tints; then again to gallop through the sage-brush, jumping where we could not turn, starting up rabbits by the score.

That little old post, now long since abandoned, marked a pleasant epoch in our life. From the ranches scattered around we could procure butter and squabs and young vegetables, and the soldiers cultivated great garden patches, and our small dinners and breakfasts live in delightful memory.

At the end of two years spent so pleasantly with the people of the First Cavalry, our company was again ordered to Angel Island [California]. But a second very active campaign in Arizona and Mexico, against Geronimo, took our soldiers away from us, and we passed through a period of considerable anxiety. June of '86 saw the entire regiment ordered to take station in Arizona once more.

We travelled to Tucson in a Pullman car. It was hot and uninteresting. I had been at Tucson before, but the place seemed unfamiliar. I looked for the old tavern; I saw only the railroad restaurant. We went in to take breakfast, before driving out to the post of Fort Lowell, seven miles away. Everything seemed changed. Iced cantaloupe was served by a spick-span alert waiter; then, quail on toast. "Ice in Arizona?" It was like a dream, and I remarked to Jack, "This isn't the same Arizona we knew in '74," and then, "I don't believe I like it as well, either; all this luxury doesn't seem to belong to the place."

After a drive behind some smart mules, over a flat stretch of seven miles, we arrived at Fort Lowell, a rather attractive post, with a long line of officers' quarters, before which ran a level road shaded by beautiful great trees. We were assigned a half of one of these sets of quarters, and as our half had no conveniences for house-keeping, it was arranged that we should join a mess with General and Mrs. Kautz and their family. We soon got settled down to our life there, and we had various recreations; among them, driving over to Tucson and riding on horseback are those which I remember best. We made a few acquaintances in Tucson, and they sometimes drove out in the evenings, or more frequently rode out on horseback. Then we would gather together on the Kautz piazza and everybody sang to the accompaniment of Mrs. Kautz's guitar. It was very hot, of course; we had all expected that, but the luxuries obtainable through the coming of the railroad, such as ice, and various summer drinks, and lemons, and butter, helped out to make the summer there more comfortable.

We slept on the piazzas, which ran around the houses, on a level with the ground. At that time the fad for sleeping out of doors, at least amongst civilized people, did not exist, and our arrangements were entirely primitive.

Our quarters were surrounded by a small yard and a fence; the latter was dilapidated, and the gate swung on one hinge. We were seven miles from anywhere, and surrounded by a desolate country. I did not experience the feeling of terror that I had had at Camp Apache, for instance, nor the grewsome fear of the Ehrenberg grave-yard, nor the appalling fright I had known in crossing the Mogollon range or in driving through Sanford's Pass. But still there was a haunting feeling of insecurity which hung around me, especially at night. I was awfully afraid of snakes, and no sooner had we lain ourselves down on our cots to sleep, than I would hear a rustling among the dry leaves that had blown in under our beds. Then all would be still again; then a crackling and a rustling—in a flash

I would be sitting up in bed. "Jack, do you hear that?" Of course I did not dare to move or jump out of bed, so I would sit, rigid, scared. "Jack! what is it?" "Nonsense, Mattie, go to sleep; it's the toads jumping about in the leaves." But my sleep was fitful and disturbed, and I never knew what a good night's rest was.

One night I was awakened by a tremendous snort right over my face. I opened my eyes and looked into the wild eyes of a big black bull. I think I must have screamed, for the bull ran clattering off the piazza and out through the gate. By this time Jack was up, and Harry and Katherine, who slept on the front piazza, came running out, and I said: "Well, this is the limit of all things, and if that gate isn't mended to-morrow, I will know the reason why."

Now I heard a vague rumor that there was a creature of this sort in or near the post, and that he had a habit of wandering around at night, but as I had never seen him, it had made no great impression on my mind. Jack had a great laugh at me, but I did not think then, nor do I now, that it was anything to be laughed at.

We had heard much of the old Mission of San Xavier del Bac, away the other side of Tucson. Mrs. Kautz decided to go over there and go into camp and paint a picture of San Xavier. It was about sixteen miles from Fort Lowell.

So all the camp paraphernalia was gotten ready and several of the officers joined the party, and we all went over to San Xavier and camped for a few days under the shadow of those beautiful old walls. This Mission is almost unknown to the American traveller.

Exquisite in color, form and architecture, it stands there a silent reminder of the Past.

The curious carvings and paintings inside the church, and the precious old vestments which were shown us by an ancient custodian, filled my mind with wonder. The building is partly in ruins, and the little squirrels were running about the galleries, but the great dome is intact, and many of the wonderful figures which ornament it. Of course we know the Spanish built it about the middle or last of the sixteenth century, and that they tried to christianize the tribes of Indians who lived around in the vicinity. But there is no sign of priest or communicant now, nothing but a desolate plain around it for miles. No one can possibly understand how the building of this large and beautiful mission was accomplished, and I believe history furnishes very little information. . . .

After a few delightful days, we broke camp and returned to Fort Lowell.

And now the summer was drawing to a close, and we were anticipating the delights of the winter climate at Tucson, when, without a note of warning, came the orders for Fort Niobrara. We looked, appalled, in each other's faces, the evening the telegram came, for we did not even know where Fort Niobrara was.

We all rushed into Major Wilhelm's quarters, for he always knew everything. We (Mrs. Kautz and several of the other ladies of the post, and myself) were in a state of tremendous excitement. We pounded on Major Wilhelm's door and we heard a faint voice from his bedroom (for it was after ten o'clock); then we waited a few moments and he said, "Come in."

We opened the door, but there being no light in his quarters we could not see him. A voice said: "What in the name of—" but we did not wait for him to finish; we all shouted: "Where is Fort Niobrara?" "The Devil!" he said. "Are we ordered there?" "Yes, yes," we cried; "where is it?" "Why, girls," he said, relapsing into his customary moderate tones, "It's a hell of a freezing cold place, away up north in Nebraska."

We turned our backs and went over to our quarters to have a consultation, and we all retired with sad hearts.

Now, just think of it! To come to Fort Lowell in July, only to move in November! What could it mean? It was hard to leave the sunny South, to spend the winter in those congealed regions in the North. We were but just settled, and now came another break-up!

Our establishment now, with two children, several servants, two saddle horses, and additional household furnishings, was not so simple as in the beginning of our army life, when three chests and a box or two contained our worldly goods. Each move we made was more difficult than the last; our allowance of baggage did not begin to cover what we had to take along, and this added greatly to the expense of moving.

The enormous waste attending a move, and the heavy outlay incurred in travelling and getting settled anew, kept us always poor; these considerations increased our chagrin over this unexpected change of station. There was nothing to be done, however. Orders are relentless, even if they seem senseless, which this one did, to the women, at least, of the Eighth Infantry.

Mary Hartwell Catherwood

(1847–1902)

IN 1857, a majority of the Supreme Court decided in *Dred Scott v. Sanford* that blacks were not citizens and therefore could not sue for their freedom. Furthermore, Chief Justice Roger B. Taney declared the Missouri Compromise to be unconstitutional. This decision and its ramifications increased the enmity between slaveholding and nonslaveholding states, and helped push the country into civil war.

That same year, traffic was heavy on the National Road, the major east-west route from Maryland to Missouri followed by the emigrant wagon trains heading for the western gold fields, the fertile valleys of Oregon and California, and the prairies. The road crossed Ohio near the Licking County home of nine-year-old Mary Hartwell. The Hartwell family joined the westward migration, settling in Illinois. When Mary's mother and physician father died within two years, Mary returned to Ohio. But the West had already captured her imagination.

Mary spent the Civil War years in Ohio, and graduated from the Female College at Granville in 1868, while the recently reunited nation was in the throes of Reconstruction. Determined to be a writer, she moved closer to the New York publishing hub. Louisa May Alcott's *Little Women* and Elizabeth Ward's *Gates Ajar* were on the best-seller list. In the next four years, the country switched its attention to works featuring locales undisturbed by the recent war. Western and midwestern regional stories by Mark Twain, Bret Harte, and Edward Eggleston captivated readers. Mary followed their lead, writing realistic midwestern fiction and then historical romances set in the old French and French-Canadian frontier of the seventeenth and eighteenth centuries.

At first Catherwood wrote for newspapers and weekly magazines. Eventually, her short stories and serialized novels were published in *Century, Lippincott's,* and the *Atlantic Monthly.* Her stories deal with an assortment of frontier settings. She was one of the earliest writers of realistic regional fiction. She worked with leading American historian Francis Parkman to incorporate accurate historical details, although Catherwood was not above adding scenes and characters for dramatic reasons. Her heroines, often romantic and humorous, were never cloy-

ing or overly sentimental. They were as heroic and refreshingly independent as their settings.

Catherwood used her first trip west as the basis for *Old Caravan
Days,* a children's story. *Spanish Peggy* and *The Spirit of an Illinois
Town* portrayed prairie towns as characters with distinctive personalities. Historical romances such as *Lazarre* and *The Story of Tonty* described French-Canadian settlement and exploration along the
Mississippi River south to St. Louis. *Mackinac and Lake Stories* focused
on the Great Lakes region. In "The Skeleton on Round Island," included
here, Catherwood is ahead of her time: she treats her Native
American–French protagonist as an individual rather than a caricature.

Mary Hartwell married James Catherwood in 1877, and they returned west, settling in Hoopston, Illinois. They had one daughter. A
prolific writer, Catherwood continued to publish until her death at fifty-
five.

ॐ

The Skeleton on Round Island

*On the 15th day of March, 1897, Ignace Pelott died at Mackinac
Island, aged ninety-three years.*

*The old quarter-breed, son of a half-breed Chippewa mother and
French father, took with him into silence much wilderness lore of the
Northwest. He was full of stories when warmed to recital, though at the
beginning of a talk his gentle eyes dwelt on the listener with anxiety, and
he tapped his forehead—"So many things gone from there!" His habit of
saying "Oh God, yes," or "Oh God, no," was not in the least irreverent,
but simply his mild way of using island English.*

*While water lapped the beach before his door and the sun smote
sparkles on the strait, he told about this adventure across the ice, and his
hearer has taken but few liberties with the recital.*

I AM TO CARRY Mamselle Rosalin of Green Bay from Mackinac to Cheboygan that time, and it is the end of March, and the wind have turn
from east to west in the morning. A man will go out with the wind in the
east, to haul wood from Boblo, or cut a hole to fish, and by night he cannot get home—ice, it is rotten; it goes to pieces quick when the March
wind turns.

I am not afraid for me—long, tall fellow then; eye that can see to
Point aux Pins; I can lift more than any other man that goes in the boats
to Green Bay or the Soo; can swim, run on snow-shoes, go without eating two, three days, and draw my belt in. Sometimes the ice-floes carry
me miles, for they all go east down the lakes when they start, and I have
landed the other side of Drummond. But when you have a woman with
you—Oh God, yes, that is different.

The way of it is this: I have brought the mail from St. Ignace with my
traino—you know the train-au-galise—the birch sledge with dogs. It is
flat, and turn up at the front like a toboggan. And I have take the traino
because it is not safe for a horse; the wind is in the west, and the strait
bends and looks too sleek. Ice a couple of inches thick will bear up a
man and dogs. But this old ice a foot thick, it is turning rotten. I have
come from St. Ignace early in the afternoon, and the people crowd about
to get their letters, and there is Mamselle Rosalin crying to go to

Cheboygan, because her lady has arrive there sick, and has sent the letter a week ago. Her friends say:

"It is too late to go to-day, and the strait is dangerous."

She say: "I make a bundle and walk. I must go when my lady is sick and her husband the lieutenant is away, and she has need of me."

Mamselle's friends talk and she cry. She runs and makes a little bundle in the house and comes out ready to walk to Cheboygan. There is nobody can prevent her. Some island people are descend from noblesse of France. But none of them have travel like Mamselle Rosalin with the officer's wife to Indiana, to Chicago, to Detroit. She is like me, French.[7] The girls use to turn their heads to see me walk in to mass; but I never look grand as Mamselle Rosalin when she step out to that ice.

I have not a bit of sense; I forget maman and my brothers and sisters that depend on me. I run to Mamselle Rosalin, take off my cap, and bow from my head to my heel, like you do in the dance. I will take her to Cheboygan with my traino—Oh God, yes! And I laugh at the wet track the sledge make, and pat my dogs and tell them they are not tired. I wrap her up in the fur, and she thank me and tremble, and look me through with her big black eyes so that I am ready to go down in the strait.

The people on the shore hurrah, though some of them cry out to warn us.

"The ice is cracked from Mission Point to the hook of Round Island, Ignace Pelott!"

"I know that," I say. "Good-day, messieurs!"

The crack from Mission Point—under what you call Robinson's Folly—to the hook of Round Island always comes first in a breaking up; and I hold my breath in my teeth as I skurry the dogs across it. The ice grinds, the water follows the sledge. But the sun is so far down in the southwest, I think "The wind will grow colder. The real thaw will not come before to-morrow."

I am to steer betwixt the east side of Round Island and Boblo. When we come into the shadow of Boblo we are chill with damp, far worse than the clear sharp air that blows from Canada. I lope beside the traino, and not take my eyes off the course to Cheboygan, except that I see the islands look blue, and darkness stretching before its time. The sweat drop off my face, yet I feel that wind through my wool clothes, and am glad of the shelter between Boblo and Round Island, for the strait outside will be the worst.

There is an Indian burying-ground on open land above the beach on that side of Round Island. I look up when the thick woods are pass, for the sunset ought to show there. But what I see is a skeleton like it is sliding down hill from the graveyard to the beach. It does not move. The earth is wash from it, and it hangs staring at me.

I cannot tell how that make me feel! I laugh, for it is funny; but I am ashame, like my father is expose and Mamselle Rosalin can see him. If I do not cover him again I am disgrace. I think I will wait till some other day when I can get back from Cheboygan; for what will she say if I stop the traino when we have such a long journey, and it is so near night, and the strait almost ready to move? So I crack the whip, but something pull, pull! I cannot go on! I say to myself, "The ground is froze; how can I cover up that skeleton without any shovel, or even a hatchet to break the earth?"

But something pull, pull, so I am oblige to stop, and the dogs turn in without one word and drag the sledge up the beach of Round Island.

"What is the matter?" says Mamselle Rosalin. She is out of the sledge as soon as its stops.

I not know what to answer, but tell her I have to cut a stick to mend my whip-handle. I think I will cut a stick and rake some earth over the skeleton to cover it, and come another day with a shovel and dig a new grave. The dogs lie down and pant, and she looks through me with her big eyes like she beg me to hurry.

But there is no danger she will see the skeleton. We both look back to Mackinac. The island have its hump up against the north, and the village in its lap around the bay, and the Mission eastward near the cliff; but all seem to moving! We run along the beach of Round Island, and then we see the channel between that and Boblo is moving too, and the ice is like wet loaf-sugar, grinding as it floats.

We hear some roars away off, like cannon when the Americans come to the island. My head swims. I cross myself and know why something pull, pull, to make me bring the traino to the beach, and I am oblige to that skeleton who slide down hill to warn me.

When we have seen Mackinac, we walk to the other side and look south and southeast towards Cheboygan. All is the same. The ice is moving out of the strait.

"We are strand on this island!" says Mamselle Rosalin. "Oh, what shall we do?"

I tell her it is better to be prisoners on Round Island than on a cake of ice in the strait, for I have tried the cake of ice and know.

"We will camp and build a fire in the cove opposite Mackinac," I say. "Maman and the children will see the light and feel sure we are safe."

"I have done wrong," says she. "If you lose your life on this journey, it is my fault."

Oh God, no! I tell her. She is not to blame for anything, and there is no danger. I have float many a time when the strait breaks up, and not save my hide so dry as it is now. We only have to stay on Round Island till we can get off.

"And how long will that be?" she ask.

I shrug my shoulders. There is no telling. Sometimes the strait clears very soon, sometimes not. Maybe two, three days.

Rosalin sit down on a stone.

I tell her we can make camp, and show signals to Mackinac, and when the ice permit, a boat will be sent.

She is crying, and I say her lady will be well. No use to go to Cheboygan anyhow, for it is a week since her lady sent for her. But she cry on, and I think she wish I leave her alone, so I say I will get wood. And I unharness the dogs, and run along the beach to cover that skeleton before dark. I look and cannot find him at all. Then I go up to the graveyard and look down. There is no skeleton anywhere. I have seen his skull and his ribs and his arms and legs, all sliding down hill. But he is gone!

The dusk close in upon the islands, and I not know what to think—cross myself, two, three times; and wish we had land on Boblo instead of Round Island, though there are wild beasts on both.

But there is no time to be scare at skeletons that slide down and disappear, for Mamselle Rosalin must have her camp and her place to sleep. Every man use to the bateaux have always his tinder-box, his knife, his tobacco, but I have more than that; I have leave Mackinac so quick I forget to take out the storekeeper's bacon that line the bottom of the sledge, and Mamselle Rosalin sit on it in the furs! We have plenty meat, and I sing like a voyageur while I build the fire. Drift, so dry in summer you can light it with a coal from your pipe, lay on the beach, but is now winter-soaked, and I make a fire-place of logs, and cut pine branches to help it.

It is all thick woods on Round Island, so close it tear you to pieces if you try to break through; only four-footed things can crawl there. When the fire is blazing up I take my knife and cut a tunnel like a little room, and pile plenty evergreen branches. This is to shelter Mamselle Rosalin, for the night is so raw she shiver. Our tent is the sky, darkness, and clouds. But I am happy. I unload the sledge. The bacon is wet. On long sticks the slices sizzled and sing while I toast them, and the dogs come close and blink by the fire, and lick their chops. Rosalin laugh and I laugh, for it smell like a good kitchen; and we sit and eat nothing but toasted meat—better than lye corn and tallow that you have when you go out with the boats. Then I feed the dogs, and she walk with me to the water edge, and we drink with our hands.

It is my house, when we sit on the fur by the fire. I am so light I want my fiddle. I wish it last like a dream that Mamselle Rosalin and me keep house together on Round Island. You not want to go to heaven when the one you think about all the time stays close by you.

But pretty soon I want to go to heaven quick. I think I jump in the lake if maman and the children had anybody but me. When I light my pipe she smile. Then her great big eyes look off towards Mackinac, and I turn and see the little far-away lights.

"They know we are on Round Island together," I say to cheer her, and she move to the edge of the fur. Then she say "Good-night," and get up and go to her tunnel-house in the bushes, and I jump up too, and spread the fur there for her. And I not get back to the fire before she make a door of all the branches I have cut, and is hid like a squirrel. I feel I dance for joy because she is in my camp for me to guard. But what is that? It is a woman that cry out loud by herself! I understand now why she sit down so hopeless when we first land. I have not know much about women, but I understand how she feel. It is not her lady, or the dark, or the ice break up, or the cold. It is not Ignace Pelott. It is the name of being prison on Round Island with a man till the ice is out of the straits. She is so shame she want to die. I think I will kill myself. If Mamselle Rosalin cry out loud once more, I plunge in the lake—and then what become of maman and the children?

She is quieter; and I sit down and cannot smoke, and the dogs pity me. Old Sauvage lay his nose on my knee. I do not say a word to him, but I pat him, and we talk with our eyes, and the bright camp-fire shows each what the other is say.

"Old Sauvage," I tell him, "I am not good man like the priest. I have been out with the boats, and in Indian camps, and I not had in my life a chance to marry, because there are maman and the children. But you know, old Sauvage, how I have feel about Mamselle Rosalin, it is three years."

Old Sauvage hit his tail on the ground and answer he know.

"I have love her like a dog that not dare to lick her hand. And now she hate me because I am shut on Round Island with her while the ice goes out. I not good man, but it pretty tough to stand that."

Old Sauvage hit his tail on the ground and say, "That so." I hear the water on the gravel like it sound when we find a place to drink; then it is plenty company, but now it is lonesome. The water say to people on Mackinac, "Rosalin and Ignace Pelott, they are on Round Island." What make you proud, maybe, when you turn it and look at it the other way, make you sick. But I cannot walk the broken ice, and if I could, she would be lef alone with the dogs. I think I will build another camp.

But soon there is a shaking in the bushes, and Sauvage and his sledge-mates bristle and stand up and show their teeth. Out comes Mamselle Rosalin with a scream to the other side of the fire.

I have nothing except my knife, and I take a chunk of burning wood and go into her house. Maybe I see some green eyes. I have handle vild-cat skin too much not to know that smell in the dark.

I take all the branches from Rosalin's house and pile them by the fire, and spread the fur robe on them. And I pull out red coals and put more logs on before I sit down away off between her and the spot where she hear that noise. If the graveyard was over us, I would expect to see that skeleton once more.

"What was it?" she whisper.

I tell her maybe a stray wolf.

"Wolves not eat people, mamselle, unless they hunt in a pack; and they run from fire. You know what M'sieu' Cable tell about wolves that chase him on the ice when he skate to Cheboygan? He come to great wide crack in ice, he so scare he jump and skate right on! Then he look back, and see the wolves go in, head down, every wolf caught and drown in the crack. It is two days before he come home, and the east wind have blow to freeze that crack over—and there are all the wolf tails, stick up, froze stiff in a row! He bring them home with him—but los them on the way, though he show the knife that cut them off!"

"I have hear that," says Rosalin. "I think he lie."

"He say he take his oat on a book," I tell her, but we both laugh, and she is curl down so close to the fire her cheeks turn rosy. For a camp-fire will heat the air all around until the world is like a big dark room; and we are shelter from the wind. I am glad she is begin to enjoy herself. And all the time I have a hand on my knife, and the cold chills down my back where that hungry vild-cat will set his claws if he jump on me; and I cannot turn around to face him because Rosalin thinks it is nothing but a cowardly wolf that sneak away. Old Sauvage is uneasy and come to me, his fangs all expose, but I drive him back and listen to the bushes be-hind me.

"Sing, M'sieu' Pelott," says Rosalin.

Oh God, yes! it is easy to sing with a vild-cat watch you on one side and a woman on the other!

"But I not know anything except boat songs."

"Sing boat songs."

So I sing like a bateau full of voyageurs, and the dark echo, and that vild-cat must be astonish. When you not care what become of you, and your head is light and your heart like a stone on the beach, you not mind vild-cats, but sing and laugh.

I cast my eye behin sometimes, and feel my knife. It make me smile to think what kind of creature come to my house in the wilderness, and I say to myself: "Hear my cat purr! This is the only time I will ever have a home of my own, and the only time the woman I want sit beside my fire."

Then I ask Rosalin to sing to me, and she sing "Malbrouck," like her father learn it in Kebec. She watch me, and I know her eyes have more danger for me than the vild-cat's. It ought to tear me to pieces if I forget maman and the children. It ought to be scare out the bushes to jump on a poor fool like me. But I not stop entertain it—Oh God, no! I say things that I never intend to say, like they are pull out of my mouth. When your heart has ache, sometimes it break up quick like the ice.

"There is Paul Pepin," I tell her. "He is a happy man; he not trouble himself with anybody at all. His father die; he let his mother take care of herself. He marry a wife, and get tired of her and turn her off with two children. The priest not able to scare him; he smoke and take his dram and enjoy life. If I was Paul Pepin I would not be torment."

"But you are not torment," says Rosalin. "Everybody speak well of you."

"Oh God, yes," I tell her; "but a man not live on the breath of his neighbors. I am thirty years old, and I have take care of my mother and brothers and sisters since I am fifteen. I not made so I can leave them, like Paul Pepin. He marry when please. I not able to marry at all. It is not far I can go from the island. I cannot get rich. My work must be always the same."

"But why you want to marry?" says Rosalin, as if that surprise her. And I tell her it is because I have seen Rosalin of Green Bay; and she laugh. Then I think it is time for the vild-cat to jump. I am thirty years old, and have nothing but what I can make with the boats or my traino; the children are not grown; my mother depend on me; and I have pro-pose to a woman, and she laugh at me!

But I not see, while we sing and talk, that the fire is burn lower, and old Sauvage has crept around the camp into the bushes.

That end all my courtship. I not use to it, and not have any business to court, anyhow. I drop my head on my breast, and it is like when I am little and the measle go in. Paul Pepin he take a woman by the chin and smack her on the lips. The women not laugh at him, he is so rough. I am as strong as he is, but I am afraid to hurt; I am oblige to take care of what need me. And I am tie to things I love—even the island—so that I cannot get away.

"I not want to marry," says Rosalin, and I see her shake her head at me. "I not think about it at all."

"Mamselle," I say to her, "You have not any inducement like I have, that torment you three years."

"How you know that?" she ask me. And then her face change from laughter, and she spring up from the blanket couch, and I think the camp go around and around me—all fur and eyes and claws and teeth—and I not know what I am doing, for the dogs are all over me—yell—yell—yell; and then I am stop stabbing, because the vild-cat has let go of Sauvage, and Sauvage has let go of the vild-cat, and I am looking at them and know they are both dead, and I cannot help him any more.

You are confuse by such things where there is noise, and howling creatures sit up and put their noses in the air, like they call their mate back out of the dark. I am sick for my old dog. Then I am proud he has kill it, and wipe my knife on its fur, but feel ashame that I have not check him driving it into camp. And then Rosalin throw her arms around my neck and kiss me.

It is many years I have tell Rosalin she did that. But a woman will deny what she know to be the trut. I have tell her the courtship had end, and she begin it again herself, and keep it up till the boats take us off Round Island. The ice not run out so quick any more now like it did then. My wife say it is a long time we waited, but when I look back it seem the shortest time I ever live—only two days.

Oh God, yes, it is three years before I marry the woman that not want to marry at all; then my brothers and sisters can take care of themselves, and she help me take care of maman.

It is when my boy Gabriel come home from the war to die that I see the skeleton on Round Island again. I am again sure it is wash out, and I go ashore to bury it, and it disappear. Nobody but me see it. Then before Rosalin die I am out on the ice-boat, and it give me warning. I know what it mean; but you cannot always escape misfortune. I cross myself when I see it; but I find good luck that first time I land; and maybe I find good luck every time, after I have land.

Mary Hallock Foote
(1848–1938)

WALLACE STEGNER'S Pulitzer Prize–winning novel, *Angle of Repose,*
contains the larger details of Mary Hallock Foote's life. She was
born to a Quaker family that lived and farmed along the Hudson River
near Milton, New York. She attended art school in New York and became one of the most successful wood-block artists in the country. Her
illustrations accompanied works by Hawthorne, Longfellow, and
Whittier.

In 1873, at a New Year's party at the home of Harriet Beecher
Stowe's uncle, Lyman Beecher, Mary Hallock met engineer Arthur
Foote. The two corresponded for three years while Arthur went west to
work for mining and construction companies. During this time, Mary
also began to publish autobiographical prose to accompany her illustrations. "The Picture in the Fire-Place Bedroom" came out in *St. Nicholas*
magazine in 1875. Although Mary was unsure about a union that would
require her to leave her career, family, and close friends, she married
Foote in the winter of 1876. While Arthur returned to California to
build their first home, Mary prepared for an unwelcome move. Five
months later she crossed the country alone to meet him near the shores
of San Francisco Bay.

Their future together was often strained by Arthur's stubbornness
and arrogance. A brilliant engineer and inventor, he had trouble working for others. In the interim between Arthur's jobs, Mary returned to
her family in New York, where their first two children were born. But
she always rejoined Arthur in remote corners of the West.

Because she viewed herself as an easterner, Mary was able to depict
the western scene with an objective voice. Encouraged by her two best
friends, Helena de Kay Gilder and Richard Watson Gilder, the de facto
editor of *Scribner's,* Mary began to write and illustrate western stories
and articles for the magazine. The first article, "A California Mining
Camp," described her surroundings and her neighbors at New Almaden,
a quicksilver, that is, mercury, mine in California where Arthur worked
as a mining engineer. Mary portrayed the mine later in "How the Pump
Stopped at the Morning Watch," this time creating a short story from an
incident at the mine. She found she was as facile with words as with

paint, and supplied the growing market for realistic stories and sketches, such as "Pictures of the Far West."

Following the mining booms, the Footes moved from California to Colorado, Mexico to Idaho, and back to California. In Leadville, Colorado, their one-room cabin, far above the lawless camp, was a stopping place for geologists and engineers mapping the West. Clarence King, Samuel Emmons, Rossiter Raymond, and innumerable others talked geology long into the night. Mary listened and drew. Her romantic novels, such as *The Led Horse Claim* (1882–1883), *John Bodewin's Testimony* (1885–1886), and *The Last Assembly Ball* (1889), first serialized in *Scribner's* and *Century* magazines, were set in mining camps. The protagonists often fell in love with engineers modeled on the men she met through Arthur's work. Her stories were so popular that she received letters from miners around the world commenting on the authenticity of the scenes she described.

On a bluff above the Boise River, within a wooden fence, lies the foundation of the "house in the canyon," the home Arthur DeWint Foote built for his family in the fall of 1885. A marker carries a sun-bleached diagram of the house constructed of basalt blocks quarried from the surrounding cliffs. The house itself is gone. In its place, black-eyed Susans nod in the hot July breeze. Across the river another marker shows a picture of the two-story house with its veranda. There, for three years, Mary Hallock Foote wrote stories and created the wood-block illustrations for which she was famous. But the stark beauty of mesa, cañon, and river could not compensate for the lack of privacy and the isolation—conditions exacerbated by the difficult birth of her third child. Worse, while Arthur struggled with alcoholism and fought to finance and construct a canal that would turn the Boise Valley into a thriving agricultural center, the monetary, marital, and emotional stresses took their toll on Mary's art. It was one of the lowest and least productive times of her life.

If Boise Canyon was a low point in Mary's life, the subsequent move back to Boise signaled regeneration. The Footes moved in with Mary's sister, Bessie, and her family. Backing for the canal project had dried up, but Arthur refused to abandon the venture. Mary's art now supported the family.

Eventually, Arthur found a permanent mining job in Grass Valley, California. Mary continued to write novels well into the twentieth century. Two of her best were *Edith Bonham,* a tribute to Helena de Kay Gilder, and *The Ground-Swell,* in remembrance of the Footes' daughter,

Agnes, who died of complications from appendicitis when she was seventeen. During the last decade of her life, Mary also wrote her autobiography, *A Victorian Gentlewoman in the Far West,* which Rodman Paul edited and published in 1972.

Mary Hallock Foote's writing focused in an unsentimental and precise fashion on subjects she knew well. Her artist's eye caught the inherent beauty, freedom, and potential of a raw land. But she did not shrink from portraying the consequences experienced by those emigrants unprepared for life beyond the structured envelope of civilization.

Mary Hallock and Arthur Foote finally returned to the East in 1932. She died in Massachusetts during her ninety-first year.

I OFTEN THINK, as I stoop to pick a cluster of white-petaled flowers, that seem the very expression of the freshness and briefness of the morning, how, in some shadowy "labór" a thousand feet below, a gang of Mexicans, finishing their night-shift, may be passing the "barrilito" from one grimy mouth to another.

If one possessed an ear-trumpet . . . by laying it on almost any spot of these steeply mounting hills and winding trails, one might hear the ringing of hammer and drill against the rock, the rumbling of cars through cavernous drifts, the dull thunder of blasts, even the voices of men burrowing in the heart of the mountain. One can walk, in the passages only of this underground world, for twenty-seven miles without treading the same path twice. Only those familiar with its blind ways from childhood may venture below in safety without a guide, for besides the danger of being lost, is that of wandering into some disused "labór," where the rotten timbers threaten a "cave." Within the last year, I am told, a part of "Mine Hill" has settled three inches, and everywhere above the "old workings" great cracks and holes show how the shell is constantly sinking. If this burrowing process goes on with the same vigor as during the last thirty years, the mountain will some day be nothing but a hollow crust,—a huge nut-shell, emptied of its kernel. Acres of its surface now cover nothing but emptiness,—caverns, hundreds of feet in length and breadth, connected by winding passages hewn out of the rock, and propped by a net-work of timbers.

"Nuevo Almadén," the mine was called, under the leisurely Mexican *régime;* then the quicksilver ore was carried in leather sacks on the miners' heads, up ladders made of notched logs, and "packed" down the mountain to the furnaces, on the backs of mules. There is an old "labór" called "La Cruz," where candles were kept burning before a shrine to the Virgin, hollowed out of the rocky wall. It was furnished with a crucifix and an image of the Queen of Heaven with a crown on her head and the Holy Child in her arms. Here the miners knelt in prayer before going to their day's or night's work. No one ever passed it without making the sign of the cross. The mule-trains, the Mexican ladders, the shrine and crucifix disappeared when the Baron family lost their claim and "Nuevo" became New Almaden. That prompt and urgent monosyllable was the key-note to the change of dynasty. What the mine may have lost in picturesqueness, it has gained, however, in general interest, from the curious mixture of races gathered here, all living under a common rule, with the same work and the same general influences, yet as distinctly national as if each occupied its own corner of the earth.

It gives me a strange feeling to see the miners go down into the underworld. The men's heads show above the top of the "skip," the bell strikes, the engineer moves a lever, the great wheels of the engine slowly swing round and the heads disappear down the black hole. I can see a hand waved and the glimmer of a candle for a little way. The spark grows fainter and a warm, damp wind blows up the shaft.

Above-ground, the colony is in three stories: The Hacienda at the foot of the mountain, the Cornish camp half-way up, and the Mexican camp on top; a long winding road leads from one to another, like a staircase.[8] From its breezy landings, looking back, one can follow the Santa Clara valley, opening out to the sea, and the long quiet lines of the Coast Range opposite, while the nearer mountains fold in around with strong lights and shadows. The mountains are not bare, but clothed chiefly with scrub-oak and live-oak, not large, yet sufficient to soften the rugged outlines. The "works" are hidden by spurs and clefts, so as to be quite inconspicuous. The shaft-houses and miners' cottages on the sides of the hills are of no more consequence than rabbit-holes. . . .

There is no undue propriety about the mining camps on the "Hill." Their domestic life has the most unrestrained frankness of expression, and their charms are certainly not obtrusive. The Mexicans have the gift of harmoniousness; they seem always to fit their surroundings, and their dingy little camp has made itself at home on the barren hills, over which it is scattered; but the charm of the Cornish camp lies partly in the vivid incongruity between its small, clamorous activities, and the repose of the vast, silent nature around it. . . .

The camp seems always to be either washing or moving, or both. Monday and May-day arrive here quite regardless of the almanac or the customs of society. The Cornish miner can hardly be said to

> fold his tent like the Arab,
> And silently steal away.

When the wind sits in the shoulder of his sail, the entire camp is aware of the fact. There is an auction of his household of his household gear, at which his neighbors are cheerfully emulous that some private good should result from the loss to the community. He departs with his wife and quiverful of children, and the house that knew him knows him no more. Another assortment of family garments flaps on the clothes-lines; another brood of chickens and children throngs his door-step.

During the long months when drought sits heavy on the land, the water-tank is one of the idyls of the Cornish Camp. It is a sort of club at which congregate all the stray dogs, donkeys, sad-eyed cows (who subsist, at this season, chiefly on hope deferred), boys with water-pails, red-shirted teamsters, and "wood-packers" with trains of jaded mules; there is nothing dubious in the nature of its benefits, and of all who gather there none depart in bitterness, unless it may be the small Cornish lads, who carry away two heavy pails and a sense of injury natural to the spirit of youth under such circumstances. Three times a day the motley crowd gathers, but I like it best at sunset, with a flushed sky overhead, against which the figures are dark; gleams of trickling water; the straw hat of a teamster, or a gaunt gray donkey, catching the waning light; while evening shadows brood already in the hollows of the mountains and deepen the mystery of the cañon beyond.

Past the store and the water-tank the road winds still upward, and passes out of sight round a spur of the mountain. It leads to the Mexican camp and into an entirely different social atmosphere. The village lies all in broadest sunlight, unrelieved by tree or shelter of any kind except here and there the shadow of a rock in which, perhaps, stands a donkey, with drooping ears and hanging lip, motionless in a patient reverie.

THE MEXICAN CAMP has little of that bustling energy which belongs to its neighbor on the floor below. It wakes up slowly in the morning,—especially if the morning be cold,—and lounges abroad on moonlight nights, when guitar-tinklings sound from the shadowy vine-flecked porches. The barest little cabin has its porch, its climbing vines and shelf of carefully tended plants. Dark-eyed women sit on the door-steps in the sun braiding a child's hair, perhaps, or chattering to a neighbor, who leans against the door-post with a baby half hidden in the folds of her shawl. They walk up and down the hilly street, letting their gowns trail in the dust, their heads enveloped in a shawl, one end of which is turned up over the shoulder; the smooth, sliding step corresponds with the accent in speaking. In passing, they look at you with a slow, grave stare like that of a child. All, even to the babies, have an air of repose; crudeness of voice or manner is almost unknown among them.

The first time I went down into the mine one of the men of the party, as is the custom, passed a bottle of whisky among the men in each "labór" we visited. The Cornish men drank in a hearty, unconstrained fashion enough, but each Mexican, before raising the bottle to his lips, turned to the two women of the party with a grave inclination and a *Buena salud, Señoras!* . . .

MY LAST VISIT to the Mexican camp was during the yellow hazy July weather; it was after a fire had swept away all the houses lying below and around the rock, which rises like a fortress at the north-west end of camp. The bare sun-baked rock stood out, with all its reddish-yellow lights and purple-brown shadows, in strong relief against the solid blue of the sky. Down its sides were the blackened lines of brick which marked the foundations of the ruined houses. Below, was the little street silent and deserted, with its quiet afternoon shadows stretching across it. It seemed old enough for anything. It might have been a little Pompeiian street lying so still in the broad sunlight, under that intensely blue-bright sky. I sat under the shadow of a Mexican cabin on the high bank over-looking the street. A little girl named Amelia, too slight and small to carry the child she held wrapped in an old shawl, stood beside me and told me the Spanish words for rock, and sky, and picture, and the names of her brothers and sisters. The mother, leaning on the railing of the rough balcony above, smiled down at me and counted them on her fin-gers—six in all—and then crossed both hands on her breast with a proud and gentle gesture of triumph in the possession of the six. The cheerfulness of the whole family,—brown, ragged, ill-fed, sickly and nu-merous as they were,—a cheerfulness which implied no hope or even un-derstanding of anything better, was the saddest thing in the whole of that warm, sunny desolation.

Early morning at New Almaden is worth getting up betimes to see. Sometimes the valley is like a great lake filled with billows of fog,—pearly white billows, tumbling and surging with noiseless motion. It is more as if the clouds had all fallen out of the sky, leaving its blue inten-sity unbroken, and heaping the valley with fleecy whiteness. On windy mornings, the fog rolls grandly out to sea along the defiles of the triple chain of hills; when there is no wind, it rises and drifts in masses over the mountains, making the clear sunlight hazy for a moment before dissolv-ing into it. After the rains, when the morning air has a frosty crispness, the mountains are outlined in sharp, dark blue against a sky of reddish-gold; even the tops of the distant red-woods may be traced, "bristling strange, in fiery light," along the horizon. As the sun lifts its head, the dark blue hills flush purple, long shadows stream across the valley, the windows and spires of San José sparkle into sight, and the bay reveals itself, a streak of silver in the far distance. There is no chorus of birds to break the stillness. . . .

I was not encouraged to investigate that camp of Chinamen below the hill, but once we went to "China Sam's" to buy a lantern. . . . [H]is wife . . . seemed not more than fourteen years old—a mere child with the smallest hands. She carried a baby slung at her back in the folds of a dark-red silk scarf, which was crossed over her breast. The baby had a tiny black cap worked with embroidery on its head,—a chubby little thing, fast asleep, swaying from side to side as the small mother trotted about. She examined my dress, hands and ornaments, and, pointing to her baby, put her fingers on her under teeth and held up two fingers to tell me it had two teeth. Whenever I tried to say anything to her she laughed and said, "No sabe." She was very delicately formed, her hands small as a child's and perfect in shape, yet when she took one of mine to look at a ring which had caught her eye, I felt uncomfortable at the touch of those slim, tawny fingers. She offered a cigar to my companion, which he accepted and held carefully, but as we left the house, I noticed that he tossed it into the bushes. In an inner closet where the day was shut out, we saw the glimmer of candle-light on some brilliantly colored papers on the wall. This was the family altar.

Several years ago Sam was head cook at the boarding-house on the "Hill." Another Chinaman tried to get his place by underhand means. Sam carefully noted his movements; there was a journey to San José, which ended badly for the other Chinaman, and not too well for Sam, as he was tried soon after for murder. He spent a few months in jail, but he had only killed another Chinaman, and he was an excellent cook,— probably a much better one than his rival,—so he was finally acquitted. Two or three years ago he sent to China for his wife; she excused herself from coming on the plea of being too old for so long a journey, and sent this young girl instead. Sam says his young wife is "heap fool! Allee time play chile [with the child]!" and he beats the "chile" because it is a girl.

TOWARD THE CLOSE of the dry season, when brown and dusty August burns into browner, dustier September, a keen remembrance of all cool, watery joys takes possession of one's thoughts. The lapping of ripples in pebbly coves, the steady thump of oars in row-locks, the smell of apple-blossoms on damp spring evenings, old mill-races mossy and dripping, the bleating of frightened lambs at a sheep-washing and the hoarse, stifled complaint of their mothers mingled with the rushing of the stream—all these once common sounds and sights haunt the memory. Every day the dust-cloud grows thicker in the valley, the mountains fade almost out of sight against a sky which is all glare without color; a dry wind searches over the bare, brown hills for any lingering drop of moisture the sun may have left there; but morning and evening still keep a spell which makes one forget the burden of the day. At the sunset the dust-cloud in the valley becomes a bar of color stretching across the base of the mountains, deep rose and orange, shading by softest gradations into cool blue. I remember one sunset especially. The clouds of dust rolling up from the valley below were transformed by the light into level bars of color like a horizontal rainbow sweeping across the entire valley; above it the mountains rose; a wonderful variety of constantly changing hues made them look like something unreal. Then there came a sudden darkening of the lower part of the mountains so that the sun-lit peaks seemed to float in the air above the bars of sun-colored dust, with a strip of cool shadow between. All is quiet; as in the morning, no birds chirp and twitter themselves to sleep; the stillness is only broken by the dull throbbing of the engine like a stifled breath in the distant shaft-house. . . .

II

The Coming of Winter

ONE YEAR'S OCCUPATION of a quarter-section of wild land means but a slight foothold in a new country—a cabin, rude as a magpie's nest; a crop of wild hay, if the settler is near a river-bottom; the tools and stock he brought with him; a few chickens not yet acclimated; a few seeds and slips from the last home; probably a new baby.

Now that the wild-geese are beginning to fly, a chance shot may furnish a meal, where every meal counts. The young wife holds the baby's blanket close to its exposed ear to deaden the report of the gun. She is not so sure of the marksman's aim as she would have been a year before she married him. He is one of an uncertain crop of husbandmen that springs up quickly on new soil, but nowhere strikes deep roots.

The prettiest girl of his native village, somewhere in the South-west, will have fancied him, and have consented to take her place beside him on the front seat of his canvas-topped wagon when the inevitable vague westward impulse seized him. As the miles lengthen behind them and "their garments and their shoes become old by reason of the long journey," she will lose her interest in the forward outlook and spend more and more of her time among the bedquilts and hen-coops in the rear of the wagon, half asleep, or watching listlessly the plains they crawl across and the slow rise and fall of the strange hills they climb.

When the settlers stop, it is not because they have reached the place to which they meant to go, but because they have found a sheltered valley with water and wild grass. The wagon needs mending, they and their cattle are tired. While they rest, they build a rude cabin, the baby is born, summer has passed. It is too late to move that winter.

The home-seeker, with all the West before him, will be wary of the final choice which costs him the freedom of the road. He is like a child in a great toy-shop full of high-priced, remotely imaginable joys, and with but a single penny in his pocket. So long as he nurses the penny unspent he is the potential possessor; a man of much wider scope, much larger resources, than the actual possessor. Birds in the bush that beckon and call are not of the same species as the bird that lies tamely in hand.

Teamsters, toiling across the great lava beds, on their way to the mountain mining-towns, make camp near the cabin in the willow-brake, sit by the settler's fire, and their talk is the large talk of the men of the road—of placer claims on the rivers far to the north, where water is plentiful all the year; of the grass, how rich and tall it grows in Long Valley, and how few stock-men with their herds have got into that region as yet.

The settler's eye is brilliant as he listens. He is losing time; he yearns for the spring, and the dawn of new chances. But he is a restless, not a resolved man, and with spring come back the birds of promise, the valley rings with their music, the seeds are up in the garden, and the baby is learning to walk.

Out of the poorest thousand in Manasseh was Gideon chosen. It may be that the child, so soon escaping out of the languid mother's arms, may be one of the mighty men in the new country where his parents waited to rest a while before moving farther on.

How the Pump Stopped at the Morning Watch

THE MAIN SHAFT OF the Morning Watch is an incline, sunk on the vein to a depth below daylight of eighteen hundred feet. There are lower workings still, in the twenty-one hundred; for the mine is one of the patriarchs of the golden age in northern California, and its famous vein, though small, has been richly persistent.

The shaft is a specimen of good early construction in deep-mining; it has two compartments, answering to the two vital functions of pumping and hoisting. A man walking up the hoist may step into the pump-shaft between timbers to avoid a car, but he must then be wary of the pump-rod.

The pump-rod at the Morning Watch is half a mile long. With a measured movement, mighty, conclusive, slow, it crawls a little way up the shaft, waits a breath, then lunges down, and you hear subterranean sobs and gulpings where the twelve pumps at their stations are sucking water from the mine. These are the water-guard, which is never relieved. Nights and Sundays, frost or flood or dry, the pumps never rest. Each lifts his load to the brother above him, sweating cold sweat and smeared with grease and slime, fighting the climbing waters. The stroke of the pump-rod is the pulse of the mine. If the pulse should stop and the waters rise, the pumps, as they go under, are "drowned." In their bitter costliness, in the depths from which they rise, though born in sunlight, the waters of the "sump" might typify the encroaching power of evil in man's nature—a power that springs from good, that yet may be turned to good, but over which conscience, like the pumps, must keep unsleeping watch and ward.

Between the Cornish miner and the Cornish pump there is a constitutional affinity and an ancient, hereditary understanding. Both are governed and driven by the power on top; both have held their own, underground, from generation to generation, without change or visible improvement. They do their work by virtue of main strength and dogged constancy, and neither one can be hurried.

On this last head, the pump-man will answer for his pump—speaking of it as an old comrade, in the masculine singular, if you ask how many beats of the great connecting-rod are normal:

"'E 'ave been as 'igh as seven and a quarter; 'e *'ave* been, but it do strain 'im. Seven, about seven, is what 'e can bear."

John Tiernay of Penzance, spoken of familiarly as "old John," was pump-man, first and last, at the Morning Watch. He was there when the first pump-station was put in and the rod was but four hundred feet long. He saw that mighty member grow, section by section, pump added to pump, as the shaft went down. Each new pump was as a child born to him; there was room in his pride always for one more. If one had a failing more than another, he made a study of its individual crankiness, and learned to spare the fault he could not remedy or hide. To the mining captain, to whom he was forced to go for supplies, he might confess that "No. 5 'e do chaw up more packin' than all the pumps in the mine"; but in general it was like touching upon delicate family matters with old John to question the conduct of his pumps.

He was a just man, Tiernay, but not perfect; he had his temporal bonds. It went hard with him on the Lord's day to choose between the public duty of worship in the miners' church, above-ground, and his private leaning toward his pumps, below. Can a man do his work in this world too well? Excessive devotion to the interests of the mine was not a common fault with its employees. The boys at the Morning Watch made friendly sport of the old enthusiast, declaring that he took his pumps to bed with him, and dreamed at night of their kicking and bucking. It is true that the thought of Sammy Trebilcox, and what he might be doing or not doing as his substitute underground, took the heart out of his Sabbath observances and made his day of rest, when he gave himself one, the longest of the seven. Wherefore his little old wife, "a good bit older nor 'e," and a woman of grave disposition, saddened by the want of children, sat mournful in church without her man, and thought of his clean shirts folded in the drawer at home, and of him, in his week-day livery of mud, earning unblessed wages below ground. She knew it was not the extra day's pay that ensnared him; her prayer was that he be delivered from pride in carnal labors, and that he make not unto himself a graven image and an idol of "they pumps."

A pump-man has his regular shifts; but so well known was the quality of John's service that not a man about the mine, from the oldest tributer to the new superintendent, would have questioned his appearance above-ground at any irregular hour of day or night. He looked, when he came on top, like some old piece of mining machinery that has been soaking underground for half a century—plastered with the pallid mud of the deepest levels, coated with grease, and stained with rust from fondlings of his pumps, the recognizably human parts of him—his un-sunned face and hands—pitted and drawn with steam.

The day's-pay men were lively in the stopes; the car-boys romped with the landing-men, and chalked the names of one another's sweethearts on the sides of refractory cars. Every tributer in the old workings had his partner to help him hammer out a "crushin'." The contractors tunneled and drifted and argued in gangs; but old John, in the bowels of the mine, with death within a foot of him on each side, kept his one-man watch alone. In his work there was no variety, no change of surroundings or of season, no irrelevant object to rest his fixed attention; solitude, monot-ony, and ceaseless, nagging vigilance, imprisoned in a tube of darkness, between the crash of the cars on the one hand and the squeeze of the rod on the other.

Iron will crystallize after years of such use, lose its elasticity and co-hesive strength. Old John had ceased to find pleasure in society or sun-light. He chose the darkest paths going home through the woods, the old roads, deep in pine-needles, undisturbed by passing feet. The sound of a boy's whoop or a man's hearty halloo drove him deeper into the shade. If spoken to, he had no answer ready, but would whisper one to himself as he went on alone, with his eyes on the ground.

Once the night-shift, going down, saw the old man bareheaded in the hoist-shaft, standing motionless on the track, his hand up as if listening. He appeared not to hear the noise of the car, or to have heard it from some imaginary direction. They waved, they roared to him, and he van-ished in the pump-shaft. Afterward they remembered his stare of bewil-derment as if he had come awake suddenly in a strange place, uncertain how he had got there. Sometimes he would pop up like a stage-ghost in the hoisting-works, haggard and panting, as if in urgent haste. Greeted with jocular questioning, he would gaze about him vaguely, turn, and plunge down again without a word.

The wife began to hear, from relatives and neighbors, disquieting comments on her husband's looks.

"It 's more than a whole month 'e 'ave n't 'ad a Sunday off," said the buxom wife of one of the shift-bosses. "Whatever's the sense in 'im workin' so 'ard, and you only two in family? A rest is what 'e need."

"Rest, dear! 'Ave n't I telled 'im so, scores and scores of time! An' 'e just like a fish out o' watter when 'e 's parted from they pumps. 'E talk of 'em the same as they were humans—made off the same piece wi' 'is own flesh and blood."

"Eh! It 's a bad lookout when a man can't leave his work behind 'im when the day is done. We belongs to 'ave our rest sometime. Why don't 'ee coax 'im out more? 'T would do 'im good to see the folks.'"

"''E never was one to be coaxed. What 'e think right that 'e 'll do; man nor woman can't make 'im do other," Mrs. Tiernay would boast, proud of a husband's will unbroken after forty years of marriage.

One morning there was a summons for the mistress at the kitchen door of the superintendent's house.

"Clem' want see you—kitch'," was the Chinese cook's sketchy way of transmitting the message.

Clemmo was there, the gardener and general utility-man. The two do not go together unless the man is good-natured, as Clemmo was. He stood, hat in hand, in his deferential way, perspiring and quite notice-ably pale. There was a catch in his breath from running. He had come to borrow an umbrella.

The mistress looked at him in surprise. It was cloudless midsummer weather, the hot valley steaming up in the face of the foothills, dust on the cloaking pine woods, red dust inches deep on all the roads and trails, dust like a steamer's smoke hovering in the wake of ore-teams miles away. The shadows of the mine buildings were short and black where a group of men had gathered, though the twelve bell had not yet struck. A sun-umbrella, did he mean?

"Any kind, ma'am; any old one will do," Clemmo repeated apologet-ically. "It 's just to hold over Mr. Tiernay when they 're carryin' him home. Yes, ma'am, he was hurt in the shaft just now—an hour ago. Oh, yes, ma'am, the doctor 's seen him. He 's pretty bad. It was an empty car struck him; dragged him quite a ways before the shaft-men heard him scream. They can't tell just how it happened; he has n't spoke since they brought him up. Yes, ma'am, one of the boys has gone on to tell the wife. They 've got an old mattress to carry him on; they have brandy. No, ma'am, there ain't anything, thank you—only the umbrella. Any old one will do."

When the umbrella was brought and it proved to be a silk one, Clemmo took it reluctantly, protesting that "any old one—" But the mis-tress cut him short. He went off with it, finally, assuring her over his shoulder that he would carry it himself and see that it came "right back."

The Chinaman looked on calmly. "I think he pretty ole—he die pretty soon," he remarked.

Three little children were frolicking in the swing under the pine-trees. Their mother quieted them, out of respect for what was soon to pass the house; but she could not moderate the morning's display of pink-faced roses, nor suggest to the sun to go under a brief cloud. All was heartless radiance and peace as the forlorn little procession came down the road—the workers carrying him home whose work was done; three men on a side, and between their stout backs, and faces red with exertion, a broken shape stretched out, and a stark white profile crowned with a bloody cloth.

What had the old man been doing in the hoist? "Fixin' up the bell-rope," the mining captain said; "but it did n't look like any of John's work," he added meaningly. "He was n't all there when he rigged up that thing. He 'd slipped a cog, somehow. Yes, sir, you bet, a man in a shaft he 's got to keep his eye out. He can watch for forty year, and the minute he forgets himself, that minute he 's gone."

ABOUT THE TURN of night, when the old man was nearing his end, he gave a loud cry and sprang up in the bed, where he had lain speechless and helpless three days. The startled watchers flew to his side.

"Take your 'ands off me, women!" he panted. "I must up. Th' pump—'e 's stopped!"

"Don't 'ee, deary!" The wife trembled at the look in his pinched gray face. "Don't 'ee be thinkin' o' they pumps no more. 'Owever could 'ee 'ear them, two mile away? Hark, now! 'T is all as still as still."

It was so still, that windless summer night, they could hear the clock tick across the passage, and the hoarse straining of the dying man's breath as they struggled to hold him down. His weakness, not their strength, prevailed. He fell back on his pillows, and a passive, awe-struck stare succeeded the energy of horror and resistance. His eyes were fixed, as one who watches spellbound the oncoming of a great disaster. They touched his still face; it was damp and cold. His chest pumped hard and slow.

"Two thousan'—gone under! Drowned, drowned!" he whispered.

"'T is all nothin' but they pumps!" the old wife grieved distractedly. She knew his time was short. "Oh, dear Saviour, don't mind it of 'im! 'E were a hard worker, and a good man to me."

At that same hour, the night of John's release, when he had given his loud cry, the watchman at the mine heard above the roar of forty stamp-heads a sound like cannon smothered within walls. He rushed across to the hoisting-works. There lay the great crown-wheel of the pump, in pieces on the floor. The pump-rod, settled on its chucks, had stopped midway of its last stroke.

One little cog, worn out, had dropped from its place; then two cogs came together, tooth to tooth, and the ten-ton wheel burst with a groan that had arrested the passing soul of the pump-man, duty-bound to the last.

An old mine, or an old man, that is nearly worked out may run on for years, at small expense, if no essential part give way; but the cost of heavy repairs is too great a strain upon halting faith and an exhausted treasury. Even so small a thing as the dropping out of one little cog, in a system worth thousands to rebuild, may decide the question whether to give up or keep on.

In that moment of ultimate consciousness, the mystery of which is with the dead, it may be that old John beheld the whole sequence of disaster that was to follow the breaking of the pump. If he did foresee it all, as his ghostly eyes seemed to say, he accepted it, as well; and that look of awestruck, appealing submission in the face of immeasurable calamity he carried to the grave. Perhaps he had seen beyond the work of this world to some place of larger recompense, where the unpaid increment of such service as his is waiting on the books. Perhaps he heard already the Master's patient "Well done."

While they were preaching the funeral sermon, his old enemy, the water of the black deeps, was creeping up, regaining ground which he and the pumps had fought for and defended, inch by inch and year by year.

"Two thousan'—gone under!" The lowest pump is lost. Leave it where it drowned, at its post. Now there is hurry and rush of tearing up tracks before the levels are flooded; the order to shut down has come late. Pull out the pumps; the fight is over! They have taken up the track in the main incline; the water has reached the nine hundred, like the chill creeping up the limbs of a dying man. The old tributers take down their muddy mine-suits from the change-house walls; families will live poorer this winter for all that water in the mine. They go trooping home, boots and bundles over the shoulder, by the paths their own feet have made. They meet no night-shift coming on. Another year, and those paths of labor will be deep in hushing pine-needles; shadows of morning and evening will be the only change of shifts. The pay-rolls are closed; the last crushing has gone through the mill. The grave of ten millions is for sale cheap, with a thousand feet of water in it.

Rose Hartwick Thorpe

(1850–1939)

THE PIONEERS AND their offspring were a mobile group. They moved
west, bought land or homesteaded, farmed, ranched or set up shop.
After a few years, drought, locusts, clouded land titles, sickness, failed
businesses, or restlessness motivated them to seek greener pastures. In
the *Little House* books, Laura Ingalls Wilder dramatized the life of one
family searching for the American dream in Wisconsin, Minnesota,
Kansas, and South Dakota. Abraham Lincoln had a similar story. So did
Rose Hartwick Thorpe.

In 1850, Rose Hartwick was born to pioneer parents in Mishawka,
Indiana. When she was ten, her father, a tailor, suffered business set-
backs. The Hartwicks joined family in Kansas, where drought killed
their farming prospects. In 1861, they moved to Litchfield, Michigan.
There, the insecure, imaginative schoolgirl composed poetry on slate
and scraps of paper. At sixteen, she read an anonymous story in
Peterson's magazine that triggered the poem "Curfew Must Not Ring
To-night"—a melodramatic ballad of love, danger, civil war, and a
woman's courage. Although the poem was not published until three
years later, it became one of the most famous ballads of the late nineteenth century, reprinted and illustrated in Europe as well as America.
As with Poe's "Raven," students across the country recited "Curfew,"
and popular poets such as Carolyn Wells parodied it. "Curfew" was included in most late–nineteenth-century anthologies. But the naive
schoolgirl was never paid for the work.

In 1871, Rose Hartwick married Edmund Carson Thorpe, a carriage
maker. The following year they had a daughter. At a time when wives
were expected to keep house and pay social visits to neighbors, Rose was
timid and retiring. She preferred writing to socializing.

In her mid-twenties Rose was paid for a poem published in *Youth's
Companion*. Despite frail health, she helped support her husband and
daughter by selling articles and poetry to newspapers, children's magazines such as *St. Nicholas,* and religious periodicals. She also wrote and
edited children's stories and monthly magazines with temperance, religious, and moralistic themes. A collection of her early poems, *Ringing
Ballads,* was published in 1887.

When Edmund Thorpe contracted tuberculosis, the family moved to San Antonio for four years before relocating in San Diego. The California climate helped them both physically and emotionally. In return, Rose sent glowing accounts of southern California life to the eastern periodicals. She also published *The Poetical Works of Rose Hartwick Thorpe* and *The White Lady of La Jolla,* a mix of travel commentary, poetry, and ghost story.

Throughout her adult life, Thorpe worked as a writer. Yet, none of her conventional work would ever again strike as deep and universal a chord as did "Curfew."

Curfew Must Not Ring To-night

England's sun was slowly setting o'er the hill-tops far away,
Filling all the land with beauty at the close of one sad day;
And its last rays kissed the forehead of a man and maiden fair,—
He with steps so slow and weary; she with sunny, floating hair;
He with bowed head, sad and thoughtful; she, with lips so cold and white,
Struggled to keep back the murmur, "Curfew must not ring to-night."

"Sexton," Bessie's white lips faltered, pointing to the prison old,
With its walls so tall and gloomy, moss-grown walls dark, damp and cold,—
"I've a lover in that prison, doomed this very night to die
At the ringing of the curfew; and no earthly help is nigh.
Cromwell will not come till sunset;" and her lips grew strangely white,
As she spoke in husky whispers, "Curfew must not ring to-night."

"Bessie," calmly spoke the sexton (every word pierced her young heart
Like a gleaming death-winged arrow, like a deadly poisoned dart),
"Long, long years I've rung the curfew from that gloomy, shadowed tower;
Every evening, just at sunset, it has tolled the twilight hour.
I have done my duty ever, tried to do it just and right:
Now I'm old, I will not miss it. Curfew bell must ring to-night!"

Wild her eyes and pale her features, stern and white her thoughtful brow;
And within her heart's deep centre Bessie made a solemn vow.
She had listened while the judges read, without a tear or sigh,—
"At the ringing of the curfew Basil Underwood *must die.*"
And her breath came fast and faster, and her eyes grew large and bright;
One low murmur, faintly spoken, "Curfew *must not* ring to-night!"

She with quick step bounded forward, sprang within the old church-door,
Left the old man coming slowly, paths he'd trod so oft before.
Not one moment paused the maiden, but with cheek and brow aglow,
Staggered up the gloomy tower, where the bell swung to and fro;
As she climbed the slimy ladder, on which fell no ray of light,
Upward still, her pale lips saying, "Curfew *shall not* ring to-night!"

She has reached the topmost ladder; o'er her hangs the great, dark bell;
Awful is the gloom beneath her, like the pathway down to hell.
See! the ponderous tongue is swinging; 'tis the hour of curfew now,
And the sight has chilled her bosom, stopped her breath, and paled her brow.
Shall she let it ring? No, never! Her eyes flash with sudden light,
As she springs and grasps it firmly: "Curfew *shall not* ring to-night!"

Out she swung,—far out. The city seemed a speck of light below,—
There 'twixt heaven and earth suspended, as the bell swung to and fro.
And the sexton at the bell-rope, old and deaf, heard not the bell,
Sadly thought that twilight curfew rang young Basil's funeral knell.
Still the maiden, clinging firmly, quivering lip and fair face white,
Stilled her frightened heart's wild beating: *"Curfew shall not ring to-night!"*

It was o'er, the bell ceased swaying; and the maiden stepped once more
Firmly on the damp old ladder, where, for hundred years before,
Human foot had not been planted. The brave deed that she had done
Should be told long ages after. As the rays of setting sun
Light the sky with golden beauty, aged sires, with heads of white,
Tell the children why the curfew did not ring that one sad night.

O'er the distant hills comes Cromwell. Bessie sees him; and her brow,
Lately white with sickening horror, has no anxious traces now.
At his feet she tells her story, shows her hands all bruised and torn;
And her sweet young face, still haggard, with the anguish it had worn,
Touched his heart with sudden pity, lit his eyes with misty light.
"Go! your lover lives," cried Cromwell. "Curfew shall not ring to-night."

Wide they flung the massive portals, led the prisoner forth to die,
All his bright young life before him. 'Neath the darkening English sky,
Bessie came, with flying footsteps, eyes aglow with lovelight sweet;
Kneeling on the turf beside him, laid his pardon at his feet.
In his brave, strong arms he clasped her, kissed the face upturned and white,
Whispered, "Darling you have saved me, Curfew will not ring to-night."

THE FAITHFUL LITTLE motor puffs impatiently, and throbs in labored breathings preparatory to carrying its burden of expectant humanity on one of its tri-daily trips from San Diego to the famous sea-side resort, La Jolla. There are picnic parties out from the city for a day on the beach. There are tourists from beyond the Rockies, and from the Old World. Some of these are of such decided individuality that they present unmistakable characteristics of state and nationality. The intellectual Bostonian, severely precise in every detail of dress and speech, perceptibly shocked at the western idioms, southern vernacularism, and wanton disregard of correct English that pulsate the air on all sides of her; the two ruddy Englishmen lounging in indolent comfort apparently unconscious of the fact that a delicate woman, with the fatal hectic flush on her cheeks, is standing in the aisle near them, having failed to secure a seat in the crowded coach; the family from Michigan, noisy boys and laughing girls, enjoying their outing with rollicking spontaneity; the woman from Colorado, dominative and self-assertive, the majesty of whose presence submerges and overwhelms the timid Hoosier school marm who has offered the royal lady a seat beside her; the sweet-faced mother and elderly gentleman from "the blue grass country;" the loud voiced Texan; the eastern capitalist; the Kansas farmer; the languid-eyed Mexican; the tawny Scotchman. It is, indeed, a miscellaneous company representing many of the states, and all conditions of life. It is, in fact, California in miniature, for California is peopled, not only with the overflow of the states, but with that of the whole world.

Of all this constant stream of humanity drifting in and out of La Jolla but few have heard of the beautiful white lady who stands at the mouth of one of the caves. To some she is only an accidental formation of nature, but she is a marvel and a mystery to those who, having known her in life, recognize an acquaintance in the specter of the caves.

Nature made La Jolla and man can neither add to nor take from the charm of her attractions. The pretty sea-side cottages that crown the high-lands, overlooking the ocean, with their wide porches and variety of architecture are an interesting spectacle, but these are not La Jolla.

The boom, boom of gigantic breakers beating their unconquerable strength against the rocks, and dashing the foam of their rage hundreds of feet in the air, with the marvelous ocean ever surging back of them, hold you with a mystic fascination, but these are not La Jolla. The merry bathers in the surf, and the little children with their bright dresses making dashes of color on shell beach from June to June the year's long day, are ever a pleasure and a delight, but they are not La Jolla. All these are common to sea-side resorts, but the magnificent handiwork of that grand old sculptor, Father Pacific, in his peculiar formations and ornamentations of the huge rocks which Mother Nature has placed convenient for his use: Cathedral Rock, the Fisherman's Bridge, Alligator Head, and especially the deep, mysterious caves from whence its name originated, these are the most attractive features of La Jolla. These are La Jolla. . . .

The murmur of the sea is in your ears, its saline fingers cling to your garments, and touch your lips with soft caresses. Your practical other self slips away from you under the mesmeric influence of this dream inviting presence, and wandering on and on you enter the great caves, and become fascinated with the novelties of the animal and vegetable life in the solitudes of these rock-ribbed caverns. You take no heed of the passage of time, or the distance over which your eager feet have traveled.

Here upon a rock is a specimen of sea-weed, pink as the heart of a rose, its delicate tracery like finest lace-work, yonder is a whole community of squirming inhabitants carrying their houses on their backs, and conducting their affairs of state after their own best approved methods. A step farther and another interest attracts your attention, absorbing your thoughts with animated speculation. Presently becoming weary of the rock-walled, rock-floored cavern, you turn your face to its entrance and are startled by the spectacle that meets your gaze.

There, in the mouth of the cave, filling its entire space, stands a tall, white lady. She is robed in shimmering garments of light, wrapped in a misty veil, and on her head is a wreath like a coronet of orange blossoms. You see at a glance that she is beautiful, and stately as a queen, for though her features are not visible, the outlines of her graceful form are perfect in every detail. She stands in an expectant attitude, with her face turned to the right as if listening. One hand is partly raised, and you know instinctively that she is in search of some one. Her dress falls in rain-bow tinted folds to her feet, and sweeps in a long, billowy train over the uneven surface of the rock-strewn entrance.

You stand breathless with amazement. Heretofore your philosophy admitted no credence of the white lady of La Jolla, but can your eyes deceive you? Behold, she stands before you trailing her bridal robes over the slimy stones. She has taken possession of the cave with her radiant presence, whose only substance is light. You can see the foam-flecked waters tossing back of her, and, looking directly through her discover a row boat drifting idly with the tide while matters of greater importance than its guidance occupy the couple whose heads lean closer as hearts speak through the windows of the soul. Presently the boat drifts past, and once more the white lady holds solitary possession of the entrance. As you stand there lost in amazement and conjecture, a wave rushes past her, submerges her train, and creeping in, touches the hem of your dress with damp, chilly fingers. You are startled from your surprised discovery with a sudden premonition of danger, and hastily seeking a place of safety you recall the story of the white lady, as related to you that morning.

Mrs. Trumbar is one of the many lodging-house keepers in San Diego, and although only an ordinary woman to all appearances she is, in fact, an unabridged volume of reminiscences connected with the old Spanish-American settlement of San Diego, and adjacent country. Nothing escapes her observation, and she never forgets.

There is much of the supernatural connected with the romantic history of San Diego, and it is often difficult to discern just where the real event is merged in the imaginative. Tradition affirms that departed spirits habitually wander about lonely places at all hours after sunset, and startle the belated tourist in his search for curious specimens of land and sea to add to his collection. Who has not heard of the cowled padre of the San Diego mission who, on moonlight nights, wanders restlessly up and down, over and under the ruined aqueduct beyond the mission walls, as if inspecting the work, and assuring himself that his army of Indian laborers are performing it satisfactorily? And who has not heard of the beautiful Indian maiden searching for her recreant lover through the canyons and among the tangled growth of Point Loma? Parties camping in Mission Valley have seen the old padre, and tourists have caught fleeting glimpses of the Indian maiden.

And there are other stories. Mrs. Trumbar can tell you all about them, relating each story in detail, and giving you minute directions how and when to approach the scene of the ghostly wanderings in order to obtain the best results and be convinced that she has not deceived you.

As you prepare for your day's outing Mrs. Trumbar approaches from the kitchen, wiping the dish-water from her brown fingers on her apron (she is always washing dishes, it seems to you), and begins:

"What place do you visit today?" adding, before you can reply, "I might suggest—oh, it's La Jolla, is it[?] Well, you'll enjoy the day out there, I can tell you. Let me see—" whisking the daily paper from a pile of like literature on the stand in the corner of the room, and finding the tide table. Her moist forefinger follows down the column and finally halts with a satisfactory pressure, and the anxiety lifts from her face as she announces that you have chosen the right day to visit La Jolla, regardless of the fact that in planning your trip you have evidently consulted the tide table for yourself.

"It is all right," she informs you. "It will be low tide at noon. You are just in luck. You can see the white lady best at the noon hour."

"Ever heard of the white lady of the caves?" she continues as you fasten a coil of your hair in place, and proceed with other details of your toilet. You are a little fearful that her narrative may crowd upon your time, but the slight negative movement of your head is sufficient encouragement. She accordingly settles herself comfortably in the generous rocker that sways her ample figure to and fro as she relates the story.

"Never heard of her? Well, now. I must tell you, or you'll miss half the interest of the trip. It's like visiting Europe without a guide, or any knowledge of the places you're going to see, to go to La Jolla without having heard the story of the beautiful bride, and—oh, yes, her husband, too, of course.

"It was long before 'the boom,' before the railroad came, and almost before the world knew that there *was* such a place as San Diego. There were only a few families of us living here then, in what was San Diego, but is now called Old Town, and we used to get what comfort we could out of life in this lonesome corner of the world. Some families had come over to New Town, but we were not among them.

"One year between Thanksgiving and Christmas time a young couple came down in the stage from Los Angeles and stopped at my house. All the best people stopped at my house in them days, but the big hotels have fairly crowded me out since the boom. Though, to be sure," with an apprehensive glance at you, and a quick indrawing of the breath, "the best people often stop with me now.

"These young folks I was speaking about were on their wedding trip; though, dear sakes alive! it must have been a hard one, all the way down from Los Angeles in that bumpy old stage. I can't imagine what ever induced them to come a traipsin' away down here to the end of the earth, unless it was to get away from everybody, and be all by themselves. I can see the bride this minute as she came up the walk that day, as tall as any queen, and every bit as handsome, too. Her eyes were as blue as the gentian flowers I used to gather when I was a little girl, and somehow I always thought of them whenever I looked at her. And her dresses! Why a queen might well have envied them, they were that fine. I remember of telling Maria (Maria was my sister, and lived with me then, but she has died since, poor dear); I remember well of telling her that I thought it a burning shame to waste all of them pretty dresses in an out-of-the-way corner like this. But I don't imagine she had them made specially for San Diego, and being a bride she had to have them anyhow.

"Yes, I know you'll have to be off pretty soon, so I'll hasten with the story. The bride—their name was Hathaway, to match their fine clothes, but I always called her 'the bride'—she wanted to visit every lonely place she could hear of, and couldn't hardly content herself to rest up from that tiresome trip down from Los Angeles. I fixed up my best bedroom for them, and laid myself out to make her feel at home. I flatter meself that I succeeded, too, for the morning they started for La Jolla she was as chipper as a bird, the poor dear.

"Mr. Hathaway engaged Trumbar to drive them to La Jolla, and I put up a lunch for them good enough to make a king's mouth water, if I do say it. There was cold turkey left over from Sunday's dinner, and pickle-lily, and pound cake, and olives raised on a tree of our own, and mince pie in a tin can to keep it from mussin', and—I can't begin to remember half of the good things I put in that basket, but there wasn't a bite of it eaten by any one, for they, poor souls, never came back again, and Trumbar was that frightened and worried that he never even opened the basket, or thought of eating."

A moment of impressive silence, and Mrs. Trumbar resumes:

"It was pitch dark before Trumbar got home that night, and I was nearly beside myself with anxiety, but the minute I set eyes on him I knew that some terrible thing had happened, for he looked like an old man, and shook as if he had an ague chill all the while he was telling me about it. He said that as soon as they reached La Jolla the young couple went off hunting for shells and sea things along the beach, and finally wandered off in the direction of the caves.

After he had unhitched and fed the horses he found a comfortable place, and smoked for a while, then feeling drowsy, stretched out in the sunshine and took a nap. He said he must have slept a long time for when he awakened he was sort of numb all over. He had hardly whipped the feeling back into his fingers when he heard a cry of terror coming from the direction of the caves, and he knew in a minute that it was the bride calling to her husband. He ran to the place where he could see the caves, and there, away at almost at the fartherest one stood Mrs. Hathaway at the entrance. He saw that the tide had turned and was running in so strong that a wave splashed over her feet, and seemed to catch at her with its awful white fingers. She was so timid about venturing near the water that he knew something had happened to whip up her courage to that extent, for the roaring of the sea behind her, and the darkness of the caves must have appalled her. Probably Mr. Hathaway had left her with the story book she had brought with her, while he went inside, and become so intent on what he was finding that he hadn't noticed the tide was rising. It was rolling in pretty strong before she discovered it, and becoming frightened at her husband's long stay, had gone in search of him.

"Trumbar tried to get to her, but he was a long distance away with a lot of climbing to do getting down to her. When he came to the bluff overlooking the caves, he called to her to come back at once, for he could see that a monstrous wave was coming, but it was useless, as he knew, for no sound of his voice could reach her through all that distance. She began flinging her arms about and wringing her hands, and just at that moment a big wave rushed in with an awful sound, and"— with a hush in her voice, and a spasmodic catch in her breath, "and that was all. Trumbar never saw either of them after that, though he waited about, calling and watching, hoping to see their bodies, if nothing more.

"It was almost night before he started for home, and by that time the caves were full of water, and he knew there was no use waiting any longer.

"The next day Trumbar and two of our neighbors drove to La Jolla, though they knew before they started that it was useless, and that they would never see the young couple again, unless the waves washed their bodies ashore. They spent the whole day searching the caves and the rocks, but they found no trace of them, not even so much as the book Mrs. Hathaway had left on the rocks when she went in search of her husband, for the tide had been uncommon high during the night, and had washed even that away.

"When the searchers came home that night we knew that we must try to find the friends of the young couple, and in looking over their belongings we found the address of her folks. We wrote to them at once, telling them of the dreadful thing that had happened to their daughter and her husband. After a few weeks (it took a long time in them days to make the trip) her brother came on, and nothing would do but he must go to the place where his sister had lost her life. So one day Trumbar and I drove him over to La Jolla.

"I put up a good lunch for I knew we would need considerable sustaining during the ordeal that was before us, to say nothing of the long, tiresome ride through the sage brush. The minute we got to La Jolla the young man (Ross Willard was his name, and he was tall and handsome like his sister) was for going right on to the cave where Trumbar had last seen her. The nearest way was down an almost perpendicular gully of loose shale, and the most we could do was to slide from top to bottom. Ross Willard went ahead, and as we was a-slipping and a-sliding down that awful place I could not help thinking how like a funeral procession it was, with this young man who had come so many miles to visit the only grave his poor sister would probably ever have, and we two, who had learned to like the young couple so much in the little while we had known them, following along behind. I was pretty tired when we got to the bottom, for there wasn't any steps to make it easy for one in them days as there is now, and if I'd been as heavy as I am now I never could have got down in the world. When we reached the bottom I would like to have rested a bit and got my breath, but Ross Willard rushed ahead, and we followed as fast as we could.

"He hurried into the cave as though he expected to find his sister there. He disappeared into the one where Trumbar had last seen her, and as he turned to speak to us a look came into his face that I'll never forget if I live a hundred years. We were following him, and our backs were to the light, but his face was toward the opening, and as he turned it suddenly went white, and he cried out:

"My sister! Look there! It is Bertha in her wedding dress!"

"We turned, and there she stood in the mouth of the cave, on the very spot where death had found her. She didn't have on the traveling dress she wore that day, but was dressed in her wedding gown. We could see the orange wreath in her hair, and her long train spread out over the stones. It was as if the whole entrance had formed her shape. It wasn't just the outlines of a woman. It was Mrs. Hathaway. You come to know a woman as much by her form as by her face, and Mrs. Hathaway was rather uncommon in her build. She was taller and more graceful than most women, carrying her head erect with a dignity that would have seemed haughty if it had not been for the sweet graciousness of her manner.

"When I saw her, standing there like life, I was that frightened you could have knocked me down with a feather, but all Ross Willard seemed to think of was to get to her at once. He pushed Trumbar aside and started for the place where she was standing. We turned and followed, but all at once she disappeared, and the opening was just like any other.["]

Mrs. Trumbar's voice is hushed. The clock ticks loudly on the mantel. The piping voice of a mocking-bird drifts in through the open window. Little awesome chills creep up your back, and you find that in spite of your philosophy the story you have mentally designated as a pretty invention has strangely impressed you.

"We are quite sure," Mrs. Trumbar continues after a momentary pause, during which her fingers have pulled nervously at a broken splint in the chair, "that the one place where the bride is visible is the spot where her young husband stood when he heard her voice calling to him, and looking up discovered her with the great wave rolling in at her back, on that fatal day. It may be that the ocean repents the destruction of those two young lives, and has chiseled her form from the edges of the rocks, and set it in the entrance of the cave as a warning to others, but I will never admit that the likeness is just accidental. It is too perfect."

Carrie Adell Green Strahorn

(1854–1925)

A s WAVES OF PIONEERS opened up the frontier west of Iowa and Missouri, the slavery issue became the focal point of fierce debate. Congress struggled both to organize new territories and to maintain the balance of power between slave and free states. Sen. Stephen A. Douglas proposed allowing residents of each new state to vote on the slavery issue—the concept of "popular sovereignty." Yet, problems arose over division of the Nebraska Territory into two new states. The Nebraska Territory, part of the Louisiana Purchase, lay north of latitude 36°30' where slavery was prohibited by the Missouri Compromise of 1820. Congress could not legally allow one of the new states to vote for slavery. Congress solved the problem by passing the Kansas-Nebraska Act on May 30, 1854, which repealed the Missouri Compromise and paved the way for bloody fighting in Kansas over the future of slavery in that state. More than two hundred people died in the conflict, a tragic prelude to the Civil War. But on January 29, 1861, as the South broke away from the Union, Kansas was admitted as a free state.

The year Congress passed the Kansas-Nebraska Act, Carrie Adell Green was born in Marengo, Illinois, a small town in the Mississippi Valley. After the war, her father, John, a surgeon and Civil War veteran, and mother, Louise, moved to the Midwest. Carrie, the middle of three daughters, studied music at the University of Michigan and overseas. In 1877, she married Robert Edmund "Pard" Strahorn, a printer, newspaper reporter, editor, Sioux War correspondent, railroad agent, builder of northwest railroads, and executive. Jay Gould hired him as a "literary agent" for the Union Pacific Railroad the same year. Pard insisted on taking his wife along on his adventures, and she contributed to the pamphlets and guidebooks he wrote to promote tourism and western settlement.

When Carrie went west in 1877, there was only one railroad linking the East and West Coasts: the Union Pacific and Central Railroad. The Strahorns traveled not only by rail but also by stagecoach, horse, wagon, and foot. Pard ostensibly toured the backcountry to describe the glories of the frontier, but all the while was secretly searching out potential railroad routes. "Dell's" book was not written until the twentieth century, when the tracks were in and the need for secrecy was past.

Fifteen Thousand Miles by Stage, published three years after Martha Summerhayes's *Vanished Arizona,* is part travel guide, part memoir. Strahorn purposefully omits "the excessive fatigue and hardships" of her journeys, stressing the positive aspects of every place. The tone is uniformly bright, the adventures in every western state and territory told with understated humor and captured in drawings by Charles M. Russell. Carrie Strahorn was the first white woman to completely explore Yellowstone. Readers followed her through Glacier and Rocky Mountain National Parks, across the Bannock War lines in 1878, and into the depths of a Montana mine. She encountered bandits, Indians, runaway horses, and overturned stages; hiked Gray's Peak in an electrical storm; forded rivers; and slept on bare ground. The only negative notes are when she patronizes Native Americans and castigates Mormon men for enslaving their wives.

The Strahorns had no children. Instead, they founded towns across southern Idaho and eastern Oregon, moving on when the fledgling settlements took root. Hailey, Shoshone, Caldwell, Mountain Home, Payette, and Ontario were a few of their projects. All still exist. In 1898, enthralled by the beauty of eastern Washington, they settled in Spokane.

After *Fifteen Thousand Miles by Stage,* Strahorn continued to publish articles on western life until her death at age seventy-one.

ॐ From *Fifteen Thousand Miles by Stage: A Woman's Unique Experience during Thirty Years of Path Finding and Pioneering from the Missouri to the Pacific and from Alaska to Mexico*

Chapter III

Black Hawk and Central—Georgetown and Gray's Peak

IT WAS PAST THE middle of November when we left Denver on a bright Sunday morning to enjoy the glories of Clear Creek Canyon and to penetrate the mysteries of the Black Hawk mines. I felt especially interested in this trip because it was there and at Central City in 1871 that Pard had worked at the printer's case so arduously, and made a record far beyond his co-workers in the number of "ems" he could correctly set up in a given time, always working early and late that he might supply his invalid father with help for family needs.

The wonders of Clear Creek Canyon are not so unknown to the world now, and do not need minute description. The narrow-gauge rail line was considered a most wonderful achievement in engineering, with its towering cliffs on the one side, and the torrents of rushing waters on the other. We crossed and re-crossed the rocky gorge, reviewing the frowning cliffs and foamy depths, gaining a glimpse of our engine as we rounded some sharp curve, or rolled under a projecting shelf that threatened to fall upon the baby train. . . .

In the party for that day was a retired banker from Boston, a man genial and companionable, who entered into the spirit of enjoyment with great zest, but he amazed everybody by asking if we were *west of Omaha*. When he saw the consternation depicted on the several faces, he said he really did not know where he was, that he had bought a round-trip ticket to the Coast including several intermediate trips, but he did not know how far he was along although he had spent several days in Denver.

Our train was carrying a "Pinafore" company up to the mountain towns that morning, and as it was waiting at the forks of Clear Creek for the down express we heard an altercation between a man and his wife belonging to the company which suddenly culminated in the man rushing from the car saying "Good-bye"; he sprang to the platform, and, before any one realized his intent he stepped up on to the framework of the bridge and jumped into the creek. The water was very high and the current running with a fall of a hundred and fifty feet to the mile. He made frantic efforts to save himself, but to no avail, and even his body could not be recovered. It was a great shock to the company with whom he was a general favorite as their "Dick Dead Eye." It seemed impossible that he meant to do more than frighten his wife, for he was such a clever, good-natured man, always doing something to entertain the company. The distracted (?) wife offered $25 reward for the return of the body if covered with the new suit of clothes which he wore when he was drowned.

Ever and anon dark holes in the mountainsides would prove the love of man for gold, and his untiring efforts to draw out the very vitals of our mother-earth. Mother Grundy beamed upon us as we whizzed past, while the donkey pictured in the pinnacles above had more the appearance of wishing himself nearer that he might enjoy his hereditary amusement of landing all intruders at the foot of the hills. The "old frog" seemed ready to begin his evening melody as soon as the shadows lengthened, but he looked as contented as though he had not been sitting bolt upright on his stony hind legs for ages and criticised by every passing man, woman, and child.

The high, towering cliffs were as grand and majestic as though the storms of centuries had not fought and striven to crush them to the earth; and who can tell how many centuries they may yet hold their mighty sway over the dark shadows of the canyon with its mass of human habitants. The unruly waters of the creek went rushing and seething over the rocks in their wild race to the sea. The mountains, the pictured rocks, and the roaring waters wove around us such a spell that the cry of the brakeman for Black Hawk seemed like a sacrilegious intrusion in the sanctum of our deepest and purest thoughts. But the spell was broken and we descended to earth to find ourselves still of the earth with human beings round about us.

When we made the first trip up this canyon the track was laid only to Black Hawk. While the Central City station was only a mile farther up the gulch, the rail line had to circuit about and zigzag for four miles among the gold mines on the mountainside to make the grade. Workmen were busy all along the distance hurrying the work to completion.

The altitude of Central City is 8300 feet above sea-level or nearly twice that of Denver. There was no hotel in Black Hawk, but at Central City the "Teller House," built by our good friend Senator Teller, was as fine as any country hotel in the State. Most streets of Central City were not over twenty feet wide, and the houses looked like bird cages hung on hooks jutting out from the mountainsides. Nearly every house was reached by a flight of stairs, and though it might be two or three stories high on the lower side, there would be an entrance on a level with the top floor on the upper side. Pard pointed out one rickety building where, in 1871, his dextrous fingers picked type out of the case at the rate of seven dollars per day, which amount, however, he found harder to collect than to set the type. But the more thrifty looking Central City *register* Office, where Col. Frank Hall did the newspaper business on a cash basis, furnished many a remittance to Pard's sick folks at home.

The Hill Smelting Works were then in this canyon, and covered four acres of ground. Professor Hill (later Colorado's United States Senator) took great pride in explaining the remarkable twenty-seven stages of treating the ore before it was lumped into the beautiful stacks of bullion piled on the office floor. Fifty-two tons of ore were treated daily and that was considered a large day's turnout at that time. Fifty cords of wood were daily consumed in smelting the fifty tons of ore. The expense of running the smelter was on an average of five hundred dollars per day.

The Bobtail gold mine tunnel was in the western part of the town. With lighted torches and rubber clothing we penetrated twenty-two hundred feet into the secret chest of mother-earth to see where she stored her wealth. We also visited other mines and scenic places. Pard to gather his statistics of productions, and I to study the people and the social ways, and both to marvel at the wondrous handiwork of our great Creator.

Next morning by half-past seven o'clock we were on our way through Virginia Canyon to Idaho Springs, a distance of only seven miles, but wonderful in its scenic grandeur. It was over this route that the stage drivers made some memorable records on the last four miles, sometimes making that distance in twelve minutes. General Grant and his daughter Nellie were put through at a four-minute gait, and when the General protested against such speed the driver coolly said his own neck was as dear as anybody's and the General need not worry.

It was here also that Horace Greeley paid an extra fare to be taken to Idaho Springs in time to catch a train to Denver. There had been a cloudburst down the north fork and it had washed out the track below Black Hawk, and the great Horace had an appointment to meet and he needed speed. Driving like a madman down the steep grade was too much, however, for Mr. Greeley; he tried to call the driver down, while striving also to hold himself on the coach, but the man with the ribbons called to him: "Keep your seat Horace, you will be there in time. You won't have to walk."

The wind blew a gale, but over one mountain and another we sped along, passing Old Chief, Squaw, and Papoose mountains, swinging the curves and corners of the road, glancing nervously at the depths and heights and wishing we might moderate the pace as earnestly as Horace Greeley or General Grant could have done, yet with no more influence over the Jehu than the squirrels of the woods chirping their incense at human intrusion.

About midway of the canyon lived a peculiar hermit, in an old long cabin, and the man's possessions were chiefly his dog and horse. The queer old man would find a mine and sell it for some price, then get drunk and stay drunk while the money lasted. When he started off on his spree he turned his horse and dog loose on the hills to care for themselves. The dog would follow the horse all day and drive it to the barn at night, watch by the door until morning, when they would both start out together again. We saw the horse feeding on the mountain grass and his faithful attendant lying a few feet away, waiting for the master's return. No one could learn what the dog subsisted on, for he never left his duty to forage. . . .

On another trip in summer we made the ride over to Bear Creek which was full of romance and grandeur. A gradual ascent over a smooth road along the bank of Bear Creek was a joy not to forget. Wild roses bloomed in profusion, sweet syringa, wild columbine, daisies, and purple flagg grew in confusion along the rocks and hedges. The most remarkable flower to me was that of the soap plant, or soap weed, an unromantic name given it because of the soapy quality of its root. The stalks grew about twenty inches high, and many had fully forty blossoms on a stem that looked like so many water lilies on a stalk. These weeds were very plentiful and would make a fine showing in any Eastern collection of house plants. The leaves of the plant are long and narrow, with very sharp points, and are used extensively in the manufacture of paper.

The only defacement in this canyon was a frequent sign warning the followers of Isaak Walton that no fishing was allowed. One cunning nimrod made himself famous by ingeniously reaching the head waters and wading down the bed of the creek. A wrathy ranchman discovered the young man, clad to the neck in rubber, coolly casting his fly and unmindful of all threats that the irate rancher could hurl at him. At last the infuriated owner lunged into the water to drag out the trespasser, but the hook and line man only went into deeper water, and continued to pull up the speckled beauties. He said he came with the water from the mountain top and had a right to stay with it, then deftly he lured the irate landowner into a deep hole, at the same time telling him that when he was wet enough he had better get out of the water. It was a most exasperating condition for the landowner and he left the water and the river vowing vengeance in "blue hot air," as he went dripping into the woods towards his cabin. . . .

Georgetown, a few miles above Idaho Springs, was then the heart of the mining section, and there General Marshall provided us with riding horses, and with his son for a guide we made the climb to the head of Clear Creek, where the waters were indeed as clear as molten crystal. We could look down on the "Silver Queen," as Georgetown was often called, with her four thousand inhabitants, where she made a mere speck in the distant valley. We visited many a "prospect" and "salted" mine, but the point of greatest interest was the Colorado Central mine. At a depth of two hundred and fifty feet we took a pick and hacked out pieces of silver ore from a vein that averaged $450 to the ton. The top of this mine was at an elevation of 12,000 feet above the sea-level, and it was entered through a tunnel 1360 feet long at the end of which 800 feet of mother-earth hung over us. The tunnel also led to the underground hall where was held one of the grandest and most unique balls ever given. There were eight rows of lights extending full length of the tunnel, and the silver walls were draped in bunting from end to end. The ball-room, thus cut out of the heart of the mountain, and which was later the machinery hall, was a blaze of light and beauty, for many ladies from the capital city and other towns of the West came in their richest gowns and made the function one of the most beautiful, novel, and weird known in mining history.

To one reared on Illinois prairies the wooded hills and timber chutes were intensely interesting. Often a chute is several thousand feet long that the timber cut on the mountain can be run to the bottom with lightening speed. It rains every day in and above Georgetown, just a shower about noon. The shower was as sure as the strike of a clock all summer long, and its great regularity rendered irrigation or sprinkling unnecessary to crops or lawns. One man along our way had a four-acre patch of potatoes which netted him $2500 a year. The sun shines only about six hours for the longest day in Georgetown, then the mountains hide it and there is only a mellow twilight after 3 P.M. . . .

To visit the summit of the universe was an inspiration not to be neglected and Gray's Peak with its altitude of 14,341 feet was then supposed to be the nearest point to heaven that one could reach on horseback. It was the dome of our continental divide, and its electrical summit had not sufficient terror to deter us from scaling its dizzy heights. From Georgetown the drive was a charming one. The carriage was luxurious and for ten miles along the beautiful toll road to the Kelso ranch the receding lowlands spread out in wondrous glory below us. Our carriage was well loaded, for aside from having four people in the party we had to carry our saddles for the ride to the summit. We spent a joyous evening at the ranch before a huge grate fire, where several fine dogs surrounding the fireplace made a picture of comfort that any artist might have coveted. . . .

One Mr. Case, the Union Pacific ticket agent of Idaho Springs, and my sister were with us and shared some peculiar phenomena away up in the clouds that came wondrously near leaving our friend Mr. Case on the summit, and gave us a scare that put lightening in our heels to get down from our pedestal. . . .

The peak was covered with small, flat stones from base to summit, making the trail a shifting one and affording only a loose sliding foothold. Near the top is a large spring where one can refresh himself, and where comfort would dictate to spread the lunch, unless one carries timber along for a fire on the summit, where it is intensely cold.

The clouds were full of freaks that drew forth loud exclamations of wonder and surprise. They would wind their snowy sheets round the base of the peak and intertwine among the lesser hills, then rise and fall full of rainbow splendor. At one time a seeming wall reached thousands of feet above us and extending to the base of the mountains slowly approached us. It seemed that nothing could save us—that we must be crowded off our pedestal and dashed on the rocks. There was no break in the moving mass, and nearer and nearer it came. We stood in terror and awe of what might happen, yet in defiance we waited its approach, until with all the gentleness of a Mother's arms we were enveloped in a sheet of blinding snow. So softly it fell, so still was the air, that no one spoke, and scarcely had our senses begun to shape themselves to earthly things again than the clouds rolled on in their great white purity, leaving us numb with fear and cold.

The little cabin on the summit was half full of snow and ice, the glass in the windows all broken; even the roof had long since given way on one side from its weight of snow, and its fallen timbers confined the clear space of the room to one corner. We clapped our hands, we danced, and jumped about to get warm, then we spread our lunch which we had brought with us. There was not a sliver of wood to make the least bit of a fire, but we drank our cold coffee and ate our sandwiches with a relish that an epicure might envy.

Some one had evidently been there before us, and not satisfied with leaving his name and address on a stone slab, he added a further identification of himself in the statement that he was the "first d—— fool of the season."

While enjoying the novel experience of our surroundings we suddenly heard a crackling in one corner of the roof that sounded like a bunch of rattlesnakes. Not stopping to think that snakes could not live in that altitude, we rushed madly from the cabin, looked upon the roof, and around the ground on the new fallen snow, but saw no evidence of any living thing. The men looked after the horses to see if they were securely tied and found them showing great evidences of fear. When they were gently patted to assure them of their safety, the men were subjected to such thrills of electric currents that they were nearly struck dumb. One declared his mustache assumed life, the other that every individual hair on his head stood up straight. In trying to point to the location of the first noise, flames flew from the finger tips, and every pat on a horse's body would bring out fire. It surely was an electrical storm that we had not been advised about, and therefore knew not the danger we were in. When miners realize that one of these storms is coming on they lose no time in getting down to timberline, but ignorance was bliss and fortunately no more serious effects occurred than to have Mr. Case stunned enough to fall, and though he was soon restored we could not dispel the strange feelings that had so nearly overpowered the entire party.

The snow-storm that had passed over us had dropped into the valley and become black as night from which forks of ragged lightening sent its glimmering lights back to us. The storm clouds seemed to fairly bump against a mountain in the great abyss below, causing them to rebound and float back over the same locality again until they struck another mountain, then to be whirled through a canyon away out of sight.

We had been so absorbed in watching the grand panorama below that we had failed to see a second wall coming toward us. This time it was not the fleecy white of unfallen snow, but a wall as black as the starless midnight. We saw the lightning flash in it and clouds whirl among themselves as they came steadily on.

The great black mass came floating toward us with tokens of danger not to be trifled with. There was no need of words for haste; we snatched our bridles, not waiting to mount, but hurried down the trail, fairly dragging the poor horses who stumbled at every step in their haste over the loose shale trail. Over a mile was left behind when we stopped for a moment's rest; we, too, tumbled and tripped over the rocky way intent only on reaching lower ground. The lightning flashed and the thunder reverberated round about us, echoing from peak to peak. Then the storm began to break in fury. We mounted our horses the first moment that we could make any time by doing so, but we could not escape the torrents of water that came pouring down upon us, and we raced madly on until we reached the Kelso ranch. Tired and wet as we were, we dared not delay, and quickly getting the horses into harness again continued the race with the elements to Georgetown. Such a cloudburst in the canyons and valleys below, and we must keep ahead of it if possible. The roar of the oncoming waters was like wings to our horses' feet, and we turned from the course of the storm not more than three minutes ahead of the great waterspout that tore up the road behind us and filled the canyons with floods and débris. It was a race for life, and when we turned from its course we sent up a shout of joy that echoed far down the Georgetown street.

Susette La Flesche
(Bright Eyes) (Omaha)
(1854–1903)

S USETTE LA FLESCHE was born in a watershed year for the Omaha tribe. In 1854, the Omaha ceded roughly three million acres of land to the U.S. government in exchange for a parcel one-tenth that size. To the south lay the Oregon and Mormon Trails, paths west that followed the shallow, braided ribbons of the Platte. Each summer, thousands of settlers pushed across Indian lands in search of gold, a desert utopia, or rich farmlands. The earliest pioneers had little effect on the Plains Indians' way of life. But by the 1850s and '60s, with the best bottom-land taken, emigrants settled farther from the trails, killed off the game, and relegated Native Americans to the least desirable tracts. Eventually, developers threatened to take even those.

The Omaha chose to maintain peaceful relations with the whites. Recognizing the futility of fighting, the Omaha turned to agriculture to supplement their foraging and hunting. Their neighbors, the Sioux, maintained the opposite stance, until, in the aftermath of the Battle of the Little Big Horn, they were hunted down and forcibly restricted. Yet, the Omahas' fate was almost as severe.

In 1877, the Ponca, sister tribe to the Omaha, were forcibly removed from their Dakota reservation by the U.S. government and resettled in Indian Territory (now Oklahoma). The trek south was a death march. The survivors, abandoned without food or shelter in inhospitable terrain, suffered malaria and starvation. One Ponca chief, Standing Bear, refused to stay, and in 1879 started home with thirty supporters. They were arrested in Omaha, Nebraska. Gen. George Crook, who was designated to cart them back to Indian Territory, enlisted the help of journalist Thomas Henry Tibbles. Tibbles, a former preacher and an abolitionist, accepted the task of finding an answer to the Ponca question—only one strand of the tangled "Indian problem." Yet, it proved the end that, once grasped, led to the eventual unraveling of the informal network of corrupt Indian agents and their friends known as the "Indian Ring."

Tibbles sought help from Omaha chief Joseph "Iron Eye" La Flesche, kinsman of the Ponca. Iron Eye did not speak English, but he agreed to have his oldest daughter, Susette, and her half brother, Francis, describe the history of the problem for Tibbles and testify in the case.

Susette had been schooled by missionaries on the reservation. At seventeen, she journeyed to New Jersey to continue her education. When she graduated, she returned to Nebraska and her family. There, she was unable to find work. The Indian agent would not hire an Indian as a teacher. Researching government records and statutes, she discovered that hiring preference was to be given to Indians for jobs on the reservations. After threatening to take her case to the court and to the press, she was given the job of assistant teacher, although at a reduced salary. But the experience taught her how to work within the system to solve Indian problems. She was the perfect complement to Tibbles, who could foment unrest and public support through articles and editorials in local and national papers. Susette's written history of the Ponca troubles served as the basis for a legal challenge of the government's right to imprison Standing Bear and his followers and, later, of the government's assignment of Ponca lands. In a landmark decision, the judge decided that Indians were men subject to the laws and regulations of the United States. They could not be imprisoned without cause; they must have recourse through the courts. They had rights. They were citizens of the United States, not wards of the government.

Although free, Standing Bear could not legally return to his old territory. Tibbles took their case on the road in 1879. Because Standing Bear did not speak English, Susette went along as interpreter. She appended her own plea for Indian rights and support after translating his words for eastern audiences that included the elite society of New York, Boston, and Washington, D.C. Francis La Flesche went along as chaperon. It was on this speaking tour that Longfellow's "Minehaha" and the eastern establishment's "Indian Princess" met Helen Hunt Jackson and Alice Fletcher. All three lives would be irrevocably altered by the contact.

With Helen Hunt Jackson's help, Susette was called to testify before Congress, and Standing Bear's Ponca were allowed to return to their lands. Unfortunately, the decision did not apply to the Ponca Indians who had stayed in Indian Territory. Families were divided. Those on the reservations could not leave without the agents' permission.

Tibbles's first wife died while the group was on tour. Two years later, in the fall of 1881, Tibbles and Susette La Flesche were married on the Omaha reservation before heading back to tour the East. That fall, they also introduced Alice Fletcher to the Omaha and Sioux cultures, although they eventually broke with her when she helped Iron Eye and one faction of the Omaha who wanted to gain title, in the form of allotments, to the land they had left. By the Dawes Act of 1887, those Indians who accepted allotments also became citizens of the United States.

Tibbles and La Flesche toured England in 1887 to raise funds for the Omaha, who had found that farming would not protect them from the lean years brought on by drought and locust infestations. But the unrelenting campaigning weakened Susette's health. A quiet and reserved person, the years in the spotlight sapped her energy. She went back to the Omaha reservation to try to farm her eighty-acre allotment. Tibbles returned to journalism to make ends meet. Bright Eyes and Tibbles were with Elaine Goodale and Charles Eastman when the Wounded Knee survivors were brought to the Pine Ridge Agency chapel.

Susette turned to writing and illustration to help whites understand the character and life of the Omaha. In addition to newspaper articles, she wrote the introduction to *Ploughed Under: The Story of an Indian Chief*, a novel by Tibbles, and "Nedawi," a short story for children. She illustrated *Oo-Mah-Ha Ta-Wa-tha*, Fanny Reed Giffen's story of the Omaha.

Susette La Flesche Tibbles never regained her health after her fight to preserve the rights of the Ponca and the Omaha. Bright Eyes died at Bancroft, Nebraska, at age forty-nine.

৯৭

Nedawi

(An Indian Story from Real Life)

"NEDAWI!" called her mother, "take your little brother while I go with your sister for some wood." Nedawi ran into the tent, bringing back her little red blanket, but the brown-faced, roly-poly baby, who had been having a comfortable nap in spite of being all the while tied straight to his board, woke with a merry crow just as the mother was about to attach him, board and all, to Nedawi's neck. So he was taken from the board instead, and, after he had kicked in happy freedom for a moment, Nedawi stood in front of her mother, who placed Habazhu on the little girl's back, and drew the blanket over him, leaving his arms free. She next put into his hand a little hollow gourd, filled with seeds, which served as a rattle; Nedawi held both ends of the blanket tightly in front of her, and was then ready to walk around with the little man.

Where should she go? Yonder was a group of young girls playing a game of *konci* or dice. The dice were five plum-seeds, scorched black, and had little stars and quarter-moons instead of numbers. She went over and stood by the group, gently rocking herself from side to side, pretty much as white children do when reciting the multiplication table. The girls would toss up the wooden bowl, letting it drop with a gentle thud on the pillow beneath, the falling dice making a pleasant clatter which the baby liked to hear. The stakes were a little heap of beads, rings, and bracelets. The laughter and exclamations of the girls, as some successful toss brought down the dice three stars and two quarter-moons (the highest throw), made Nedawi wish that she, too, were a young girl, and could win and wear all those pretty things. How gay she would look! Just then, the little glittering heap caught baby's eye. He tried to wriggle out of the blanket to get to it, but Nedawi held tight. Then he set up a yell. Nedawi walked away very reluctantly, because she wanted to stay and see who would win. She went to her mother's tent, but found it deserted. Her father and brothers had gone to the chase. A herd of buffalo had been seen that morning, and all the men in the tribe had gone, and would not be back till night. Her mother, her sister, and the women of the household had gone to the river for wood and water. The tent looked enticingly cool, with the sides turned up to let the breeze sweep through, and the straw mats and soft robes seemed to invite her to lie down on them and dream the afternoon away, as she was too apt to do. She did not yield to the temptation, however, for she knew Mother would not like it, but walked over to her cousin Metai's tent. She found her cousin "keeping house" with a number of little girls, and stood to watch them while they put up little tents, just large enough to hold one or two girls.

"Nedawi, come and play," said Metai. "You can make the fire and cook. I 'll ask Mother for something to cook."

"But what shall I do with Habazhu?" said Nedawi.

"I 'll tell you. Put him in my tent, and make believe he's our little old grandfather."

Forthwith he was transferred from Nedawi's back to the little tent. But Habazhu had a decided objection to staying in the dark little place, where he could not see anything, and crept out of the door on his hands and knees. Nedawi collected a little heap of sticks, all ready for the fire, and went off to get a fire-brand to light it with. While she was gone, Habazhu crawled up to a bowl of water which stood by the intended fire-place, and began dabbling in it with his chubby little hands, splashing the water all over the sticks prepared for the fire. Then he thought he would like a drink. He tried to lift the bowl in both bands, but only succeeded in spilling the water over himself and the fire-place.

When Nedawi returned, she stood aghast; then, throwing down the brand, she took her little brother by the shoulders and, I am sorry to say, shook him violently, jerked him up, and dumped him down by the door of the little tent from which he had crawled. "You bad little boy!" she said. "It 's too bad that I have to take care of you when I want to play."

You see, she was no more perfect than any little white girl who gets into a temper now and then. The baby's lip quivered, and he began to cry. Metai said to Nedawi: "I think it 's real mean for you to shake him, when he does n't know any better."

Metai picked up Baby and tried to comfort him. She kissed him over and over, and talked to him in baby language. Nedawi's conscience, if the little savage could be said to have any, was troubling her. She loved her baby brother dearly, even though she did get out of patience with him now and then.

"I 'll put a clean little shirt on him and pack him again," said she, suddenly. Then she took off his little wet shirt, wrung it out, and spread it on the tall grass to dry in the sun. Then she went home, and, going to a pretty painted skin in which her mother kept his clothes, she selected the red shirt, which she thought was the prettiest. She was in such a hurry, however, that she forgot to close and tie up the skin again, and she carelessly left his clean shirts lying around as she had laid them out. When Baby was on her back again, she walked around with him, giving directions and overseeing the other girls at their play, determined to do that rather than nothing.

The other children were good-natured, and took her ordering as gracefully as they could. Metai made the fire in a new place, and then went to ask her mother to give her something to cook. Her mother gave her a piece of dried buffalo meat, as hard as a chip and as brittle as glass. Metai broke it up into small pieces, and put the pieces into a little tin pail of water, which she hung over the fire. "Now," she said, "when the meat is cooked and the soup is made, I will call you all to a feast, and Habazhu shall be the chief."

They all laughed. But alas for human calculations! During the last few minutes, a shy little girl, with soft, wistful black eyes, had been watching them from a little distance. She had on a faded, shabby blanket and a ragged dress.

"Metai," said Nedawi, "let 's ask that girl to play with us; she looks so lonesome."

"Well," said Metai, doubtfully, "I don't care; but my mother said she did n't want me to play with ragged little girls."

"My father says we must be kind to poor little girls, and help them all we can; so I'm going to play with her if you don't," said Nedawi, loftily.

Although Metai was the hostess, Nedawi was the leading spirit, and had her own way, as usual. She walked up to the little creature and said, "Come and play with us, if you want to." The little girl's eyes brightened, and she laughed. Then she suddenly drew from under her blanket a pretty bark basket, filled with the most delicious red and yellow plums. "My brother picked them in the woods, and I give them to you," was all she said. Nedawi managed to free one hand, and took the offering with an exclamation of delight, which drew the other girls quickly around. Instead of saying "Oh! Oh!" as you would have said, they cried "Hin! Hin!" which expressed their feeling quite as well, perhaps.

"Let us have them for our feast," said Metai, taking them.

Little Indian children are taught to share everything with one another, so it did not seem strange to Nedawi to have her gift looked on as common property. But, while the attention of the little group had been concentrated on the matter in hand, a party of mischievous boys, passing by, caught sight of the little tents and the tin pail hanging over the fire. Simultaneously, they set up a war-whoop and, dashing into the deserted camp, they sent the tent-poles scattering right and left, and snatching up whatever they could lay hands on, including the tin pail and its contents, they retreated. The little girls, startled by the sudden raid on their property, looked up. Rage possessed their little souls. Giving shrieks of anger, they started in pursuit. What did Nedawi do? She forgot plums, baby, and everything. The ends of the blanket slipped from her grasp, and she darted forward like an arrow after her companions.

Finding the chase hopeless, the little girls came to a stand-still, and some of them began to cry. The boys had stopped, too; and seeing the tears flow, being good-hearted boys in spite of their mischief, they surrendered at discretion. They threw back the articles they had taken, not daring to come near. They did not consider it manly for big boys like themselves to strike or hurt little girls, even though they delighted in teasing them, and they knew from experience that they would be at the mercy of the offended party if they went near enough to be touched. The boy who had the dinner brought the little pail which had contained it as near as he dared, and setting it down ran away.

"You have spilt all our soup. There's hardly any of it left. You bad boys!" said one of the girls.

They crowded around with lamentations over their lost dinner. The boys began to feel remorseful.

"Let's go into the woods and get them some plums to make up for it."

"Say, girls, hand us your pail, and we'll fill it up with plums for you."

So the affair was settled.

But, meanwhile, what became of the baby left so unceremoniously in the tall grass? First he opened his black eyes wide at this style of treatment. He was not used to it. Before he had time, however, to make up his mind whether to laugh or cry, his mother came to the rescue. She had just come home and thrown the wood off her back, when she caught sight of Nedawi dropping him. She ran to pick him up, and finding him unhurt, kissed him over and over. Some of the neighbors had run up to see what was the matter. She said to them:

"I never did see such a thoughtless, heedless child as my Nedawi. She really has 'no ears.' I don't know what in the world will ever become of her. When something new interests her, she forgets everything else. It was just like her to act in this way."

Then they all laughed, and one of them said: "Never mind—she will grow wiser as she grows older," after which consoling remark they went away to their own tents.

It was of no use to call Nedawi back. She was too far off.

Habazhu was given over to the care of the nurse, who had just returned from her visit. An hour or two after, Nedawi came home.

"Mother!" she exclaimed, as she saw her mother frying bread for supper, "I am so hungry. Can I have some of that bread?"

"Where is your little brother?" was the unexpected reply.

Nedawi started. Where *had* she left him? She tried to think.

"Why, Mother, the last I remember I was packing him, and—and oh, Mother! you *know* where he is. Please tell me."

"When you find him and bring him back to me, perhaps I shall forgive you," was the cold reply.

This was dreadful. Her mother had never treated her in that way before. She burst into tears and started out to find Habazhu, crying all the way. She knew that her mother knew where baby was, or she would not have taken it so coolly; and she knew also that her mother expected her to bring him home. As she went stumbling along through the grass, she felt herself seized and held in somebody's strong arms, and a great, round, hearty voice said:

"What's the matter with my little niece? Have all her friends deserted her that she is wailing like this? Or has her little dog died? I thought Nedawi was a brave little woman."

It was her uncle Two Crows. She managed to tell him, through her sobs, the whole story. She knew, if she told him herself, he would not laugh at her about it, for he would sympathize in her troubles, though he was a great tease. When she ceased, he said to her: "Well, your mother wants you to be more careful next time, I suppose; and, by the way, I think I saw a little boy who looked very much like Habazhu, in my tent."

Sure enough, she found him there with his nurse. When she got home with them, she found her mother,—her own dear self,—and, after giving her a big hug, she sat quietly down by the fire, resolved to be very good in the future. She did not sit long, however, for soon a neighing of horses, and the running of girls and children through the camp to meet the hunters, proclaimed their return. All was bustle and gladness throughout the camp. There had been a successful chase, and the led horses were laden with buffalo meat. These horses were led by the young girls to the tents to be unpacked, while the boys took the hunting-horses to water and tether in the grass. Fathers, as they dismounted, took their little children in their arms, tired as they were. Nedawi was as happy as any in the camp, for her seventeen-year-old brother, White Hawk, had killed his first buffalo, and had declared that the skin should become Nedawi's robe, as soon as it was tanned and painted.

What a pleasant evening that was to Nedawi, when the whole family sat around a great fire, roasting the huge buffalo ribs, and she played with her little brother Habazhu, stopping now and then to listen to the adventures of the day, which her father and brothers were relating! The scene was truly a delightful one, the camp-fires lighting up the pleasant family groups here and there, as the flames rose and fell. The bit of prairie where the tribe had camped had a clear little stream running through it, with shadowy hills around, while over all hung the clear, star-lit sky. It seemed as if nature were trying to protect the poor waifs of humanity clustered in that spot. Nedawi felt the beauty of the scene, and was just thinking of nestling down by her father to enjoy it dreamily, when her brothers called for a dance. The little drum was brought forth, and Nedawi danced to its accompaniment and her brothers' singing. She danced gravely, as became a little maiden whose duty it was to entertain the family circle. While she was dancing, a little boy, about her own age, was seen hovering near. He would appear, and, when spoken to, would disappear in the tall, thick grass.

It was Mischief, a playmate of Nedawi's. Everybody called him "Mischief," because mischief appeared in every action of his. It shone from his eyes and played all over his face.

"You little plague," said White Hawk; "what do you want?"

For answer, the "little plague" turned a somersault just out of White Hawk's reach. When the singing was resumed, Mischief crept quietly up behind White Hawk, and, keeping just within the shadow, mimicked Nedawi's grave dancing, and he looked so funny that Nedawi suddenly laughed, which was precisely Mischief's object. But before be could get out of reach, as he intended, Thunder, Nedawi's other brother, who had been having an eye on him, clutched tight hold of him, and Mischief was landed in front of the fire-place, in full view of the whole family. "Now," said Thunder, "you are my prisoner. You stay there and dance with Nedawi." Mischief knew there was no escape, so he submitted with a good grace. He went through all sorts of antics, shaking his fists in the air, twirling suddenly around and putting his head close to the ground, keeping time with the accompaniment through it all.

Nedawi danced staidly on, now and then frowning at him; but she knew of old that he was irrepressible. When Nedawi sat down, he threw into her lap a little dark something and was off like a shot, yelling at the top of his voice, either in triumph at his recent achievements or as a practice for future war-whoops.

"Nedawi, what is it?" said her mother.

Nedawi took it to the fire, when the something proved to be a poor little bird.

"I thought he had something in his hand when he was shaking his fist in the air," said Nedawi's sister, Nazainza, laughing.

"Poor little thing!" said Nedawi; "it is almost dead."

She put its bill into the water, and tenderly tried to make it drink. The water seemed to revive it somewhat.

"I'll wrap it up in something warm," said Nedawi, "and may be it will sing in the morning."

"Let me see it," said Nedawi's father.

Nedawi carried it to him.

"Don't you feel sorry for it, daughter?"

"Yes, Father," she answered.

"Then take it to the tall grass, yonder, and put it down where no one will step on it, and, as you put it down, say: 'God, I give you back your little bird. As I pity it, pity me.'"

"And will God take care of it?" said Nedawi, reverently, and opening her black eyes wide at the thought.

"Yes," said her father.

"Well, I will do as you say," said Nedawi, and she walked slowly out of the tent.

Then she took it over to the tall, thick grass, and making a nice, cozy little nest for it, left it there, saying just what her father had told her to say. When she came back, she said:

"Father, I said it."

"That was right, little daughter," and Nedawi was happy at her father's commendation.

Nedawi always slept with her grandmother and sister, exactly in the middle of the circle formed by the wigwam, with her feet to the fireplace. That place in the tent was always her grandmother's place, just as the right-hand side of the tent was her father's and mother's, and the left-hand her brothers'. There never was any confusion. The tribe was divided into bands, and every band was composed of several families. Each band had its chief, and the whole tribe was ruled by the head-chief, who was Nedawi's father. He had his own particular band besides.

Every tent had its own place in the band, and every band had its own particular place in the great circle forming the camp. Each chief was a representative, in council, of the men composing his band, while over all was the head-chief. The executive power was vested in the "soldiers' lodge," and when decisions were arrived at in council, it was the duty of its soldiers to execute all its orders, and punish all violations of the tribal laws. The office of "town-crier" was held by several old men, whose duty it was "to cry out" through the camp the announcements of councils, invitations to feasts, and to give notice of anything in which the whole tribe were called on to take part.

Well, before Nedawi went to sleep this evening, she hugged her grandmother, and said to her:

"Please tell me a story."

Her grandmother said:

"I cannot, because it is summer. In the winter I will tell you stories."

"Why not in summer?" said Nedawi.

"Because, when people tell stories and legends in summer, the snakes come around to listen. You don't want any snakes to come near us tonight, do you?"

"But," said Nedawi, "I have not seen any snakes for the longest times, and if you tell it right softly they wont hear you."

"Nedawi," said her mother, "don't bother your grandmother. She is tired and wants to sleep."

Thereupon Grandmother's heart felt sorry for her pet, and she said to Nedawi:

"Well, if you will keep still and go right to sleep when I am through, I will tell you how the turkeys came to have red eyelids.

"Once upon a time, there was an old woman living all alone with her grandson, Rabbit. He was noted for his cunning and for his tricks, which he played on every one. One day, the old woman said to him, 'Grandson, I am hungry for some meat.' Then the boy took his bow and arrows, and in the evening he came home with a deer on his shoulders, which he threw at her feet, and said, 'Will that satisfy you?' She said, 'Yes, grandson.' They lived on that meat several days, and, when it was gone, she said to him again, 'Grandson, I am hungry for some meat.' This time he went without his bow and arrows, but he took a bag with him. When he got into the woods, he called all the turkeys together. They gathered around him, and he said to them: 'I am going to sing to you, while you shut your eyes and dance. If one of you opens his eyes while I am singing, his eyelids shall turn red.' Then they all stood in a row, shut their eyes, as he had told them, and began to dance, and this is the song he sang to them while they danced:

> "'Ha! wadamba thike
> Inshta zhida, inshta zhida,
> Imba theonda,
> Imba theonda.'

[The literal translation is:

> "Ho! he who peeps
> Red eyes, red eyes,
> Flap your wings,
> Flap your wings."]

"Now, while they were dancing away, with their eyes shut, the boy took them, one by one, and put them into his bag. But the last one in the row began to think it very strange that his companions made no noise, so he gave one peep, screamed in his fright, 'They are making 'way with us!' and flew away. The boy took his bag of turkeys home to his grandmother, but ever after that the turkeys had red eyelids."

Nedawi gave a sigh of satisfaction when the story was finished, and would have asked for more, but just then her brothers came in from a dance which they had been attending in some neighbor's tent. She knew her lullaby time had come. Her brothers always sang before they slept either love or dancing songs, beating time on their breasts, the regular beats making a sort of accompaniment for the singing. Nedawi loved best of all to hear her father's war-songs, for he had a musical voice, and few were the evenings when she had gone to sleep without hearing a lullaby from her father or brothers. Among the Indians, it is the fathers who sing, instead of the mothers. Women sing only on state occasions, when the tribe have a great dance, or at something of the sort. Mothers "croon" their babies to sleep, instead of singing.

Gradually the singing ceased, and the brothers slept as well as Nedawi, and quiet reigned over the whole camp.

Gertrude Franklin Horn Atherton
(1857–1948)

IN 1542, the Spanish viceroy sent Juan Rodríguez Cabrillo to explore the coast north of Baja California. He entered the Bay of San Miguel on September 27, becoming the first European to land in California. Other Spanish, English, and Russian explorers followed, without leaving their mark on the landscape. When Sebastian Vizcaíno sailed from Acapulco in 1602 to retrace Cabrillo's route, he renamed the bay San Diego de Alcala de Henares. But the first profound changes to Alta California came through the establishment of the California missions more than two hundred years after Cabrillo's expedition.

On July 1, 1769, Franciscan missionary Father Junipero Serra, after walking up the Baja California peninsula, erected a cross near San Diego Bay, establishing the first in a chain of twenty-one missions stretching north along *el Camino Real,* the King's Highway. Nine of the missions were founded by Serra, who died in 1784 at Mission San Carlos Borromeo near Monterey. The Spanish flag was lowered at Monterey in the spring of 1822. The last of the Franciscan "string-of-pearls" was Mission San Francisco Solano, completed in Sonoma two years after the political turmoil that marked Mexico's struggle for independence from Spain culminated in Augustín de Iturbide's successful Mexican Revolution.

Following the Mexican government's edict of secularization in 1834, mission lands were stolen or sold. Those mission priests who stayed in California starved alongside the Indians they had trained to cultivate the European crops and animals that replaced indigenous sources of food. Both the Mexican and the American settlers that flooded into California evicted tribes from their land. By the end of the nineteenth century, the Indian population had been decimated.

The religio-pastoral mission communities that laid the foundation for settlement in California lasted only sixty years. But around them grew the cities, towns, and culture of Spanish California—a culture that lives today in place-names and folklore. Helen Hunt Jackson wrote articles and reports on Fray Junipero Serra, colonial Los Angeles, and the California missions. Gertrude Atherton mined that golden age for her historical novels and short stories.

Gertrude Horn was born in San Francisco. In the mid-nineteenth century, the "City by the Bay" was a boomtown where vigilante justice maintained order among the saloons, dance halls, opium dens, and the waterfront district. Horn's parents divorced when she was three. A grandfather raised her until 1876, when she married George Atherton. Atherton, a native of Chile, was a member of a prominent family for whom the peninsula town was named. The marriage was not happy, but produced two children. Only one of them reached adulthood.

Gertrude began publishing short fiction and novels in her early twenties, focusing on the scandals, secrets, and lives of the San Francisco elite. The works sold well, although they alienated her peers.

In 1888, Atherton's husband died while sailing to South America. She did not marry again, but enjoyed the life of an affluent and independent widow. She moved first to New York, then overseas in 1895. She wrote stories with European locales, but her most popular subjects continued to be the life and characters of California. Recognizing that Spanish California had not been explored in American fiction, Atherton researched the history of her native state and wrote some of her best short stories, including "The Vengeance of Padre Arroyo." These were collected in *Before the Gringo Came* and *The Splendid Idle Forties,* an enlarged version of *Gringo.* To gather background material, she visited the old Spanish families, stayed at their haciendas, talked to them of former days, and captured the color, drama, and musical language of the era. In retelling the tragic love stories of Californios and Russian soldiers, she romanticized an era and popularized historical events. To each story she added a twist, like that at the end of "Padre Arroyo."

In Lawrence Clark Powell's opinion, Atherton pioneered the genre of biographical novels with *The Conquerer,* the life of Alexander Hamilton. She continued this form in *Rezanov, The Immortal Marriage,* and *The Jealous Gods.* She also produced nonfiction, such as *California: An Intimate History, My San Francisco,* and her autobiography, *Adventures of a Novelist* (1932).

The grande dame of California novelists continued writing until her death at ninety.

The Vengeance of Padre Arroyo

I

PILAR, from her little window just above the high wall surrounding the big adobe house set apart for the women neophytes of the Mission of Santa Ines, watched, morning and evening, for Andreo, as he came and went from the rancheria. The old women kept the girls busy, spinning, weaving, sewing, but age nods and youth is crafty. The tall young Indian who was renowned as the best huntsman of all the neophytes, and who supplied Padre Arroyo's table with deer and quail, never failed to keep his ardent eyes fixed upon the grating so long as it lay within the line of his vision. One day he went to Padre Arroyo and told him that Pilar was the prettiest girl behind the wall—the prettiest girl in all the Californias—and that she should be his wife. But the kind, stern old padre shook his head.

"You are both too young. Wait another year, my son, and if thou art still in the same mind thou shalt have her."

Andreo dared make no protest, but he asked permission to prepare a home for his bride. The padre gave it willingly, and the young Indian began to make the big adobes, the bright red tiles. At the end of a month he had built him a cabin among the willows of the rancheria a little apart from the others: he was in love, and association with his fellows was distasteful. When the cabin was builded his impatience slipped from its curb, and once more he besought the priest to allow him to marry.

Padre Arroyo was sunning himself on the corridor of the Mission, shivering in his heavy brown robes, for the day was cold.

"Orion," he said, sternly—he called all his neophytes after the celebrities of earlier days, regardless of the names given them at the font—"have I not told thee thou must wait a year? Do not be impatient, my son. She will keep. Women are like apples: when they are too young they set the teeth on edge; when ripe and mellow they please every sense; when they wither and turn brown it is time to fall from the tree into a hole. Now go and shoot a deer for Sunday; the good padres from San Luis Obispo and Santa Barbara are coming to dine with me."

Andreo, dejected, left the padre. As he passed Pilar's window and saw a pair of wistful black eyes behind the grating his heart took fire. No one was within sight. By a series of signs he made his lady understand that he would place a note beneath a certain adobe in the wall.

Pilar, as she went to and fro under the fruit-trees in the garden, or sat on the long corridor weaving baskets, watched that adobe with fascinated eyes. She knew that Andreo was tunneling it, and one day a tiny hole proclaimed that his work was accomplished. But how to get the note? The old women's eyes were very sharp when the girls were in front of the gratings. Then the civilizing development of Christianity upon the heathen intellect triumphantly asserted itself. Pilar, too, conceived a brilliant scheme. That night the padre, who encouraged any evidence of industry, no matter how eccentric, gave her a little garden of her own—a patch where she could raise sweet peas and Castilian roses.

"That is well, that is well, my Nausicaa," he said, stroking her smoken braids. "Go cut the slips and plant them where thou wilt. I will send thee a package of sweet pea seeds."

Pilar spent every spare hour bending over her "patch," and the hole, at first no bigger than a pin's point, was larger at each setting of the sun behind the mountain, while the old women, scolding on the corridor, called to her not to forget vespers.

On the third evening, kneeling on the damp ground, she drew from the little tunnel in the adobe a thin slip of wood covered with the labor of sleepless nights. She hid it in her smock—that first of California's love-letters—then ran with shaking knees and prostrated herself before the altar. That night the moon streamed through her grating, and she deciphered the fact that Andreo had loosened eight adobes above her garden, and would await her every midnight.

Pilar sat up in bed and glanced about the room with terrified delight. It took her but a moment to decide the question; love had kept her awake too many nights. The neophytes were asleep; as they turned now and again, their narrow beds of hide, suspended from the ceiling, swung too gently to awaken them. The old women snored loudly. Pilar slipped from her bed and looked through the grating. Andreo was there, the dignity and repose of primeval man in his bearing. She waved her hand and pointed downward to the wall; then, throwing on the long, coarse gray smock that was her only garment, crept from the room and down the stair. The door was protected against hostile tribes by a heavy iron bar, but Pilar's small hands were hard and strong, and in a moment she stood over the adobes which had crushed her roses and sweet peas.

As she crawled through the opening, Andreo took her hand bashfully, for they had never spoken. "Come," he said: "we must be far away before dawn."

They stole past the long Mission, crossing themselves as they glanced askance at the ghostly row of pillars; past the guard-house, where the sentries slept at their post; past the rancheria; then, springing upon a waiting mustang, dashed down the valley. Pilar had never been on a horse before, and she clung in terror to Andreo, who bestrode the unsaddled beast as easily as a cloud rides the wind. His arm held her closely: fear vanished, and she enjoyed the novel sensation. Glancing over Andreo's shoulder she watched the mass of brown and white buildings, the winding river, fade into the mountain. Then they began to ascend an almost perpendicular steep. The horse followed a narrow trail; the crowding trees and shrubs clutched the blanket and smock of the riders; after a time trail and scene grew white: the snow lay on the heights.

"Where do we go?" she asked.

"To Zaca lake, on the very top of the mountain, miles above us. No one has ever been there but myself. Often I have shot deer and birds beside it. They will never find us there."

The red sun rose over the mountains of the east. The crystal moon sank in the west. Andreo sprang from the weary mustang and carried Pilar to the lake. A sheet of water, round as a whirlpool, but calm and silveren, lay amidst the sweeping willows and pine-forested peaks. The snow glittered beneath the trees, but a canoe was on the lake, a hut on the marge.

II

Padre Arroyo tramped up and down the corridor, smiting his hands together. Then Indians bowed lower than usual, as they passed, and hastened their steps. The soldiers scoured the country for the bold violators of Mission law. No one asked Padre Arroyo what he would do with the sinners, but all knew that punishment would be sharp and summary: the men hoped that Andreo's mustang had carried him beyond its reach; the girls, horrified as they were, wept and prayed in secret for Pilar.

A week later, in the early morning, Padre Arroyo sat on the corridor. The Mission stood on a plateau overlooking a long valley forked and silvered by the broad river. The valley was planted thick with olive-trees, and their silver leaves sparkled in the rising sun. The mountain-peaks about and beyond were white with snow, but the great red poppies blossomed at their feet. The padre, exiled from the luxury and society of his dear Spain, never tired of the prospect: he loved his Mission children, but he loved Nature more.

Suddenly he leaned forward on his staff and lifted the heavy brown hood of his habit from his ear. Down the road winding from the eastern mountains came the echo of galloping footfalls. He rose expectantly and waddled out upon the plaza, shading his eyes with his hand. A half-dozen soldiers, riding closely about a horse bestridden by a stalwart young Indian supporting a woman, were rapidly approaching the Mission. The padre returned to his seat and awaited their coming.

The soldiers escorted the culprits to the corridor; two held the horse while they descended, then led it away, and Andreo and Pilar were alone with the priest. The bridegroom placed his arm about the bride and looked defiantly at Padre Arroyo, but Pilar drew her long hair about her face and locked her hands together.

Padre Arroyo folded his arms and regarded them with lowered brows, a sneer on his mouth.

"I have new names for you both," he said, in his thickest voice. "Antony, I hope thou hast enjoyed thy honeymoon. Cleopatra, I hope thy little toes did not get frost-bitten. You both look as if food had been scarce. And your garments have gone in good part to clothe the brambles, I infer. It is too bad you could not wait a year and love in your cabin at the rancheria, by a good fire, and with plenty of frijoles and tortillas in your stomachs." He dropped his sarcastic tone, and, rising to his feet, extended his right arm with a gesture of malediction. "Do you comprehend the enormity of your sin?" he shouted. "Have you not learned on your knees that the fires of hell are the rewards of unlawful love? Do you not know that even the year of sackcloth and ashes I shall impose here on earth will not save you from those flames a million times hotter than the mountain fire, than the roaring pits in which evil Indians torture one another? A hundred years of their scorching breath, of roasting flesh, for a week of love! Oh, God of my soul!"

Andreo looked somewhat staggered, but unrepentant. Pilar burst into loud sobs of terror.

The padre stared long and gloomily at the flags of the corridor. Then he raised his head and looked sadly at his lost sheep.

"My children," he said, solemnly, "my heart is wrung for you. You have broken the laws of God and of the Holy Catholic Church, and the punishments thereof are awful. Can I do anything for you, excepting to pray? You shall have my prayers, my children. But that is not enough; I cannot—ay! I cannot endure the thought that you shall be damned. Perhaps"—again he stared meditatively at the stones, then, after an impressive silence, raised his eyes. "Heaven vouchsafes me an idea, my children. I will make your punishment here so bitter that Almighty God in his mercy will give you but a few years of purgatory after death. Come with me."

He turned and led the way slowly to the rear of the Mission buildings. Andreo shuddered for the first time, and tightened his arm about Pilar's shaking body. He knew that they were to be locked in the dungeons. Pilar, almost fainting, shrank back as they reached the narrow spiral stair which led downward to the cells. "Ay! I shall die, my Andreo!" she cried. "Ay! my father, have mercy!"

"I cannot, my children," said the padre, sadly. "It is for the salvation of your souls."

"Mother of God! When shall I see thee again, my Pilar?" whispered Andreo. "But, ay! the memory of that week on the mountain will keep us both alive."

Padre Arroyo descended the stair and awaited them at its foot. Separating them, and taking each by the hand, he pushed Andreo ahead and dragged Pilar down the narrow passage. At its end he took a great bunch of keys from his pocket, and raising both hands commanded them to kneel. He said a long prayer in a loud, monotonous voice which echoed and re-echoed down the dark hall and made Pilar shriek with terror. Then he fairly hurled the marriage ceremony at them, and made the couple repeat after him the responses. When it was over, "Arise," he said.

The poor things stumbled to their feet, and Andreo caught Pilar in a last embrace.

"Now bear your incarceration with fortitude, my children; and if you do not beat the air with your moans I will let you out in a week. Do not hate your old father, for love alone makes him severe, but pray, pray, pray."

And then he locked them both in the same cell.

Milicent Washburn Shinn

("M. W. S.")

(1858–1940)

T HE OFF-YEAR ELECTORAL race of 1858 placed the slavery issue squarely in the middle of the table. On the night of June 16, in his hometown of Springfield, Illinois, country lawyer-turned-politician Abraham Lincoln denounced the institution of slavery in a speech before the Republican State Convention that had just nominated him for the United States Senate. Pointing out that the Kansas-Nebraska Act of 1854 had fomented rather than squelched national controversy over the slavery issue, Lincoln quoted from the New Testament. "'A house divided against itself cannot stand,'" he said. "I believe this government cannot endure permanently half slave and half free."[9]

The issue of slavery and its future status in the territorial expansion of the United States became the focal point of the campaign that followed. Lincoln and Stephen A. Douglas debated aspects of the issue seven times between August and October. Lincoln won the popular vote, but lost the race. The national exposure, however, paved the way for a regional split in the Democratic Party. This split, mirroring the divided nation, helped Lincoln defeat Douglas in the presidential race of 1860.

In that year of the Lincoln-Douglas debates, Milicent Washburn Shinn was born on a farm in Niles, in Alameda County, California. Her parents had emigrated from Austin, Texas, in 1856, with Milicent's brother, Charles Howard Shinn. Charles became a writer, journalist, editor, foreign correspondent for European papers, teacher, horticulturist, and economist. Milicent followed in his footsteps, writing for and editing San Francisco periodicals before switching to academic research.

Milicent Shinn attended the University of California, Berkeley. She taught in district schools and edited a San Francisco newspaper to earn enough money to complete her education. After graduation in 1880, she continued to teach and edit, but she also contributed poetry and short stories to the *Californian*. When Bret Harte left San Francisco in 1882, she took his place as editor of the *Californian*. In 1883, she bought the magazine and merged it with the *Overland Monthly*.

For the next eleven years, Shinn was the driving force behind the *Overland Monthly*. As editor, she published and corresponded with the leading western writers of her day, including Helen Hunt Jackson, Ina Coolbrith, Mary Austin, Charles Warren Stoddard, George W. Stewart, and Mark Twain. During those years, she published her own editorials, book reviews, short stories, poetry, and essays such as "Summer Cañons." Her brother, Charles, after finishing his education at Johns Hopkins, returned to California in 1885 as the magazine's business manager. In 1890, the year his daughter, Ruth, was born, he left to join the agricultural department of the University of California. In 1894, Milicent sold the magazine and entered graduate school at Berkeley.

Milicent Shinn earned her Ph.D. in 1898, the first woman to do so at Berkeley. The focus of her doctoral research and later writing was child psychology and development. She recorded her niece's physical, verbal, and intellectual development during the first three years of life, using those observations as the basis for three studies: *Notes on the Development of a Child, The Biography of a Baby,* and *The Development of the Senses in the First Three Years of Childhood.* These works were crucial early studies in the field of child development.

Although her poetry reveals at least one deep romantic attachment, Shinn remained an independent single woman. She died on the family ranch in Niles, a town absorbed in the twentieth century by the urban sprawl of Fremont, California. Houses, freeways, and strip malls replaced the almond groves and pastoral scenes Shinn described. But an old three-story brick building at 120 Sutter Street, dwarfed by San Francisco business-district skyscrapers, marks the site where Shinn published the *Overland Monthly* more than a century ago.

[THE] WEST WIND, all the summer months, begins every afternoon—or oftener yet, shortly before noon—like surf in the trees; a warm, sleepy, indefinite wind, rising and falling in long pulses, yet keeping, for all its warmth, just a touch of the sea about it, which makes it good to breathe. . . .

In the summer months, the round foothills that border much of our farming country are colored as richly as the plain, and far more effectively, because of the blue background. "The hills are green," we say, to characterize our wet season; "the hills are brown," to characterize our dry season. But who with an eye for color will lose interest in the hills as soon as they cease to be green. The "brown" of the summer months is really an endless variety of warm yellows and russets and bronze and gold shades innumerable. The wheat and barley fields extend in strips and blocks and all manner of irregular patches up on these hills; and the uncultivated parts are covered with grasses that are not dead, but ripened and cured on the stem at this season. Even after the grain is cut, the stubble will keep its richness of color for a while, before stubble and wild grass and everything weather into the uniform dun color of autumn. The distant hills soften their blue with white, and sink their cañons and ridges out of sight, thus bringing all the blue in the landscape—for the sky is softened too—far better into key with the yellows than these same mountains would be in their sharp sapphire of April. . . .

In the coast hills, north and south of San Francisco, among the redwood forests, the genuine, tawny, lowland summer does not enter. But at the inland sides of Santa Clara and Alameda and Contra Costa counties you will find the true summer cañons that I want to give a little idea of—cañons that, like the lowlands, are burning now in the last stages of that slow fire we call life. One reaches them by unsuspected roads leading among the hills—well-made, much-traveled roads, which constantly reveal an unsuspected population in these remote places. Every mile or two the steep hillsides draw back and leave a little room beside the stream—for it is a stream, of course, that decides the existence of the pass—and here a farm-house finds room with grain fields stretching up over the slopes behind, and grape-vines or orchard close about it, some-times. Through and through, these hills are penetrated with roads, each of which finds out, not merely spots for farm-houses, or even for tiny clusters of them, but level valleys several miles in extent, crossed by con-siderable streams, and filled with grain fields and orchards. One is sur-prised to pierce deep into a range of hills that he had supposed a barren, uninhabited country, by a road whose existence he had not suspected, and come across a pleasant dwelling, obviously Spanish, and obviously thirty or more years old, with well-grown orchard, grape-vines climbing over the balcony that runs around the upper story, and adobe barn, get-ting pretty ruinous, near by. It is always in some especially good nook, with convenient springs, that such a dwelling is discovered. . . .

There are other roads among these neighboring foothills—roads that instead of creeping through the grain-sown passes—taking lifts from the streams whenever they chance to be going the same way and winding over low "divides"—cut steeply over some ridge that separates large val-leys; for when the larger streams cleave their way through a ridge, they offer no help to roads; their way lies between abrupt sides, and their channels are strewn with great fragments of rock that they have brought down upon themselves from the steep slopes. These roads lay open at every curve wilder views than one could dream lay within fifty miles of San Francisco, over deep valleys, winding between rugged ridges, fold-ing, intersecting, rising abruptly to imposing heights, plunging down into sharp ravines; pine-trees, too, thinly scattered over some of the hill-sides; and an abundance of thicket through which the road cuts. . . .

They are warm places, these cañons—crevices between the great, tawny, sunny wrinkles of the foothills as they are. The daily trade-wind reaches them, but milder, sleepier, breathing less of the sea than even on the warm lowlands. When the high fog blankets the lowland sky all night, it shuts off the stars above the cañon just before daylight comes to extinguish them, and breaks up and melts away during the morning. You may sling your hammock there, between two of the lilac-and-sycamore stems, and feel sure that even the hours just before dawn will not infuse a chill into the sweet, clean, dry air. It is one of the best of places to be at night; in the daytime, with the sleepy wind rising and falling in the trees, and the warmth collected and poured down by the spreading sides of the cañon, life will be little more than lying in the shade close to the stream, where a little cool breath always comes creep-ing between the ranks of alder that touch branches overhead across the water. But at night, if you discard tents and traps—as the camper always should unless the climate makes it a positive imprudence—you may find life—oh! most full. I defy you to carry an anxiety or disappointment into the wilderness that the mountain stream will not smooth into quietness if you will lie in the still, starlit darkness, and listen to it. The wind goes down with sunset. The treetops above your hammock stand motionless against the stars; the great mountain flanks rise darker and more motionless on either hand—so steep and high that you hardly need turn more than your eyes to look from one dark crest to the other. The stream plunges down half a dozen little rapids within hearing; and you will never know how many tones there are in the chord of a mountain stream till you lie and listen beside it all night, without so much as a tent wall between. There is a great deal of change, too, in the tones: there will chime in a hollow tinkling noise for two minutes, and then cease, as if some tricklet had found a new way to fall, and lost it again; now the nearest "riffle" will drown the sound of a remote one, and then lull till both are blending their sounds. But under all variation is the soothing monotone. Goethe might have lain beside a mountain stream at night, and translated its spirit into words when he wrote the "Wanderer's Nachtlied" of Longfellow's translation: "O'er all the hilltops Is quiet now."

It lays cool hands of sound on the hot and aching heart, and smooths away, slowly, monotonously, imperceptibly, the heat and ache, as a patient nurse would smooth them out of the temples. The crickets chirp quietly; from somewhere in the bushes a cicada sends up a faint, shadowy reminiscence of the dizzying "*biz-z-z-z*" he has been shrilling out during the day. Nothing else makes any sound. Close your eyes, and let the running water fill your consciousness; open them, to see the great gulf of heaven above, and to meet the eyes of the stars whenever you choose to look; to see the pale, motionless foliage of the trees, in perfect rest, bathing in starlight and in the mild coolness of the night air. Away from home and shelter? In the wilderness? You have but just come home; you have been in a foreign land among strangers who vexed you and perplexed you; and now you are come back to go to sleep under your own chamber-roof again, and you may relax every nerve, and let the sense of peace and perfect safety flow through you. Out of dim hereditary instinct from our half-human days when the woods were our refuge and our home and our life; or out of the soothing effect on the senses of sound and sight; or out of perhaps nothing more mysterious than the perfect oxygenation by this fragrant air of the blood that goes to your nerves and brains—there comes to you the sense of a great protecting presence in this Nature—this Mother Earth—this much-suspected and guarded-against order of the universe, this inanimate collection of rocks and trees and water running down hill; a presence in whose arms you may nestle down, and drop your anxieties, and shut your eyes to sleep as safely as a baby in its mother's lap.

ॐ

A Cycle

I

Spring-time—is it spring-time?
Why, as I remember spring,
Almonds bloom and blackbirds sing;
Such a shower of tinted petals drifting to the clover floor,
Such a multitudinous rapture raining from the sycamore;
And among the orchard trees—
Acres musical with bees—
Moans a wild dove, making silence seem more silent than before.

Yes, that is the blackbird's note;
Almond petals are afloat;
But I had not heard nor seen them, for my heart was far away.
Birds and bees and fragrant orchards—ah! They can not bring the May;
For the human presence only,
That has left my ways so lonely,
Ever can bring back the spring-time to my autumn of to-day.

II

Autumn—is it autumn?
I remember autumn yields
Dusty roads and stubble-fields,
Weary hills, no longer rippled o'er their wind-swept slopes with grain,
Trees all gray with dust, that gathers even thicker till the rain;
And where noisy waters drove
Downward from the heights above,
Only bare white channels wander stonily across the plain.

Yes, I see the hills are dry,
Stubble-fields about me lie.
What care I when in the channels of my life once more I see

Sweetest founts, long sealed and sunken, bursting upward, glad and free?
Hills may parch or laugh in greenness,
Sky be sadness or sereneness,
Thou my life, my best belovéd, all my spring-time comes with thee.

II. *Before Burial*

Alas to lie here, cold in heart and brain,
With hands already folded for the grave,
And, like a bit of drift the backward wave
Has left ashore—a mocking symbol vain—
The purple pansies mourning on the breast
Whence surging thought and grief have ebbed away:—
All pulse of hope in hopeless, blank arrest,
All chance of better fortune gone for aye;—

So all-bereft that if you came today
With late relenting, with warm hands and strong
Of reparation, meeting pulses numb,
I should not know. Yet hath this power to lay
A deeper loss on death's most utter wrong:
—That, even too late, you surely will not come.

AT THIS STAGE the babies of grandpa's line have always been seated on the floor in a horse-collar, as befitted farm babies; and this latest one [baby Ruth] went into the collar at four months old, like the rest of us in our day, and spent much of her fifth month sitting there, sucking or brandishing her rattle, and looking happily about her. It is really a comfortable seat for a baby not yet quite ready to sit alone. . . . Sitting as usual in her horse-collar, she was bending herself back over it, a thing that she had done before; but . . . she kept it up so persistently, and bent herself back with such exertion, that at last the back of her head touched the floor. She righted herself with an expression of great surprise. Evidently she had been experimenting in new muscular sensations only, and (as happens to all experimenters sometimes) had got an extra result that she did not bargain for and did not understand. She bent back again, with her head screwed around to see what had given her the touch. In this position, she did not reach the floor. She sat up again, looked at me with a perplexed face, and tried it over, a full dozen times, till her mother picked her up to stop it, on the ground that the baby was more valuable than the experiment, and that she would break her little back. For days, however, the baby returned to the investigation, doubling herself back over the arm of any one who held her till her head hung, or over the horse-collar till it rested on the floor. . . .

Talk before you go, Your tongue will be your overthrow, says the old saw. But perhaps our baby did not earn the ill omen, it was such a faint foreshadowing of speech that she was guilty of. Probably she would not have been detected in it at all, had not ten months' practice made us pretty good detectives. Indeed, but for the notebook, by which I could compare from day to day the wavering approach to some meaning in her use of this or that syllable, I should not have dared to be sure there really was a meaning. It is in these formless beginnings of a beginning that we get our best clues (as in all evolutionary studies) to the real secrets of the origin of language. . . .

In the last four days of the tenth month we began to suspect a faint consistency in the use of several of the most common sounds. We began to think that . . . a favorite old murmur of "M-gm" or "Ng-gng" recurred so often when something disappeared from sight that we could not but wonder if we had not here an echo of our frequent "All gone!" . . . It was used as loosely as it was pronounced: the baby murmured "Ng-gng!" pensively when some one left the room; when she dropped something; when she looked for something she could not find; when she had swallowed a mouthful of food; when she heard a door close. She wounded her father's feelings by commenting "M-gâ!" as her little hands wandered about the unoccupied top of his head. . . .

And now our little girl was entered on the last month of the year—a month of the most absorbing activity, yet perhaps rather in practicing the powers she already had than in developing new ones. She added to the list of words she understood till it was impossible to make record of them all—new ones cropped up at every turn. . . .

It was about the middle of the twelfth month that the little one added the useful sign of nodding to her means of communicating. She had been taught to nod as a mere trick the month before, and took to it at once, jerking her whole little body at every nod and priding herself mightily on it. Perhaps because of this pride and pleasure, it became after a time a sort of expression of approval: she greeted us with nodding in sign of pleasure when we came in; she nodded like a mandarin when she heard she was to go to ride. So now, when a pleasant suggestion was made, "Would Ruth like a cracker?" "Does Ruth want to go see the kitties?" her nod of approval soon passed into the meaning of assent; indeed, it began now to be joined with the grunt of "E!" that I have mentioned. She had a perfectly intelligible negative grunt, too, just such as grumpy grown people use, out of the primitive stock of their remotest ancestry, no doubt.

I was nearly taken in at one time by this cheerful nodding and "E!" The little lady used them so intelligently when she was offered something she wanted, and refused so consistently when offered what she knew she did not want, that I began to set down any question as understood if she said yes to it. But presently I had an inkling that when she did not know whether she wanted it or not, she said yes, on the chance—since most things prefaced by "does Ruth want?" proved pleasant. So I asked her alluringly, "Does Ruth want a course in higher mathematics?"

The rosy baby looked at me gravely, waited with a considering air, as she always did, taking it in, nodded gravely, and said decisively, "E!"

"Does Ruth want to go and be a missionary in Raratonga?"

"E!" with no less decision.

I saved her confidence in my good faith by substituting something else as good, and more immediately practicable, for the mysterious attractions I had offered, and used due caution thereafter in recording her answers. . . .

Charlotte Anna Perkins Stetson Gilman
(1860–1935)

AFTER THE ELECTION of Abraham Lincoln in the fall of 1860, South Carolina voted, on December 20, to secede from the United States. Ten other states followed, eight of them before Lincoln's inauguration on March 4, 1861. Less than six weeks later, Pierre Beauregard fired upon Fort Sumter, South Carolina, forcing the president-elect to declare an "insurrection." The Civil War lasted four years, and took the lives of more than half a million men. Robert E. Lee surrendered at Appomattox Court House on April 9, 1865. But Lincoln presided over a reunited country for only five days before John Wilkes Booth fatally shot him at Ford's Theater.

Charlotte Anna Perkins was born on July 3, 1860, in Hartford, Connecticut. Through her father, Frederick Beecher Perkins, Charlotte was related to the Beecher family of preachers, social activists, and intellectuals including Lyman Beecher, her great-grandfather, and abolitionist Harriet Beecher Stowe, her great-aunt. Although Charlotte was too young to comprehend the Civil War's political, social, and economic causes, its divisiveness was mirrored in her own life when her father deserted the family.

Charlotte's rootless and impoverished childhood in Rhode Island, coupled with her mother's emotional detachment, produced an intellectual and objective adult determined to be self-supporting. After graduating from art school in 1880, Perkins worked in commercial illustration and tutored children. In her free time, she taught herself German and French, wrote poetry and short stories. When she was twenty-four, she married artist Charles Walter Stetson, and subsequently lapsed into depression. After their daughter, Katherine, was born in 1885, Charlotte's condition was enhanced by postpartum depression. The prescribed cure—complete rest, no writing—was worse than the affliction, but triggered Charlotte's most famous short story, "The Yellow Wallpaper."

Charlotte took Katherine to Pasadena, California, where the physical and intellectual climate was more agreeable. In southern California, Charlotte wrote, tutored art, lectured, and ran a boardinghouse—as Mary Main does in "An Honest Woman." After Stetson and Perkins divorced, Charlotte sent Katherine to live with her father and his second wife. Charlotte threw herself into her writing. She published *In This Our World,* a collection of poems in 1893, the year her mother died of cancer.

Women and Economics, a sociological study of the problems hindering women's advancement, made Perkins famous. She became an international voice for women's rights, lecturing on her proposed solutions to repressive male-dominated societies of the day. Later books—*The Home, Human Work,* and *The Man-made World*—elucidated those social themes. In part to maintain complete editorial control over her writing, she launched a magazine, the *Forerunner,* in 1909. For the next seven years, she published articles, utopian novels, short stories, essays, and poetry through this and other outlets. *Herland,* the most famous of these serialized novels, introduced Perkins's ideas of social reform via the adventures of three American men who encounter a 2,000-year-old female civilization not subject to Darwinian laws. Although *Forerunner*'s circulation was small, and the writing never again equaled the artistry of "The Yellow Wallpaper," the vehicle helped make Perkins one of the most well-known advocates of woman's rights at the turn of the century.

In 1900, Perkins married her first cousin, George Houghton Gilman. Their marriage, a happy one, lasted until his death in 1934. Charlotte, who had learned that she had breast cancer in 1932, planned to commit suicide when the agony became too great. She took her life in 1935. *The Living of Charlotte Perkins Gilman: An Autobiography* was published posthumously.

California Colors

Colors of a winter country,
Southern, snowless, auburn country,
Dove, fawn umber, dull gold country,
Purple-tipped and dun.
Only over those soft colors,
Skies of a Saharan summer—
Gorgeous summer sun.
Only, while the northern forests
Gray and stark are seen,
Here the live oak, manzanita,
Eucalyptus and grevillia,
Fringing pepper, fragrant orange—
Wear eternal green.

Summer trees by winter meadows,
Rose-bloom never done;
Knee-deep green of sudden springtime,
Nine months' peaceful golden weather,
Then swift rain and glowing sunshine—
Fall and spring made one.
Only winter in the orchards,
Few short leafless weeks of winter,
With those tender winter colors
under the warm sun.

❧
Santa Clara Hills

Oh bare, round-bosomed, dimpling hills!
With fawn and golden heights and violet hollows,
Where the warm sunlight lingeringly flows,
Dawn flush, noon gold, soft fire of evening rose,
And tender moonlight follows.

An Honest Woman

"THERE'S AN HONEST woman if ever there was one!" said the young salesman to the old one, watching their landlady whisk inside the screen door and close it softly without letting in a single fly—those evergreen California flies not mentioned by real estate men.

"What makes you think so?" asked Mr. Burdock, commonly known as "Old Burdock," wriggling forward, with alternate jerks, the two hind legs which supported his chair, until its backward tilt was positively dangerous.

"Think!" said young Abramson with extreme decision, "I happen to know. I've put up here for three years past, twice a year; and I know a lot of people in this town—sell to 'em right along."

"Stands well in the town, does she?" inquired the other with no keen interest. He had put up at the Main House for eight years, and furthermore he knew Mrs. Main when she was a child; but he did not mention it. Mr. Burdock made no pretense of virtue, yet if he had one in especial it lay in the art of not saying things.

"I should say she did!" the plump young man replied, straightening his well-curved waistcoat. "None better. She hasn't a bill standing—settles the day they come in. Pays cash for everything she can. She must make a handsome thing of this house; but it don't go in finery—she's as plain as a hen."

"Why I should call Mrs. Main rather a good looking woman," Burdock gently protested.

"Oh yes, good looking enough; but I mean her style—no show—no expense—no dress. But she keeps up the house all right—everything first class, and reasonable prices. She's got good money in the bank they tell me. And there's a daughter—away at school somewhere—won't have her brought up in a hotel. She's dead right, too."

"I dunno why a girl couldn't grow up in a hotel—with a nice mother like that," urged Mr. Burdock.

"Oh come! You know better'n that. Get talked about in any case—probably worse. No sir! You can't be too careful about a girl, and her mother knows it."

"Glad you've got a high opinion of women. I like to see it," and Mr.

Burdock tilted softly backward and forward in his chair, a balancing foot thrust forth. He wore large, square-toed, rather thin shoes with the visible outlines of feet in them.

The shoes of Mr. Abramson, on the other hand, had pronounced outlines of their own, and might have been stuffed with anything—that would go in.

"I've got a high opinion of good women," he announced with finality. "As to bad ones, the less said the better!" and he puffed his strong cigar, looking darkly experienced.

"They're doin' a good deal towards reformin' 'em, nowadays, aint they?" ventured Mr. Burdock.

The young man laughed disagreeably. "You can't reform spilled milk," said he. "But I do like to see an honest, hard-working woman succeed."

"So do I, boy," said his companion, "so do I," and they smoked in silence.

The hotel bus drew up before the house, backed creakingly, and one passenger descended, bearing a large, lean suitcase showing much wear. He was an elderly man, tall, well-built, but not well carried; and wore a long, thin beard. Mr. Abramson looked him over, decided that he was neither a buyer nor a seller, and dismissed him from his mind.

Mr. Burdock looked him over and brought the front legs of his chair down with a thump.

"By Heck!" said he softly.

The newcomer went in to register. Mr. Burdock went in to buy another cigar.

Mrs. Main was at the desk alone, working at her books. Her smooth, dark hair curved away from a fine forehead, both broad and high; wide-set, steady gray eyes looked out from under level brows with a clear directness. Her mouth, at thirty-eight, was a little hard.

The tall man scarcely looked at her, as he reached for the register book; but she looked at him, and her color slowly heightened. He signed his name as one of considerable importance, "Mr. Alexander E. Main, Guthrie, Oklahoma."

"I want a sunny room," he said, "A south room, with a fire when I want it. I feel the cold in this climate very much."

"You always did," remarked Mrs. Main quietly.

Then he looked; the pen dropping from his fingers and rolling across the untouched page, making a dotted path of lessening blotches.

Mr. Burdock made himself as small as he could against the cigar stand, but she ruthlessly approached, sold him the cigar he selected, and waited calmly till he started out, the tall man still staring.

Then she turned to him.

"Here is your key," she said. "Joe, take the gentleman's grip."

The boy moved off with the worn suitcase, but the tall man leaned over the counter towards her.

Mr. Burdock was carefully closing the screen door—so carefully that he could still hear.

"Why Mary! Mary! I must see you," the man whispered.

"You may see me at any time," she answered quietly. "Here is my office."

"This evening!" he said excitedly. "I'll come down this evening when it's quiet. I have so much to tell you, Mary."

"Very well," she said. "Room 27, Joe," and turned away.

Mr. Burdock took a walk, his cigar still unlighted.

"By Heck!" said he. "By—Heck!—And she as cool as a cucumber— That confounded old skeezicks!—Hanged if I don't happen to be passin'."

A STURDY LONG-LEGGED little girl was Mary Cameron when he first did business with her father in a Kansas country store. Ranch born and bred, a vigorous, independent child, gravely selling knives and sewing silk, writing paper and potatoes "to help father."

Father was a free thinker—a man of keen, strong mind, scant education, and opinions which ran away with him. He trained her to think for herself, and she did; to act up to her beliefs, and she did; to worship liberty and the sacred rights of the individual, and she did.

But the store failed, as the ranch had failed before it. Perhaps "old man Cameron's" arguments were too hot for the store loafers; perhaps his free thinking scandalized them. When Burdock saw Mary again she was working in a San Francisco restaurant. She did not remember him in the least; but he knew one of her friends there and learned of the move to California—the orange failure, the grape failure, and unexpected death of Mr. Cameron, and Mary's self-respecting efficiency since.

"She's doin' well already—got some money ahead—and she's just as straight!" said Miss Josie. "Want to meet her?"

"Oh no." said Mr. Burdock, who was of a retiring disposition. "No, she wouldn't remember me at all."

When he happened into that restaurant again a year later Mary had gone, and her friend hinted dark things.

"She got to goin' with a married man!" she confided. "Man from Oklahoma—name o' Main. One o' these Healers—great man for talkin.' She's left here, and I don't know where she is."

Mr. Burdock was sorry, very sorry—not only because he knew Mary, but because he knew Mr. Main. First—where had he met that man first? When he was a glib young phrenologist in Cincinnati. Then he'd run against him in St. Louis—a palmist this time; and then in Topeka—"Dr. Alexander," some sort of an "opathist." Dr. Main's system of therapy varied, it appeared, with circumstances; he treated brains or bones as it happened, and here in San Francisco had made quite a hit; had lectured, had written a book on sex.

That Mary Cameron, with her hard sense and high courage, should take up with a man like that!

But Mr. Burdock continued to travel, and some four years later, coming to a new hotel in San Diego, he had found Mary again, now Mrs. Mary Main, presiding over the affairs of the house, with a small daughter going to school sedately.

Nothing did he say, to or about her; she was closely attending to her business, and he attended to his; but the next time he was in Cincinnati he had no difficulty in hearing of Mrs. Alexander Main—and her three children—in very poor circumstances indeed.

Of Main he had heard nothing for many years—till now.

He returned to the hotel, and walked near the side window of the office. No one there yet. Selecting chewing gum for solace, as tobacco might betray him, he deliberately tucked a camp stool under the shadow of the overhanging rose bush and sat there, somewhat thornily, but well hidden.

"It's none o' my business, but I mean to get the rights o' this," said Mr. Burdock.

She came in about a quarter of ten, as neat, as plain, as quiet as ever, and sat down under the light with her sewing. Many pretty things Mrs. Main made lovingly, but never wore.

She stopped after a little, folded her strong hands in her lap, and sat looking straight before her.

"If I could only see what she's looking at, I'd get the hang of it," thought Mr. Burdock, occasionally peering.

What she was looking at was a woman's life—and she studied it calmly and with impartial justice.

A fearless, independent girl, fond of her father but recognizing his weaknesses, she had taken her life in her own hands at about the age of twenty, finding in her orphanhood mainly freedom. Her mother she hardly remembered. She was not attractive to such youths as she met in the course of business, coldly repellant to all casual advances, and determined inwardly not to marry, at least not till she had made something of herself. She had worked hard, kept her health, saved money, and read much of the "progressive literature" her father loved.

Then came this man who also read—studied—thought; who felt as she felt, who shared her aspirations, who "understood her." (Quite possibly he did—he was a person of considerable experience.)

Slowly she grew to enjoy his society, to depend upon it. When he revealed himself as lonely, not over strong, struggling with the world, she longed to help him; and when, at last, in a burst of bitter confidence, he had said he must leave her, that she had made life over for him but that he must tear himself away, that she was life and hope and joy to him, but he was not free—she demanded the facts.

He told her a sad tale, seeming not to cast blame on any but himself; but the girl burned deep and hot with indignation at the sordid woman, older than he, who had married him in his inexperienced youth, drained him of all he could earn, blasted his ideals, made his life an unbearable desert-waste. She had—but no, he would not blacken her who had been his wife.

"She gives me no provable cause for divorce," he told her. "She will not loosen her grip. I have left her, but she will not let me go."

"Were there any—children?" she asked after a while.

"There was one little girl—" he said with a pathetic pause. "She died—"

He did not feel it necessary to mention that there were three little boys—who had lived, after a fashion.

Then Mary Cameron made a decision which was more credit to her heart than to her head, though she would have warmly denied such a criticism.

"I see no reason why your life—your happiness—your service to the community—should all be ruined and lost because you were foolish as a boy."

"I was," he groaned. "I fell under temptation. Like any other sinner, I must bear my punishment. There is no escape."

"Nonsense," said Mary. "She will not let you go. You will not live with her. You cannot marry me. But I can be your wife—if you want me to."

It was nobly meant. She cheerfully risked all, gave up all, to make up to him for his "ruined life"; to give some happiness to one so long un-happy and when he vowed that he would not take advantage of such sublime unselfishness, she said that it was not in the least unselfish—for she loved him. This was true—she was quite honest about it.

And he? It is perfectly possible that he entered into their "sacred com-pact" with every intention of respecting it. She made him happier than anyone else ever had, so far.

There were two happy years when Mr. and Mrs. Main—they took themselves quite seriously—lived in their little flat together and worked and studied and thought great thoughts for the advancement of human-ity. Also there was a girl child born, and their contentment was com-plete.

But in time the income earned by Mr. Main fell away more and more; till Mrs. Main went forth again and worked in a hotel, as efficient as ever, and even mere [more] attractive.

Then he had become restless and had gone to Seattle to look for em-ployment—a long search, with only letters to fill the void.

And then—the quiet woman's hands were clenched together till the nails were purple and white—then The Letter came.

She was sitting alone that evening, the child playing on the floor. The woman who looked after her in the daytime had gone home. The two "roomers" who nearly paid the rent were out. It was a still, soft evening.

She had not had a letter for a week—and was hungry for it. She kissed the envelope—where his hand had rested. She squeezed it tight in her hands—laid her cheek on it—pressed it to her heart.

The baby reached up and wanted to share in the game. She gave her the envelope. . . .

He was not coming back—ever. . . . It was better that she should kpow [know] at once. . . . She was a strong woman—she would not be overcome. . . . She was a capable woman—independent—he need not worry about her in that way. . . . They had been mistaken. . . . He had found one that was more truly his. . . . She had been a Great Boon to him. . . . Here was some money for the child. . . . Good-bye.

She sat there, still, very still, staring straight before her, till the child reached up with a little cry.

Then she caught that baby in her arms, and fairly crushed her with passionate caresses till the child cried in good earnest, and had to be comforted. Stony-eyed, the mother soothed and rocked her till she slept, and laid her carefully in her little crib. Then she stood up and faced it.

"I suppose I am a ruined woman," she said.

She went to the glass and lit the gas on either side, facing herself with fixed gaze and adding calmly. "I don't look it!"

She did not look it. Tall, strong, nobly built, softer and richer for her years of love, her happy motherhood; the woman she saw in the glass seemed as one at the beginning of a splendid life, not at the end of a bad one.

No one could ever know all that she thought and felt that night, bracing her broad shoulders to meet this unbelievable blow.

If he had died she could have borne it better; if he had disappeared she would at least have had her memories left. But now she had not only grief but shame. She had been a fool—a plain, ordinary, old-fashioned, girl fool, just like so many others she had despised. And now?

Under the shock and torture of her shattered life the brave, practical soul of her struggled to keep its feet, to stand erect. She was not a demonstrative woman. Possibly he had never known how much she loved him, how utterly her life had grown to lean on his.

This thought struck her suddenly and she held her head higher. "Why should he ever know?" she said to herself, and then, "At least I have the child!" Before that night was over her plans were made.

The money he had sent, which her first feeling was to tear and burn, she now put carefully aside. "He sent it for the child," she said. "She will need it." She sublet the little flat and sold the furniture to a young couple, friends of hers, who were looking for just such a quiet home. She bought a suit of mourning, not too cumbrous, and set forth with little Mollie for the South.

In that fair land to which so many invalids come too late, it is not hard to find incompetent women, widowed and penniless, struggling to make a business of the only art they know; emerging from the sheltered harbor of "keeping house" upon the troubled sea of "keeping boarders."

Accepting moderate terms because of the child, doing good work because of long experience, offering a friendly sympathy out of her own deep sorrow, Mrs. Main made herself indispensable to such a one.

When her new employer asked her about her husband, she would press her handkerchief to her eyes and say, "He has left me. I cannot bear to speak of him."

This was quite true.

In a year she had saved a little money, and had spent it for a ticket home for the bankrupt lady of the house, who gladly gave her "the goodwill of the business" for it.

Said goodwill was lodged in an angry landlord, a few discontented and largely delinquent boarders, and many unpaid tradesmen. Mrs. Main called a meeting of her creditors in the stiff boarding house parlor.

She said, "I have bought this business, such as it is, with practically my last cent. I have worked seven years in restaurants and hotels and know how to run this place better than it has been done so far. If you people will give me credit for six months, and then, if I make good, for six months more, I will assume these back debts—and pay them. Otherwise I shall have to leave here, and you will get nothing but what will come from a forced sale of this third hand furniture. I shall work hard for I have this fatherless child to work for." She had the fatherless child at her side—a pretty thing, about three years old.

They looked the house over, looked her over, talked a little with the boarder of longest standing, and took up her offer.

She made good in six months; at the end of the year had begun to pay debts; and now—

Mrs. Main drew a long breath and came back to the present.

Mollie, dear Mollie, was a big girl now, doing excellently well at a good school. The Main House was an established success—had been for years. She had some money laid up—for Mollie's college expenses. Her health was good, she liked her work, she was respected and esteemed in the town, a useful member of a liberal church, of the Progressive Woman's Club, of the City Improvement Association. She had won Comfort, Security and Peace.

His step on the stairs—restrained—uncertain—eager.

Her door was open. He came in, and closed it softly behind him. She rose and opened it.

"That door stands open," she said. "You need not worry. There's no one about."

"Not many, at any rate," thought the unprincipled Burdock.

She sat down again quietly. He wanted to kiss her, to take her in his arms; but she moved back to her seat with a decided step, and motioned him to his.

"You wanted to speak to me, Mr. Main. What about?"

Then he poured forth his heart as he used to, in a flow of strong, convincing words.

He told of his wanderings, his struggles, his repeated failures; of the misery that had overwhelmed him in his last fatal mistake.

"I deserve it all," he said with the quick smile and lift of the head that once was so compelling. "I deserve everything that has come to me. . . .

Once to have had you. . . . And to be so blind a fool as to let go your hand! I needed it, Mary, I needed it."

He said little of his intermediate years as to facts; much as to the waste of woe they represented.

"Now I am doing better in my business," he said. "I have an established practice in Guthrie, but my health is not good and I have been advised to come to a warmer climate at least for a while."

She said nothing but regarded him with a clear and steady eye. He seemed an utter stranger, and an unattractive one. That fierce leap of the heart, which, in his presence, at his touch, she recalled so well—where was it now?

"Will you not speak to me, Mary?"

"I have nothing to say."

"Can you not—forgive me?"

She leaned forward, dropping her forehead in her hands. He waited breathless; he thought she was struggling with her heart.

In reality she was recalling their life together, measuring its further prospects in the light of what he had told her, and comparing it with her own life since. She raised her head and looked him squarely in the eye.

"I have nothing to forgive," she said.

"Ah you are too generous, too noble!" he cried. "And I? The burden of my youth is lifted now. My first wife is dead—some years since—and I am free. You are my real wife, Mary, my true and loving wife. Now I can offer you the legal ceremony as well."

"I do not wish it," she answered.

"It shall be as you say," he went on. "But for the child's sake—I wish to be a father to her."

"You are her father," said she. "That cannot be helped."

"But I wish to give her my name."

"She has it. I gave it to her."

"Brave, dear woman! But now I can give it to you."

"I have it also. It has been my name ever since I—according to my conscience—married you."

"But—but—you have no *legal* right to it, Mary."

She smiled, even laughed.

"Better read a little law, Mr. Main. I have used that name for twelve years, am publicly and honorably known by it; it is mine, legally."

"But Mary, I want to help you."

"Thank you. I do not need it."

"But I want to do for the child—my child—our little one!"

"You may," said she. "I want to send her to college. You may help if you like. I should be very glad if Mollie could have some pleasant and honorable memories of her father." She rose suddenly. "You wish to marry me now, Mr. Main?"

"With all my heart I wish it, Mary. You will?—"

He stood up—he held out his arms to her.

"No," said she, "I will not. When I was twenty-four I loved you, I sympathized with you. I was willing to be your wife—truly and faithfully your wife; even though you could not legally marry me—because I loved you. Now I will not marry you because I do not love you. That is all."

He glanced about the quiet, comfortable room; he had already estimated the quiet, comfortable business; and now, from some forgotten chamber of his honey-combed heart, welled up a fierce longing for this calm, strong, tender woman whose power of love he knew so well.

"Mary! You will not turn me away! I love you—I love you as I never loved you before!"

"I'm sorry to hear it," she said again. "It does not make me love you again."

His face darkened.

"Do not drive me to desperation," he cried. "Your whole life here rests on a lie, remember. I could shatter it with a word."

She smiled patiently.

"You can't shatter facts, Mr. Main. People here know that you left me years ago. They know how I have lived since. If you try to blacken my reputation here I think you will find the climate of Mexico more congenial."

On second thoughts, this seemed to be the opinion of Mr. Main, who presently left for that country.

It was also agreed with by Mr. Burdock, who emerged later, a little chilly and somewhat scratched, and sought his chamber.

"If that galoot says anything against her in this town, he'll find a hotter climate than Mexico—by Heck!" said Mr. Burdock to his boots as he set them down softly. And that was all he ever said about it.

Elaine Goodale Eastman

(1863–1953)

IN THE YEARS FOLLOWING George Armstrong Custer's defeat at the Little Big Horn, the U.S. government forced nomadic Sioux and Cheyenne onto reservations in the Dakota Territory. The practical extinction of the buffalo, accompanied by territorial restriction of the Indian tribes, required a change from the traditional hunting-and-gathering lifestyle to dryland farming. Ideally, the Indians were given yearly allowances of food, grain, farm implements, and household goods. In reality, Indian agents—political appointees who were ill equipped to teach Indians how to farm—siphoned off the bulk of the resources. Worse still, in the late 1880s, drought and locusts defeated those who attempted to farm. Frustration, malnutrition, fear, and a yearning for the old ways created fertile ground for a new messianic religion.

The Ghost Dance movement originated in western Nevada with a Paiute named Wovoka. Messengers such as Sitting Bull, who claimed to have seen the messiah—a blonde, blue-eyed, stigmata-bearing Christ-figure—carried the word east. The new messiah's apocalyptic message proclaimed the end of the white man's civilization, the return of the buffalo to the Plains, and the triumph of Native Americans over white civilization. Sioux followers of the Ghost Dance religion believed that this would happen when the grass turned green in the spring of 1891—as long as the people continued to perform the Ghost Dance around a sacred tree. The army and Indian agents in the Dakotas, fearing an uprising, forbade the Ghost Dance. It continued. Tensions mounted until, in December 1890, white soldiers murdered Sitting Bull.

On December 29, 1890, at Wounded Knee Creek on the Pine Ridge Indian Reservation, South Dakota, American troops massacred roughly 250 to 300 unarmed Sioux. Elaine Goodale, the first superintendent of education for the Dakota reservations, heard "the distant thunder of big guns, some eighteen miles away" from where she wrapped Christmas gifts at the Chapel of the Holy Cross at the Pine Ridge Agency. The wounded, few of whom survived the ordeal, were taken to the church. They were tended by Goodale, Susette La Flesche, and a Santee Sioux doctor, Charles Eastman *(Ohiyesa)*. Dr. Eastman, raised in Canada and educated in the East, had just returned to work among his people.

Within weeks, the Ghost Dance religion went underground. So did Sioux dreams of the return of the buffalo culture to the Plains.

Who was this single white woman with an official post who traveled freely and fearlessly among the Sioux and spoke their language? Elaine Goodale was born in 1863 on Sky Farm in the Berkshire Mountains of Massachusetts. Her mother, who homeschooled the four children, was a poet and musician. She passed on her love of literature to her offspring. Elaine and her younger sister, Dora, published poems, including "Ashes of Roses," in *St. Nicholas* in 1877, when Elaine was thirteen. Beginning in 1878, they put out four books of poetry and mixed prose and poetry.

At twenty, when Sky Farm was sold, the independent Elaine taught at the Hampton Institute, a missionary school for "Negroes" and Indians. In 1885, while touring the Sioux agencies in the Dakota Territory (with geologist Florence Bascum), Elaine noticed the empty schoolhouses. She returned a year later to open a day school on the White River. In her philosophy, acculturation would be accomplished more efficiently and less painfully if children attended day schools rather than being separated from their families and sent to boarding schools, the preferred method at that time. During her years of teaching and supervising education in the Dakotas—a position she accepted in 1890—Elaine wrote articles and poems for newspapers and magazines such as the *New York Evening Post* and the *Independent*. She also became well known as a lecturer on Indian education.

Shortly after Wounded Knee, Elaine Goodale married Eastman. She quit her job to support her husband and to raise their six children. But she did not stop writing. She collaborated with Charles on nine books and numerous articles, only a few of which bear her name. They moved frequently, and after thirty years, they quietly separated. Charles Eastman published no more books or articles. On her own, Elaine Goodale Eastman wrote children's books, including *Indian Legends Retold* and *Pratt: The Red Man's Moses*. Her memoir, *Sister to the Sioux*, was published twenty-five years after her death.

Ashes of Roses

Soft on the sunset sky
Bright daylight closes,
Leaving, when light doth die,
Pale hues that mingling lie—
Ashes of roses.

When love's warm sun is set,
Love's brightness closes;
Eyes with hot tears are wet,
In hearts there linger yet
Ashes of roses.

The Wood-Chopper to His Ax

My comrade keen, my lawless friend,
When will your savage temper mend?
I wield you, powerless to resist;
I feel your weight bend back my wrist,
Straighten the corded arm,
Caress the hardened palm.

War on these forest tribes they made,
The men who forged your sapphire blade;
Its very substance thus renewed
Tenacious of the ancient feud.
In crowding ranks uprose
Your ambushed, waiting foes.

This helve, by me wrought out and planned,
By long use suited to this hand,
Was carved, with patient, toilsome art,
From stubborn hickory's milk-white heart;

Its satin gloss makes plain
The fineness of the grain.

When deeply sunk, an entering wedge,
The live wood tastes your shining edge;
When, strongly cleft from side to side,
You feel its shrinking heart divide,
List not the shuddering sigh
Of that dread agony.

Yon gaping mouth you need not miss,
But close it with a poignant kiss;
Nor dread to search, with whetted knife,
The naked mystery of life,
And count on shining rings
The ever-widening springs.

Hew, trenchant steel, the ivory core,
One mellow, resonant stroke the more
Loudly the cracking sinews start,
Unwilling members wrenched apart—
Dear ax, your 'complice I
In love and cruelty!

Pima Tales

Children of the Cloud

THERE WAS SORROW on the Casa Grande (the Great Pueblo), for the prettiest woman in the village would accept no man for her husband. Her suitors were many and impatient, but her black glossy locks were still wound above her ears in the manner of virgins, and she steadily refused to allow them to hang down in the matron's coils.

One day a great Cloud came out of the east, looked down upon the maiden and wished to marry her, for she was very beautiful. A second time and a third he floated silently overhead, and at last he found her tired out with work and lying asleep at her mat-weaving. He let fall a single drop of rain upon her, and by and by twin boys were born.

Now when the boys were about ten years old, they began to notice that other boys had fathers whom they welcomed home from war and the chase. "Mother," said they, "who shall we call our father?"

"In the morning look to the east," their mother answered, "and you will see a stately white cloud towering heaven-ward. That cloud is your father."

Then they begged to go visit their father, and she refused, for she was afraid; but when the boys grew large and strong she could no longer keep them, since they were determined to go. She told them to journey four full days to the eastward and not to stop once on the way.

Her sons followed her instructions, and in four days they came to the house of the Wind. "Are you our father?" asked they.

"No," replied Wind, "I am your uncle. Your father lives in the next house; go and find him."

They did so, but Cloud sent them back to Wind, telling them that he was really the one whom they sought. Again Wind sent them to Cloud. Four times they went back and forth, and the fourth time Cloud saw that they were persistent and he said to them: "You say that you are my sons. Prove it!"

Instantly the younger son sent forked lightning leaping across the heavens, while the elder caused the heat lightning to flash in the distance. The skies opened and rain came down in torrents, enough to drown a mere mortal, but the boys only laughed at the roar and rush of the tempest. Then Cloud saw that they were in truth his children, and he took them to his house.

After they had been there a long time, they began to miss their mother sorely, and finally they wished to return to earth. Their father gave each a magic bow and arrows, strictly charging them to avoid any whom they might meet on the homeward path.

First the Eagle on mighty wing swooped toward them, and they turned aside. Then came the Hawk, and afterward the Raven, but the boys managed to elude all of these. Last the Coyote sought to intercept them, and whichever way they turned, he was always before them. So they stepped out of the road and stood one on either side to allow him to pass. But when Coyote came opposite to them, each was changed into a plant of the mescal, the sacred agave, which is both food and drink to the Indian.

&

The Naughty Grandchildren

AN OLD WOMAN had set her pot on the fire with the soup for dinner, and as her two grandchildren were playing near, she cautioned them not to upset the pot. The boy and girl were in a frolicsome mood, chasing one another with shouts of laugher; and as they ran they heedlessly struck against the pot, which rolled over and broke in pieces, spilling the rich broth into the ashes.

Now when their grandmother saw the mischief they had done in spite of her warning, she caught and whipped them both. Thereupon the children determined to run away.

As soon as she missed them, the old woman followed the runaways out into the desert, calling loudly upon them to come back, for she had only punished them for their own good and loved them both dearly. However, run as fast as she might, she could never come up with them. The two children were never seen again; but it is said that they were turned into two giant cacti and still stand side by side upon the plain.

૪

Bluebird and Coyote

IN THE OLD DAYS the animals wore no such fine clothing as now, and the bluebird was of an ugly dun color, which made him very unhappy. One fine morning he came to a lake shining like turquoise, and something told him to bathe in the water.

Lightly he skimmed above the waves and dipped his wings four times, singing as he did so:

> "Here is blue water—
> I go in—
> I am all blue!"

The fourth time that he sang the verse and shook the water from his feathers, they really became bright blue!

Just then Coyote appeared, in time to see the transformation. "If you can make yourself beautiful by bathing in the lake, I can do as much," said he, and accordingly he took the plunge. Coyote could not swim, and he choked and strangled and was almost drowned. When at last he contrived to get upon dry land, he was shivering with cold. He rolled and rolled in the warm sand, which stuck to his fur, and he became dirt color, just as you see him now.

Edith Maude Eaton
(Sui Sin Far)
(1865–1914)

CONSTRUCTION OF THE first transcontinental railroad in the 1860s, and all subsequent rail lines, created jobs for skilled and unskilled laborers. Due to the Civil War, a labor shortage developed that was answered not only by importation of foreign workers but also by recruitment from previously untapped American labor pools. The Irish, escaping a potato famine, represented the largest contingent of European immigrants. Thousands entered the United States through the northeastern seaboard and Canada and helped construct the Union Pacific tracks westward from Omaha, Nebraska, to Utah. Chinese workers were recruited at first from Chinese neighborhoods in California, where they had settled during and after the gold rush. All of the mining districts had Chinese quarters—separate ghettos with separate graveyards. So did cities such as Los Angeles, Sacramento, and San Francisco. But when supply was not great enough to meet demand, the Central Pacific Railroad sent agents to China. Once the main railroads were finished the Chinese stayed and brought family members from China.

The United States was not the only Western country to have a Chinese population. The British Empire included Hong Kong, and some Chinese emigrated to England and Canada where "yellow" skin made assimilation difficult.

Edith Maude Eaton, who wrote under the pen name Sui Sin Far (the Chinese Lily), had an English father and a Chinese mother. The oldest girl in a family of fourteen distinguished and talented children, she supported herself as a writer from an early age. When she was seven, the family moved from England to New York, and then to Montreal, Canada. Prejudice in the New World was just as profound as in the Old. Although Eaton could have passed herself off as pure white or Japanese, a more acceptable heritage in Western minds, she chose to learn as much about her Chinese heritage as possible. It is clear from one of her most famous works, "Leaves from the Mental Portfolio of an Eurasian," that the two sides warred constantly.

For health reasons, Eaton moved to the western United States. In San Francisco, Los Angeles, and Seattle, she wrote articles on Chinese neighborhoods and short stories set among the Chinese population. Her plots emphasized the problems suffered by immigrants and their offspring, children of two cultures. Her settings invoked the flavor of Chinatown. She was the first woman of Chinese heritage to write fiction in the United States. Her work was published in leading journals and magazines, including the *Overland Monthly, Century,* the *Independent, Good Housekeeping,* and *Out West.* Most of her stories from the last decade of the nineteenth century and the first decade of the twentieth were collected in *Mrs. Spring Fragrance,* a gem published in 1912.

As a Eurasian, Eaton identified with both heritages. Asian and non-Asian males of her day saw her as either half-white or half-Asian. She preferred to stay single rather than marry a man who could not accept both sides of her heritage.

Leaves from the Mental Portfolio of an Eurasian

WHEN I LOOK BACK over the years I see myself, a little child of scarcely four years of age, walking in front of my nurse, in a green English lane, and listening to her tell another of her kind that my mother is Chinese. "Oh, Lord!" exclaims the informed. She turns me around and scans me curiously from head to foot. Then the two women whisper together. Tho the word "Chinese" conveys very little meaning to my mind, I feel that they are talking about my father and mother and my heart swells with indignation. When we reach home, I rush to my mother and try to tell her what I have heard. I am a young child. I fail to make myself intelligible. My mother does not understand, and when the nurse declares to her, "Little Miss Sui is a story-teller," my mother slaps me.

Many a long year has past over my head since that day—the day on which I first learned that I was something different and apart from other children, but tho my mother has forgotten it, I have not.

I see myself again, a few years older. I am playing with another child in a garden. A girl passes by outside the gate. "Mamie," she cries to my companion. "I wouldn't speak to Sui if I were you. Her mamma is Chinese."

"I don't care," answers the little one beside me. And then to me, "Even if your mamma is Chinese, I like you better than I like Annie."

"But I don't like you," I answer, turning my back on her. It is my first conscious lie.

I am at a children's party, given by the wife of an Indian officer whose children were school fellows of mine. I am only six years of age, but have attended a private school for over a year, and have already learned that China is a heathen country, being civilized by England. However, for the time being, I am a merry romping child. There are quite a number of grown people present. One, a white haired old man, has his attention called to me by the hostess. He adjusts his eyeglasses and surveys me critically. "Ah, indeed!" he exclaims, "Who would have thought it at first glance. Yet now I see the difference between her and other children. What a peculiar coloring! Her mother's eyes and hair and her father's features, I presume. Very interesting little creature!"

I had been called from my play for the purpose of inspection. I do not return to it. For the rest of the evening I hide myself behind a hall door and refuse to show myself until it is time to go home.

My parents have come to America. We are in Hudson City, N.Y., and we are very poor. I am out with my brother, who is ten months older than myself. We pass a Chinese store, the door of which is open. "Look!" says Charlie, "Those men in there are Chinese!" Eagerly I gaze into the long low room. With the exception of my mother, who is English bred with English ways and manner of dress, I have never seen a Chinese person. The two men within the store are uncouth specimens of their race, drest in working blouses and pantaloons with queues hanging down their backs. I recoil with a sense of shock.

"Oh, Charlie," I cry, "Are we like that?"

"Well, we're Chinese, and they're Chinese, too, so we must be!" returns my seven-year-old brother.

"Of course you are," puts in a boy who has followed us down the street, and who lives near us and has seen my mother: "Chinky, Chinky, Chinaman, yellow-face, pig-tail, rat-eater." A number of other boys and several little girls join in with him.

"Better than you," shouts my brother, facing the crowd. He is younger and smaller than any there, and I am even more insignificant than he; but my spirit revives.

"I'd rather be Chinese than anything else in the world," I scream.

They pull my hair, they tear my clothes, they scratch my face, and all but lame my brother; but the white blood in our veins fights valiantly for the Chinese half of us. When it is all over, exhausted and bedraggled, we crawl home, and report to our mother that we have "won the battle."

"Are you sure?" asks my mother doubtfully.

"Of course. They ran from us. They were frightened," returns my brother.

My mother smiles with satisfaction.

"Do you hear?" she asks my father.

"Umm," he observes, raising his eyes from his paper for an instant. My childish instinct, however, tells me that he is more interested than he appears to be.

It is tea time, but I cannot eat. Unobserved I crawl away. I do not sleep that night. I am too excited and I ache all over. Our opponents had been so very much stronger and bigger than we. Toward morning, however, I fall into a doze from which I awake myself, shouting:

"Sound the battle cry;
See the foe is nigh."

My mother believes in sending us to Sunday school. She has been brought up in a Presbyterian college.

The scene of my life shifts to Eastern Canada. The sleigh which has carried us from the station stops in front of a little French Canadian hotel. Immediately we are surrounded by a number of villagers, who stare curiously at my mother as my father assists her to alight from the sleigh. Their curiosity, however, is tempered with kindness, as they watch, one after another, the little black heads of my brothers and sisters and myself emerge out of the buffalo robe, which is part of the sleigh's outfit. There are six of us, four girls and two boys; the eldest, my brother, being only seven years of age. My father and mother are still in their twenties. "Les pauvres enfants," the inhabitants murmur, as they help to carry us into the hotel. Then in lower tones: "Chinoise, Chinoise."

For some time after our arrival, whenever we children are sent for a walk, our footsteps are dogged by a number of young French and English Canadians, who amuse themselves with speculations as to whether, we being Chinese, are susceptible to pinches and hair pulling, while older persons pause and gaze upon us, very much in the same way that I have seen people gaze upon strange animals in a menagerie. Now and then we are stopt and plied with questions as to what we eat and drink, how we go to sleep, if my mother understands what my father says to her, if we sit on chairs or squat on floors, etc., etc., etc.

There are many pitched battles, of course, and we seldom leave the house without being armed for conflict. My mother takes a great interest in our battles, and usually cheers us on, tho I doubt whether she understands the depth of the troubled waters thru which her little children wade. As to my father, peace is his motto, and he deems it wisest to be blind and deaf to many things.

School days are short, but memorable. I am in the same class with my brother, my sister next to me in the class below. The little girl whose desk my sister shares shrinks close against the wall as my sister takes her place. In a little while she raises her hand.

"Please, teacher!"

"Yes, Annie."

"May I change my seat?"

"No, you may not!"

The little girl sobs. "Why should she have to sit beside a—"

Happily my sister does not seem to hear, and before long the two little girls become great friends. I have many such experiences.

My brother is remarkably bright; my sister next to me has a wonderful head for figures, and when only eight years of age helps my father with his night work accounts. My parents compare her with me. She is of sturdier build than I, and, as my father says, "Always has her wits about her." He thinks her more like my mother, who is very bright and interested in every little detail of practical life. My father tells me that I will never make half the woman that my mother is or that my sister will be. I am not as strong as my sisters, which makes me feel somewhat ashamed, for I am the eldest little girl, and more is expected of me. I have no organic disease, but the strength of my feelings seems to take from me the strength of my body. I am prostrated at times with attacks of nervous sickness. The doctor says that my heart is unusually large; but in the light of the present I know that the cross of the Eurasian bore too heavily upon my childish shoulders. I usually hide my weakness from the family until I cannot stand. I do not understand myself, and I have an idea that the others will despise me for not being as strong as they. Therefore, I like to wander away alone, either by the river or in the bush. The green fields and flowing water have a charm for me. At the age of seven, as it is today, a bird on the wing is my emblem of happiness.

I have come from a race on my mother's side which is said to be the most stolid and insensible to feeling of all races, yet I look back over the years and see myself so keenly alive to every shade of sorrow and suffering that it is almost a pain to live.

If there is any trouble in the house in the way of a difference between my father and mother, or if any child is punished, how I suffer! And when harmony is restored, heaven seems to be around me. I can be sad, but I can also be glad. My mother's screams of agony when a baby is born almost drive me wild, and long after her pangs have subsided I feel them in my own body. Sometimes it is a week before I can get to sleep after such an experience.

A debt owing by my father fills me with shame. I feel like a criminal when I pass the creditor's door. I am only ten years old. And all the while the question of nationality perplexes my little brain. Why are we what we are? I and my brothers and sisters. Why did God make us to be hooted and stared at? Papa is English, Mamma is Chinese. Why couldn't we have been either one thing or the other? Why is my mother's race despised? I look into the faces of my father and mother. Is she not every bit as dear and good as he? Why? Why? She sings us the songs she learned at her English school. She tells us tales of China. Tho a child when she left her native land she remembers it well, and I am never tired of listening to the story of how she was stolen from her home. She tells us over and over again of her meeting with my father in Shanghai and the romance of their marriage. Why? Why?

I do not confide in my father and mother. They would not understand. How could they? He is English, she is Chinese. I am different to both of them—a stranger, tho their own child. "What are we?" I ask my brother. "It doesn't matter, sissy," he responds. But it does. I love poetry, particularly heroic pieces. I also love fairy tales. Stories of everyday life do not appeal to me. I dream dreams of being great and noble; my sisters and brothers also. I glory in the idea of dying at the stake and a great genie arising from the flames and declaring to those who have scorned us: "Behold, how great and glorious and noble are the Chinese people!"

My sisters are apprenticed to a dressmaker; my brother is entered in an office. I tramp around and sell my father's pictures, also some lace which I make myself. My nationality, if I had only known it at the time, helps to make sales. The ladies who are my customers call me "The Little Chinese Lace Girl." But it is a dangerous life for a very young girl. I come near to "mysteriously disappearing" many a time. The greatest temptation was in the thought of getting far away from where I was known, to where no mocking cries of "Chinese!" "Chinese!" could reach.

Whenever I have the opportunity I steal away to the library and read every book I can find on China and the Chinese. I learn that China is the oldest civilized nation on the face of the earth and a few other things. At eighteen years of age what troubles me is not that I am what I am, but that others are ignorant of my superiority. I am small, but my feelings are big—and great is my vanity.

My sisters attend dancing classes, for which they pay their own fees. In spite of covert smiles and sneers, they are glad to meet and mingle with other young folk. They are not sensitive in the sense that I am. And yet they understand. One of them tells me that she overhead a young man say to another that he would rather marry a pig than a girl with Chinese blood in her veins.

In course of time I too learn shorthand and take a position in an office. Like my sister, I teach myself, but, unlike my sister, I have neither the perseverance nor the ability to perfect myself. Besides, to a temperament like mine, it is torture to spend the hours in transcribing other people's thoughts. Therefore, altho I can always earn a moderately good salary, I do not distinguish myself in the business world as does she.

When I have been working for some years I open an office of my own. The local papers patronize me and give me a number of assignments, including most of the local Chinese reporting. I meet many Chinese persons, and when they get into trouble am often called upon to fight their battles in the papers. This I enjoy. My heart leaps for joy when I read one day an article signed by a New York Chinese in which he declares "The Chinese in America owe an everlasting debt of gratitude to Sui Sin Far for the bold stand she has taken in their defense."

The Chinaman who wrote the article seeks me out and calls upon me. He is a clever and witty man, a graduate of one of the American colleges and as well a Chinese scholar. I learn that he has an American wife and several children. I am very much interested in these children, and when I meet them my heart throbs in sympathetic tune with the tales they relate of their experiences as Eurasians. "Why did papa and mamma born us?" asks one. Why?

I also meet other Chinese men who compare favorably with the white men of my acquaintance in mind and heart qualities. Some of them are quite handsome. They have not as finely cut noses and as well developed chins as the white men, but they have smoother skins and their expression is more serene; their hands are better shaped and their voices softer.

Some little Chinese women whom I interview are very anxious to know whether I would marry a Chinaman. I do not answer No. They clap their hands delightedly, and assure me that the Chinese are much the finest and best of all men. They are, however, a little doubtful as to whether one could be persuaded to care for me, full-blooded Chinese people having a prejudice against the half white.

Fundamentally, I muse, all people are the same. My mother's race is as prejudiced as my father's. Only when the whole world becomes as one family will human beings be able to see clearly and hear distinctly. I believe that some day a great part of the world will be Eurasian. I cheer myself with the thought that I am but a pioneer. A pioneer should glory in suffering.

"You were walking with a Chinaman yesterday," accuses an acquaintance.

"Yes, what of it?"

"You ought not to. It isn't right."

"Not right to walk with one of my own mother's people? Oh, indeed!"

I cannot reconcile his notion of righteousness with my own.

I AM LIVING IN a little town away off on the north shore of a big lake. Next to me at the dinner table is the man for whom I work as a stenographer. There are also a couple of business men, a young girl and her mother.

Some one makes a remark about the cars full of Chinamen that past that morning. A transcontinental railway runs thru the town.

My employer shakes his rugged head. "Somehow or other," says he, "I cannot reconcile myself to the thought that the Chinese are humans like ourselves. They may have immortal souls, but their faces seem to be so utterly devoid of expression that I cannot help but doubt."

"Souls," echoes the town clerk. "Their bodies are enough for me. A Chinaman is, in my eyes, more repulsive than a nigger."

"They always give me such a creepy feeling," puts in the young girl with a laugh.

"I wouldn't have one in my house, " declares my landlady.

"Now, the Japanese are different altogether. There is something bright and likeable about those men," continues Mr. K.

A miserable, cowardly feeling keeps me silent. I am in a Middle West town. If I declare what I am, every person in the place will hear about it the next day. The population is in the main made up of working folks with strong prejudices against my mother's countrymen. The prospect before me is not an enviable one—if I speak. I have no longer an ambition to die at the stake for the sake of demonstrating the greatness and nobleness of the Chinese people.

Mr. K turns to me with a kindly smile.

"What makes Miss Far so quiet?" he asks.

"I don't suppose she finds the 'washee washee men' particularly interesting subjects of conversation," volunteers the young manager of the local bank.

With a great effort I raise my eyes from my plate. "Mr. K.," I say, addressing my employer, "the Chinese people may have no souls, no expression on their faces, be altogether beyond the pale of civilization, but whatever they are, I want you to understand that I am—I am a Chinese."

There is silence in the room for a few minutes. Then Mr. K. pushes back his plate and standing up beside me, says:

"I should not have spoken as I did. I know nothing whatever about the Chinese. It was pure prejudice. Forgive me!"

I admire Mr. K.'s moral courage in apologizing to me; he is a conscientious Christian man, but I do not remain much longer in the little town.

I AM UNDER A tropic sky, meeting frequently and conversing with persons who are almost as high up in the world as birth, education and money can set them. The environment is peculiar, for I am also surrounded by a race of people, the reputed descendants of Ham, the son of Noah, whose offspring, it was prophesied, should be the servants of the sons of Shem and Japheth. As I am a descendant, according to the Bible, of both Shem and Japheth, I have a perfect right to set my heel upon the Ham people; but tho I see others around me following out the Bible suggestion, it is not in my nature to be arrogant to any but those who seek to impress me with their superiority, which the poor black maid who has been assigned to me by the hotel certainly does not. My employer's wife takes me to task for this. "It is unnecessary," she says, "to thank a black person for a service."

The novelty of life in the West Indian island is not without its charm. The surroundings, people, manner of living, are so entirely different from what I have been accustomed to up North that I feel as if I were "born again." Mixing with people of fashion, and yet not of them, I am not of sufficient importance to create comment or curiosity. I am busy nearly all day and often well into the night. It is not monotonous work, but it is certainly strenuous. The planters and business men of the island take me as a matter of course and treat me with kindly courtesy. Occasionally an Englishman will warn me against the "brown boys" of the island, little dreaming that I too am of the "brown people" of the earth.

When it begins to be whispered about the place that I am not all white, some of the "sporty" people seek my acquaintance. I am small and look much younger than my years. When, however, they discover that I am a very serious and sober-minded spinster indeed, they retire quite gracefully, leaving me a few amusing reflections.

One evening a card is brought to my room. It bears the name of some naval officer. I go down to my visitor, thinking he is probably some one who, having been told that I am a reporter for the local paper, has brought me an item of news. I find him lounging in an easy chair on the veranda of the hotel—a big, blond, handsome fellow, several years younger than I.

"You are Lieutenant—?" I inquire.

He bows and laughs a little. The laugh doesn't suit him somehow—and it doesn't suit me, either.

"If you have anything to tell me, please tell it quickly, because I'm very busy."

"Oh, you don't really mean that," he answers, with another silly and offensive laugh. "There's always plenty of time for good times. That's what I am here for. I saw you at the races the other day and twice at King's House. My ship will be here for——weeks."

"Do you wish that noted?" I ask.

"Oh, no! Why—I came just because I had an idea that you might like to know me. I would like to know you. You look such a nice little body. Say, wouldn't you like to go out for a sail this lovely night? I will tell you all about the sweet little Chinese girls I met when we were at Hong Kong. They're not so shy!"

I LEAVE EASTERN CANADA for the Far West, so reduced by another attack of rheumatic fever that I only weigh eighty-four pounds. I travel on an advertising contract. It is presumed by the railway company that in some way or other I will give them full value for their transportation across the continent. I have been ordered beyond the Rockies by the doctor, who declares that I will never regain my strength in the East. Nevertheless, I am but two days in San Francisco when I start out in search of work. It is the first time that I have sought work as a stranger in a strange town. Both of the other positions away from home were se-cured for me by home influence. I am quite surprised to find that there is no demand for my services in San Francisco and that no one is particu-larly interested in me. The best I can do is to accept an offer from a rail-way agency to typewrite their correspondence for $5 a month. I stipulate, however, that I shall have the privilege of taking in outside work and that my hours shall be light. I am hopeful that the sale of a story or newspaper article may add to my income, and I console myself with the reflection that, considering that I still limp and bear traces of sickness, I am fortunate to secure any work at all.

The proprietor of one of the San Francisco papers, to whom I have a letter of introduction, suggests that I obtain some subscriptions from the people of Chinatown, that district of the city having never been canvassed. This suggestion I carry out with enthusiasm tho I find that the Chinese merchants and people generally are inclined to regard me with suspicion. They have been imposed upon so many times by unscrupulous white people. Another drawback—save for a few phrases, I am unacquainted with my mother tongue. How, then, can I expect these people to accept me as their own countrywoman? The Americanized Chinamen actually laugh in my face when I tell them that I am of their race. However, they are not all "doubting Thomases." Some little women discover that I have Chinese hair, color of eyes and complexion, also that I love rice and tea. This settles the matter for them—and for their husbands.

My Chinese instincts develop. I am no longer the little girl who shrunk against my brother at the first sight of a Chinaman. Many and many a time, when alone in a strange place, has the appearance of even an humble laundryman given me a sense of protection and made me feel quite at home. This fact of itself proves to me that prejudice can be eradicated by association.

I meet a half Chinese, half white girl. Her face is plastered with a thick white coat of paint and her eyelids and eyebrows are blackened so that the shape of her eyes and the whole expression of her face is changed. She was born in the East, and at the age of eighteen came West in answer to an advertisement. Living for many years among the working class, she had heard little but abuse of the Chinese. It is not difficult, in a land like California, for a half Chinese, half white girl to pass as one of Spanish or Mexican origin. This the poor child does, tho she lives in nervous dread of being "discovered." She becomes engaged to a young man, but fears to tell him what she is, and only does so when compelled by a fearless American girl friend. This girl, who knows her origin, realizing that the truth sooner or later must be told, and better soon that late, advises the Eurasian to confide in the young man, assuring her that he loves her well enough not to allow her nationality to stand, a bar sinister, between them. But the Eurasian prefers to keep her secret, and only reveals it to the man who is to be her husband when driven to bay by the American girl, who declares that if the half-breed will not tell the truth she will. When the young man hears that the girl he is engaged to has Chinese blood in her veins, he exclaims: "Oh, what will my folks say?" But that is all. Love is stronger than prejudice with him, and neither he nor she deems it necessary to inform his "folks."

The Americans, having for many years manifested a much higher regard for the Japanese than for the Chinese, several half Chinese young men and women, thinking to advance themselves, both in a social and business sense, pass as Japanese. They continue to be known as Eurasians; but a Japanese Eurasian does not appear in the same light as a Chinese Eurasian. The unfortunate Chinese Eurasians! Are not those who compel them to thus cringe more to be blamed than they?

People, however, are not all alike. I meet white men, and women, too, who are proud to mate with those who have Chinese blood in their veins, and think it a great honor to be distinguished by the friendship of such. There are also Eurasians and Eurasians. I know of one who allowed herself to become engaged to a white man after refusing him nine times. She had discouraged him in every way possible, had warned him that she was half Chinese; that her people were poor, that every week or month she sent home a certain amount of her earnings, and that the man she married would have to do as much, if not more; also, most uncompromising truth of all, that she did not love him and never would. But the resolute and undaunted lover swore that it was a matter of indifference to him whether she was a Chinese or a Hottentot, that it would be his pleasure and privilege to allow her relations double what it was in her power to bestow, and as to not loving him—that did not matter at all. He loved her. So, because the young woman had a married mother and married sisters, who were always picking at her and gossiping over her independent manner of living, she finally consented to marry him, recording the agreement in her diary thus:

"I have promised to become the wife of —— —— on —— ——, 189 , because the world is so cruel and sneering to a single woman—and for no other reason."

Everything went smoothly until one day. The young man was driving a pair of beautiful horses and she was seated by his side, trying very hard to imagine herself in love with him, when a Chinese vegetable gardener's cart came rumbling along. The Chinaman was a jolly-looking individual in blue cotton blouse and pantaloons, his rakish looking hat being kept in place by a long queue which was pulled upward from his neck and wound around it. The young woman was suddenly possest with the spirit of mischief. "Look!" she cried, indicating the Chinaman, "there's my brother. Why don't you salute him?"

The man's face fell a little. He sank into a pensive mood. The wicked one by his side read him like an open book.

"When we are married," said she, "I intend to give a Chinese party every month."

No answer.

"As there are very few aristocratic Chinese in this city, I shall fill up with the laundrymen and vegetable farmers. I don't believe in being exclusive in democratic America, do you?"

He hadn't a grain of humor in his composition, but a sickly smile contorted his features as he replied:

"You shall do just as you please, my darling. But—but—consider a moment. Wouldn't it be just a little pleasanter for us if, after we are married, we allowed it to be presumed that you were—er—Japanese? So many of my friends have inquired of me if that is not your nationality. They would be so charmed to meet a little Japanese lady."

"Hadn't you better oblige them by finding one?"

"Why—er—what do you mean?"

"Nothing much in particular. Only—I am getting a little tired of this," taking off his ring.

"You don't mean what you say! Oh, put it back, dearest! You know I would not hurt your feelings for the world!"

"You haven't. I'm more than pleased. But I do mean what I say."

That evening the "ungrateful" Chinese Eurasian diaried, among other things, the following:

"Joy, oh, joy! I'm free once more. Never again shall I be untrue to my own heart. Never again will I allow any one to 'hound' or 'sneer' me into matrimony."

I secure transportation to many California points. I meet some literary people, chief among whom is the editor of the magazine who took my first Chinese stories. He and his wife give me a warm welcome to their ranch. They are broad-minded people, whose interest in me is sincere and intelligent, not affected and vulgar. I also meet some funny people who advise me to "trade" upon my nationality. They tell me that if I wish to succeed in literature in America I should dress in Chinese costume, carry a fan in my hand, wear a pair of scarlet beaded slippers, live in New York, and come of high birth. Instead of making myself familiar with the Chinese-Americans around me, I should discourse on my spirit acquaintance with Chinese ancestors and quote in between the "Good mornings" and "How d'ye dos" of editors,

> "Confucius, Confucius, how great is Confucius,
> Before Confucius, there never was Confucius,
> After Confucius, there never came Confucius,"
> etc., etc., etc.,

or something like that, both illuminating and obscuring, don't you know. They forget, or perhaps they are not aware that the old Chinese sage taught "The way of sincerity is the way of heaven."

My experiences as an Eurasian never cease; but people are not now as prejudiced as they have been. In the West, too, my friends are more advanced in all lines of thought than those whom I know in Eastern Canada—more genuine, more sincere, with less of the form of religion, but more of its spirit.

So I roam backward and forward across the continent. When I am East, my heart is West. When I am West, my heart is East. Before long I hope to be in China. As my life began in my father's country it may end in my mother's.

After all I have no nationality and am not anxious to claim any. Individuality is more than nationality. "You are you and I am I," says Confucius. I give my right hand to the Occidentals and my left to the Orientals, hoping that between them they will not utterly destroy the insignificant "connecting link." And that's all.

Mary Hunter Austin
(1868–1934)

"FERVENT PARTICIPATION in mineral rushes and land rushes, in timber booms and cattle speculation deepened the impression that the
determination of white Americans to develop the West's natural resources left very little room for the development of their souls," wrote
Patricia Nelson Limerick in 1996.[10] But although an acknowledged secular impetus drove most pioneers, it also engendered in those independent and self-sufficient people a strong ethical code and a spiritual
attachment to the land. By 1889, when Mary Hunter published her first
article, "One Hundred Miles on Horseback," there was a growing audience for short stories, poems, and essays that dealt with the westerner's
mystical relationship with the landscape.

Mary Hunter was born and raised in Carlinville, Illinois. She was a
sensitive, artistic, and psychically attuned child who learned to read and
write at an early age. She progressed so rapidly in school that by age
eight she was in the same class as her ten-year-old brother. Two years
later she was devastated by the deaths of her father and younger sister,
Jennie. English-born Civil War veteran George Hunter succumbed to tuberculosis, Jennie to diphtheria. Austin was left in the care of her
mother, Susanna Hunter, who constantly pressured Mary to lose her eccentric ways. Mary escaped inward, away from her mother and two
brothers.

Hunter was a natural observer, fascinated by the entire gamut of her
surroundings. A talented artist, she was more comfortable outdoors
than cooped up inside rooms that lacked proportion, privacy, and
warmth. But in college, she chose biology over art. After she graduated
from Blackburn College in 1888, the family decided (over Mary's objections) to homestead in the desolate southern San Joaquin Valley of
California. The new surroundings awakened Hunter's latent writing talent. Mary named and described the elements of her new world with passion, magic, and song. She also made friends with Gen. Edward Beale,
owner of the vast Tejon Ranch. He allowed her to roam at will, alone or
with his foreman as guide. Her studies of the natural world, including its
human inhabitants, filled notebooks and served as the foundation for

fiction, poetry, and essays. Her experiences also engendered a deep and lasting spiritual connection with the earth.

In the wake of a drought that cost the Hunters their homesteads, Mary tutored farm children and taught school, writing when she could find time. She married Stafford Wallace Austin, a mining engineer and the son of a wealthy family from Hawaii. After attempts at ranching and viniculture failed, they moved from place to place, job to job, ending up on the east side of the Sierra Nevada. There, Wallace worked for the irrigation company, and they taught school. Their only child, Ruth, was born mentally impaired.

Artistically and scientifically, Mary was a trained observer. Like Alice Cary, she had always lived outside the circle. A misfit in her birth family, Austin created a family out of the raw materials of earth, sky, animals, and people who lived apart from civilization. She was a naturist who extended her study from the earth, plants, and animals to include native people and more recent emigrants. She ignored man-made boundaries, substituting geographic and topographic features for fences and roads. When the Austins moved to Independence, California, Mary extended her terrain to include not only the Sierra Nevada that rose sheer behind her brown house but also the entire western basin and range: the Panamint Mountains and White-Inyos to the east, the Owens and Walker Valleys, the Mojave Desert. She learned the secrets of this forbidding place, and shared them in *The Land of Little Rain* (1903), a collection of essays that made her famous.

Mary Austin felt stifled in her life with Wallace. She left him in 1906. Wallace divorced her in 1914, although they continued to correspond until his death in 1932. Meanwhile, Mary joined the art colony at Carmel-by-the-Sea, which included writers George Sterling, Jack London, Lincoln Steffens, and Robinson Jeffers. In that stimulating environment she composed short stories, children's stories, poems, novels, and essays set in southern California and eastern Nevada, including *The Basket Woman, The Flock,* and *The Ford.* Bolstered by her success, she moved again, this time to New York.

Separated from the source of her inspiration, Austin's work, although prolific, began to grow stale. To recapture the magic, she took a trip in 1918 with Daniel T. MacDougal through the Sonoran Desert around Tucson, up over the Mogollon Rim and into New Mexico. She fell in love with this country and produced *The Land of Journey's Ending,* a paean to the desert and its people.

In 1918, Austin also joined the growing arts colony in Santa Fe, settling into an adobe house she named La Casa Querida—Beloved House. During the last sixteen years of her life, she fought to preserve and publicize Native American art, music, and culture. Although she has been criticized for patronizing both aboriginal and Hispanic Americans, and for Americanizing their art, her efforts reinvigorated dying crafts and made them commercially successful.

Austin paved the way for later nature writers such as Edward Abby, Aldo Leopold, Annie Dillard, Frank Waters, and Terry Tempest Williams. Her work, where it focuses on the western landscape and people, is timeless. "Pahawitz-Na'an" demonstrates Austin's love for Native Americans, the rhythm of their storytelling, and the sense of magic she, and they, lived with daily. "Neither Spirit nor Bird (Shoshone Love Song)" is not a literal translation of Indian poetry, but Austin's way of capturing the essence of their song.

Mary Austin's brown house still sits at the foot of Kearsarge in Independence, California. Her ashes are cemented into a hill above Santa Fe; her spirit dwells at Inscription Rock, New Mexico, and throughout the Southwest.

Preface to The Land of Little Rain

I CONFESS TO A great liking for the Indian fashion of name-giving: every man known by that phrase which best expresses him to whoso names him. Thus he may be Mighty-Hunter, or Man-Afraid-of-a-Bear, according as he is called by friend or enemy, and Scar-Face to those who knew him by the eye's grasp only. No other fashion, I think, sets so well with the various natures that inhabit in us, and if you agree with me you will understand why so few names are written here as they appear in the geography. For if I love a lake known by the name of the man who discovered it, which endears itself by reason of the close-locked pines it nourishes about its borders, you may look in my account to find it so described. But if the Indians have been there before me, you shall have their name, which is always beautifully fit and does not originate in the poor human desire for perpetuity.

Nevertheless there are certain peaks, cañons, and clear meadow spaces which are above all compassing of words, and have a certain fame as of the nobly great to whom we give no familiar names. Guided by these you may reach my country and find or not find, according as it lieth in you, much that is set down here. And more. The earth is no wanton to give up all her best to every comer, but keeps a sweet, separate intimacy for each. But if you do not find it all as I write, think me not less dependable nor yourself less clever. There is a sort of pretense allowed in matters of the heart, as one should say by way of illustration, "I know a man who . . . ," and so give up his dearest experience without betrayal. And I am in no mind to direct you to delectable places toward which you will hold yourself less tenderly than I. So by this fashion of naming I keep faith with the land and annex to my own estate a very great territory to which none has a surer title.

The country where you may have sight and touch of that which is written lies between the high Sierras south from Yosemite—east and south over a very great assemblage of broken ranges beyond Death Valley, and on illimitably into the Mojave Desert. You may come into the borders of it from the south by a stage journey that has the effect of involving a great lapse of time, or from the north by rail, dropping out of the overland route at Reno. The best of all ways is over the Sierra passes by pack and trail, seeing and believing. But the real heart and core of the country are not to be come at in a month's vacation. One must summer and winter with the land and wait its occasions. Pine woods that take two and three seasons to the ripening of cones, roots that lie by in the sand seven years awaiting a growing rain, firs that grow fifty years before flowering,—these do not scrape acquaintance. But if ever you come beyond the borders as far as the town that lies in a hill dimple at the foot of Kearsarge, never leave it until you have knocked at the door of the brown house under the willow-tree at the end of the village street, and there you shall have such news of the land, of its trails and what is astir in them, as one lover of it can give to another.

Pahawitz-Na'an

HAIWAI LIES IN A hill dimple at the foot of Tonopah, and eastward, straight away as the crow flies, rises the high ridge which divides that country from the valley of Bitter Springs. Over that ridge, called Waban, go all the Indian inhabitants of Haiwai at the time of the first hoar frost, to the piñon gathering. The broad, low-heading trees grow thickly, midway of the east slope of Waban, and, in the dry flats where no trees are, grow *chia,* wild cabbage, and foodful roots. High on Waban, among the tamarack pines, are deer for the killing, and quail troop at all seasons on the downward slopes.

The piñon season makes a little exodus at Haiwai. There is work to be done at good wages, white men's work on the farms and about the mines; but when the quail begin to flock and frosts to nip, a call comes out of the hills that no Paiute can deny.

The strong men go to the hunting of deer, the strong women to beat down the round, brown cones from the unwilling trees, old men to tend the fires for roasting, and old women to keep the camp.

As for the children, they are incredibly busy, getting themselves nicely varnished over with crystal-clear resin, and growing so fat on the oily kernels that it is a wonder how they keep on seeing out of their small, beady eyes. With the tribe goes their flock, goats and sheep two score, up by the way of Waban Pass to feed in the high meadows; and, because he was accounted fit for nothing else, Limpy was set to watch them. Any Paiute of Haiwai would have told you that the child should have been glad that he was able to do so much for his keep, but to Limpy it was the very badge and trumpeter of his affliction. It was a post of no labor and much lying in the sun; the meadows were small, well fenced by barrens over which the sheep had no desire to stray, and, for help, a dog that had the flock upon his conscience.

At the foot of Waban begins the Soshone country, and time was when the Paiutes harvested piñons at peril. But in these pacific days there is little traffic of any sort between Paiutes and Soshone, except that they steal from each other with the greatest good-will if occasion offers. And though Limpy dreamed dreams of holding his flock in the face of their warlike hordes, he knew he was quite safe against any such chance. Mornings and evenings Chopo helped him from meadow to camp, that was seldom too far for a long cry to reach. When the small children could be spared, he coaxed them with him for company, and the wild things of Waban showed him many a wonder. But because he could not, Limpy longed to be breaking his back with the heavy baskets, and wearying his legs with trotting to and fro with the pitchy, shiny cones. Limpy, however, had learned the logic of necessity, and tended sheep; and since there was no one who belonged to him in particular, there was no one to find out how sore a heart he had. In truth, Limpy would have been of little use at the piñon gathering, for one-half of his body was paralyzed, stiffened and shriveled into all but uselessness. He could stoop with difficulty, and lift and carry not at all. Moreover, the boy was a public charge in the Campoodie, where nobody loved him and nobody was unkind. Because they pitied him, the Paiutes took no notice of his infirmity, and because he had the heart of a man, Limpy made no moan, but, being a Paiute, felt the primitive shame of physical deformity, and the desire to do great things and win a man's name. The name he was known by he had accepted from the Whites for whom he did errands, they needing something to call him by. Those of his own people who understood it thought it a good enough name, being true; the more so since there is no need of one having a particular name who has done nothing in particular worth naming. Small chance of that, thought the Paiutes of Haiwai since there was to be no more fighting with Whites or each other, though no lack of causes to fight for. So Limpy minded sheep, hopping about with incredible spryness on his peg leg, and made merry at the piñon gathering.

The young men had gone to the high passes hunting the deer, and only old men and women kept the camp at Hidden Waters, on the sunrise slope of Waban. Limpy was having a particularly good time, having coaxed the younger children to the herding-meadow by a tale of a woodchuck that came out of its hole and spoke to him. The woodchuck had not spoken that day, but it might have, and there was the fun of expecting it; so they brought home the flock merrily through the slanting light, garlanded with wild flowers, and laughing an echo to the laughter of the women coming it [in] with the baskets.

The flock was shut in the wattled corral at the end of the swale, and by moonrise the camp at Hidden Waters was sleeping the sleep of the well-fed. Meanwhile Limpy's hour approached.

The first that was known of it was when Chopo loosed the flock and cried out that two were missing—two he-goats of the flock—and never a dog had barked, nor an owl hooted louder than its wont.

Limpy knew, and the boys that were with him knew, that they had all come in from the feeding-ground. Chopo laid his eyes to the ground, squinting along the trampled grass; meantime the old men wagged their heads with surmisings. Chopo neither wagged nor spoke. The hair of his head stood up; his nostrils were drawn and lifted at the outer corners; his eyes narrowed to fine points of fire. He was following a trail. He slid out of the golden patch by the springs into the twilight pines. The old men went about to gather sticks; they would have a council fire; perhaps they would make medicine. They shook with excitement, their old eyes glittered beadily; but they did not talk. Limpy hopped about on his peg leg, helping. He kn[e]w better than to question his elders, but as guardian of the flock he felt that somewhat devolved upon him. The women were forbidden from the harvesting.

"It would be well," suggested Limpy to old Tuyo, the arrow-maker, "if the young men came home from the hunting."

The arrow-maker was not sure. Young men were needful if there was fighting, but this—Ah! Ah! and he fell to mumbling and shaking his head. What, oh, what is it? Limpy questioned with his eyes. The arrow-maker leaned over to him. They were very good friends; perhaps there was also a matter of secret sympathy between them, for the arrow-maker was not valued of his tribe as he had been.

"*Pahawitz na'an,*" he said with his lips to the boy's ear. Limpy's own eyes glittered. He left gathering sticks, and made a little council for himself, back of a brown boulder by the spring, with the other boys ready to hear a wonder. *Pahawitz na'an!* He that was reputed to be the father of Paiutes, believed by some to be an evil spirit, going about in the form of a beast with the thoughts of a man. *Pahawitz na'an!* But none of them dared say it above a whisper, lest the man-bear should hear.

They had heard tales of him by the winter fire, but it had been long and long since the bear that walked like a man had been seen of any Paiute. Hunters who came not back from their hunting were supposed to have met with him. One, Chico, reported having seen the tracks of him five winters ago, when the snow was deep on Tonopah, and had come away in a great fright; but this tale was not much believed. "He would have run away from the tracks of a real bear just the same," explained the arrow-maker. But now the arrow-maker had seen also. All the camp at Hidden Waters kept close and went softly; the fear of

Pahawitz na'an was on them all. It wore off as it drew near noon; it was so bright and clear a day, the late flowers made a pleasant glow in the sun, the sheep bleated cheerfully in the corral, and the pleasant smell of roasting cones hung in the air. Limpy took a blackened stick and began to draw upon the rocks. He drew the *Mahalas* gathering cones, the young men hunting the deer, white men as he remembered them.

"Now," he said, "I will draw *Pahawitz na'an*." Sallie's Tomee, who stood as high as Limpy's shoulder and was as broad as long, broke into a howl of terror.

"Ho," cried Limpy, "who's afraid of *Pahawitz na'an?*" Tomee stamped with rage and fright.

"Don't you say that name some more," he cried.

"Coyote," jeered Limpy; "look, there is Chopo! The bear has not eaten him."

In fact Chopo and the man-bear had not come together. The Indian had followed the trail until he lost it in a stony place. But *Pahawitz na'an* it was. He had come into the camp and gone out of it on all fours, but through the pines he stood up and walked like a man, driving the goats. Did ever a bear the like? Moreover the dogs had not barked.

That night the arrow-maker made Medicine. He burned strange smelling things in the fire, muttering, the while, things that one must not venture to hear. It was not very strong Medicine, but it sufficed. *Pahawitz na'an* came no more to the sheepfolds for that time.

The third day the young men returned, and, though they heard the news with headshakings and snorts of disbelief, the camp was moved from Hidden Waters to Passowai, and the harvesting went on.

And now it was for Limpy to say if he would have help at the herding or no, and that he would not; for since it was thought worthy the courage of a man, there was no Paiute so jealous of his work as the little, lame lad. He had moments of heart-sinking when he heard things stirring in the wood, and looked ever sidewise as he went among the gloaming pines. But the cool October days moved on, and the fear faded. Limpy forged with the flocks into farther and farther meadows. And in time *Pahawitz na'an* came back for more sheep.

It was near mid-afternoon. Limpy lay on the sunward side of a boulder, mocking the tell-tale jays in the Tamarack pines.

Suddenly the jays left quarreling to clear out of the timber on the upper side of the meadow, crying, "Thief, a thief! Who comes? A thief, a thief!" The chipmunks heard and stopped in mid career, motionless as the rocks they perched upon. The woodchucks heard and got back to their doors; the dogs moved uneasily to put themselves between the flock and whatever came out of the wood.

Limpy saw the hair of their backs rise, and there fell a silence in the glen—such a silence as moves before an enemy or a stranger in the wood—and out of the silence, moving stilly, too cautiously by far for a bear that was not half a man, came *Pahawitz na'an.*

And yet it was no man that came out of the wood, but a bear, brown and shaggy as bears should be, walking on four feet as other bears.

Limpy slid from his rock to the shadow of it; the dogs bristled more and more, but they did not bark, and *Pahawitz na'an* spoke to them. Yes! And in the Paiute tongue, since they understood no other. Limpy did not hear, but he saw them slink, bristling still, but abashed. *Pahawitz na'an* nosed among the indifferent sheep, parting out the best of them. Never a bear did as this one did. He drove the yearlings out of the meadow, and, as he went, he rose up like a man, and went walking and driving the sheep among the tamarack pines. And after him, from bole to bole of the shadowing trees, from bush to boulder, followed a peg-legged little Indian, sometime keeper of the flock. For as Limpy lay in the shadow of the rock, his strength came back to him, and with it a little of his man's spirit and sturdy sense. The sheep were not eaten and the dogs had not barked; *Pahawitz na'an* had spoken and they had obeyed him. Clearly the man-bear wanted sheep, and at the thought Limpy's wrath arose. The sheep were his, his in trust as shepherd, his by right of his interest in the property of the campoodie. A scant flock meant scant living at Haiwai!

It was too far to go to the camp for help; the flock was safe with the dogs against any other chance than just the one that had befallen them. Limpy would have his sheep again, or at the least know where they went. Besides, a curiosity greater than the fear drew him to the edge of the wood; but though he had courage for following, he did not follow fast.

If *Pahawitz na'an* were a man, he could be none other than an Indian by the wit he showed in covering his track, doubling and turning so that it was a weary little Paiute that came to the end of it where it dropped over the rim of an exceedingly steep, deep gully, in which boulders, huge as houses, lay tumbled thick together amid masses and windy caves of shade. The sound of the sheep came up from them, and Limpy, peering over the edge, saw *Pahawitz na'an* going about man-wise to drive his last steal into a pen and make it fast with stones. Then from a recess of the rocks he drew a knife long and shining, and Limpy's awed gaze clung to it in the gathering gloom. Then on a sudden there was a scurry of bare feet on the pine needles, the pad, pad of a little peg-leg, and away into the woods fled Limpy, for with a quick motion of the knife at his own throat, *Pahawitz na'an* had thrown off his bear's skin and stood forth a man.

About the hour of sunset, Chopo set out to help the tardy Limpy home with the sheep, and met them half way of the trail, straggling and lagging, the dogs doing their work half-heartedly, for the puzzle of the man-bear worked mischief in their heads. Chopo counted the flock—two missing—and Limpy! Here was strange work. He got the remnant to the camp and spread the news; but with the best speed they could make, it was too late when the young men came to the herding meadow to do more than piece out the circumstance. Peer as they might into the darkling wood, they could read only that Limpy and the sheep went away walking with *Pahawitz na'an,* he going on two feet and making a track very like a bear's, but such as no bear ever made. By that time the dark fell on camp, and the fear that walketh in darkness.

There was a council fire at Passowai that night, the children huddling by their mothers, and all ears alert for sounds from the wood. The old men spoke oftenest and at greatest length; it was their time come again. Nevertheless there were young men to whom the whole thing seemed of human contriving. In the end, according to the wisdom of the fathers, they made Big Medicine.

They cleared a space around the fire, and the arrow-maker leaped in the dim-lit circle, nearly naked, and bedaubed with a paste of white flour, for he had left his Medicine-bags at Haiwai. There was no light but the fire. The old men made them rattles of willow wands, split and peeled, and the click of these and the droning voices reached far across the night. Around the squatting circle ran little movements of fervor, of appreciation, shoves and nudges, laughter of sheer delight. Vague excitement flickered and flared up in the faces of the old, old men, mumbling like dogs who hunt in dreams. Clear across the open space the firelight glittered on the throats of the young men where the pulse moved, fluttering, sliding, snake-like, as in the throat of wild animals about to spring. One—two hours the rhythmic, hypnotic dance went on, rose in a scale, and the heart pounded heavily against the glistening ribs—and far out in the pines arose a small sobbing cry.

One caught it in the outer circle of listeners and froze into an attitude of listening. The sense of approaching presence ran like a thing palpable around the circle. A cry, and then another, struck through the tense preoccupation of the dancers, and stilled the clack of the rattles. It came from the far side of the camp toward the wood, and insensibly the circle melted and massed again, putting the fire between it and whatever might come out of the dark.

The cry grew and was answered by the tethered flock and the dogs; afterward came the pad, pad of a peg-leg—Limpy!

He came into the circle, wan and scared, breaking into tears and sobbing. His was a tale marvelous beyond belief, such as would serve for big talk for time to come. "And at the last," said Limpy, "he cut himself with the knife and came out a man."

"Ah! Ehu! Heard you ever the like?"

"So," said High Jack, "what kind of a man?"

"Indian man."

"Paiute?"

"No, not Paiute. Maybe Soshone."

"Ah! a—a—ah!"

"Dressed?" said High Jack. Like a flash it came to Limpy that the man who came out of the bear's skin in the glen wore blue overalls such as the men bought in the shops. A little breath of laughter ran about the camp; a spirit in overalls!

"And the place," said High Jack, "could you find it again? Then eat and sleep. Presently we may have need of you." He took Limpy bodily by the shoulders and turned him out of the council. And this time it was the young men who talked.

Two hours later the moon rose. Limpy had not turned his side in bed for the heaviness of slumber when the men called him. It was clear; it was cold and gloriously light; the wood was deeply still. One of the men gave him an old coat with long ragged tails that hung down and warmed his legs. High Jack came behind and thrust his shoulders between the boy's knees. Six figures, singly and still, threaded the aisles of the pines, and on the shoulders of the foremost rode the little lame shepherd, pointing the way.

They went forward at a great pace, without words. They were young men brought up on the borders of White life, thinking thoughts other than their fathers had, but as they went in the moonlight they grew more and more like what their fathers were. Their faces fell into set, fierce lines. They crouched and moved stealthily. Nearing the gully of Big Rocks, they drew off their boots and went lightly as the night wind. At the head of the gully where the trail went down, they left Limpy, very glad at first not to go near the man-bear, very frightened to be alone as soon as they had dropped down among the shadows.

Pahawitz na'an was asleep in his bear's skin for warmth, thinking no harm. He neither saw nor heard the six Paiutes feeling toward him, but the sheep heard and waked him with their blether. He wormed through the hollows of the rocks like a wild thing, but the click of the bear's claws betrayed him. It was Indian set to catch Indian—wild thing against his kind. He made the trail first, knowing the tricks of the place, and up to the rim of the wall, not fairly on it, for there the moonlight shone, but a little to one side where the bluff was dark and more sheer. There, as he raised himself, dreadful to behold with his own head close by the bear's head hanging over his shoulder, suddenly there shot up from the scrub, where Limpy huddled in his loose long coat with flapping tails, with a terrible, amazed howl, an impish figure with wind-spread wings, dancing black and large against the moon. The man-bear slipped. The superstitions he had played upon undid him. He groped for a hold, but the bear's skin prevented him. He fell out from the cliff and backward, making no sound, but clutching wildly at the throat of his lying dress as his body plunged into the shadow of the gulf.

When the Paiutes came and looked upon his face they said, each man of them in his own way, "Soshone," as one might say dog, coyote, or what not; and they buried him where he lay.

It was dawn-end, and a light breaking over Soshone Land when the Paiutes came back to Passowai, driving their sheep, and one, who had brought away the bear skin, capering in it to the great delight of the camp. High on the shoulders of the young men rode Limpy, bepraised and called out of his name. Hours after, deep in the slumber that paid out the night watch, the boy smiled the smile of a satisfied heart. For the name they had called him by, the name he had made for himself at the gully of Big Rocks, was *Pahawitz na'an*.

Neither Spirit nor Bird (Shoshone Love Song)

Neither spirit nor bird;
That was my flute you heard
Last night by the River.
When you came with your wicker jar
Where the river drags the willows,
That was my flute you heard,
Wacoba, Wacoba,
Calling, Come to the willows!

Neither the wind nor a bird
Rustled the lupin blooms,
That was my blood you heard
Answer your garment's hem
Whispering through the grasses;
That was my blood you heard
By the wild rose under the willows.

That was no beast that stirred,
That was my heart you heard
Pacing to and fro
In the ambush of my desire,
To the music my flute let fall.
Wacoba, Wacoba,
That was my heart you heard
Leaping under the willows.

Sharlot Mabridth Hall

(1870–1943)

S ANTA FE, founded in 1609 by Basque explorer Juan de Oñate and five hundred Spanish colonists, lies more than fifteen hundred miles north of Vera Cruz, Mexico, the official port of entry for goods during the era of Spanish rule. Although Santa Fe and its mission were largely self-supporting, yearly caravans from the South transported those supplies that could not be grown, raised, or manufactured in the valley of the Rio Grande. Spanish settlers had little choice but to pay the exorbitant prices demanded by traveling merchants, for it was illegal to trade with the Americans.

In 1821, William Becknell, accompanied by a few men and a pack train loaded with trade goods, blazed a trail from Independence, on the Missouri River, to Santa Fe. They entered foreign territory shortly after Mexico achieved independence from Spain. Instead of being arrested by the first column of Mexican soldiers they encountered, they received a warm welcome and were escorted to Santa Fe. Becknell's commercial venture proved so successful that the next spring he returned with a larger party equipped with wagons. This second venture blazed a route across the Cimarron Desert—accessible by wagon, but short on water. Despite the hardship, the trip proved that wagon trains could ferry goods and people into Mexico and still reap substantial profit. In the next few years, as the route was improved, American caravans annually made the trek across the frontier. Supply stations such as Council Grove and Bent's Fort grew up along the Santa Fe Trail, and the American government established Fort Leavenworth to house and supply troops escorting the traders.

In 1846, eighteen-year-old newlywed Susan Shelby Magoffin accompanied her merchant husband over the Santa Fe Trail. She kept a diary of the journey, which was edited and published by Stella Drumm eighty years later. Compared to other women pioneers, Magoffin traveled in style with her husband, brother-in-law, and servants. But the trip had its hardships. She miscarried at Bent's Fort, and later was caught up in the hostilities of the Mexican War. Although Magoffin was the first white woman to journey over the trail, she was not the first American woman.

Magoffin's pack train passed an unidentified African American woman, alone, driving her wagon north out of Mexico.

By the time eleven-year-old Sharlot Mabridth Hall and her family drove a herd of horses over the trail from Kansas to New Mexico Territory in late 1881, the land had belonged to the United States for thirty years. From Santa Fe, the Halls continued on to Lynx Creek, where they worked a family placer gold operation. James Hall, Sharlot's father, then moved the family and stock a few miles away to Lonesome Valley, southeast of Prescott, the territorial capital of Arizona. Eight years later, the family built Orchard Ranch, one of the largest homesteads in the area.

Sharlot Hall began writing poetry as a child, encouraged by her mother, a former schoolteacher. Hall hid her thoughts and poems from her father, an irascible and emotionally unstable rancher who did not see the value in books or writing. Ranch work allowed little time for formal schooling, but Sharlot attended a year of high school in Prescott when she was sixteen. Because of her mother's frail health, Sharlot returned home to help manage the homestead. But she kept writing. In 1891 she began to publish prose and poetry in periodicals.

Sharlot elected to remain single, a decision arising from her independent nature, the dysfunctional relationship between her parents, and the tenets of the free-thought movement that swept the country at the end of the last century. At twenty-four, however, she fell in love with Samuel P. Putnam, the charismatic leader of the free-thought movement. Her spiritual and emotional attachment to him continued even after Putnam's death in 1896.

That same year, Sharlot submitted poems to *Land of Sunshine* editor Charles Lummis. Thereafter, her short stories, articles, and poetry appeared regularly in his California magazine and in other national publications, including the *Atlantic Monthly, Ladies' Home Journal,* and *Everybody's* magazine. Hall's poem "Out West" both named and graced the first page of Lummis's revamped *Land of Sunshine.* Hall became a staff writer, and eventually assistant editor, for *Out West.* But she refused to move to California. Instead, she commuted, staying with Lummis and his wife at El Alisal, their unique home on the outskirts of Pasadena. Through her association with *Out West* she met other writers, such as Mary Austin, another Lummis protegée.

Under Lummis's influence, Hall developed an interest in history, archaeology, and ethnology. By extolling the Arizona climate, the rich mines and fertile soil, and the history and beauty of the cañon country,

Sharlot encouraged both tourism and immigration. The governor chose Hall as the first territorial historian in 1909, a post she held for three years. She used the position to research Native American culture and folklore and to record the reminiscences of Arizona's pioneer families. In articles, and in the poem "Arizona," which she mailed to every member of Congress, Hall fought for admission of Arizona as a state separate from New Mexico. She succeeded. In 1912, both states were admitted to the Union.

Hall is best known for her poetry, western odes that lauded the strength of the pioneers and praised the landscape. She published a collection of her poems, *Cactus and Pine: Songs of the Southwest* (1910), which she revised eleven years later. *Poems of a Ranch Woman,* a collection of her later poetry, was published posthumously. Two books containing prose excerpts have also come out since her death: *Sharlot Herself: Selected Writings of Sharlot Hall* and *Sharlot Hall on the Arizona Strip,* her diary of a wagon trip in 1911.

After Sharlot lost her position as state historian, she returned home to oversee Orchard Ranch and to care for her parents. The workload, which included coping with an increasingly irrational father, left no time or energy for publishing. Her father's death, twelve years after her mother's, gave Sharlot the freedom to resume her writing life. She moved back to Prescott, bought the old Governor's Mansion—a log house—and began the great task of protecting and refurbishing it. Today, this centerpiece of the Sharlot Hall Museum stands as a monument both to the writer and to the state she helped create. And in Phoenix, her office under the dome of the Arizone State Capitol Museum rotunda is preserved as it was when she worked there.

Out West (The West)

When the world of waters was parted by the stroke of a mighty rod,
Her eyes were first of the lands of earth to look on the face of God;
The white mists robed and throned her, and the sun in his orbit wide
Bent down from his ultimate pathway and claimed her his chosen bride;
And He that had formed and dowered her with the dower of a royal queen,
Decreed her the strength of mighty hills, the peace of the plains between;
The silence of utmost desert, and cañons rifted and riven,
And the music of wide-flung forests where strong winds shout to heaven.

Then high and apart He set her, and bade the grey seas guard,
And the lean sands clutching her garment's hem keep stern and solemn ward.
What dreams she knew as she waited! What strange keels touched her shore!
And feet went into the stillness, and returned to the sea no more.
They passed through her dream like shadows—till she woke one pregnant
morn,
And watched Magellan's white-winged ships swing round the ice-bound
Horn;
She thrilled to their masterful presage, those dauntless sails from afar,
And laughed as she leaned to the ocean till her face shone out like a star.

And men who toiled in the drudging hives of a world as flat as a floor
Thrilled in their souls to her laughter, and turned with hand to the door;
And creeds as hoary as Adam, and feuds as old as Cain,
Fell deaf on the ear that harkened and caught that far refrain;
Into dungeons by light forgotten, and prisons of grim despair,
Hope came with pale reflection of her star on the swooning air;
And the old, hedged, human whirlpool, with its seething misery,
Burst through—as a pent-up river breaks through to the healing sea.

Calling—calling—calling—resistless, imperative, strong—
Soldier, and priest, and dreamer—she drew them, a mighty throng.
The unmapped seas took tribute of many a dauntless band,
And many a brave hope measured but bleaching bones in the sand;
Yet for one that fell, a hundred sprang out to fill his place,
For death at her call was sweeter than life in a tamer race.

Sinew and bone she drew them; steel-thewed—and the weaklings shrank—
Grim-wrought of granite and iron were the men of her foremost rank.

Stern as the land before them, and strong as the waters crossed;
Men who had looked on the face of defeat nor counted the battle lost;
Uncrowned rulers and statesmen, shaping their daily need
To the law of brother with brother, till the world stood by to heed;
The sills of a greater empire they hewed and hammered and turned,
And the torch of a larger freedom from their blazing hill-tops burned;
Till the old ideals that had led them grew dim as a childhood's dream,
And Caste went down in the balance, and Manhood stood supreme.

The wanderers of earth turned to her—outcast of the older lands—
With a promise and hope in their pleading, and she reached them pitying
hands;
And she cried to the Old-World cities that drowse by the Eastern main;
"Send me your weary, house-worn broods and I'll send you Men again!
Lo, here in my wind-swept reaches, by my marshalled peaks of snow,
Is room for a larger reaping than your o'er-tilled fields can grow;
Seed of the Man-Seed springing to stature and strength in my sun,
Free with a limitless freedom no battles of men have won."

For men, like the grain of the cornfields, grow small in the huddled crowd,
And weak for the breath of spaces where a soul make speak aloud;
For hills, like stairways to heaven, shaming the level track;
And sick with the clang of pavements and the marts of the trafficking pack.
Greatness is born of greatness, and breadth of a breadth profound;
The old Antæan fable of strength renewed from the ground
Was a human truth for the ages; since the hour of the Eden-birth
That man among men was strongest who stood with his feet on the earth!

Nations are men grown greater—with the course of their destinies
Fore-shaped in the womb that bore them to the ultimate fall or rise;
Doomed by a dull horizon, or damned by a tread-mill path
To sink into stolid slumber, or trample the grapes of wrath:
But shamed by Her tameless grandeur, what soul could be mean and poor?
Upheld by Her lofty courage, what heart would fail to endure?
As the blood of the breast that suckled, the sons in their manhood are—
She has mothered a brood of lion's cubs, and they bear Her name afar.

His Place

To the enduring memory of Clarence H. Shaw, who knew the desert as
few men know it, alike in its grimmest phases and its most beautiful, and
who found, of choice, his last resting place in it.

This is his place—here where the mountains run,
Naked and scarred and seamed, up to the face of the sun;
His place—reaches of wind-blown sand, brown and barren and old,
Where the creosote, scorched and glazed, clings with a stubborn hold;
And tall and solemn and strange the fluted cactus lifts
Its arms like a cross that pleads from the lonely, rock-hedged rifts;
His place—where the great near stars lean low, and burn, and shine,
Still and steady and clear, like lamps at the door of a shrine.

This is his land—his land—where the great skies bend
Over the wide, clean sweep of a world without measure or end;
His land—where, across and between, the pale swift whirlwinds go
Like souls that may not rest—by their quest sent to and fro;
And down the washes of sand the vague mirages lay
Their spell of enchanted light, moving in ripple and spray
Of waters that gleam and glisten, with joy and color rife—
Streams where no mouth may drink, but fair as the River of Life.

This is his place—the mesquite, like a thin, green mist of tears,
Knows the way of his wish—keeps the hope of his years;
Till, one appointed day, comes the with-holden spring—
Then, miracle wrought in gold—that swift, rare blossoming!
This is his place—where silence eternal fills
The still white sun-drowsed plain and the slumbering, iron-rimmed hills;
Where Today and Forever mingle and Changeless and Change are one.
Here, in his own land he waits till Today and Forever are done.

Arizona

No beggar she in the mighty hall where her bay-crowned sisters wait,
No empty-handed pleader for the right of a free-born state,
No child, with a child's insistence, demanding a gilded toy;
But a fair-browed, queenly woman, strong to create or destroy—
Wise for the need of the sons she has bred in the school where weaklings fail,
Where cunning is less than manhood, and deeds, not words, avail—
With the high, unswerving purpose that measures and overcomes,
And the faith in the Farthest Vision that builded her hard-won homes.

Link her, in her clean-proved fitness, in her right to stand alone—
Secure for whatever future in the strength that her past has won—
Link her, in her morning beauty, with another, however fair?
And open your jealous portal and bid her enter there
With shackles on wrist and ankle, and dust on her stately head,
And her proud eyes dim with weeping? No! Bar your doors instead
And seal them fast forever! but let her go her way—
Uncrowned if you will, but unshackled, to wait for a larger day.

Ay! Let her go bare-handed, bound with no grudging gift,
Back to her own free spaces where her rock-ribbed mountains lift
Their walls like a sheltering fortress—back to her house and blood.
And we of her blood will go our way and reckon your judgment good.
We will wait outside your sullen door till the stars you wear grow dim
As the pale dawn-stars that swim and fade o'er our mighty Cañon's rim.
We will lift no hand for the bays ye wear, nor covet your robes of state—
But ah! by the skies above us all, we will shame ye while we wait!

We will make ye the mold of an empire here in the land ye scorn,
While ye drowse and dream in your well-housed ease that States at your nod
are born.
Ye have blotted your own beginnings, and taught your sons to forget
That ye did not spring fat-fed and old from the powers that bear and beget.
But the while ye follow your smooth-made roads to a fireside safe of fears,
Shall come a voice from a land still young, to sing in your age-dulled ears
The hero song of a strife as fine as your fathers' fathers knew,
When they dared the rivers of unmapped wilds at the will of a bark canoe—

The song of the deed in the doing, of the work still hot from the hand;
Of the yoke of man laid friendly-wise on the neck of a tameless land.
While your merchandise is weighing, we will bit and bridle and rein
The floods of the storm-rocked mountains and lead them down to the plain;
And the foam-ribbed, dark-hued waters, tired from that mighty race,
Shall lie at the feet of palm and vine and know their appointed place;
And out of that subtle union, desert and mountain-flood,
Shall be homes for a nation's choosing, where no home else had stood.

We will match the gold of your minting, with its mint-stamp dulled and marred
By the tears and blood that have stained it and the hands that have clutched too hard,
With the gold that no man has lied for—the gold no woman has made
The price of her truth and honor, plying a shameless trade—
The clean, pure, gold of the mountains, straight from the strong, dark earth,
With no tang or taint upon it from the hour of its primal birth.
The trick of the money-changer, shifting his coins as he wills,
Ye may keep—no Christ was bartered for the wealth of our lavish hills.

"Yet we are a little people—too weak for the cares of state!"
Let us go our way! When ye look again, ye shall find us, mayhap, too great.
Cities we lack—and gutters where children snatch for bread;
Numbers—and hordes of starvelings, toiling but never fed.
Spare pains that would make us greater in the pattern that ye have set;
We hold to the larger measure of the men that ye forget—
The men who, from trackless forests and prairies lone and far,
Hewed out the land where ye sit at ease and grudge us our fair-won star.

"There yet be men, my masters," though the net that the trickster flings
Lies wide on the land to its bitter shame, and his cunning parleyings
Have deafened the ears of Justice, that was blind and slow of old.
Yet time, the last Great Judge, is not bought, or bribed, or sold;
And Time and the Race shall judge us—not a league of trafficking men,
Selling the trust of the people, to barter it back again;
Palming the lives of millions as a handful of easy coin,
With a single heart to the narrow verge where craft and state-craft join.

The Fruit of the Yucca Tree

THE SUN, a dull red ball seen through the dust haze, slid behind the sky line, flinging back a last glow of beauty over the land he loved best. The haze deepened to a luminous purple on the peaks and foothills, cut with masses of rich-toned shadow in the rugged cañons that furrowed their sides and crept down into the desert like wrinkles in some age-worn face.

Above the horizon a great band of orange and flame grew slowly, fading up and up into pink and pale-green and dying away in vague depths of softened blue.

For half an hour a veil of filmy gold rested on the mesas where the dust-filled air caught and held the light.

The thick, sharp, sabre-like clusters of leaves on the yucca trees were touched with the reflection, like the play of fire on a drawn sword. Down across the sand-washes the day slowly retreated, leaving the mesquite and ironwood trees in shadow.

The smoke, rising through the branches of a tall, shaggy yucca, was lost in gathering darkness, but the fire sent its glimmer far through the forest.

It was not often that a fire burned there and the few wild things to whom the place was home drew close in wonder and curiosity, or fled in fear, according to their kind.

A strange little jumping mouse had discovered a crumb of bread and was dragging it stealthily away to eke out his hoard of yucca seeds. Somewhere out in the inky sand-hills a coyote sent up his call, "Ya-i-ah! I-ah! I-ah! Ya-e-ah! e-e-e-e!" rising and swelling, chopped short with vicious snaps and yells, and rising again till his lean mate flung it back weirdly multiplied.

Just beyond the campfire a covered traveling-wagon stood in the circle of light, the harness thrown idly across the tongue and a span of dust-coated mules tied to the hind wheels. By the front wheel, next the fire, a roll of bedding had been put down and a man was lying on it, his head propped on his arm, watching a woman trim the uncouth branches of the yucca trees with garlands of mistletoe.

The dainty leaves were flushed with red and the long, berry-set sprays were like ropes of pink pearls. It seemed too exquisite, too fragile in its ethereal beauty, to be a child of the desert. Yet they had gathered it that day, where the yard-long clusters clung to the mesquite and ironwood trees along the sand washes.

The woman stepped down from the cracker-box, on which she had been standing to reach the higher limbs. The firelight played over her, showing the gold in her brown hair and the half-whimsical, half-anxious curve of her mouth.

"Isn't it lovely? Don't it make you feel Christmas in the air?"

The man laughed, with a note of teasing in his voice.

"Christmas? Here? Lost on the outside edge of Nowhere, without even a jack-rabbit for dinner or a blaze on the trunk of a yucca to show us the way out? I can't say that it does; unless you intend to compound a mistletoe pudding."

"Don't joke! Isn't it lovely? It is twelve hours before we have to begin trying to get out; please let it be Christmas till then. See, here are your things. Don't look too much; you mustn't know until morning." She touched one garlanded branch from which half a dozen parcels hung.

"Such a time as I've had hiding them; you are the worst prowler."

"Oh! And I have nothing for you!" he said regretfully.

"Yes you have; you are going to be well again. That is my best gift; everything else can wait till we get out."

There was a quick step across the dry yucca leaves beyond the wagon. "Pardon me! Your fire has been my guide this hour. I can put you on your road; I know the desert as a man knows his own dooryard."

He came forward as he spoke; a man very tall, very brown, as one long unhoused from sun and wind, and with a strange, withdrawn remoteness in his eyes.

He looked at the woman wistfully, almost reverently, and past her to the wreathed yucca tree, on which her hand still rested. "You are the first woman I have seen in two years," he said, as her eyes filled with wonder. "And you have trimmed a Christmas tree! Here! In the desert! And all unbidden you have your Christmas guest."

"But not unwelcome," she answered. "Are you alone?"

"No; I have two comrades." He whistled a low note and they came out from the yuccas into the circle of light—a large gray burro and a strange, beautiful animal with the graceful head of a deer and big, dark eyes that were almost human in their softness. Both were packed—the burro with a prospector's outfit of food and blankets, with tools and rifle strapped on top; the other with a worn and dusty canvas case.

"Unpack your animals and stay with us tonight," said the man on the bed. "We can give you a Christmas supper of bread and coffee."

"I've had supper, thank you; but I'd be glad to talk awhile. It's a good many months since I've heard any voice but my own."

He led the burro outside the camp and took off the pack, then he unfastened the canvas case and came back to the fire.

The burro began picking the coarse grass among the cactus clumps, but the other one followed his master into the light, as if questioning his safety in that strange company.

"What is it?" asked the woman.

"A deer, a mule deer. See the long ears. They have no horns, and here in the desert they are always the color of the sand. Go Amigo; go and find your supper," and he turned the beautiful head toward the forest.

"There goes my friend. Jack is the best servant a man could ask; but Amigo is more—he is a friend. He never leaves me; he will stop feeding at night to come and lie at my feet and keep guard. He comes of brave blood; it is 'like mother, like son.'

"I found him three years ago in the Hacuavar mountains. Some hunter had shot the mother and she had fallen on the trail as she tried with her last strength to lead her fawn to the one water-hole on that side of the desert. She died trying to give the little fellow his chance for life; her nose, stiff and cold, was laid over his back when I found them.

"I carried him ten miles to the water on my shoulders—and last summer he paid it back. A rattlesnake had coiled almost at my head while I slept. Amigo came in from feeding and saw it. He drew all four feet together and leaped on the thing and crushed its life out before I knew my danger. Now he never leaves me after I spread the blankets at night. You see each of us owes his life to the other; we are blood brothers. But how do you come so far out of the way?"

"They sent us on an old road from Plumosa to Congress; they said it was shorter. We've followed every old pack-trail on the desert, I think; if we've missed one we're sure to find it tomorrow." The man laughed, shifting his head on the roll of bedding. "I wouldn't mind it but our grub-box is empty—and my pocket, too, for that matter. I'm a lot stronger, though. I'll get work at Congress."

"Not yet!" cried the woman, throwing the end of a blanket across his shoulders. "I'll earn our next 'grub-stake'; they always want cooks at a mine like that. You shall not take the risk now, just when we've made the chance sure."

She had forgotten the stranger in this, which was plainly an old anxiety. Unconsciously she was telling him all. It was a relief to talk to this quiet man who lay beside the fire, questioning now and then with the directness of one long used to the largeness of hills and desert.

While she talked, he had drawn something out of the dusty canvas case at his side. When she was done, he lifted it to his shoulder—a violin, the dark old wood reflecting the fire-light like ebony and the carven head, a misshapen hunchback, with sunken, uncouth cheeks wrapped in a monkish cowl, resting against his hand.

He touched the bow to the strings, softly at first, then surely. The woman leaned back against the gray trunk of the yucca tree; the anxious lines in her face relaxing, the whimsical smile half curving her lips. It was as if he had said: "You shall have Christmas, even here. Be still! I am bringing it."

The music slipped out through his hands like a released spirit—lilting carols—lullabies—fragments of play-songs—tender old hymns. He might have been leading her by the hand through the holly-wreathed memories. It was only when she threw out her hand against the grim, sabre-leaved yucca limb that she knew he was playing for himself at last, and forgetful of her.

The dark old wood seemed to throb like a living thing; she would have sworn that the carven hunchback moved, raised his head, reached a thin, eager hand to the strings.

The music seemed to sweep up to the great, low-hung stars; it beat and surged and overflowed through the forest till the desert was filled, and yet too narrow to hold that mighty cry of a tormented soul.

Now despairing, now pleading, now defiant; it rose at last through heart-breaking anguish into triumph that thrilled and called her like an army of bugles. He played it over and over—that strong, heart-wrung, inevitable triumph at the end.

The desert was gone. The yucca forest with the dim, low-flickering camp-fire widened out to a great room ablaze with light. And they that heard were not just a man on whom death had set his mark and a woman lost in dreams against the gray-ribbed trunk of a yucca tree. Jewels blazed there on the white shoulders of women, and the thronging men paid scarcely more homage to one in uniform with a broad scarf across his shoulder and many orders of honor on his breast, than to him who stood on the dim stage waiting.

He lifted his bow; a hush fell on the house; the man in uniform leaned far out of his box to listen, and tears were shining on the cheeks of the women. When it was done, the crash of applause shook the stage and that forgotten name that was once his was on every lip—no just-won name, but one honored through half a world.

How the dark old wood had throbbed! How the carven hunchback had striven to rise and touch again the beloved strings! The hunchback monk—the music-mad wretch who had sold his soul to the devil for the secret of that dark, resonant wood and those graceful, mysterious curves! His hand had set his own image there on the head, to mar and mangle the tone for all but a master's touch, to sweep the strings with the harmony of his own wild soul when kindred fingers held the bow, they said. And it might have been his long-dead self that played that night.

Very quietly the player laid down the bow and put the violin back in the dusty canvas case. The man was asleep on the roll of bedding; the woman was sitting with her head on her hand, staring into the coals of the camp-fire.

He roused her and told her the road they must take in the morning, drawing a map of it in the ashes that she might show her husband. Then he picked up the case and held out his hand.

"I will say good-night now; I may not see you in the morning. Will you shake hands with me? It is a long time since I have touched a woman's hand. I wish you a happy Christmas—the happiest possible— and a safe journey to Congress. It has been my Christmas gift to meet you."

"But you must not!" she cried, confusedly. "You must come back to the world. Come with us. Your music—"

He shook his head. His eyes had in them the old, withdrawn aloofness that had died out while he played. She felt as if she was looking across interminable stretches of desert where the gray sand blew and drifted.

MORNING DOES NOT come in the desert as it comes in other lands. There is an hour of pale, dust-sifted light, always increasing, before the sun comes. An hour when the earth seems wrapped in mystery; and the air has a faint, other-worldly fragrance, haunting and intangible, like a breath of incense blown through some still, far-doomed temple.

The hills that were red at sunset are now blue—pale, translucent, like hills seen in a dream—and the long sand-washes and mesas between are gray like sea water on a cloudy day.

The woman had watched it many times. To herself she called it her "hour of peace," slipped in between the anxiety of yesterday and lost with the night and anxiety of today waiting to begin with the sunrise. She stopped heaping the pile of dry yucca leaves on the ashes of the camp-fire and looked across the valley.

The eastern hills, notched and serrated into huge, jagged peaks, were turning a deeper blue and stood out boldly as if hewn from blocks of lapis lazuli. Through the lowest notch a thin shaft of sunshine broke and traveled across the valley. She watched its progress; it seemed so like some living thing choosing its way. It came down over the wagon and the camp-fire and was all but lost in the shaggy yucca leaves.

She watched it shining through the pearly mistletoe berries and among her little parcels on the limb. Then it slipped on across the sand and she saw that something else, a worn pouch of buckskin, was hanging just above the rest. A note addressed to herself was pinned with a cactus thorn to the flap.

The letters were strange and foreign and the paper thin and creased, as if something had been wrapped in it and carried a long while in a man's pocket. It was dim in places as if traced by the uncertain light of a camp-fire. She read it slowly:

"Dear Madame:—It will be Christmas morning when you read this. For the sake of the day accept the fruit which a stranger leaves on your tree. Take the pouch to H—— H——, at Congress; tell him you have met the 'desert fiddler' and give him the note you will find inside. Do what he tells you. Do not let your husband work; he must rest. May there be many happy Christmas days for you both.

"Your unbidden guest,

"The Desert Fiddler."

There was nothing more—no clue. He had gone in the night while they slept. The pouch was half full of gold in dust and nuggets, twenty ounces perhaps—the slow hoard of years.

THERE IS A little nook in the cañon below the mine at Congress, hedged in by granite boulders and over-grown grove-like with giant cactus. They lift their clumsy branches above the great, many-fluted trunks like arms and there is something human in their waiting attitude. Spring crowns them with a brief glory of clustered blossoms like carven snow, honey-sweet and rich and tempting the wild bees and birds.

They had blossomed twice, overlooking the low, brown house at their feet, when a man came up the narrow trail through the desert twilight, followed by a gray burro. He carried a dusty canvas case in his hand and, as he drew near, a woman opened the door and came out—alone.

He touched her hand a moment; then he sat down on the step and began to play.

It was the music of the yucca forest, that heart-wrung triumph of a soul in battle; but tempered now with something infinitely sad, infinitely tender.

"Will you keep Jack for me?" he said, when it was done. "Amigo is dead—I cannot tell you now. I cannot stay in the desert. I am going back to the world."

Willa Sibert Cather
(1873–1947)

"THE WORLD BROKE apart in 1922," Willa Cather wrote in the introduction to *Not Under Forty,* a collection of essays published during the Great Depression. World War I had rent the fabric of life in the West. Immigrant sons had been buried on the battlefields of Europe. Others had come home, but not to the midwestern towns and farms that reared them, choosing instead to find jobs in the cities. The small prairie towns that had provided the backdrop, focus, and characters for Cather's stories declined.

Willela Sibert Cather was born in the Back Lick Valley, not far from Winchester, Virginia. Cathers and Boaks, her mother's family, fought on both sides of the Civil War that had ranged back and forth across the Virginia countryside. Her father ran her grandfather Cather's sheep ranch. Willa, the oldest of the seven Cather children, accompanied her father on his rounds, learning the forest and setting traps for rabbits, more comfortable outdoors than in. Her maternal grandmother, Rachel Boak, lived with them and taught her to read and write. "Old Mrs. Harris," perhaps Cather's most famous short story, depicted her relationship with Rachel and with Virginia ("Jennie") Cather, Willa's mother.

Willa Cather was nine when Willow Grove, her grandfather Cather's farm near Winchester, was sold. Willa emigrated with her family by train and wagon to the edge of the frontier, a remote farm on the Nebraska plains. Grandfather Cather had gone ahead of them to farm the rich glacial soil near Red Cloud. Willa's initial shock, when faced with the treeless expanse so different from the ancient limestone hills and deciduous forests of her birthplace, was replaced gradually over the next eighteen months. Through solitary horseback rides to neighboring farms of European immigrants, Cather became enthralled not only with the endless sky and more subtle life of the red-grass prairies but also with the people who had left family, culture, and history behind to start over in the West.

After two years on the farm, Cather's father moved the family into Red Cloud. There, immigrant neighbors introduced her to Latin, Greek, and world literature. She read voraciously from their libraries, at the same time observing and absorbing every detail of the world around her. Town also offered the theater with performances by traveling troupes of actors. Willa fell in love with the stage. She wrote plays and performed in them with her siblings and friends.

An introspective child, Cather developed into a supreme individualist. In her early teens she decided to be a surgeon. She cut her hair short, dressed like a boy, accompanied the town doctors on their rounds, and called herself Willie. She did not adopt more conventional feminine attire until midway through her schooling at the University of Nebraska, Lincoln.

While at Lincoln, Cather switched from science to literature. Her first short story, "Peter," was published when she was eighteen. Poetry, essays, and more short stories followed. The land and the people of those formative Nebraska years imbued Willa's stories with a sense of place. Tangible, sensory images dragged the reader into plots, gave depth and motivation to characters and events. The West remained a source of inspiration throughout her life.

After graduation in 1895, she worked in a succession of journalist, teaching, and editorial jobs in Nebraska, Pittsburgh, and New York. In 1906, S. S. McClure asked her to help edit his magazine, *McClure's,* one of the foremost in the country. The job left her little time to write fiction. Prompted by positive comments from Sarah Orne Jewett, a respected writer of realistic fiction, Willa left editing in 1911 to write full-time. *O Pioneers!* which was her first critically acclaimed novel, was published in 1913. Like *My Ántonia,* published five years later, it was a lyrical, dramatic tribute to the Midwest and its people.

On her first trip to Arizona in 1912, Cather fell in love with the Southwest. *The Song of the Lark* reflects that emotional-mystical attachment. Three years later she visited the Enchanted Bluff, Acoma Pueblo, thus fulfilling the dreams of her fictional characters. She returned to the Southwest numerous times, visiting Mary Austin, Mabel Dodge Luhan, and Alice Corbin Henderson. *Death Comes to the Archbishop,* one of her most popular novels, came out of those visits.

Willa Cather's fiction drew on other areas of the country as well. *Sapphira and the Slave Girl,* her last novel, returned to the land of her birth. *A Shadow on the Rocks* depicted historic French Canada. *One of Ours,* which won the Pulitzer Prize, was set in Europe and the Midwest. Both *One of Ours* and *A Lost Lady* decried the passing of the pioneer era in the West.

Cather chose a career over marriage, although she became infatuated with one young man during a 1912 vacation in Winslow, Arizona. She described him in *The Song of the Lark,* and remembered him in a poem, "Spanish Johnny." Otherwise, her deep emotional attachments were with women: Carrie and Irene Miner, Louise Pound, Isabelle McClung Hambourg, Sarah Orne Jewett, and Edith Lewis. Lewis and Cather lived together during the last forty years of Cather's life.

Cather often wrote in a tent pitched in a field in Jaffrey, New Hampshire, the town in which she is buried. Her headstone bears the following quote from *My Ántonia:* "That is happiness; to be dissolved into something complete and great."

Prairie Dawn

A crimson fire that vanquishes the stars;
A pungent odor from the dusty sage;
A sudden stirring of the huddled herds;
A breaking of the distant table-lands
Through purple mists ascending, and the flare
Of water ditches silver in the light;
A swift, bright lance hurled low across the world;
A sudden sickness for the hills of home.

Prairie Spring

Evening and the flat land,
Rich and somber and always silent;
The miles of fresh-plowed soil,
Heavy and black, full of strength and harshness;
The growing wheat, the growing weeds,
The toiling horses, the tired men;
The long empty roads,
Sullen fires of sunset, fading,
The eternal, unresponsive sky.
Against all this, Youth,
Flaming like the wild roses,
Singing like the larks over the plowed fields,
Flashing like a star out of the twilight;
Youth with its insupportable sweetness,
Its fierce necessity,
Its sharp desire,
Singing and singing,
Out of the lips of silence,
Out of the earthy dusk.

Part IV

The Ancient People

I

THE SAN FRANCISCO Mountain lies in northern Arizona, above Flagstaff, and its blue slopes and snowy summit entice the eye for a hundred miles across the desert. About its base lie the pine forests of the Navajos, where the great red-trunked trees live out their peaceful centuries in the sparkling air. The *piñons* and scrub begin only where the forest ends, where the country breaks into open, stony clearings and the surface of the earth cracks into deep canyons. The great pines stand at a considerable distance from each other. Each tree grows alone, murmurs alone, thinks alone. They do not intrude upon each other. The Navajos are not much in the habit of giving or of asking help. Their language is not a communicative one, and they never attempt an interchange of personality in speech. Over their forests there is the same inexorable reserve. Each tree has its exalted power to bear.

That was the first thing Thea Kronborg felt about the forest, as she drove through it one May morning in Henry Biltmer's democrat wagon—and it was the first great forest she had ever seen. She had got off the train at Flagstaff that morning, rolled off into the high, chill air when all the pines on the mountain were fired by sunrise, so that she seemed to fall from sleep directly into the forest.

Old Biltmer followed a faint wagon trail which ran southeast, and which, as they traveled, continually dipped lower, falling away from the high plateau on the slope of which Flagstaff sits. The white peak of the mountain, the snow gorges above the timber, now disappeared from time to time as the road dropped and dropped, and the forest closed behind the wagon. More than the mountain disappeared as the forest closed thus. Thea seemed to be taking very little through the wood with her. The personality of which she was so tired seemed to let go of her. The high, sparkling air drank it up like blotting-paper. It was lost in the thrilling blue of the new sky and the song of the thin wind in the *piñons*. The old, fretted lines which marked one off, which defined her,—made her Thea Kronborg, Bowers's accompanist, a soprano with a faulty middle voice,—were all erased.

So far she had failed. Her two years in Chicago had not resulted in anything. She had failed with Harsanyi, and she had made no great progress with her voice. She had come to believe that whatever Bowers had taught her was of secondary importance, and that in the essential things she had made no advance. Her student life closed behind her, like the forest, and she doubted whether she could go back to it if she tried. Probably she would teach music in little country towns all her life. Failure was not so tragic as she would have supposed; she was tired enough not to care.

She was getting back to the earliest sources of gladness that she could remember. She had loved the sun, and the brilliant solitudes of sand and sun, long before these other things had come along to fasten themselves upon her and torment her. That night, when she clambered into her big German feather bed, she felt completely released from the enslaving desire to get on in the world. Darkness had once again the sweet wonder that it had in childhood.

The Enchanted Bluff

WE HAD OUR swim before sundown, and while we were cooking our supper the oblique rays of light made a dazzling glare on the white sand about us. The translucent red ball itself sank behind the brown stretches of corn field as we sat down to eat, and the warm layer of air that had rested over the water and our clean sand-bar grew fresher and smelled of the rank ironweed and sunflowers growing on the flatter shore. The river was brown and sluggish, like any other of the half-dozen streams that water the Nebraska corn lands. On one shore was an irregular line of bald clay bluffs where a few scrub oaks with thick trunks and flat, twisted tops threw light shadows on the long grass. The western shore was low and level, with corn fields that stretched to the sky-line, and all along the water's edge were little sandy coves and beaches where slim cottonwoods and willow saplings flickered.

The turbulence of the river in spring-time discouraged milling, and, beyond keeping the old red bridge in repair, the busy farmers did not concern themselves with the stream; so the Sandtown boys were left in undisputed possession. In the autumn we hunted quail through the miles of stubble and fodder land along the flat shore, and, after the winter skating season was over and the ice had gone out, the spring freshets and flooded bottoms gave us our great excitement of the year. The channel was never the same for two successive seasons. Every spring the swollen stream undermined a bluff to the east, or bit out a few acres of corn field to the west and whirled the soil away to deposit it in spumy mud banks somewhere else. When the water fell low in midsummer, new sand-bars were thus exposed to dry and whiten in the August sun. Sometimes these were banked so firmly that the fury of the next freshet failed to unseat them; the little willow seedlings emerged triumphantly from the yellow froth, broke into spring leaf, shot up into summer growth, and with their mesh of roots bound together the moist sand beneath them against the batterings of another April. Here and there a cottonwood soon glittered among them, quivering in the low current of air that, even on breathless days when the dust hung like smoke above the wagon road, trembled along the face of the water.

It was on such an island, in the third summer of its yellow green, that we built our watch-fire; not in the thicket of dancing willow wands, but on the level terrace of fine sand which had been added that spring; a little new bit of world, beautifully ridged with ripple marks, and strewn with the tiny skeletons of turtles and fish, all as white and dry as if they had been expertly cured. We had been careful not to mar the freshness of the place, although we often swam out to it on summer evenings and lay on the sand to rest.

This was our last watch-fire of the year, and there were reasons why I should remember it better than any of the others. Next week the other boys were to file back to their old places in the Sandtown High School, but I was to go up to the Divide to teach my first country school in the Norwegian district. I was already homesick at the thought of quitting the boys with whom I had always played; of leaving the river, and going up into a windy plain that was all windmills and corn fields and big pastures; where there was nothing wilful or unmanageable in the landscape, no new islands, and no chance of unfamiliar birds—such as often followed the watercourses.

Other boys came and went or used the river for fishing or skating, but we six were sworn to the spirit of the stream, and we were friends mainly because of the river. There were the two Hassler boys, Fritz and Otto, sons of the little German tailor. They were the youngest of us; ragged boys of ten and twelve, with sunburned hair, weather-stained faces, and pale blue eyes. Otto, the elder, was the best mathematician in the school, and clever at his books, but he always dropped out in the spring term as if the river could not get on without him. He and Fritz caught the fat, horned catfish and sold them about the town, and they lived so much in the water that they were as brown and sandy as the river itself.

There was Percy Pound, a fat, chubby boy with freckled cheeks, who took half a dozen boys' story-papers and was always being kept in for reading detective stories behind his desk. There was Tip Smith, destined by his freckles and red hair to be the buffoon in all our games, though he walked like a timid little old man and had a funny, cracked laugh. Tip worked hard in his father's grocery store every afternoon, and swept it out before school in the morning. Even his recreations were laborious. He collected cigarette cards and tin tobacco-tags indefatigably, and would sit for hours humped up over a snarling little scroll-saw which he kept in his attic. His dearest possessions were some little pill-bottles that purported to contain grains of wheat from the Holy Land, water from the Jordan and the Dead Sea, and earth from the Mount of Olives. His father had bought these dull things from a Baptist missionary who peddled them, and Tip seemed to derive great satisfaction from their remote origin.

The tall boy was Arthur Adams. He had fine hazel eyes that were almost too reflective and sympathetic for a boy, and such a pleasant voice that we all loved to hear him read aloud. Even when he had to read poetry aloud at school, no one ever thought of laughing. To be sure, he was not at school very much of the time. He was seventeen and should have finished the High School the year before, but he was always off somewhere with his gun. Arthur's mother was dead, and his father, who was feverishly absorbed in promoting schemes, wanted to send the boy away to school and get him off his hands; but Arthur always begged off for another year and promised to study. I remember him as a tall, brown boy with an intelligent face, always lounging among a lot of us little fellows, laughing at us oftener than with us, but such a soft, satisfied laugh that we felt rather flattered when we provoked it. In after-years people said that Arthur had been given to evil ways even as a lad, and it is true that we often saw him with the gambler's sons and with old Spanish Fanny's boy, but if he learned anything ugly in their company he never betrayed it to us. We would have followed Arthur anywhere, and I am bound to say that he led us into no worse places than the cat-tail marshes and the stubble fields. These, then, were the boys who camped with me that summer night upon the sand-bar.

After we finished our supper we beat the willow thicket for driftwood. By the time we had collected enough, night had fallen, and the pungent, weedy smell from the shore increased with the coolness. We threw ourselves down about the fire and made another futile effort to show Percy Pound the Little Dipper. We had tried it often before, but he could never be got past the big one.

"You see those three big stars just below the handle, with the bright one in the middle?" said Otto Hassler; "that's Orion's belt, and the bright one is the clasp." I crawled behind Otto's shoulder and sighted up his arm to the star that seemed perched upon the tip of his steady forefinger. The Hassler boys did seine-fishing at night, and they knew a good many stars.

Percy gave up the Little Dipper and lay back on the sand, his hands clasped under his head. "I can see the North Star," he announced, contentedly, pointing toward it with his big toe. "Any one might get lost and need to know that."

We all looked up at it.

"How do you suppose Columbus felt when his compass didn't point north anymore?" Tip asked.

Otto shook his head. "My father says that there was another North Star once, and that maybe this one won't last always. I wonder what would happen to us down here if anything went wrong with it?"

Arthur chuckled. "I wouldn't worry, Ott. Nothing's apt to happen to it in your time. Look at the Milky Way! There must be lots of good dead Indians."

We lay back and looked, meditating, at the dark cover of the world. The gurgle of the water had become heavier. We had often noticed a mutinous, complaining note in it at night, quite different from its cheerful daytime chuckle, and seeming like the voice of a much deeper and more powerful stream. Our water had always these two moods: the one of sunny complaisance, the other of inconsolable, passionate regret.

"Queer how the stars are all in sort of diagrams," remarked Otto. "You could do most any proposition in geometry with 'em. They always look as if they meant something. Some folks say everybody's fortune is all written out in the stars, don't they?"

"They believe so in the old country," Fritz affirmed.

But Arthur only laughed at him. "You're thinking of Napoleon, Fritzey. He had a star that went out when he began to lose battles. I guess the stars don't keep any close tally on Sandtown folks."

We were speculating on how many times we could count a hundred before the evening star went down behind the corn fields, when some one cried, "There comes the moon, and it's as big as a cart wheel!"

We all jumped up to greet it as it swam over the bluffs behind us. It came up like a galleon in full sail; an enormous, barbaric thing, red as an angry heathen god.

"When the moon came up red like that, the Aztecs used to sacrifice their prisoners on the temple top," Percy announced.

"Go on, Perce. You got that out of *Golden Days*. Do you believe that, Arthur?" I appealed.

Arthur answered, quite seriously: "Like as not. The moon was one of their gods. When my father was in Mexico City he saw the stone where they used to sacrifice their prisoners."

As we dropped down by the fire again some one asked whether the Mound-Builders were older than the Aztecs. When we once got upon the Mound-Builders we never willingly got away from them, and we were still conjecturing when we heard a loud splash in the water.

"Must have been a big cat jumping," said Fritz. "They do sometimes. They must see bugs in the dark. Look what a track the moon makes!"

There was a long, silvery streak on the water, and where the current fretted over a big log it boiled up like gold pieces.

"Suppose there ever *was* any gold hid away in all this old river?" Fritz asked. He lay like a little brown Indian, close to the fire, his chin on his hand and his bare feet in the air. His brother laughed at him, but Arthur took his suggestion seriously.

"Some of the Spaniards thought there was gold up here somewhere. Seven cities chuck full of gold, they had it, and Coronado and his men came up to hunt it. The Spaniards were all over this country once."

Percy looked interested. "Was that before the Mormons went through?"

We all laughed at this.

"Long enough before. Before the Pilgrim Fathers, Perce. Maybe they came along this very river. They always followed the watercourses."

"I wonder where this river really does begin?" Tip mused. That was an old and a favorite mystery which the map did not clearly explain. On the map the little black line stopped somewhere in western Kansas; but since rivers generally rose in mountains, it was only reasonable to suppose that ours came from the Rockies. Its destination, we knew, was the Missouri, and the Hassler boys always maintained that we could embark at Sandtown in flood-time, follow our noses, and eventually arrive at New Orleans. Now they took up their old argument. "If us boys had grit enough to try it, it wouldn't take no time to get to Kansas City and St. Joe."

We began to talk about the places we wanted to go to. The Hassler boys wanted to see the stock-yards in Kansas City, and Percy wanted to see a big store in Chicago. Arthur was interlocutor and did not betray himself.

"Now it's your turn, Tip."

Tip rolled over on his elbow and poked the fire, and his eyes looked shyly out of his queer, tight little face. "My place is awful far away. My uncle Bill told me about it."

Tip's Uncle Bill was a wanderer, bitten with mining fever, who had drifted into Sandtown with a broken arm, and when it was well had drifted out again.

"Where is it?"

"Aw, it's down in New Mexico somewheres. There aren't no railroads or anything. You have to go on mules, and you run out of water before you get there and have to drink canned tomatoes."

"Well, go on, kid. What's it like when you do get there?"

Tip sat up and excitedly began his story.

"There's a big red rock there that goes right up out of the sand for about nine hundred feet. The country's flat all around it, and this here rock goes up all by itself, like a monument. They call it the Enchanted Bluff down there, because no white man has ever been on top of it. The sides are smooth rock, and straight up, like a wall. The Indians say that hundreds of years ago, before the Spaniards came, there was a village away up there in the air. The tribe that lived there had some sort of steps, made out of wood and bark, hung down over the face of the bluff, and the braves went down to hunt and carried water up in big jars swung on their backs. They kept a big supply of water and dried meat up there, and never went down except to hunt. They were a peaceful tribe that made cloth and pottery, and they went up there to get out of the wars. You see, they could pick off any war party that tried to get up their little steps. The Indians say they were a handsome people, and they had some sort of a queer religion. Uncle Bill thinks they were Cliff-Dwellers who had got into trouble and left home. They weren't fighters, anyhow.

"One time the braves were down hunting and an awful storm came up—a kind of waterspout—and when they got back to their rock they found their little staircase had been all broken to pieces, and only a few steps were left hanging away up in the air. While they were camped at the foot of the rock, wondering what to do, a war party from the north came along and massacred 'em to a man, with all the old folks and women looking on from the rock. Then the war party went on south and left the village to get down the best way they could. Of course they never got down. They starved to death up there, and when the war party came back on their way north, they could hear the children crying from the edge of the bluff where they had crawled out, but they didn't see a sign of a grown Indian, and nobody has ever been up there since."

We exclaimed at this dolorous legend and sat up.

"There couldn't have been many people up there," Percy demurred. "How big is the top, Tip?"

"Oh, pretty big. Big enough so that the rock doesn't look nearly as tall as it is. The top's bigger than the base. The bluff is sort of worn away for several hundred feet up. That's one reason it's so hard to climb."

I asked how the Indians got up, in the first place.

"Nobody knows how they got up or when. A hunting party came along once and saw that there was a town up there, and that was all."

Otto rubbed his chin and looked thoughtful. "Of course there must be some way to get up there. Couldn't people get a rope over someway and pull a ladder up?"

Tip's little eyes were shining with excitement. "I know a way. Me and Uncle Bill talked it all over. There's a kind of rocket that would take a rope over—life-savers use 'em—and then you could hoist a rope-ladder and peg it down at the bottom and make it tight with guy-ropes on the other side. I'm going to climb that there bluff, and I've got it all planned out."

Fritz asked what he expected to find when he got up there.

"Bones, maybe, or the ruins of their town, or pottery, or some of their idols. There might be 'most anything up there. Anyhow, I want to see."

"Sure nobody else has been up there, Tip?" Arthur asked.

"Dead sure. Hardly anybody ever goes down there. Some hunters tried to cut steps in the rock once, but they didn't get higher than a man can reach. The Bluff's all red granite, and Uncle Bill thinks it's a boulder the glaciers left. It's a queer place, anyhow. Nothing but cactus and desert for hundreds of miles, and yet right under the bluff there's good water and plenty of grass. That's why the bison used to go down there."

Suddenly we heard a scream above our fire and jumped up to see a dark, slim bird floating southward far above us—a whooping-crane we knew by her cry and her long neck. We ran to the edge of the island, hoping we might see her alight, but she wavered southward along the rivercourse until we lost her. The Hassler boys declared that by the look of the heavens it must be after midnight, so we threw more wood on our fire, put on our jackets, and curled down in the warm sand. Several of us pretended to doze, but I fancy we were really thinking about Tip's Bluff and the extinct people. Over in the wood the ring-doves were calling mournfully to one another, and once we heard a dog bark, far away. "Somebody getting into old Tommy's melon patch," Fritz murmured, sleepily, but nobody answered him. By and by Percy spoke out of the shadow.

"Say, Tip, when you go down there will you take me with you?"

"Maybe."

"Suppose one of us beats you down there, Tip?"

"Whoever gets to the Bluff first has got to promise to tell the rest of us exactly what he finds," remarked one of the Hassler boys, and to this we all readily assented.

Somewhat reassured, I dropped off to sleep. I must have dreamed about a race for the Bluff, for I awoke in a kind of fear that other people were getting ahead of me and that I was losing my chance. I sat up in my damp clothes and looked at the other boys, who lay tumbled in uneasy attitudes about the dead fire. It was still dark, but the sky was blue with the last wonderful azure of night. The stars glistened like crystal globes, and trembled as if they shone through a depth of clear water. Even as I watched, they began to pale and the sky brightened. Day came suddenly, almost instantaneously. I turned for another look at the blue night, and it was gone. Everywhere the birds began to call, and all manner of little insects began to chirp and hop about in the willows. A breeze sprang up from the west and brought the heavy smell of ripened corn. The boys rolled over and shook themselves. We stripped and plunged into the river just as the sun came up over the windy bluffs.

When I came home to Sandtown at Christmas time, we skated out to our island and talked over the whole project of the Enchanted Bluff, renewing our resolution to find it.

Although that was twenty years ago, none of us have ever climbed the Enchanted Bluff. Percy Pound is a stockbroker in Kansas City and will go nowhere that his red touring-car cannot carry him. Otto Hassler went on the railroad and lost his foot braking; after which he and Fritz succeeded their father as the town tailors.

Arthur sat about the sleepy little town all his life—he died before he was twenty-five. The last time I saw him, when I was home on one of my college vacations, he was sitting in a steamer-chair under a cottonwood tree in the little yard behind one of the two Sandtown saloons. He was very untidy and his hand was not steady, but when he rose, unabashed, to greet me, his eyes were as clear and warm as ever. When I had talked with him for an hour and heard him laugh again, I wondered how it was that when Nature had taken such pains with a man, from his hands to the arch of his long foot, she had ever lost him in Sandtown. He joked about Tip Smith's Bluff, and declared he was going down there just as soon as the weather got cooler; he thought the Grand Cañon might be worth while, too.

I was perfectly sure when I left him that he would never get beyond the high plank fence and the comfortable shade of the cottonwood. And, indeed, it was under that very tree that he died one summer morning.

Tip Smith still talks about going to New Mexico. He married a slatternly, unthrifty country girl, has been much tied to a perambulator, and has grown stooped and gray from irregular meals and broken sleep. But the worst of his difficulties are now over, and he has, as he says, come into easy water. When I was last in Sandtown I walked home with him late one moonlight night, after he had balanced his cash and shut up his store. We took the long way around and sat down on the schoolhouse steps, and between us we quite revived the romance of the lone red rock and the extinct people. Tip insists that he still means to go down there, but he thinks now he will wait until his boy, Bert, is old enough to go with him. Bert has been let into the story, and thinks of nothing but the Enchanted Bluff.

Natalie Curtis Burlin
(1875–1921)

Twenty-two of the contiguous United States lie west of the Mississippi River. Yet, in 1875, when Natalie Curtis was born in New York City, half of these states had not been admitted to the Union. In her short life, the organization of the West would be completed, eleven states formally recognized, and the territories of Alaska and Hawaii added. She witnessed the end of an expansionist era, the end of the Indian wars, the breakdown of the traditional Native American way of life, and the usurpation of Indian land. Attempts at their forced assimilation into mainstream American life marked the latter quarter of the nineteenth century and the beginning of the twentieth.

Natalie Curtis was the daughter of a successful New York City doctor. Music was her creative passion; she studied piano and composition in America and Europe, preparing for a concert career. But on a trip to the Southwest with her brother in 1900, she heard the music and chants of Native Americans for the first time and witnessed the pressures from church and government to eradicate Indian culture. Indian children were routinely sent to English-speaking boarding schools to separate them from cultural and family units (*see* Zitkala-Sa). In the wake of the Ghost Dance war, Indians were forbidden to speak their native languages or perform traditional ceremonies.

Determined to preserve what she called America's original folk music, Curtis sought permission from President Theodore Roosevelt, a family friend, to record Indian songs, chants, oral history, and legends. She traveled to eighteen tribes, transcribing songs in standard musical notation. Her work was so precise that she could teach the songs of one tribe to another. For posterity, she included English translations beneath the Indian lyrics. In her effort to preserve vanishing cultures, she was a pioneer in the study of musical ethnography. Yet, her vision and her vocation were altruistic. Curtis called her compendium *The Indians' Book,* and took no credit for the thousands of miles she had traveled to dusty corners of the West, or for the hours she had spent editing the histories of the tribes she encountered. She called herself "the white friend," or "the interpreter." The authors, she insisted, were the Indians themselves.

Curtis's lyrical and metered prose absorbed much from the cultures she interviewed. The text of *The Indians' Book* sings, reflecting both her passion for music and the specific rhythms she transcribed. Her journeys brought her closer to the earth through contact with people who lived with and from the land. In the simplicity of her writing, she allows us to see her soul.

In addition to *The Indians' Book*, Curtis produced *Songs of Ancient America*, a collection of Pueblo Indian songs, articles on Native American poets and artists, and a review of cowboy songs. Recognizing the need to preserve black folk music, she recorded more than four hundred songs and published them in 1919. She also founded a music school in Harlem for African Americans.

In 1914, Natalie Curtis married artist Paul Burlin, an artist eleven years her junior. For the next seven years they lived in Santa Fe while he painted desert landscapes and Native Americans and she studied folk music. In 1921, rebelling against the virulent post–World War I criticism of American abstract artists, Burlin and Curtis moved to France. Curtis used the opportunity to present Native American music to an enthusiastic Paris audience. A few days later, she was struck and killed by a car. She was forty-six.

The Song of the Hopi Chief

LOLOLOMAI, chief of the Hopi village of Oraibi, was well named Lolo-lomai (Very-Good), for he had ever been the watchful father of his people. Eighty summers had shone upon him, yet he bore himself with the dignity of chieftaincy. Unlike many Hopis, he had travelled far and had been to see the great chief in Washington, in the land where "there were many clouds and the sun looked like the moon."

To The Indian's Book is here given the account of the white friend's talk with Lololomai, word for word, as written shortly after the visit:

I sought Lololomai to tell him of my purpose with the Hopi songs. My interpreter was a Hopi lad, who, though blind, led with sure foot the way up the steep, rocky trail to the village. The chief was seated on his house-top, spinning, for in Hopi-land it is the men who spin and weave. He rose and met us at the head of the ladder that led to where he sat.

"I have come to talk with you, friend, on something that concerns your people," I said.

"Ancha-a ('Tis well)," he answered, solemnly, and motioned me to sit down with him.

"Lololomai," I said, "the Hopi children are going to school; they are learning new ways and are singing new songs—American songs instead of Hopi. Some of the children are very young—so young that there have been, perhaps, but three corn-plantings since they came into the world. These little ones will never sing the songs of their fathers. They will not sing of the corn, the bean-blossoms, and the butterflies. They will know only American songs. Hopi songs are beautiful; it is sad that they should be forgotten."

To all of this the old chief said, "Hao, hao (Even so, even so)," and nodded slowly.

"But," I continued, "there is one thing in the school good for all to have and to know, and that is *books*. Books can be of many kinds, Hopi as well as English. As yet your people have no books nor do they read or write. That is why your songs will be forgotten, why even your language may some day pass away.

"When you sing, your song is heard, then dies like the wind that sweeps the cornfields and is gone, none knows whither. But if you could

write, your could put your song into a book, and your people, even to
the children of their children, could know your song as if you yourself
were singing. They could look upon the written page and say: 'thus sang
Lololomai, our chief, in the long ago. Thus sings Lololomai to-day.'"

The head drooped lower and the aged face was grave.

"But until the time shall come," I said, "when the Hopis shall themselves record their stories and their songs, some one must do this for
them, else much will be lost—lost forever, like a wind-blown trail. So I
have come from my far-distant home by the 'great waters' in the East to
write the Hopi songs."

There was a pause. Then the old chief turned to me pathetically.
There was a wistful yearning in the aged eyes, a cloud of trouble on the
wrinkled brow.

"It is well," he said, "but will not the superintendent be angry if you
do this thing? Are you sure that you will not bring trouble upon us?
White people try to stop our songs and dances so I am fearful of your
talk."

"Be at rest, my friend," I said, "the great chief at Washington is father
of all the people in this country, as you are father of all in this village.[11]
He has given his permission for the writing of the Hopi songs. He is glad
to have them written, for he, too, knows that Hopi songs are beautiful."

"Then it is well," replied Lololomai—"then it is well, indeed. But will
you, friend, explain to me that which I cannot understand? Why do the
white people want to stop our dances and our songs? Why do they trouble us? Why do they interfere with what can harm them not? What ill do
we to any white man when we dance?"

"Lololomai, white men do not understand your dances or your songs.
They do not even know one word of your language. When I have written your songs, I will write English words as well as Hopi, that white
men may know of what you sing. When they understand, they will perhaps no longer want to stop your dances and your songs. To you,
Lololomai, the Hopi Chief, will I give the Hopi songs when they are
written. You will keep them for your people with the other sacred things
that are your trust. Then in the days to come the younger Hopis will
read, and so the songs never will be forgotten."

Lololomai bowed his head. "Lolomai," he said, "pas lolomai (good,
very good)."

"And now will you sing one of your own songs, that I may write it?"
I asked. "Sing a song of your own making, for Lololomai's song should
be the first."

The chief rested his chin on his hand and gazed before him over the desert in deep thought. "I am old," he said, "and I have made many songs and have forgotten many songs. It is as you say, the songs I made when I was young I remember now no longer. I will sing the last song that I made."

He rose and beckoned me to another sunny corner on the house-top, spreading a blanket for a seat.

"This song," Lololomai explained, "was sung during our ceremony of thank-offering after the corn was garnered for the year.[12] The men go from one kiva to another, all night long, dancing and singing. This is the song of the men from my kiva, the chief kiva.[13] It tells how my kiva the chief and his men are praying to make the corn to grow next year for all the people. That is the meaning of my song."

Then in rhythmic monotone the old man crooned beside me. Long and diligently I worked at the recording, with the glare of the hot sun on my paper. It was no light task to fix the chant in musical notation.

I saw this question in the chief's eyes: "I have sung the song; why does it take so long to make those black marks on the paper?" And I said, "Lololomai, you know that when the Hopi sets a trap for the blackbird, sometimes it is long before he can catch his fluttering prey. Your song is a wild blackbird to me, and it may be that the sun will move far along the sky before I have captured it."

When I had finished, I showed Lololomai the written page[.] The old man scanned the mysterious tracings, and, nodding slowly, repeated again and again, "Ancha-a, ikwatchi, ancha-a (It is well, my friend, it is well)." Then drawing his blanket around him, Lololomai stepped to the edge of the roof, and, facing the sun, sank upon his knees with head bowed in his hands. What his act meant I knew not, for I had heard that Hopis stood erect to pray. But the swift instinct of sympathy said—the aged father of the village thus consecrates the new task for the Hopis.

The shadows on the village street grew long. The sun was sinking. Here and there a lone Hopi was returning from below with laden burro. Soon the trail would be dotted with home-coming Indians. We sat long in silence, Lololomai, the blind boy, and I. I watched the glow enfold the desert with the mystery of dying day. The chief's song was that sung when the corn was garnered. And I—with book and pencil I was gleaning in the Hopi fields in this the sunset hour of the people's native life. The time is short before night shall fall forever on the spirit of spontaneous song within the Indian.

Silent still, the blind boy and I took our downward way upon the rocky trail. To my companion, in his night, the deepening shadow bore no import, but a twilight sadness lay upon my spirit. I thought of the garnered Hopi corn. Will there be many more plantings of poetry and harvestings of song? Darkness closed in. But off beyond in silver glory rose the moon.

To Lololomai had been promised the songs of his people. But before the pledge could be fulfilled the old chief followed the western sun. The silent desert never again will waken to his voice. But for Hopis yet unborn The Indians' Book holds the song of the long-loved chieftain of Oraibi.

৯৹

Lololomai's Prayer

A Leaf from the Recorder's Diary

IT WAS SUNSET when for the last time I climbed the steep trail to the village of Oraibi. The level desert seemed a lilac sea, and the outlines of the craggy table-lands were sharp against the flaming sky. Many weeks had passed since I had left the railroad to take the long two-days' drive across the "Painted Desert" to the Hopi villages, and in those weeks I had learned to know and to love the "People of Peace." To-morrow I must leave the desert and its freedom for my distant Eastern home, and so I sought Lololomai, the aged chief, to say to him and to his household a parting word. Thus I passed on a farewell visit through the ancient town, with its terraces of roofs, its open dance-plazas, and its odd corners.

The chief's house was near the end of the village. I opened the low door and entered a dark chamber of stone. The pale light of dying day came faintly through the narrow windows; a smouldering fire on the hearth threw flicker of light and shadow on a group of Indians seated on the floor. A nephew of the chief stood before the hearth; the firelight showed the brown, handsome face, velvet clothes and buckskin leggings. He had passed me on the trail on his fleet white horse, flourishing his riding quirt, and singing as he rode.

"Where is your uncle, the chief, Lololomai?" I asked of the young man, when I had made my greetings.

"He has gone with some men to clear the springs," was the answer. "The sand has filled the springs and our animals have no water."

"Then I shall not see him," I said, sadly. "I had come to bid him good-bye."

But Ponianömsi, the chief's sister, said, "I will bear your message to Lololomai, if you will leave your words with me."

Ponianömsi was of high importance in the village, for, with the Hopi, descent is reckoned on the female side, and as the chief is the father of his people, so is his sister the mother. Ponianömsi had the gentle courtesy of the Hopi and the added dignity of her position. Her shoulders were square and firm; they had not bent beneath the weight of the water-jar carried daily by the Hopi women from the springs up the steep trail to the village. Mules had hauled water for the household of the chief; Ponian[ö]msi's small form was erect.

The hostess spread a roll of sheepskin on the floor for me to sit upon, and I joined the group by the fire. I had brought, as a farewell gift, a jar of gray sand from the shores of the Atlantic. The Navajos, neighbors to the Hopis, had asked me the year before to bring them such sand. They had said, "If, in our ceremonies, we use sand that comes from where there is so much water, that sand will surely bring water to us here; it must help us in our prayers for rain."

I had brought enough sand for Hopis as well as Navajos. "See," I said to the group at the fireside, "I have brought you something from the great waters, even some of the very ground that lies beneath the waters. The sand is silver there, not golden, like yours upon the desert."

I opened the jar and poured the gray particles into Ponianömsi's outstretched palm. She stooped by the fire the better to see, and slowly let fall the shining stream from one hand into the other.

"Where I live," I continued, "there is much sand like this and there are great waters, so great that a man standing on the edge can see no land upon the other side."

Ponianömsi closed her fingers over the sand and looked at me with earnest eyes. The other Indians, too, children of the desert, all gazed upon me with fixed look. The sand was passed from hand to hand. Each Indian fingered it with reverence.

"There is a great water to the west of California: that you know. But my home is by the Eastern waters, towards the rising sun. And in my home the fields are green with grass, and trees grow tall. The mountains there are not barren rocks like yours; they are covered with waving forests. The sun does not shine always, as with you; there are many clouds, and much rain falls. Sometimes it rains for many days; then the skies are gray, not blue."

"And are you going back to those great waters and that Eastern land?" said Ponianömsi.

"To-morrow I must go," I said. Then spoke Talaskwaptiwa, brother of the chief, with true Indian hospitality. "But you will come to see us many times?"

"Ah no," I answered, "I cannot come back soon again, nor can I come back often, for my home is far away."

"How far?" said Talaskwaptiwa. "How many days must a Hopi run before he find your land?"

"A Hopi must run for many moons to reach the great waters of the East," I answered. "The railroad train runs four days and four nights without rest, and the train runs in one hour as far as a Hopi does in a day."

The Indians fingered the sand in silence. It had come a long way.

"You would be surprised at so much green, if you could see my country," I said. "But my people would be as much surprised if they could see your corn. With us, corn is all yellow and white, not many colored, as with you. We have never seen corn blue and red and black like yours. Will you, in friendship, give me of your corn an ear of every color to take to my people?"

Ponianömsi rose, and with her Talaskwaptiwa. At the embers they lit a tiny bit of candle and picking up a woven basket-tray went to the store-room where the corn was neatly stacked in sorted piles of different colors. They brought me the full tray. Ponianömsi held it in the light of the fire. "See," she said, picking up in turn an ear of each color, "the blue, the black, the spotted, the pink, the red, the yellow, the white, the lilac, I have brought one of each kind."

All light had faded from the windows. The room was lit by the fire alone; night had come. Outside, the white horse whinnied and stirred the dust impatiently. I rose to go; Ponianömsi took my hand. "You will not forget me," I said. Ponianömsi answered, "We will pray for you, our friend, and when you are in your far-off home by those great waters, will you pray for the Hopis, that they may have rain?"

"I will pray for the Hopis that they may have rain and that they may be 'good in their hearts,'" I answered, using the Hopis' own prayer-phrase.

Talaskwaptiwa stood by the hearth, his face grave in the fire-light. I knew that the time was drawing near when the Hopis would plant their *bahos,*—emblematic prayer-sticks, into whose feathered ends prayers are breathed. If any Hopis are absent at the time of the offering of bahos, those at home make bahos for them. So I said, "When the Hopis make their bahos, will they make one for me?"

Talaskwaptiwa looked up quickly; this was a strange request from a *Bahana*—an American. But he answered, "We are spinning now in the kivas; soon we shall make the bahos.[14] I will make a baho for you, and we will pray for you."

"Pray that I, too, may be good in my heart," I said, as I bent and kissed the cheek of Ponianömsi.

So we parted. The young nephew left with me, for he, too, lived at the foot of the mesa. Together we passed through the shadowed village, meeting here and there a hurrying barefoot Hopi flitting homeward through the dark.

The young man led his white horse by the bridle as we clambered down the rocky trail beneath the stars. "When Talaskwaptiwa has made the baho, what will he do with it?" I asked.

"He will give it to Ponianömsi," answered the Hopi, "when all the women go to plant their bahos, she will take it with her."

"And where do the women plant the bahos?"

"Over there—east!" He pointed with his whip to the cliff above. "On the edge of the mesa they will plant the bahos when the yellow line comes over the mountains."[15]

"Why do they plant them at the coming of the yellow line?"

"Because they pray, and if they pray when the sun rises, the sun will carry the prayers up, up!" His whip moved, in illustration, from horizon to zenith.

"And to whom do the Hopis pray?"

There was a pause, then, slowly, "It is that which makes the rain—that makes all things. It is the Power, and it lives behind the sun."[16]

"And the katzinas?"

"The katzinas only take the prayers. We do not pray to them."

"Does the Power that lives behind the sun look like a man, or like anything that the Hopis have ever seen?"

The Hopi looked at me in surprise. "No, it is not a man; we don't know how it looks. We only know that it *is*."

"When Lololomai, the chief, prays, how does he pray? Will you tell me?"

"He goes to the edge of the cliff and turns his face to the rising sun, and scatters the sacred corn-meal. Then he prays for all the people. He asks that we may have rain and corn and melons, and that our fields may bring us plenty. But these are not the only things he prays for. He prays that all the people may have health and long life and be happy and good in their hearts. And Hopis are not the only people he prays for. He prays for everybody in the whole world—everybody. And not people alone; Lololomai prays for all the animals. And not animals alone; Lololomai prays for all the plants. He prays for everything that has life. That is how Lololomai prays."

We trod the rest of our downward way in silence. I looked up at the sky, so vast and deep, lit by the brilliant desert stars. As we neared the foot of the trail, I glanced back at the village-crested mesa. It loomed a great black shadow on the sky. To-morrow, the Hopi world would no longer be mine. Then, as though to seal in spiritual beauty the memory of the simple people of Oraibi, the wide night seemed to echo, "He prays for the whole world—for everything that has life."

Gertrude Simmons Bonnin
(Zitkala-Sa) (Sioux)
(1876–1938)

THE INVENTION OF the telephone in 1876 marked the beginning of the communication age. A year later Thomas Edison invented the phonograph, and in 1879, he produced a practical form of electric lights. These inventions, taken together, did as much to unite the country as the transcontinental railroad had a decade earlier. Yet, the benefits of Alexander Graham Bell's and Edison's genius would take generations to reach the reservation Indians of America's heartland.

Gertrude Simmons, daughter of a Yankton Sioux mother and a white father, was born on the Pine Ridge Reservation in southwestern South Dakota. For eight years, Gertrude, who named herself Zitkala-Sa (Red Bird), lived a traditional life with her mother, who spoke no English. Against her mother's wishes, Zitkala-Sa chose to leave the reservation to pursue an education. She returned three years later, already an outsider, a child in limbo. For four years, she struggled to reattach herself to the old ways. It proved impossible.

Zitkala-Sa returned to school. Overcoming vicious prejudice, she won oratory prizes in competition with whites. When health problems prevented her from receiving a college degree, she taught at the Carlisle Indian School in Pennsylvania. Her success was dearly purchased. Caught in the tug-of-war between two civilizations, Zitkala-Sa sacrificed her relationship with her mother, yet was never fully accepted into white society.

Zitkala-Sa wrote about her western life and the family she had left in order to join the white world. In 1900, she published a series of autobiographical sketches in the *Atlantic Monthly. Old Indian Legends,* a collection of stories for children, came out in 1901. Magazines such as *Harper's* and *Everybody's* published her short fiction in 1901 and 1902. They were republished in 1921 as *American Indian Stories.*

Raised in a culture based on oral tradition, Zitkala-Sa chose to translate that tradition into writing. Once she began the process of acculturation, Zitkala-Sa could not retreat to her former life or belief system. She was, in effect, estranged from both worlds because white America ridiculed the same Native Americans it sought to educate and proselytize.

Zitkala-Sa hoped that her work would shed light on the painful accul-turation process and the inequities of life on the margins of mainstream America.

Although her early writings made her famous, in the twenty-year in-terval between her major publications, Zitkala-Sa turned to working for, and lecturing about, Indian rights—a struggle that absorbed her for the rest of her life. Assisting her in this effort was Raymond Bonnin, a Sioux whom she married in 1902. They had a son, Raymond, in 1903. While living in Utah with her family, Zitkala-Sa worked among and taught the reservation Indians. A talented violinist, she contributed her unique view and interpretation to an opera by William Hanson, *Sun Dance*, that was performed both locally and in New York.

From 1916 to 1920, Zitkala-Sa worked in Washington, D.C., as an officer of the Society of the American Indian (SAI). Despite the rulings handed down in the Ponca case (*see* Susette La Flesche), Native Americans were not considered citizens. The allotment system was still in place, employment and educational opportunities were limited, health care was minimal, and assimilation was destroying families and cultural identities. To alleviate these problems, Zitkala-Sa traveled, lectured, wrote articles, and edited the *American Indian* magazine. Upon SAI's demise, Zitkala-Sa worked through women's groups to accomplish her goals, emphasizing the patriotism of Native Americans, including her husband, who fought in World War I. In 1924, Zitkala-Sa's writing bore fruit: Native Americans gained citizen status.

Zitkala-Sa was born the year that Elizabeth Bacon Custer lost her husband to Sioux warriors at the Little Big Horn. She died during the Great Depression. She is buried in Arlington Cemetery, not far from those who fought to eradicate her people.

I

My Mother

A WIGWAM OF weather-stained canvas stood at the base of some irregularly ascending hills. A footpath wound its way gently down the sloping land till it reached the broad river bottom; creeping through the long swamp grasses that bent over it on either side, it came out on the edge of the Missouri.

Here, morning, noon, and evening, my mother came to draw water from the muddy stream for our household use. Always, when my mother started for the river, I stopped my play to run along with her. She was only of medium height. Often she was sad and silent, at which times her full arched lips were compressed into hard and bitter lines, and shadows fell under her black eyes. Then I clung to her hand and begged to know what made the tears fall.

"Hush; my little daughter must never talk about my tears"; and smiling through them, she patted my head and said, "Now let me see how fast you can run to-day." Whereupon I tore away at my highest possible speed, with my long black hair blowing in the breeze.

I was a wild little girl of seven. Loosely clad in a slip of brown buckskin, and light-footed with a pair of soft moccasins on my feet, I was as free as the wind that blew my hair, and no less spirited than a bounding deer. These were my mother's pride,—my wild freedom and overflowing spirits. She taught me no fear save that of intruding myself upon others.

Having gone many paces ahead I stopped, panting for breath, and laughing with glee as my mother watched my every movement. I was not wholly conscious of myself, but was more keenly alive to the fire within. It was as if I were the activity, and my hands and feet were only experiments for my spirit to work upon.

Returning from the river, I tugged beside my mother, with my hand upon the bucket I believed I was carrying. One time, on such a return, I remember a bit of conversation we had. My grown-up cousin, Warca-Ziwin (Sunflower), who was then seventeen, always went to the river alone for water for her mother. Their wigwam was not far from ours; and I saw her daily going to and from the river. I admired my cousin greatly. So I said: "Mother, when I am tall as my cousin Warca-Ziwin, you shall not have to come for water. I will do it for you."

With a strange tremor in her voice which I could not understand, she answered, "If the paleface does not take away from us the river we drink."

"Mother, who is this bad paleface?" I asked.

"My little daughter, he is a sham,—a sickly sham! The bronzed Dakota is the only real man."

I looked up into my mother's face while she spoke; and seeing her bite her lips, I knew she was unhappy. This aroused revenge in my small soul. Stamping my foot on the earth, I cried aloud, "I hate the paleface that makes my mother cry!"

Setting the pail of water on the ground, my mother stooped, and stretching her left hand out on the level with my eyes, she placed her other arm about me; she pointed to the hill where my uncle and my only sister lay buried.

"There is what the paleface has done! Since then your father too has been buried in a hill nearer the rising sun. We were once very happy. But the paleface has stolen our lands and driven us hither. Having defrauded us of our land, the paleface forced us away.

"Well, it happened on the day we moved camp that your sister and uncle were both very sick. Many others were ailing, but there seemed to be no help. We traveled many days and nights; not in the grand, happy way that we moved camp when I was a little girl, but we were driven, my child, driven like a herd of buffalo. With every step, your sister, who was not as large as you are now, shrieked with the painful jar until she was hoarse with crying. She grew more and more feverish. Her little hands and cheeks were burning hot. Her little lips were parched and dry, but she would not drink the water I gave her. Then I discovered that her throat was swollen and red. My poor child, how I cried with her because the Great Spirit had forgotten us!

"At last, when we reached this western country, on the first weary night your sister died. And soon your uncle died also, leaving a widow and an orphan daughter, your cousin Warca-Ziwin. Both your sister and uncle might have been happy with us today, had it not been for the heartless paleface."

My mother was silent the rest of the way to our wigwam. Though I saw no tears in her eyes, I knew that was because I was with her. She seldom wept before me.

❧

VI

The Ground Squirrel

IN THE BUSY autumn days my cousin Warca-Ziwin's mother came to our wigwam to help my mother preserve foods for our winter use. I was very fond of my aunt, because she was not so quiet as my mother. Though she was older, she was more jovial and less reserved. She was slender and remarkably erect. While my mother's hair was heavy and black, my aunt had unusually thin locks.

Ever since I knew her, she wore a string of large blue beads around her neck,—beads that were precious because my uncle had given them to her when she was a younger woman. She had a peculiar swing in her gait, caused by a long stride rarely natural to so slight a figure. It was during my aunt's visit with us that my mother forgot her accustomed quietness, often laughing heartily at some of my aunt's witty remarks.

I loved my aunt threefold: for her hearty laughter, for the cheerfulness she caused my mother, and most of all for the times she dried my tears and held me in her lap, when my mother had reproved me.

Early in the cool mornings, just as the yellow rim of the sun rose above the hills, we were up and eating our breakfast. We awoke so early that we saw the sacred hour when a misty smoke hung over a pit surrounded by an impassable sinking mire. This strange smoke appeared every morning, both winter and summer; but most visibly in midwinter it rose immediately above the marshy spot. By the time the full face of the sun appeared above the eastern horizon, the smoke vanished. Even very old men, who had known this country the longest, said that the smoke from this pit had never failed a single day to rise heavenward.

As I frolicked about our dwelling I used to stop suddenly, and with a fearful awe watch the smoking of the unknown fires. While the vapor was visible I was afraid to go very far from our wigwam unless I went with my mother.

From a field in the fertile river bottom my mother and aunt gathered an abundant supply of corn. Near our tepee they spread a large canvas upon the grass, and dried their sweet corn in it. I was left to watch the corn, that nothing should disturb it. I played around it with dolls made of ears of corn. I braided their soft fine silk for hair, and gave them blankets as various as the scraps I found in my mother's workbag.

There was a little stranger with a black-and-yellow-striped coat that used to come to the drying corn. It was a little ground squirrel, who was so fearless of me that he came to one corner of the canvas and carried away as much of the sweet corn as he could hold. I wanted very much to catch him and rub his pretty fur back, but my mother said he would be so frightened if I caught him that he would bite my fingers. So I was as content as he to keep the corn between us. Every morning he came for more corn. Some evenings I have seen him creeping about our grounds; and when I gave a sudden whoop of recognition he ran quickly out of sight.

When mother had dried all the corn she wished, then she sliced great pumpkins into thin rings; and these she doubled and linked together into long chains. She hung them on a pole that stretched between two forked posts. The wind and sun soon thoroughly dried the chains of pumpkin. Then she packed them away in a case of thick and stiff buckskin.

In the sun and wind she also dried many wild fruits,—cherries, berries, and plums. But chiefest among my early recollections of autumn is that one of the corn drying and the ground squirrel.

I have few memories of winter days at this period of my life, though many of the summer. There is one only which I can recall.

Some missionaries gave me a little bag of marbles. They were all sizes and colors. Among them were some of colored glass. Walking with my mother to the river, on a late winter day, we found great chunks of ice piled all along the bank. The ice on the river was floating in huge pieces. As I stood beside one large block, I noticed for the first time the colors of the rainbow in the crystal ice. Immediately I thought of my glass marbles at home. With my bare fingers I tried to pick out some of the colors, for they seemed so near the surface. But my fingers began to sting with the intense cold, and I had to bite them hard to keep from crying.

From that day on, for many a moon, I believed that glass marbles had river ice inside of them.

V

Iron Routine

A LOUD-CLAMORING bell awakened us at half past six in the cold winter mornings. From happy dreams of Western rolling lands and unlassoed freedom we tumbled out upon chilly bare floors back again into a pale-face day. We had short time to jump into our shoes and clothes, and wet our eyes with icy water, before a small hand bell was vigorously rung for roll call.

There were too many drowsy children and too numerous orders for the day to waste a moment in any apology to nature for giving her children such a shock in the early morning. We rushed downstairs, bounding over two high steps at a time, to land in the assembly room.

A paleface woman, with a yellow-covered roll book open on her arm and a gnawed pencil in her hand, appeared at the door. Her small, tired face was coldly lighted with a pair of large gray eyes.

She stood still in a halo of authority, while over the rim of her spectacles her eyes pried nervously about the room. Having glanced at her long list of names and called out the first one, she tossed up her chin and peered through the crystals of her spectacles to make sure of the answer "Here."

Relentlessly her pencil black-marked our daily records if we were not present to respond to our names, and no chum of ours had done it successfully for us. No matter if a dull headache or the painful cough of slow consumption had delayed the absentee, there was only time enough to mark the tardiness. It was next to impossible to leave the iron routine after the civilizing machine had once begun its day's buzzing; and as it was inbred in me to suffer in silence rather than to appeal to the ears of one whose open eyes could not see my pain, I have many times trudged in the day's harness heavy-footed, like a dumb sick brute.

Once I lost a dear classmate. I remember well how she used to mope along at my side, until one morning she could not raise her head from her pillow. At her deathbed I stood weeping, as the paleface woman sat near her moistening the dry lips. Among the folds of the bedclothes I saw the open pages of the white man's Bible. The dying Indian girl talked disconnectedly of Jesus the Christ and the paleface who was cooling her swollen hands and feet.

I grew bitter, and censured the woman for cruel neglect of our physical ills. I despised the pencils that moved automatically, and the one teaspoon which dealt out, from a large bottle, healing to a row of variously ailing Indian children. I blamed the hard-working, well-meaning, ignorant woman who was inculcating in our hearts her superstitious ideas. Though I was sullen in all my little troubles, as soon as I felt better I was ready again to smile upon the cruel woman. Within a week I was again actively testing the chains which tightly bound my individuality like a mummy for burial.

The melancholy of those black days has left so long a shadow that it darkens the path of years that have since gone by. These sad memories rise above those of smoothly grinding school days. Perhaps my Indian nature is the moaning wind which stirs them now for their present record. But, however tempestuous this is within me, it comes out as the low voice of a curiously colored seashell, which is only for those ears that are bent with compassion to hear it.

❦

VII

Incurring My Mother's Displeasure

IN THE SECOND journey to the East I had not come without some precautions. I had a secret interview with one of our best medicine men, and when I left his wigwam I carried securely in my sleeve a tiny bunch of magic roots. This possession assured me of friends wherever I should go. So absolutely did I believe in its charms that I wore it through all the school routine for more than a year. Then, before I lost my faith in the dead roots, I lost the little buckskin bag containing all my good luck.

At the close of this second term of three years I was the proud owner of my first diploma. The following autumn I ventured upon a college career against my mother's will.

I had written for her approval, but in her reply I found no encouragement. She called my notice to her neighbors' children, who had completed their education in three years. They had returned to their homes, and were then talking English with the frontier settlers. Her few words hinted that I had better give up my slow attempt to learn the white man's ways, and be content to roam over the prairies and find my living upon wild roots. I silenced her by deliberate disobedience.

Thus, homeless and heavy-hearted, I began anew my life among strangers.

As I hid myself in my little room in the college dormitory, away from the scornful and yet curious eyes of the students, I pined for sympathy. Often I wept in secret, wishing I had gone West, to be nourished by my mother's love, instead of remaining among a cold race whose hearts were frozen hard with prejudice.

During the fall and winter seasons I scarcely had a real friend, though by that time several of my classmates were courteous to me at a safe distance.

My mother had not yet forgiven my rudeness to her, and I had no moment for letter-writing. By daylight and lamplight, I spun with reeds and thistles, until my hands were tired from their weaving, the magic design which promised me the white man's respect.

At length, in the spring term, I entered an oratorical contest among the various classes. As the day of competition approached, it did not seem possible that the event was so near at hand, but it came. In the chapel the classes assembled together, with their invited guests. The high platform was carpeted, and gayly festooned with college colors. A bright white light illumined the room, and outlined clearly the great polished beams that arched the domed ceiling. The assembled crowds filled the air with pulsating murmurs. When the hour for speaking arrived all were hushed. But on the wall the old clock which pointed out the trying moment ticked calmly on.

One after another I saw and heard the orators. Still, I could not realize that they longed for the favorable decision of the judges as much as I did. Each contestant received a loud burst of applause, and some were cheered heartily. Too soon my turn came, and I paused a moment behind the curtains for deep breath. After my concluding words, I heard the same applause that the others had called out.

Upon my retreating steps, I was astounded to receive from my fellow students a large bouquet of roses tied with flowing ribbons. With the lovely flowers I fled from the stage. This friendly token was a rebuke to me for the hard feelings I had borne them.

Later, the decision of the judges awarded me the first place. Then there was a mad uproar in the hall, where my classmates sang and shouted my name at the top of their lungs; and the disappointed students howled and brayed in fearfully dissonant tin trumpets. In this excitement, happy students rushed forward to offer their congratulations. And I could not conceal a smile when they wished to escort me in a procession to the students' parlor, where all were going to calm themselves. Thanking them for the kind spirit which prompted them to make such a proposition, I walked alone with the night to my own little room.

A few weeks afterward, I appeared as the college representative in another contest. This time the competition was among orators from different colleges in our state. It was held at the state capital, in one of the largest opera houses.

Here again was a strong prejudice against my people. In the evening, as the great audience filled the house, the student bodies began warring among themselves. Fortunately, I was spared witnessing any of the noisy wrangling before the contest began. The slurs against the Indian that stained the lips of our opponents were already burning like a dry fever within my breast.

But after the orations were delivered a deeper burn awaited me. There, before that vast ocean of eyes, some college rowdies threw out a large white flag, with a drawing of a most forlorn Indian girl on it. Under this they had printed in bold black letters words that ridiculed the college which was represented by a "squaw." Such worse than barbarian rudeness embittered me. While we waited for the verdict of the judges, I gleamed fiercely upon the throngs of palefaces. My teeth were hard set, as I saw the white flag still floating insolently in the air.

Then anxiously we watched the man carry toward the stage the envelope containing the final decision.

There were two prizes given, that night, and one of them was mine!

The evil spirit laughed within me when the white flag dropped out of sight, and the hands which furled it hung limp in defeat.

Leaving the crowd as quickly as possible, I was soon in my room. The rest of the night I sat in an armchair and gazed into the crackling fire. I laughed no more in triumph when thus alone. The little taste of victory did not satisfy a hunger in my heart. In my mind I saw my mother far away on the Western plains, and she was holding a charge against me.

III

My Mother's Curse upon White Settlers

ONE BLACK NIGHT mother and I sat alone in the dim starlight, in front of our wigwam. We were facing the river, as we talked about the shrinking limits of the village. She told me about the poverty-stricken white settlers, who lived in caves dug in the long ravines of the high hills across the river.

A whole tribe of broad-footed white beggars had rushed higher to make claims on those wild lands. Even as she was telling this I spied a small glimmering light in the bluffs.

"That is a white man's lodge where you see the burning fire," she said. Then, a short distance from it, only a little lower than the first, was another light. As I became accustomed to the night, I saw more and more twinkling lights, here and there, scattered all along the wide black margin of the river.

Still looking toward the distant firelight, my mother continued: "My daughter, beware of the paleface. It was the cruel paleface who caused the death of your sister and your uncle, my brave brother. It is this same paleface who offers in one palm the holy papers, and with the other gives a holy baptism of firewater. He is the hypocrite who reads with one eye, 'Thou shalt not kill,' and with the other gloats upon the sufferings of the Indian race." Then suddenly discovering a new fire in the bluffs, she exclaimed, "Well, well, my daughter, there is the light of another white rascal!"

She sprang to her feet, and, standing firm beside her wigwam, she sent a curse upon those who sat around the hated white man's light. Raising her right arm forcibly into line with her eye, she threw her whole might into her doubled fist as she shot it vehemently at the strangers. Long she held her outstretched fingers toward the settler's lodge, as if an invisible power passed from them to the evil at which she aimed.

Elinore Pruitt Rupert Stewart
(1878?–1933)

T HE NINETEENTH AMENDMENT to the Constitution, which guaranteed a woman's right to vote, was not ratified until August 26, 1920. Wyoming Territory, however, had led the country by granting the vote to women in 1869, twenty-one years before Wyoming was admitted as the forty-fourth state. Statehood and equal rights did not yield a burgeoning population in a land characterized by ten months of winter. Although mail-order brides and housekeepers recruited through newspaper ads helped swell the female ranks, isolation and harsh physical and economical conditions took their toll. In 1909, when thirty-something Elinore Pruitt Rupert left a life of menial labor in Denver to keep house for a Scottish widower one-half mile north of the Utah border, Wyoming remained sparsely populated.

Elizabeth Pruitt Stewart told stories within the letters she sent to a former employer, Juliet Coney, a Bostonian transplanted to Denver. Coney sent the letters to the *Atlantic Monthly,* where they were published in 1913 and 1914. Two collections of the Stewart letters, *Letters of a Woman Homesteader* and *Letters on an Elk Hunt,* came out in 1914 and 1915. They focus on the land and people of one of America's last frontiers: the isolated cattle and sheep ranches of southeastern Wyoming.

Pruitt was a westerner, born in Arkansas and raised in Indian Territory, the oldest of eight children. Both parents died when she was fourteen. Although her grandmother helped raise her youngest siblings, Pruitt and five brothers worked for the railroad and at odd jobs to support themselves. When she answered Stewart's ad, Elinore was a widow with little formal schooling and a four-year-old daughter, Jerrine. A promising freelance newspaper career had ended with the death of Pruitt's husband, a civil engineer, soon after Jerrine was born. Elinore was reduced to taking in laundry, delivering coal, and cleaning houses in Denver. But she wanted to raise her daughter in the country. She needed the security of working her own land.

On February 19, 1909, Congress passed the Enlarged Homestead Act, which allowed heads of households to homestead 320 acres (half a section) of public lands in eight western states, including Wyoming.

Although cattlemen had lobbied for the bill, Pruitt Rupert saw it as a way out. By April, she was employed by Clyde Stewart and had moved to Burntfork, Wyoming. Within six weeks she had married him and filed on her adjoining acreage.

Life on the isolated flanks of the Uinta Mountains was no easier than Elinore's earlier life had been. Illness took their firstborn son, but three more survived. Blizzards killed their cattle. Economic conditions made small-scale ranching unprofitable. Yet, through it all, when the innumerable daily chores were done, Elinore wrote letters to friends and acquaintances. The consistently upbeat letters downplayed her troubles, focusing instead on the lives of those around her. The rest of the country might have entered the twentieth century, but Elinore's writing reveals the haunting beauty of a land and way of life that flowed with the rhythm of the seasons. For her, the contact with readers, however far removed, helped counteract the loneliness of that rural life. Eventually, they also brought in much-needed cash.

Elinore was severely injured in a mowing accident in 1926. Seven years later she died. Her positive spirit, strength, and humor live on in her letters.

Burnt Fork, Wyoming,
April 18, 1909.

Dear Mrs. Coney,—

Are you thinking I am lost, like the Babes in the Wood? Well, I am not and I'm sure the robins would have the time of their lives getting leaves to cover me out here. I am 'way up close to the Forest Reserve of Utah, within half a mile of the line, sixty miles from the railroad. I was twenty-four hours on the train and two days on the stage, and oh, those two days! The snow was just beginning to melt and the mud was about the worst I ever heard of.

The first stage we tackled was just about as rickety as it could very well be and I had to sit with the driver, who was a Mormon and so handsome that I was not a bit offended when he insisted on making love all the way, especially after he told me that he was a widower Mormon. But, of course, as I had no chaperone I looked very fierce (not that that was very difficult with the wind and mud as allies) and told him my actual opinion of Mormons in general and particular.

Meantime my new employer, Mr. Stewart, sat upon a stack of baggage and was dreadfully concerned about something he calls his 'Tookie,' but I am unable to tell you what that is. The road, being so muddy, was full of ruts and the stage acted as if it had the hiccoughs and made us all talk as though we were affected in the same way. Once Mr. Stewart asked me if I did not think it a 'duir gey trip.' I told him he could call it gay if he wanted to, but it did n't seem very hilarious to me. Every time the stage struck a rock or a rut Mr. Stewart would 'hoot,' until I began to wish we would come to a hollow tree or a hole in the ground so he could go in with the rest of the owls.

At last we 'arriv,' and everything is just lovely for me. I have a very, very comfortable situation and Mr. Stewart is absolutely no trouble, for as soon as he has his meals he retires to his room and plays on his bagpipe, only he calls it his 'bugpeep.' It is 'The Campbells are Coming,' without variations, at intervals all day long and from seven till eleven at night. Sometimes I wish they would make haste and get here.

There is a saddle horse especially for me and a little shotgun with which I am to kill sage chickens. We are between two trout streams, so you can think of me as being happy when the snow is through melting and the water gets clear. We have the finest flock of Plymouth Rocks and get so many nice eggs. It sure seems fine to have all the cream I want after my town experiences. Jerrine is making good use of all the good things we are having. She rides the pony to water every day.

I have not filed on my land yet because the snow is fifteen feet deep on it, and I think I would rather see what I am getting, so will wait until summer. They have just three seasons here, Winter and July and August. We are to plant our garden the last of May. When it is so I can get around I will see about land and find out all I can and tell you.

I think this letter is about to reach thirty-secondly, so I will send you my sincerest love and quit tiring you. Please write me when you have time.

Sincerely yours,
Elinore Rupert.

Burnt Fork, Wyo., Sept. 28 [1909]

Dear Mrs. Coney,—

Your second card just reached me and I am plumb glad because, although I answered your other, I was wishing I could write you for I have had the most charming adventure.

It is the custom here for as many women as care to, to go in a party over to Utah into Ashland (which is over a hundred miles away) after fruit. They usually go in September, and it takes a week to make the trip. They take wagons and camp out and of course have a good time, but the greater part of the way, there is n't even a semblance of a road and it is merely a semblance anywhere. They came over to invite me to join them. I was of two minds—I wanted to go but it seemed a little risky and a big chance for discomfort, since we would have to cross the Uinta Mountains, and a snowstorm likely any time. But I did n't like to refuse outright, so we left it to Mr. Stewart. His 'Ye 're nae gang' sounded powerful final, so the ladies departed in awed silence and I assumed a martyr-like air and acted like a very much abused woman, although he did only what I wanted him to do. At last, in sheer desperation he told me

the 'bairn canna stand the treep,' and that was why he was so determined. I knew why, of course, but I continued to look abused lest he gets
it into his head that he can boss me. After he had been reduced to the
proper plane of humility and had explained and begged my pardon and
had told me to consult only my own pleasure about going and coming
and using his horses, only not to 'expoose' the bairn, why, I forgave him
and we were friends once more.

Next day all the men left for the round-up, to be gone a week. I knew
I never could stand myself a whole week. In a little while the ladies came
past on their way to Ashland. They were all laughing and were so happy
that I really began to wish I was one of the number, but they went their
way and I kept wanting to go *somewhere*. I got reckless and determined
to do something real bad. So I went down to the barn and saddled Robin
Adair, placed a pack on 'Jeems McGregor,' then Jerrine and I left for a
camping-out expedition.

It was nine o'clock when we started and we rode hard until about
four, when I turned Robin loose, saddle and all, for I knew he would go
home and some one would see him and put him into the pasture. We had
gotten to where we could n't ride anyway, so I put Jerrine on the pack
and led 'Jeems' for about two hours longer, then, as I had come to a
good place to camp, we stopped.

While we had at least two good hours of daylight, it gets so cold here
in the evening that fire is very necessary. We had been climbing higher
into the mountains all day and had reached a level table-land where the
grass was luxuriant and there was plenty of wood and water. I unpacked
'Jeems' and staked him out, built a roaring fire, and made our bed in an
angle of a sheer wall of rock where we would be protected against the
wind. Then I put some potatoes into the embers as Baby and I are both
fond of roasted potatoes. I started to a little spring to get water for my
coffee when I saw a couple of jack-rabbits playing, so I went back for
my little shot-gun. I shot one of the rabbits, so I felt very like
Leatherstocking because I had killed but one when I might have gotten
two. It was fat and young, and it was but the work of a moment to dress
it and hang it up on a tree. Then I fried some slices of bacon, made myself a cup of coffee, and Jerrine and I sat on the ground and ate.
Everything smelled and tasted so good! This air is so tonic that one gets
delightfully hungry. Afterward we watered and re-staked 'Jeems,' I
rolled some logs onto the fire, and then we sat and enjoyed the prospect.

The moon was so new that its light was very dim, but the stars were
bright. Presently a long, quivering wail arose and was answered from a

dozen hills. It seemed just the sound one ought to hear in such a place. When the howls ceased for a moment we could hear the subdued roar of the creek and the crooning of the wind in the pines. So we rather enjoyed the coyote chorus and were not afraid, because they don't attack people. Presently we crept under our Navajos and, being tired, were soon asleep.

I was awakened by a pebble striking my cheek. Something prowling on the bluff above us had dislodged it and it struck me. By my Waterbury it was four o'clock, so I arose and spitted my rabbit. The logs had left a big bed of coals, but some ends were still burning and had burned in such a manner that the heat would go both under and over my rabbit. So I put plenty of bacon grease over him and hung him up to roast. Then I went back to bed. I did n't want to start early because the air is too keen for comfort early in the morning.

The sun was just gilding the hilltops when we arose. Everything, even the barrenness, was beautiful. We have had frosts, and the quaking aspens were a trembling field of gold as far up the stream as we could see. We were 'way up above them and could look far across the valley. We could see the silvery gold of the willows, the russet and bronze of the currants, and patches of cheerful green showed where the pines were. The splendor was relieved by a background of sober gray-green hills, but even on them gay streaks and patches of yellow showed where rabbit-brush grew. We washed our faces at the spring,—the grasses that grew around the edge and dipped into the water were loaded with ice,—our rabbit was done to a turn, so I made some delicious coffee, Jerrine got herself a can of water, and we breakfasted. Shortly afterwards we started again. We did n't know where we were going but we were on our way.

That day was more toilsome than the last but a very happy one. The meadow larks kept singing like they were glad to see us. But we were still climbing and soon got beyond the larks and sage chickens and up into the timber, where there are lots of grouse. We stopped to noon by a little lake where I got two small squirrels and a string of trout. We had some trout for dinner and salted the rest with the squirrels in an empty can for future use. I was anxious to get a grouse and kept close watch but was never quick enough. Our progress was now slower and more difficult because in places we could scarcely get through the forest. Fallen trees were everywhere and we had to avoid the branches, which was powerful hard to do. Besides, it was quite dusky among the trees long before night, but it was all so grand and awe-inspiring. Occasionally there was an opening through which we could see the snowy peaks, seemingly just beyond us, toward which we were headed.

But when you get among such grandeur you get to feel how little you are and how foolish is human endeavor, except that which reunites us with the mighty force called God. I was plumb uncomfortable, because all my own efforts have always been just to make the best of everything and to take things as they come.

At last we came to an open side of the mountain where the trees were scattered. We were facing south and east and the mountain we were on sheered away in a dangerous slant. Beyond us still greater wooded mountains blocked the way, and in the cañon between night had already fallen. I began to get scary. I could only think of bears and catamounts, so, as it was five o'clock, we decided to camp. The trees were immense. The lower branches came clear to the ground and grew so dense that any tree afforded a splendid shelter from the weather, but I was nervous and wanted one that would protect us against any possible attack. At last we found one growing in a crevice of what seemed to be a sheer wall of rock. Nothing could reach us on two sides and in front two large trees had fallen so that I could make a log-heap which would give us warmth and make us safe. So with rising spirits I unpacked and prepared for the night. I soon had a roaring fire up against the logs and, cutting away a few branches, let the heat into as snug a bedroom as any one could wish. The pine needles made as soft a carpet as the wealthiest could afford. Springs abound in the mountains, so water was plenty. I staked 'Jeems' quite near so that the fire-light would frighten away any wild thing that tried to harm him. Grass was very plentiful, so when he was made 'comfy' I made our bed and fried our trout. The branches had torn off the bag in which I had my bread, so it was lost in the forest, but who needs bread when they have good, mealy potatoes? In a short time we were eating like Lent was just over. We lost all the glory of the sunset except what we got by reflection, being on the side of the mountain we were, with the dense woods between. Big sullen clouds kept drifting over and a wind got lost in the trees that kept them rocking and groaning in a horrid way. But we were just as cozy as we could be and rest was as good as anything.

I wish you could once sleep on the kind of bed we enjoyed that night. It was both soft and firm, with the clean, spicy smell of the pine. The heat from our big fire came in and we were warm as toast. It was so good to stretch out and rest. I kept thinking how superior I was since I dared to take such an outing when so many poor women down in Denver were bent on making their twenty cents per hour in order that they could spare a quarter to go to the 'show.' I went to sleep with a powerfully self-satisfied feeling, but I awoke to realize that pride goeth before a fall.

I could hardly remember where I was when I awoke, and I could almost hear the silence. Not a tree moaned, not a branch seemed to stir. I arose and my head came in violent contact with a snag that was not there when I went to bed. I thought either I must have grown taller or the tree shorter during the night. As soon as I peered out, the mystery was explained.

Such a snowstorm I never saw! The snow had pressed the branches down lower, hence my bumped head. Our fire was burning merrily and the heat kept the snow from in front. I scrambled out and poked up the fire, then, as it was only five o'clock, I went back to bed. And then I began to think how many kinds of idiot I was. Here I was thirty or forty miles from home, in the mountains where no one goes in the winter and where I knew the snow got to be ten or fifteen feet deep. But I could never see the good of moping, so I got up and got breakfast while Baby put her shoes on. We had our squirrels and more baked potatoes and I had delicious black coffee.

After I had eaten I felt more hopeful. I knew Mr. Stewart would hunt for me if he knew I was lost. It was true, he would n't know which way to start, but I determined to rig up 'Jeems' and turn him loose, for I knew he would go home and that he would leave a trail so that I could be found. I hated to do so for I knew I should always have to be powerfully humble afterwards. Anyway it was still snowing, great, heavy flakes, they looked as large as dollars. I did n't want to start 'Jeems' until the snow stopped because I wanted him to leave a clear trail. I had sixteen loads for my gun and I reasoned that I could likely kill enough food to last twice that many days by being careful what I shot at. It just kept snowing, so at last I decided to take a little hunt and provide for the day. I left Jerrine happy with the towel rolled into a baby, and went along the brow of the mountain for almost a mile, but the snow fell so thickly that I could n't see far. Then I happened to look down into the cañon that lay east of us and saw smoke. I looked toward it a long time but could make out nothing but smoke, but presently I heard a dog bark and I knew I was near a camp of some kind. I resolved to join them, so went back to break my own camp.

At last everything was ready and Jerrine and I both mounted. Of all the times! If you think there is much comfort, or even security, in riding a pack-horse in a snowstorm over mountains where there is no road, you are plumb wrong. Every once in a while a tree would unload its snow down our backs. 'Jeems' kept stumbling and threatening to break our necks. At last we got down the mountain side where new danger confronted us,—we might lose sight of the smoke or ride into a bog. But at last, after what seemed hours, we came into a 'clearing' with a small log-house and, what is rare in Wyoming, a fireplace. Three or four hounds set up their deep baying and I knew by the chimney and the hounds that it was the home of a Southerner. A little old man came bustling out, chewing his tobacco so fast, and almost frantic about his suspenders which it seemed he could n't get adjusted.

As I rode up, he said, 'Whither, friend?' I said 'Hither.' Then he asked, 'Air you spying around for one of them dinged game wardens arter that deer I killed yisteddy?' I told him I had never even seen a game warden and that I did n't know he had killed a deer. 'Wall,' he said, 'air you spying around arter that gold mine I diskivered over on the west side of Baldy?' But after a while I convinced him that I was no more nor less than a foolish woman lost in the snow. Then he said, 'Light, stranger, and look at your saddle.' So I 'lit' and looked, and then I asked him what part of the South he was from. He answered, 'Yell County, by gum! The best place in the United States, or in the world, either.' That was my introduction to Zebulon Pike Parker.

Only two 'Johnny Rebs' could have enjoyed each other's company as Zebulon Pike and myself did. He was so small and so old, but so cheerful and so sprightly, and a real Southerner! He had a big, open fireplace with back-logs and andirons. How I enjoyed it all! How we feasted on some of the deer killed 'yisteddy,' and real corn-pone baked in a skillet down on the hearth. He was so full of happy recollections and had a few that were not so happy! He is, in some way, a kinsman of Pike of Pike's Peak fame, and he came west 'jist arter the wah' on some expedition and 'jist stayed.' He told me about his home life back in Yell County, and I feel that I know all the 'young uns.'

There was George Henry, his only brother; and there were Phœbe and 'Mothie,' whose real name is Martha; and poor little Mary Ann, whose death was described so feelingly that no one could keep back the tears. Lastly there was little Mandy, the baby and his favorite, but who, I am afraid, was a selfish little beast since she had to have her prunellas when all the rest of the 'young uns' had to wear shoes that old Uncle Buck made out of rawhide. But then 'her eyes were blue as morning glories and her hair was jist like corn silk, so yaller and fluffy.' Bless his simple, honest heart! His own eyes are blue and kind, and his poor, thin little shoulders are so round that they almost meet in front. How he loved to talk of his boyhood days! I can almost see his Father and George Henry as they marched away to the 'wah' together, and the poor little Mother's despair as she waited day after day for some word that never came.

Poor little Mary Ann was drowned in the bayou where she was trying to get water-lilies. She had wanted a white dress all her life and so, when she was dead, they took down the white cross-bar curtains and Mother made the little shroud by the light of a tallow dip. But being made by hand it took all the next day too, so that they buried her by moonlight down back of the orchard under the big elm where the children had always had their swing. And they lined and covered her grave with big, fragrant water-lilies. As they lowered the little home-made coffin into the grave the mocking birds began to sing and they sang all that dewy, moonlight night. Then little Mandy's wedding to Judge Carter's son Jim was described. She wore a 'cream-colored poplin with a red rose throwed up in it,' and the lace that was on Grandma's wedding dress. There were bowers of sweet Southern roses and honeysuckle and wisteria. Don't you know she was a dainty bride?

At last it came out that he had not heard from home since he had left it. 'Don't you ever write?' I asked. 'No, I am not an eddicated man, although I started to school. Yes 'm, I started along of the rest, but they told me it was a Yankee teacher and I was 'fraid, so when I got most to the schoolhouse I hid in the bushes with my spelling book, so that is all the learning I ever got. But my mother was an eddicated woman, yes 'm, she could both read and write. I have the Bible she give me yit. Yes 'm, you jist wait and I'll show you.' After some rummaging in a box he came back with a small leather-bound Bible with print so small it was hard to read. After turning to the record of births and deaths he handed it to me, his wrinkled old face shining with pride as he said, 'There, my mother wrote that with her own hand.' I took the book and after a little deciphered that 'Zebulon Pike Parker was born Feb. 10, 1830,' written in the stiff, difficult style of long ago and written with poke-berry ink. He said his mother used to read about some 'old feller that was jist covered with biles,' so I read Job to him, and he was full of surprise they didn't 'git some cherry bark and some sasparilly and bile it good and gin it to him.'

He had a side room to his cabin, which was his bed-room, so that night he spread down a buffalo robe and two bearskins before the fire for Jerrine and me. After making sure there were no moths in them, I spread blankets over them and put a sleepy, happy little girl to bed, for he had insisted on making molasses candy for her because they happened to be born on the same day of the month. And then he played the fiddle until almost one o'clock. He played all the simple, sweet, old-time pieces, in rather a squeaky, jerky way, I am afraid, but the music suited the time and the place.

Next morning he called me early and when I went out I saw such a beautiful sunrise, well worth the effort of coming to see. I had thought his cabin in a cañon, but the snow had deceived me, for a few steps from the door the mountains seemed to drop down suddenly for several hundred feet and the first of the snow peaks seemed to lie right at our feet. Around its base is a great swamp, in which the swamp pines grow very thickly and from which a vapor was rising that got about halfway up the snow peak all around. Fancy to yourself a big jewel-box of dark green velvet lined with silver chiffon, the snow peak lying like an immense opal in its centre and over all the amber light of a new day. That is what it looked most like.

Well, we next went to the corral where I was surprised to find about thirty head of sheep. Some of them looked like they should have been sold ten years before. 'Don't you ever sell any of your sheep?' I asked. 'No 'm. There was a feller come here once and wanted to buy some of my wethers, but I would n't sell any because I did n't need any money.' Then he went from animal to animal, caressing each and talking to them, calling them each by his name. He milked his one cow, fed his two little mules, and then we went back to the house to cook breakfast. We had delicious venison steak, smoking hot, and hoe-cakes and the 'bestest' coffee, and honey.

After breakfast we set out for home. Our pack transferred to one of the little mules, we rode 'Jeems,' and Mr. Parker rode the other mule. He took us another way down cañon after cañon so that we were able to ride all the time and could make better speed. We came down out of the snow and camped within twelve miles of home in an old, deserted ranch house. We had grouse and sage chicken for supper. I was so anxious to get home that I could hardly sleep, but at last I did and was only awakened by the odor of coffee, and barely had time to wash before Zebulon Pike called breakfast. Afterwards we fixed 'Jeems's' pack so that I could still ride, for Zebulon Pike was very anxious to get back to his 'critters.'

Poor, lonely, child-like little man! He tried to tell me how glad he had been to entertain me. 'Why,' he said, 'I was plumb glad to see you and right sorry to have you go. Why, I would jist as soon talk to you as to a nigger. Yes 'm, I would. It has been almost as good as talking to old Aunt Dilsey.' If a Yankee had said the same to me I would have demanded instant apology, but I know how the Southern heart longs for the dear, kindly old 'niggers,' so I came on homeward, thankful for the first time, that I can't talk correctly.

I got home at twelve and found, to my joy, that none of the men had returned, so I am safe from their superiority for a while, at least.

With many apologies for this outrageous letter, I am

Your ex-Washlady,
Elinore Rupert.

A N ESTIMATED NINETEEN million immigrants entered the United
States during the nineteenth century. Irish and Germans escaped
famines of the 1840s. Economic depression and overpopulation in the
1880s forced Scandinavians, Germans, British, and Irish to seek land
and jobs in the New World. In the first quarter of the twentieth century,
depression and political turmoil sent new waves of Central and Eastern
Europeans, Italians, and Russian peasants and Jews across the ocean.
These immigrants not only flooded coastal cities of the East but also
headed for western cities and carved farms from the midwestern
prairies. Those who chose the industrial opportunities of the cities
crowded into impoverished ethnic neighborhoods without basic sanitation, creating conditions ripe for the spread of malnutrition and disease.
The situation in Chicago was so severe that in 1889, Jane Addams and
Ellen Gates Starr established Hull House to study and address immigrant problems that included illiteracy, unemployment, overcrowding,
sanitation, juvenile crime, and epidemics of tuberculosis, polio, and typhoid.

The poor had no resources to escape these conditions. The wealthy,
who lived in separate enclaves but employed carriers of the diseases,
were almost as vulnerable. When they contracted "consumption," those
with money fled to sanatoriums in the dry climates of California and the
Southwest. There was no cure. Antibiotics and vaccinations against
polio and tuberculosis were not discovered until the mid-twentieth century. In Corbin's day, patients hoped that desert air would bring remis-
sion. Rose Hartwick Thorpe and her husband moved to San Diego for
"the cure." Edith Maude Eaton (Sui Sin Far) went to Los Angeles and
San Francisco. Alice Corbin chose Santa Fe. Relocation to the Southwest
saved her life and inspired some of her best work.

Alice Corbin was born in St. Louis. After the death of her mother
from tuberculosis in 1884, Corbin moved to Chicago. Although Alice's
childhood was spent in continual readjustment to new schools in
Illinois, Missouri, Indiana, Virginia, and Louisiana, she captured her re-
actions to these sojourns in verse. Her first book of poetry, *Linnet Songs,*
was published while she was still in high school in Chicago.

In 1903, after graduation from college in New Orleans, Alice returned to Chicago. There she belonged to a circle of poets who advocated an imagistic, realistic, more concise poetry. Ezra Pound, Carl Sandburg, Witter Bynner, and Harriet Monroe represented the transition from the staid conventions of nineteenth-century verse to the experimental freedom of modern poetry. With Monroe, Alice edited *Poetry: A Magazine of Verse* from Monroe's Chicago house. Alice wrote prose as well as poetry, including reviews for Chicago newspapers.

A year after Corbin settled into the writing life of Chicago, she met artist William Penhallow Henderson. They married in 1905, and had a daughter, Alice Oliver, in 1907. Alice continued to write and edit. She produced children's plays, poetry anthologies, translations of fairy tales, and another book of poetry, *The Spinning Woman of the Sky*. In 1916, tuberculosis forced her to leave Chicago for a sanatorium in Santa Fe. The temporary stay became a permanent relocation.

Alice was instrumental, along with Mabel Dodge Luhan, Mary Austin, Natalie Curtis Burlin, D. H. Lawrence, and Willa Cather in establishing Santa Fe as a center for the arts. After her recuperation, Alice returned to editing *Poetry*, as well as publishing books of poetry and anthologies of the "new poets." Like other southwestern writers, she found inspiration not only in the red-rock country but also in the architectural, linguistic, historical, religious, and ethnic melange of New Mexican culture. Her last two books are arguably her best: *Red Earth* (1920), about her adopted Southwest, and *The Sun Turns West* (1933), autobiographical poems. *Red Earth,* in particular, captures the rhythm and mysticism of the Southwest in realistic, timeless, effortless verse.

Alice Corbin Henderson survived her husband by six years. She died in the summer of 1949 at her daughter's New Mexico ranch.

Red Earth

Muy Vieja Mexicana

I've seen her pass with eyes upon the road—
An old bent woman in a bronze black shawl,
With skin as dried and wrinkled as a mummy's,
As brown as a cigar-box, and her voice
Like the low vibrant strings of a guitar.
And I have fancied from the girls about
What she was at their age, what they will be
When they are old as she. But now she sits
And smokes away each night till dawn comes round,
Thinking, beside the piñons' flame, of days
Long past and gone, when she was young—content
To be no longer young, her epic done:

For a woman has work and much to do,
And it's good at the last to know it's through,
And still have time to sit alone,
To have some time you can call your own.
It's good at the last to know your mind
And travel the paths that you traveled blind,
To see each turn and even make
Trips in the byways you did not take—
But that, *por Dios,* is over and done,
It's pleasanter now in the way we've come;
It's good to smoke and none to say
What's to be done on the coming day,
No mouths to feed or coat to mend,
And none to call till the last long end.
Though one have sons and friends of one's own,
It's better at last to live alone.
For a man must think of food to buy,
And a woman's thoughts may be wild and high;
But when she is young she must curb her pride,
And her heart is tamed for the child at her side.

But when she is old her thoughts may go
Wherever they will, and none to know.
And night is the time to think and dream,
And not to get up with the dawn's first gleam;
Night is the time to laugh or weep,
And when dawn comes it is time to sleep . . .

When it's all over and there's none to care,
I mean to be like her and take my share
Of comfort when the long day's done,
And smoke away the nights, and see the sun
Far off, a shriveled orange in a sky gone black,
Through eyes that open inward and look back.

On the Acequia Madre

Death has come to visit us today,
He is such a distinguished visitor
Everyone is overcome by his presence—
"Will you not sit down—take a chair?"
But Death stands in the doorway, waiting to depart;
He lingers like a breath in the curtains.
The whole neighborhood comes to do him honor,
Women in black shawls and men in black sombreros
Sitting motionless against white-washed walls;
And the old man with the grey stubby beard
To whom death came,
Is stunned into silence.
Death is such a distinguished visitor,
Making even old flesh important.

But who now, I wonder, will take the old horse to pasture?

El Rito de Sante Fe

This valley is not ours, nor these mountains,
Nor the names we give them—they belong,
They, and this sweep of sun-washed air,

Desert and hill and crumbling earth,
To those who have lain here long years
And felt the soak of the sun
Through the red sand and crumbling rock,
Till even their bones were part of the sun-steeped valley;
How many years we know not, nor what names
They gave to antelope, wolf, or bison,
To prairie dog or coyote,
To this hill where we stand,
Or the moon over your shoulder . . .
Let us build a monument to Time
That knows all, sees all, and contains all,
To whom these bones in the valley are even as we are:
Even Time's monument would crumble
Before the face of Time,
And be as these white bones
Washed clean and bare by the sun. . . .

Candle-Light and Sun

Candle-Light

It might have been me in the darkened room
With the shutters closed,
Lying straight and slim
In the shuttered dusk,
In the twilight dim;
Like a silken husk
When the corn is gone,
Life withdrawn.
I am living, and she is dead—
It might have been me instead.

The Mask

Death is a beautiful white mask,
That slips over the face, when the moment comes,
To hide the happiness of the soul.

Rain-Prayer

A broken ploughed field
In the driving rain,
Rain driven slant-wise
Over the plain.
I long for the rain,
The dull long rain,
For farmlands and ploughlands
and cornlands again.
O grey broken skies,
You were part of my pain!

Fame

Fame is an echo
Far off, remote—
But love is a sweetness
You taste in the throat,
Friendship a comfort
When twilight falls.
But fame is an echo
Through empty halls.

Song of Sunlight

Sunlight is in my eyes,
Every house edged with light;
Open fields are before me,
Mountains across the sky.

What have I to do with cities?

Here the gods are clean, wind-swept.
They run along the hills,
Mad with sunlight;
They tumble into a deep canyon;
They take hold of a cloud
And swing with it—listen!—
They drop far off, noiselessly,
Beyond the blue mountain.

At night they lie down under the moon.
Do you see that hill move—
Heavily, like a sleeper,
Wrinkling his skin,
Moving the contour of pines and rocks,
Resting his hips?

It is not far to the stars,
Not far for them to lean down and whisper . . .

Sunlight, I am mad with your light.
Rocks, I have never known you before.
Earth, your red canyons
Are sluiced through me,
The crests of your hills
Break over me—
I ride upward to meet them.

NOTES

1. Tony Hillerman, ed., *The Best of the West: An Anthology of Classic Writing from the American West* (New York: HarperCollins, 1991), 293.

2. Nancy Kirkpatrick Wright, ed., *Sharlot Herself: Selected Writings of Sharlot Hall*, 44.

3. Harriet Martineau was a popular British writer of the nineteenth century who wrote about her travels in America. [Ed. note]

4. Karnes came from Tennessee and joined the Texas forces at Conception '35, while very young. Yoakum [Henderson Yoakum, *History of Texas,* 2 vols. (New York: Redfield, 1855)] refers to an amusing incident of this same battle. "One who was often with him, (Karnes), and by his side at Conception, says he never knew him to swear before or since that day. But when he came into the lines, after being shot at so often, and began to load his rifle, he exclaimed with some wrath, 'The d——d rascals have shot out the bottom of my powder horn.' Karnes was quite sober and temperate . . . he had remarkable gentleness and delicacy of feeling." [Maverick's note]

5. "F." was Dr. Fayette Clapp, Louise Clappe's husband. [Ed. note]

6. Let no practical mountaineer be allured by my description into the ascent of Long's Peak. Truly terrible as it was to me, to a member of the Alpine Club it would not be a feat worth performing. [Bird's note]

7. The old fellow would not own the Chippewa. [Catherwood's note]

8. "Hacienda," as used at Almaden, describes the village where the manager lives and has his office, and where the furnaces are built for reducing the ore. When the mine was under Mexican management it was much less extended, there was no Cornish camp and the settlement was chiefly at the Hacienda. [Foote's note]

9. Allan Nevins, *The Emergence of Lincoln: Douglas, Buchanan, and Party Chaos, 1857–1859,* 361.

10. Patricia Nelson Limerick, "Believing in the American West," 208.

11. President Theodore Roosevelt, who, from the first, took great interest in the work. [Burlin's note]

12. This ceremony is called *Wuwuchim-yungya.* [Burlin's note]

13. The kiva is an underground council-chamber. There are many kivas, probably one for each clan, originally. Here the men come to meet in council or to spin and weave. Here also the new songs are learned and dances practised.

But the most important use of the kiva is as a sacred chamber where altars are placed and secret ceremonial rites performed. [Burlin's note]

14. Woolen cord, used to bind the bahos, is ceremonially spun by the men in the *kivas*—underground council chambers. [Burlin's note]

15. The Hopi expression for dawn. [Burlin's note]

16. Mrs. Matilda Cox Stevenson, of the Bureau of American Ethnology, in her classification of the Zuñi higher powers, tells of "A'wonawil'ona, the supreme, life-giving, bisexual power, who is referred to as He-She, the symbol and initiator of life, and life itself, pervading all space," also of "the Sun Father, who is directly associated with the supreme power; . . . he is the giver of light and warmth, and through the supreme power the giver of life." (See "The Zuñi Indians; Their Mythology, Esoteric Fraternities, and Ceremonies." Twenty-Third Annual Report, Bureau of American Ethnology, Washington, D. C.) [Burlin's note]

Atherton, Gertrude. "The Vengeance of Padre Arroyo." In *Before the Gringo Came: Being Eleven Stories of Old California*. New York: J. Selwin Tait and Sons, 1894.

Austin, Mary. "Neither Spirit nor Bird (Shoshone Love Song)." In *Golden Songs of the Golden State*, comp. Marguerite Wilkinson. Chicago: McClurg, 1917.

———. "Pahawitz-Na'an." *Out West* 18 (March 1903): 337–44.

———. Preface to *The Land of Little Rain*. Boston: Houghton Mifflin, 1903.

Bird, Isabella L. *A Lady's Life in the Rocky Mountains*. 7th ed. 1879. Reprint, New York: G. P. Putnam's Sons, 1882.

Bonnin, Gertrude [Zitkala-Sa, pseud.]. "Impressions of an Indian Childhood." *Atlantic Monthly* 85 (January 1900): 37–47.

———. "An Indian Teacher among Indians." *Atlantic Monthly* 85 (March 1900): 381–86.

———. "School Days of an Indian Girl." *Atlantic Monthly* 85 (February 1900): 185–94.

Burlin, Natalie Curtis. *See* Curtis Burlin, Natalie.

Carey [Cary], Alice. "My Grandfather." In *Clovernook; or, Recollections of Our Neighborhood in the West*. Clinton Hall, N.Y.: Redfield, 1852.

Cary, Alice. "An Order for a Picture." In *The Poetical Works of Alice and Phoebe Cary*. Boston: Houghton Mifflin, 1882.

Cary, Phoebe. "'The Barefoot Boy.'" In *The Poetical Works of Alice and Phoebe Cary*. Boston: Houghton Mifflin, 1882.

———. "Granny's House." In *The Poems of Alice and Phoebe Cary*. New York: Thomas Y. Crowell, 1903.

———. "Homes for All [Plea for the Homeless]." In *The Poems of Alice and Phoebe Cary*. New York: Thomas Y. Crowell, 1903.

———. "Our Homestead." In *The Poems of Alice and Phoebe Cary*. New York: Thomas Y. Crowell, 1903.

Cather, Willa Sibert. "The Enchanted Bluff." *Harper's* 118 (April 1909): 774–81.

———. "Prairie Dawn." *McClure's* 31 (June 1908): 229.

———. "Prairie Spring." *McClure's* 40 (December 1912): 226.

———. *The Song of the Lark*. Boston: Houghton Mifflin, 1915.

Catherwood, Mary Hartwell. "The Skeleton on Round Island." In *Mackinac and Lake Stories*. New York: Harper and Brothers, 1899.

Clappe, Louise [Dame Shirley, pseud.]. "California, in 1851. Letter Third. A Trip into the Mines." In *Pioneer; or, California Monthly Magazine* 1 (April 1854): 221–24.

Coolbrith, Ina D. "California." In *A Perfect Day, and Other Poems*. San Francisco: John H. Carmony, 1881.

———. "In the Grand Cañon." In *Songs from the Golden Gate*. Boston: Houghton Mifflin, 1895.

———. "Listening Back." *Sunset* 45 (December 1920): 41.

———. "With a Wreath of Laurel." In *A Perfect Day, and Other Poems*. San Francisco: John H. Carmony, 1881.

Corbin [Henderson], Alice. "Candle-Light and Sun." *Poetry: A Magazine of Verse* 13.3 (1920): 197–99.

———. "Red Earth." *Poetry: A Magazine of Verse* 13.3 (1920): 194–97.

Curtis Burlin, Natalie. "Lololomai's Prayer." In *The Indians' Book: An Offering by the American Indians of Indian Lore, Musical and Narrative, to Form a Record of the Songs and Legends of Their Race*, ed. Natalie Curtis Burlin. New York: Harper and Brothers, 1907.

———. "The Song of the Hopi Chief." In *The Indians' Book: An Offering by the American Indians of Indian Lore, Musical and Narrative, to Form a Record of the Songs and Legends of Their Race*. New York: Harper and Brothers, 1907.

Custer, Elizabeth B. *"Boots and Saddles"; or, Life in Dakota with General Custer*. New York: Harper and Brothers, 1885.

———. *Tenting on the Plains; or, General Custer in Kansas and Texas*. New York: Charles L. Webster, 1889.

Eastman, Elaine Goodale. "Ashes of Roses." *St. Nicholas* 5 (December 1877): 110.

———. "Pima Tales." In *Indian Legends Retold*. Boston: Little, Brown, 1919.

———. "The Wood-Chopper to His Ax." *Overland Monthly*, 2d ser., 2 (September 1883): 275.

Eaton, Edith Maude. *See* Far, Sui Sin.

Far, Sui Sin. "Leaves from the Mental Portfolio of an Eurasian." *Independent* 66.3138 (21 January 1909): 125–32.

Fletcher, Alice C. "Personal Studies of Indian Life: Politics and Pipe-dancing." *Century* 45 (January 1893): 441–55.

———. "Personal Studies of Indian Life: Tribal Life among the Omahas." *Century* 51 (January 1896): 450–61.

Foote, Mary Hallock. "A California Mining Camp." *Scribner's* 15.4 (February 1878): 480–93.

———. "How the Pump Stopped at the Morning Watch." *Century,* n.s., 36 (June 1899): 469–72.

———. "Pictures of the Far West." *Century* 37 (December 1888): 161–62.

Frémont, Jessie Benton. *Souvenirs of My Time.* Boston: D. Lothrop, 1887.

Fuller, S. M. *Summer on the Lakes, in 1843.* Boston: Charles C. Little and James Brown; New York: Charles S. Francis, 1844.

Gage, Frances Dana. "Address to Woman's Rights Convention, Akron, Ohio, May 28, 1851." In *History of Woman Suffrage, 1848–1861,* by Elizabeth Cady Stanton, et al. Vol. 1. New York: Fowler and Wells, Publishers, 1881.

———. *Elsie Magoon; or, The Old Still-House in the Hollow: A Tale of the Past.* Philadelphia: Lippincott, 1867.

———. "Reminiscences by Frances D. Gage: Sojourner Truth." In *History of Woman Suffrage, 1848–1861,* by Elizabeth Cady Stanton, et al. Vol. 1. New York: Fowler and Wells, Publishers, 1881.

Gilman, Charlotte Perkins. "California Colors." *Forerunner* 6 (April 1915): 93.

———. "An Honest Woman." *Forerunner* 2.3 (March 1911): 59–65.

———. "Santa Clara Hills." *Forerunner* 5 (September 1914): 231.

Hall, Sharlot M. "Arizona." *Out West* 24.2 (February 1906): 67–69.

———. "The Fruit of the Yucca Tree." *Out West* 23 (December 1905): 569–75.

———. "His Place." *Out West* 28.2 (February 1908): 113.

———. "Out West." *Out West* 16.1 (January 1902): 3–5.

Henderson, Alice Corbin. *See* Corbin [Henderson], Alice.

Hopkins, Sarah Winnemucca. *See* Winnemucca, Sarah.

Jackson, Helen Hunt [H. H., pseud.]. "Cheyenne Mountain." In *Poems by Helen Jackson.* Boston: Little, Brown, 1908.

———. "Echoes in the City of Angels." *Century,* n.s., 5 (May–June 1883): 194–210.

———. *Ramona: A Story.* Boston: Roberts Brothers, 1886.

Kirkland, Caroline M. *A New Home—Who'll Follow? or, Glimpses of Western Life.* New York: C. S. Francis; Boston: J. H. Francis, 1839.

La Flesche, Susette [Bright Eyes, pseud.]. "Nedawi." *St. Nicholas* 8 (January 1881): 225–30.

Maverick, Mary A. *Memoirs of Mary A. Maverick, San Antonio's First American Woman.* Arranged by Mary A. Maverick and her son Geo. Madison Maverick. Edited by Rena Maverick Green. San Antonio: Alamo Printing, 1921.

Ruiz de Burton, María Amparo [C. Loyal, pseud.]. *The Squatter and the Don: A Novel Descriptive of Contemporary Occurrences in California.* San Francisco: [S. Carson], 1885.

Rupert [Stewart], Elinore. "Letters of a Woman Homesteader." *Atlantic Monthly* 112.4 (October 1913): 433–43.

Schoolcraft, Jane Johnston [Leelinau, pseud.]. "The Forsaken Brother: A Chippewa Tale." In *The Literary Voyager; or, Muzzeniegun,* by Henry Rowe Schoolcraft. Edited and with an introduction by Philip P. Mason. East Lansing: Michigan State University Press, 1962.

———. "The Origin of the Robin: An Oral Allegory." In *The Literary Voyager; or, Muzzeniegun,* by Henry Rowe Schoolcraft. Edited and with an introduction by Philip P. Mason. East Lansing: Michigan State University Press, 1962.

Shinn, Milicent Washburn. *The Biography of a Baby.* Boston: Houghton Mifflin, 1900.

———. "A Cycle." *Californian* 1 (June 1880): 543.

———. "Summer Cañons." *Overland Monthly,* 2d ser., 2 (August 1883): 205–10.

———. "Two Sonnets of Lost Love." *Overland Monthly,* 2d ser., 5 (February 1885): 199.

Stewart, Elinore Pruitt Rupert. *See* Rupert [Stewart], Elinore.

Strahorn, Carrie Adell. *Fifteen Thousand Miles by Stage: A Woman's Unique Experience during Thirty Years of Path Finding and Pioneering from the Missouri to the Pacific and from Alaska to Mexico.* 2d ed. New York: G. P. Putnam's Sons, Knickerbocker Press, 1915.

Summerhayes, Martha. *Vanished Arizona: Recollections of My Army Life.* Philadelphia: J. B. Lippincott, 1908.

Thorpe, Rose Hartwick. "Curfew Must Not Ring To-night." In *Rose Hartwick Thorpe and the Story of "Curfew Must Not Ring To-night,"* by George J. Wharton. Pasadena, Calif.: Radiant Life Press, 1916.

———. *The White Lady of La Jolla.* San Diego: Grandier, 1904.

Winnemucca, Sarah. "Letter from Sarah Winnemucca, an Educated Pah-Ute Woman." In *A Century of Dishonor: A Sketch of the United States Government's Dealings with Some of the Indian Tribes,* by Helen Hunt Jackson [H. H., pseud.], 395–96. New York: Harper and Brothers, Franklin Square, 1881.

———. "The Pah-Utes." *Californian* 6 (September 1882): 252–56.

REFERENCES AND SUGGESTIONS FOR FURTHER READING

Gertrude Franklin Horn Atherton

Before the Gringo Came: Being Eleven Stories of Old California. New York: J. Selwin Tait and Sons, 1894.

The Conqueror: Being the True and Romantic Story of Alexander Hamilton. New York: Macmillan, 1902.

The Splendid Idle Forties: Stories of Old California. New York: Macmillan, 1902.

Rezanov. New York: Authors and Newspapers Association, 1906.

California: An Intimate History. New York: Harper and Brothers, 1914.

The Immortal Marriage. New York: Boni and Liveright, 1927.

The Jealous Gods: A Processional Novel of the Fifth Century, B.C. (Concerning One Alcibiades). New York: H. Liveright, 1928.

Adventures of a Novelist. New York: Liveright, 1932.

Golden Gate Country. New York: Duell, Sloan, and Pearce, 1945.

My San Francisco: A Wayward Biography. Indianapolis: Bobbs–Merrill, 1946.
෴

Goetzmann, W. H., and Glyndwr Williams. *The Atlas of North American Exploration: From the Norse Voyages to the Race to the Pole.* New York: Prentice Hall, 1992.

Mainiero, Lina, ed. *American Women Writers: A Critical Reference Guide from Colonial Times to the Present.* Vol. 1. New York: Ungar, 1979.

Powell, Lawrence C. *California Classics—The Creative Literature of the Golden State: Essays on the Books and Their Writers.* Santa Barbara: Capra Press, 1982.

Weber, D. J. *The Spanish Frontier in North America.* New Haven: Yale University Press, 1992.

Mary Hunter Austin

The Land of Little Rain. Boston: Houghton Mifflin, 1903.

"Pahawitz–Na'an." *Out West* 18 (March 1903): 337–44.

The Basket Woman. Boston: Houghton Mifflin, 1904.

The Flock. Boston: Houghton Mifflin, 1906.

Lost Borders. New York: Harper and Brothers, 1909.

The Ford. Boston: Houghton Mifflin, 1917.

The Path on the Rainbow: An Anthology of Songs and Chants from the Indians of North America. Ed. George W. Cronyn. New York: Boni and Liveright, 1918.

The American Rhythm. New York: Harcourt, Brace, 1923.

The Land of Journeys' Ending. New York: Century, 1924.

Earth Horizon: An Autobiography. Boston: Houghton Mifflin, 1932.

Western Trails: A Collection of Short Stories by Mary Austin. Ed. Melody Graulich. Reno: University of Nevada Press, 1987.

"One Hundred Miles on Horseback." In *A Mary Austin Reader,* ed. Esther F. Lanigan. Tucson: University of Arizona Press, 1996.

∞

Fink, Augusta. *I–Mary: A Biography of Mary Austin.* Tucson: University of Arizona Press, 1983.

Jaycox, Faith. "Regeneration through Liberation: Mary Austin's 'The Walking Woman' and Western Narrative Formula." *Legacy* 6.1 (1989): 5–12.

Limerick, Patricia Nelson. "Believing in the American West." In *The West: An Illustrated History,* narrated by Geoffrey C. Ward, 207–13. Based on a documentary film script by Geoffrey C. Ward and Dayton Duncan; with contributions by Dayton Duncan et al. Boston: Little, Brown, 1996.

Pearce, T. M., ed. *Literary America, 1903–1934: The Mary Austin Letters.* Westport, Conn.: Greenwood Press, 1979.

Powell, Lawrence Clark. *Southwest Classics.* Tucson: University of Arizona Press, 1974.

Isabella Lucy Bird Bishop

The Englishwoman in America. 1856. Reprint, with a foreword and notes by Andrew Hill Clark, Madison: University of Wisconsin Press, 1966.

The Hawaiian Archipelago: Six Months among the Palm Groves, Coral Reefs, and Volcanoes of the Sandwich Islands. 1875. Reprint, as *Six Months in the Sandwich Islands,* Honolulu: University of Hawaii Press for Friends of the Library of Hawaii, 1964.

A Lady's Life in the Rocky Mountains. 1879–1880. Reprint, Norman: University of Oklahoma Press, 1960.

The Yangtze Valley and Beyond: An Account of Journeys in China, Chiefly in the

Province of Sze Chuan and among the Man–tze of the Somo Territory. 1899. Reprint, Boston: Beacon Press, 1987.

This Grand Beyond: The Travels of Isabella Bird Bishop. Ed. Cicely Palser Havely. London: Century, 1984.

❧

Barr, Pat. Introduction to *The Yangtze Valley and Beyond: An Account of Journeys in China, Chiefly in the Province of Sze Chuan and among the Man–tze of the Somo Territory,* by Isabella L. Bird. Boston: Beacon Press, 1987.

Boorstin, Daniel J. Introduction to *A Lady's Life in the Rocky Mountains,* by Isabella L. Bird. Norman: University of Oklahoma Press, 1960.

Gertrude Simmons Bonnin (Zitkala–Sa)

"Impressions of an Indian Childhood." *Atlantic Monthly* 85 (January 1900): 37–47.

"The School Days of an Indian Girl." *Atlantic Monthly* 85 (February 1900): 185–94.

"An Indian Teacher among Indians." *Atlantic Monthly* 85 (March 1900): 381–86.

Old Indian Legends. Boston: Ginn and Company, 1901.

"Why I Am a Pagan." *Atlantic Monthly* 90 (December 1902): 801–3.

American Indian Stories. Washington, D.C.: Hayworth Publishing House, 1921. Reprint, with a foreword by Dexter Fisher, Lincoln: University of Nebraska Press, Bison Books, 1985.

❧

Lauter, Paul, ed. *The Heath Anthology of American Literature.* Vol. 2. Lexington, Mass.: D. C. Heath, 1990.

Rappaport, Doreen. *The Flight of Red Bird: The Life of Zitkala–Sa.* New York: Dial Books, 1997.

Alice Cary and Phoebe Cary

Carey [Cary], Alice. *Clovernook; or, Recollections of Our Neighborhood in the West.* Clinton Hall, N.Y.: Redfield, 1852.

———. *Clovernook, Second Series.* Clinton Hall, N.Y.: Redfield, 1853.

———. *Clovernook Sketches and Other Stories.* Ed. Judith Fetterley. New Brunswick, N.J.: Rutgers University Press, 1987.

Cary, Alice, and Phoebe Cary. *Poems by Alice and Phoebe Cary*. Philadelphia: Moss and Brother, 1850.

———. *The Poetical Works of Alice and Phoebe Cary*. Household edition. Boston: Houghton Mifflin, 1882.

———. *The Poems of Alice and Phoebe Cary*. With an introduction and notes by Katharine Lee Bates. New York: Thomas Y. Crowell, 1903.

Cary, Phoebe. *Poems and Parodies*. Boston: Tickner, Reed, and Fields, 1854.
℘

Ames, Mary Clemmer. *A Memorial of Alice and Phoebe Cary, with Some of Their Later Poems*. New York: Hurd and Houghton; Cambridge: Riverside Press, 1873.

———. *Outlines of Men, Women, and Things*. New York: Hurd and Houghton; Cambridge: Riverside Press, 1873.

Croly, Mrs. *Sorosis: Its Origin and History*. New York: J. J. Little, 1886.

Fetterly, Judith. "Entitled to More than 'Peculiar Praise': The Extravagance of Alice Cary's *Clovernook*." Legacy 10 (1993): 103–19.

Gray, Janet, ed. *She Wields a Pen: American Women Poets of the Nineteenth Century*. Iowa City: University of Iowa Press, 1997.

Knight, Denise D., ed. *Nineteenth–Century American Women Writers: A Bio–bibliographical Critical Sourcebook*. Westport, Conn.: Greenwood Press, 1997.

Lauter, Paul, ed. *The Heath Anthology of American Literature*. Vol. 1. Lexington, Mass.: D. C. Heath, 1990.

Mainiero, Lina, ed. *American Women Writers: A Critical Reference Guide from Colonial Times to the Present*. Vol. 1. New York: Ungar, 1979.

Willa Sibert Cather

April Twilights, and Other Poems. Boston: Richard G. Badger, Gorham Press, 1903.

O Pioneers! New York: Houghton Mifflin, 1913.

The Song of the Lark. New York: Houghton Mifflin, 1915.

My Ántonia. New York: Houghton Mifflin, 1918.

One of Ours. New York: Alfred A. Knopf, 1922.

A Lost Lady. New York: Alfred A. Knopf, 1923.

Death Comes for the Archbishop. New York: Alfred A. Knopf, 1927.
℘

Gray, Dorothy. *Women of the West*. Millbrae, Calif.: Les Femmes, 1976.

Sergeant, Elizabeth Shepley. *Willa Cather: A Memoir.* Lincoln: University of Nebraska Press, 1963.

Sloate, Bernice, and Lucia Woods, eds. *Willa Cather: A Pictorial Memoir.* Lincoln: University of Nebraska Press, 1973.

Woodress, James. *Willa Cather: A Literary Life.* Lincoln: University of Nebraska Press, 1987.

Mary Hartwell Catherwood

Old Caravan Days. 1880. Reprint, Boston: D. Lothrop, 1884.

"The Old Colony House." *Lippincott's* 32 (December 1883): 578–95.

The Story of Tonty. Chicago: A. C. McClurg, 1890.

"The Spirit of an Illinois Town." *Atlantic Monthly* 78 (1896): 168–74, 338–47, 480–91.

Mackinac and Lake Stories. New York: Harper and Brothers, 1899.

Spanish Peggy: A Story of Young Illinois. Chicago: H. S. Stone, 1899.

Lazarre. Indianapolis: Bobbs–Merrill, 1901.

∞

Fairbanks, Carol. *Prairie Women: Images in American and Canadian Fiction.* New Haven: Yale University Press, 1986.

Mainiero, Lina, ed. *American Women Writers: A Critical Reference Guide from Colonial Times to the Present.* Vol. 1. New York: Ungar, 1979.

Willard, Frances Elizabeth, and Mary A. Livermore, eds. *A Woman of the Century: Fourteen Hundred Seventy Biographical Sketches Accompanied by Portraits of Leading American Women in All Walks of Life.* Buffalo: Charles Wells Moulton, 1893.

Louise Amelia Knapp Smith Clappe (Dame Shirley)

"The Equality of the Sexes." *Pioneer; or, California Monthly Magazine* 1 (February 1854): 85–88.

California in 1851–1852: The Letters of Dame Shirley. Ed. Carl I. Wheat. 2 vols. San Francisco: Grabhorn Press, 1933.

The Shirley Letters from the California Mines, 1851–1852. With an introduction and notes by Carl I. Wheat. New York: Alfred A. Knopf, 1949.

∞

Gray, Dorothy. *Women of the West.* Millbrae, Calif.: Les Femmes, 1976.

Knight, Denise D., ed. *Nineteenth–Century American Women Writers: A Bio–bibliographical Critical Sourcebook*. Westport, Conn.: Greenwood Press, 1997.

Lockhart, Sandra. "*Legacy* Profile: Louise Amelia Knapp Smith Clappe (Dame Shirley), 1819–1906." *Legacy* 8.2 (1991): 141–48.

Mainiero, Lina, ed. *American Women Writers: A Critical Reference Guide from Colonial Times to the Present*. Vol. 1. New York: Ungar, 1979: 369–70.

Powell, Lawrence Clark. *California Classics—The Creative Literature of the Golden State: Essays on the Books and Their Writers*. Santa Barbara: Capra Press, 1971.

Ina Donna Coolbrith (Josephine Donna Smith)

A Perfect Day, and Other Poems. San Francisco: John H. Carmany, 1881.

The Singer of the Sea. San Francisco: Century Club of California, 1894.

Songs from the Golden Gate. Boston: Houghton Mifflin, 1895.

Wings of Sunset. Boston: Houghton Mifflin, 1929.

∞

Atherton, Gertrude, et al. *The Spinners' Book of Fiction*. 1907. Reprint, with an introduction by Priscilla Oaks, Boston: Gregg Press, 1979.

Knight, Denise D. *Nineteenth–Century American Women Writers: A Bio–bibliographical Critical Sourcebook*. Westport, Conn: Greenwood Press, 1997.

Rhodehamel, Josephine D., and R. F. Wood. *Ina Coolbrith: Librarian and Laureate of California*. Provo: Brigham Young University Press, 1973.

Walker, Cheryl. "Ina Coolbrith and the Nightingale Tradition." *Legacy* 6.1 (1989): 27–33.

Alice Corbin Henderson

Linnet Songs. Chicago: Wind–Tryst Press, 1898.

The Spinning Woman of the Sky. Chicago: Ralph Fletcher Seymour, 1912.

Red Earth: Poems of New Mexico. Chicago: Ralph Fletcher Seymour, 1921.

The Sun Turns West. Santa Fe: Writers' Editions, 1933.

———, ed. *The Turquoise Trail: An Anthology of New Mexico Poetry*. Boston: Houghton Mifflin; Cambridge: Riverside Press, 1928.

Corbin [Henderson], Alice, and Harriet Monroe, eds. *The New Poetry: An Anthology*. New York: Macmillan, 1932.

∞

Cahill, Daniel J. *Harriet Monroe*. New York: Twayne, 1973.

Monroe, Harriet. *A Poet's Life: Seventy Years in a Changing World.* New York: Macmillan, 1938.

Pearce, T. M. *Alice Corbin Henderson.* Southwest Writers Series, no. 21. Austin: Steck–Vaughn, 1969.

Natalie Curtis Burlin

"An American–Indian Composer." *Harper's Monthly* 107 (September 1903): 626–32.

Songs of Ancient America. New York: G. Schirmer, 1905.

"The Song of the Indian Mother: By Natalie Curtis, compiler of *'The Indians' Book.'*" *Craftsman* 15.1 (October 1908): 57–63.

"Mr. Roosevelt and Indian Music." *Outlook* 121 (5 March 1919): 399–400.

"An American Indian Artist." *Outlook* 124 (14 January 1920): 64–66.

"A Western Reverie." *Nation* 3 (24 November 1920): 591–92.

"Pueblo Poetry." *El Palacio* 12.7 (1 April 1922): 95–99.

——, ed. *The Indians' Book: An Offering by the American Indians of Indian Lore, Musical and Narrative, to Form a Record of the Songs and Legends of Their Race.* New York: Harper and Brothers, 1907.

∝

Babcock, Barbara A., and Nancy J. Parezo, eds. *Daughters of the Desert: Women Anthropologists in the Southwest, 1880–1980.* Tucson: Arizona State Museum, University of Arizona, 1986.

"Natalie Curtis Burlin." *Outlook* 129 (23 November 1921): 458–59.

Sandler, Irving. *Paul Burlin.* New York: American Federation of Arts, 1962.

Elizabeth Clift Bacon Custer

"Boots and Saddles"; or, Life in Dakota with General Custer. 1885. Reprint, with an introduction by Jane R. Stewart, Norman: University of Oklahoma Press, 1961.

Tenting on the Plains; or, General Custer in Kansas and Texas. 1887. Reprint, with an introduction by Jane R. Stewart, Norman: University of Oklahoma Press, 1971.

Following the Guidon. New York: Harper and Brothers, 1890.

"The Kid." *St. Nicholas* 27 (September 1900): 964–79.

∝

Mainiero, Lina, ed. *American Women Writers: A Critical Reference Guide from Colonial Times to the Present.* Vol. 1. New York: Ungar, 1979.

Randall, Ruth Painter. *I Elizabeth: A Biography of the Girl Who Married General George Armstrong Custer of "Custer's Last Stand."* Boston: Little, Brown, 1966.

Elaine Goodale Eastman

"Ashes of Roses." *St. Nicholas* 5 (December 1877): 110.

"The Wood–Chopper to His Ax." *Overland Monthly*, 2d ser., 2 (September 1883): 275.

Indian Legends Retold. Boston: Little, Brown, 1919.

Pratt: The Red Man's Moses. Norman: University of Oklahoma Press, 1935.

Sister to the Sioux: The Memoirs of Elaine Goodale Eastman, 1885–1891. Ed. Kay Graber. Lincoln: University of Nebraska Press, 1978.

℘

Eastman, Charles A. (*Ohiyesa*), and Elaine Goodale Eastman. *Wigwam Evenings: Sioux Folk Tales Retold.* 1909. Reprint, with an introduction by Michael Dorris and Louise Erdich, Lincoln: University of Nebraska Press, 1990.

Mainiero, Lina, ed. *American Women Writers: A Critical Reference Guide from Colonial Times to the Present.* Vol. 1. New York: Ungar, 1979.

Edith Maude Eaton (Sui Sin Far)

"Leaves from the Mental Portfolio of an Eurasian." *Independent* 66.3138 (21 January 1909): 125–32.

Mrs. Spring Fragrance. Chicago: A. C. McClurg, 1912.

"The Wisdom of the New." *Legacy* 6.1 (1989): 34–49.

Mrs. Spring Fragrance and Other Writings. Ed. Amy Ling and Annette White–Parks. Urbana: University of Illinois Press, 1995.

℘

Green, Carol Hurd, and Mary Grimley Mason, eds. *American Women Writers: A Critical Reference Guide from Colonial Times to the Present.* Vol. 5. New York: Ungar, 1979.

Alice Cunningham Fletcher

"Sun Dance of the Oglalla Sioux." *Proceedings of the American Association for the Advancement of Science* 30 (1883): 580–84.

Historical Sketch of the Omaha Tribe of Indians in Nebraska. Washington, D.C.: Bureau of Indian Affairs, 1885.

"Personal Studies of Indian Life: Politics and Pipe–dancing." *Century* 45 (January 1893): 441–55.

"Personal Studies of Indian Life: Tribal Life among the Omahas." *Century* 51 (January 1896): 450–61.

Indian Story and Song from North America. Boston: Small, Maynard, 1900.

Indian Games and Dances with Native Songs: Arranged from American Indian Ceremonials and Sports. 1915. Reprint, New York: AMS Press, 1970.

Fletcher, Alice Cunningham, and Francis La Flesche, a Member of the Omaha Tribe. *The Omaha Tribe.* Smithsonian Institution, Bureau of American Ethnology, Twenty–seventh Annual Report, 1905–1906. Washington, D.C., 1911.

&

Croly, Mrs. *Sorosis: Its Origin and History.* New York: J. J. Little, 1886.

Gay, E. Jane. *With the Nez Perces: Alice Fletcher in the Field, 1889–1892.* Ed. Frederick E. Hoxie and Joan T. Mark. Lincoln: University of Nebraska Press, 1981.

Jackson, Helen Hunt. *A Century of Dishonor: A Sketch of the United States Government's Dealings with Some of the Indian Tribes.* New York: Harper and Brothers, 1881.

Mark, Joan T. *A Stranger in Her Native Land: Alice Fletcher and the American Indians.* Lincoln: University of Nebraska Press, 1988.

Nabokov, Peter, ed. *Native American Testimony: A Chronicle of Indian–White Relations from Prophecy to the Present, 1492–1992.* New York: Viking, 1991.

Tibbles, Thomas Henry. *Buckskin and Blanket Days: Memoirs of a Friend of the Indians, 1905.* Garden City, N.Y.: Doubleday, 1957.

Ward, Geoffrey C., narrator. *The West: An Illustrated History.* Based on a documentary film script by Geoffrey C. Ward and Dayton Duncan; with contributions by Dayton Duncan et al. Boston: Little, Brown, 1996.

Mary Hallock Foote

"The Picture in the Fire–Place Bedroom." *St. Nicholas* 2 (February 1875): 248–50.

"A California Mining Camp." *Scribner's Monthly* 15.4 (February 1878): 480–93.

The Led–Horse Claim: A Romance of a Mining Camp. Boston: James R. Osgood, 1883.

John Bodewin's Testimony. Boston: Ticknor, 1886.

The Last Assembly Ball: A Pseudo Romance of the Far West. Boston: Houghton Mifflin, 1889.

"Pictures of the Far West." Parts 1–10. *Century* 37.1 (November 1888): 108–9; 2 (December 1888): 162–63; 3 (January 1889): 448–49; 4 (February 1889): 500–501; 5 (March 1889): 686–87; 38.1 (May 1889): 2–4; 2 (June 1889): 298–300; 3 (July 1889): 341–43; 4 (August 1889): 501–3; 5 (October 1889): 872–74.

"How the Pump Stopped at the Morning Watch." *Century,* n.s., 36 (June 1899): 469–72.

The Little Fig–Tree Stories. Boston: Houghton Mifflin, 1899.

A Victorian Gentlewoman in the Far West: The Reminiscences of Mary Hallock Foote. Ed. Rodman W. Paul. San Marino, Calif.: Huntington Library, 1972.

∞

Johnson, Lee Ann. *Mary Hallock Foote.* Boston: Twayne, 1980.

Maguire, James H. *Mary Hallock Foote.* Western Writers Series, no. 2. Boise, Idaho: Boise State College, 1972.

Mainiero, Lina, ed. *American Women Writers: A Critical Reference Guide from Colonial Times to the Present.* Vol. 2. New York: Ungar, 1979.

Stegner, Wallace. *Angle of Repose.* Garden City, N.Y.: Doubleday, 1971.

Jessie Ann Benton Frémont

The Story of the Guard: A Chronicle of the War. Boston: Ticknor and Fields, 1863.

A Year of American Travel. New York: Harper and Brothers, 1878.

Souvenirs of My Time. Boston: D. Lothrop, 1887.

Far West Sketches. Boston: D. Lothrop, 1890.

"The Origin of the Frémont Explorations." *Century,* n.s., 19 (March 1891): 766–71.

The Will and the Way Stories. Boston: D. Lothrop, 1891.

Mother Lode Narratives. Ed. Shirley Sargent. Ashland, Oreg.: Lewis Osborne, 1970.

∞

Frémont, John Charles [and Jessie Benton Frémont]. *Memoirs of My Life.* Vol. 1. Chicago: Belford, Clarke, 1887.

Herr, Pamela. *Jessie Benton Frémont.* New York: Franklin Watts, 1987.

Nevins, Allan. *Frémont, Pathmarker of the West.* 1939. Reprint, New York: Longman, Green, 1955.

———. *Frémont, the West's Greatest Adventurer; Being a Biography from Certain Hitherto Unpublished Sources of General John C. Frémont, Together with His Wife, Jessie Benton Frémont, and Some Account of the Period of Expansion which Found a Brilliant Leader in the Pathfinder*. New York: Harper and Brothers, 1928.

Sarah Margaret Fuller Ossoli

Summer on the Lakes, in 1843. Boston: Charles C. Little and James Brown; New York: Charles S. Francis, 1844.

Woman in the Nineteenth Century. New York: Greeley and McElrath, 1845.

The Essential Margaret Fuller. Ed. Jeffrey Steele. New Brunswick, N.J.: Rutgers University Press, 1992.

The Portable Margaret Fuller. Ed. Mary Kelley. New York: Penguin Books, 1994.

ॐ

Chevigny, Bell Gale. *The Woman and the Myth: Margaret Fuller's Life and Writings*. Old Westbury, N.Y.: Feminist Press, 1976.

Knight, Denise D., ed. *Nineteenth–Century American Women Writers: A Bio–bibliographical Critical Sourcebook*. Westport, Conn.: Greenwood Press, 1997.

Lauter, Paul, ed. *The Heath Anthology of American Literature*. Vol. 1. Lexington, Mass.: D. C. Heath, 1990.

Tokovich, Nicole. "Traveling in the West, Writing in the Library: Margaret Fuller's *Summer on the Lakes*." *Legacy* 10.2 (1993): 79–102.

Frances Dana Barker Gage

Elsie Magoon; or, The Old Still–House in the Hollow: A Tale of the Past. Philadelphia: J. B. Lippincott, 1867.

ॐ

Logan, Shirley W., ed. *Pen and Voice: A Critical Anthology of Nineteenth–Century African–American Women*. Carbondale: Southern Illinois University Press, 1995.

Mainiero, Lina, ed. *American Women Writers: A Critical Reference Guide from Colonial Times to the Present*. Vol. 2. New York: Ungar, 1979.

Painter, Nell I. *Sojourner Truth: A Life, a Symbol*. New York: W. W. Norton, 1996.

Stanton, Elizabeth Cady, et al. *History of Woman Suffrage, 1848–1861.* Vol. 1. 1881. Reprint, New York: Arno Press, 1969.

Charlotte Anna Perkins Stetson Gilman

Stetson, Charlotte Perkins. "The Yellow Wallpaper." *New England Magazine* 5 (January 1892): 647–56.

———. *In This Our World.* Oakland, Calif.: McCombs and Vaughn, 1893.

———. *Women and Economics: A Study of the Economic Relation between Men and Women as a Factor in Social Evolution.* 1898. Reprint, with an introduction by Carl N. Degler, New York: Harper and Row, 1966.

Gilman, Charlotte Perkins. *The Home: Its Work and Influence.* New York: McClure, Phillips, 1903.

———. *Human Work.* New York: McClure, Phillips, 1904.

———. *Forerunner.* Vols. 1–7. Reprint, with an introduction by Ann J. Lane, New York: Pantheon, 1979.

———. *The Living of Charlotte Perkins Gilman: An Autobiography.* Foreword by Zona Gale. New York: D. Appleton–Century, 1935. Reprint, with an introduction by Ann J. Lane, Madison: University of Wisconsin Press, 1990.

———. *The Charlotte Perkins Gilman Reader.* Ed. Ann J. Lane. New York: Pantheon, 1980.

———. *The Diaries of Charlotte Perkins Gilman.* 2 vols. Ed. Denise D. Knight. Charlottesville: University Press of Virginia, 1994.

———. *The Later Poetry of Charlotte Perkins Gilman.* Ed. Denise D. Knight. Newark: University of Delaware Press; London: Associated University Presses, 1996.

Sharlot Mabridth Hall

"Out West." *Out West* 16.1 (January 1902): 3–5.

"The Fruit of the Yucca Tree." *Out West* 23 (December 1905): 569–75.

"Arizona." *Out West* 24.2 (February 1906): 67–69.

"His Place." *Out West* 28.2 (February 1908): 113.

Cactus and Pine: Songs of the Southwest. Boston: Sherman, French, 1911.

Poems of a Ranch Woman. Comp. Josephine Mackenzie. Prescott, Ariz.: Sharlot Hall Historical Society, 1989.

Sharlot Hall on the Arizona Strip: A Diary of a Journey through Northern

Arizona in 1911. Ed. C. Gregory Crampton. Flagstaff, Ariz.: Northland Press, 1975.

℘

Drumm, Stella M., ed. *Down the Santa Fe Trail and into Mexico: The Diary of Susan Shelby Magoffin, 1846–1847.* 1926. Reprint, with a foreword by Howard R. Lamar, Lincoln: University of Nebraska Press, 1982.

Maxwell, Margaret F. *A Passion for Freedom: The Life of Sharlot Hall.* Tucson: University of Arizona Press, 1982.

Wright, Nancy Kirkpatrick, ed. *Sharlot Herself: Selected Writings of Sharlot Hall.* Prescott, Ariz.: Sharlot Hall Museum Press, 1992.

Helen Maria Fiske Hunt Jackson

Verses by H. H. Boston: Fields, Osgood, 1870.

Poems by Helen Jackson. 1873. Boston: Little, Brown, 1908.

Bits of Travel at Home. Boston: Roberts Brothers, 1878.

A Century of Dishonor: A Sketch of the United States Government's Dealings with Some of the Indian Tribes. New York: Harper and Brothers, 1881.

"Echoes in the City of Angels." *Century,* n.s., 5 (May–June 1883): 194–210.

"Father Junipero and His Work: A Sketch of the Foundation, Prosperity, and Ruin of the Franciscan Missions in California." *Century* 26.1 (May 1883): 3–18; 2 (June 1883): 199–215.

"Outdoor Industries in Southern California." *Century* 26.6 (October 1883): 803–20.

Ramona: A Story. Boston: Roberts Brothers, 1886.

Glimpses of California and the Missions. Boston: Little, Brown, 1902.

Westward to a High Mountain: The Colorado Writings of Helen Hunt Jackson. Ed. Mark I. West. Denver: Colorado Historical Society, 1994.

H. H. [Helen Hunt Jackson], and Abbot Kinney. *Report of Mrs. Helen Hunt Jackson and Abbot Kinney on the Conditions and Needs of Mission Indians in 1883.* Washington, D.C.: Government Printing Office, 1883.

℘

Banning, Evelyn I. *Helen Hunt Jackson.* New York: Vanguard Press, 1973.

Dorris, Michael. Introduction to *Ramona,* by Helen Jackson. New York: NAL Penguin, Signet Classic, 1988.

Knight, Denise D., ed. *Nineteenth-Century American Women Writers: A Bio-bibliographical Critical Sourcebook.* Westport, Conn.: Greenwood Press, 1997.

Mainiero, Lina, ed. *American Women Writers: A Critical Reference Guide from Colonial Times to the Present.* Vol. 2. New York: Ungar, 1979.

"Mrs. Helen Jackson (H. H.)." *Century* 31.2 (December 1885): 251–59.

Odell, Ruth. *Helen Hunt Jackson.* New York: D. Appleton–Century, 1939.

Orzeck, Martin, and Robert Weisbuch, eds. *Dickinson and Audience.* Ann Arbor: University of Michigan Press, 1996.

Powell, Lawrence Clark. *California Classics—The Creative Literature of the Golden State: Essays on the Books and Their Writers.* Santa Barbara: Capra Press, 1971.

Vroman, A. C. "The Story of Ramona." *Out West,* n.s., 7 (1914): 17–25.

Whitaker, Rosemary. *Helen Hunt Jackson.* Western Writers Series, no. 78. Boise, Idaho: Boise State University Printing and Graphics Services, 1987.

———. "*Legacy* Profile: Helen Hunt Jackson, 1830–1885." *Legacy* 3.1 (1986): 56–62.

Caroline Matilda Stansbury Kirkland

A New Home, Who'll Follow?; or, Glimpses of Western Life. New York: C. S. Francis; Boston: J. H. Francis, 1839.

Forest Life, by the Author of A New Home. 2 vols. New York: C. S. Francis, 1842.

Western Clearings. 2 vols. New York: Wiley and Putnam, 1845.

℘

Fairbanks, Carol. *Prairie Women: Images in American and Canadian Fiction.* New Haven: Yale University Press, 1986.

Knight, Denise D., ed. *Nineteenth-Century American Women Writers: A Bio-bibliographical Critical Sourcebook.* Westport, Conn.: Greenwood Press, 1997.

Lauter, Paul, ed. *The Heath Anthology of American Literature.* Vol. 1. Lexington, Mass.: D. C. Heath, 1990.

Mainiero, Lina, ed. *American Women Writers: A Critical Reference Guide from Colonial Times to the Present.* Vol. 2. New York: Ungar, 1979.

Spencer, Stacy L. "*Legacy* Profile: Caroline Kirkland, 1801–1864." *Legacy* 8.2 (1991): 133–40.

Western Literature Association. *A Literary History of the American West.* Fort Worth: Texas Christian University Press, 1987.

Zagarell, Sandra A. Introduction to *A New Home, Who'll Follow?; or, Glimpses of Western Life,* by Mrs. Mary A. Clavers, an Actual Settler [Caroline Kirkland]. New Brunswick, N.J.: Rutgers University Press, 1990.

Susette La Flesche (Bright Eyes)

"Nedawi." *St. Nicholas* 8 (January 1881): 225–30.

☙

Giffen, Fannie Reed. *Oo–Ma–Ha Ta–Wa–tha*. Lincoln: privately printed, 1898.

Green, Norma Kidd. *Iron Eye's Family: The Children of Joseph La Flesche*. Lincoln, Nebr.: Johnsen Publishing, 1969.

Mark, Joan T. *A Stranger in Her Native Land: Alice Fletcher and the American Indians*. Lincoln: University of Nebraska Press, 1988.

Nabokov, Peter, ed. *Native American Testimony: A Chronicle of Indian–White Relations from Prophecy to the Present, 1492–1992*. New York: Viking, 1991.

Tibbles, Thomas Henry. *Buckskin and Blanket Days: Memoirs of a Friend of the Indians*. 1905. Reprint, Garden City, N.Y.: Doubleday, 1957.

——. *Ploughed Under: The Story of an Indian Chief*. New York: Fords, Howard, and Hurlbert, 1881.

Who Was Who in America: Historical Volume, 1607–1896. Chicago: A. N. Marquis, 1963.

Mary Ann Adams Maverick

Memoirs of Mary A. Maverick: San Antonio's First American Woman. Ed. Rena Maverick Green. 1921. Reprint, with an introduction by Sandra L. Myres, Lincoln: University of Nebraska Press, 1989.

☙

Crawford, Ann Fears, and Crystal Sasse Ragsdale. *Women in Texas: Their Lives, Their Experiences, Their Accomplishments*. Austin: State House Press, 1992.

María Amparo Ruiz de Burton

Who Would Have Thought It? 1872. Reprint, ed. Rosaura Sánchez and Beatrice Pita, Houston: Arte Público Press, 1995.

[C. Loyal.] *The Squatter and the Don: A Novel Descriptive of Contemporary Occurrences in California*. San Francisco: [S. Carson], 1885.

The Squatter and the Don. Ed. Rosaura Sánchez and Beatrice Pita. Houston: Arte Público Press, 1995.

☙

Dana, Richard Henry. *Two Years before the Mast: A Personal Narrative of Life at Sea*. New York: Harper, 1840.

Elinore Pruitt Rupert Stewart

"Letters of a Woman Homesteader." Parts 1–6. *Atlantic Monthly* 112 (October 1913) 433–43; (November 1913): 589–98; (December 1913): 820–30; 113 (January 1914): 17–26; (February 1914): 170–77; (April 1914): 525–32.

Letters of a Woman Homesteader. Foreword by Jessamyn West. Boston: Houghton Mifflin, 1914.

"Letters on an Elk Hunt." Parts 1–5. *Atlantic Monthly* 115 (February 1915): 152–60; (March 1915): 316–22; (April 1915): 481–87; (May 1915): 620–27; (June 1915): 768–76.

Letters on an Elk Hunt by a Woman Homesteader. 1915. Reprint, with a foreword by Elizabeth Fuller Ferris, Lincoln: University of Nebraska Press, 1979.
℞

Mainiero, Lina, ed. *American Women Writers: A Critical Reference Guide from Colonial Times to the Present.* Vol. 4. New York: Ungar, 1979.

Jane Johnston Schoolcraft (Bame–wa–wa–ge–zhik–a–quay)

Lauter, Paul. *The Heath Anthology of American Literature.* Vol. 1. Lexington, Mass.: D. C. Heath, 1990.

Schoolcraft, Henry Rowe. *Algic Researches, Comprising Inquiries Respecting the Mental Characteristics of the North American Indians.* Vol. 1. New York: Harper and Brothers, 1839.

———. *The Literary Voyager; or, Muzzeniegun.* Ed. Philip P. Mason. East Lansing: Michigan State University Press, 1962.

Milicent Washburn Shinn

Shinn, Milicent Washburn. "A Cycle." *Californian* 1 (June 1880): 543.

———. "Summer Cañons." *Overland Monthly,* 2d ser., 2 (August 1883): 205–11.

———. "Two Sonnets of Lost Love." *Overland Monthly,* 2d ser., 5 (February 1885): 199.

———. *Notes on the Development of a Child.* 1893–1899. Reprint, New York: Johnson Reprint Corporation, 1966.

———. *The Biography of a Baby.* Boston: York: Houghton Mifflin, 1900.

———. *Notes on the Development of a Child.* Vol. 2, *The Development of the Senses in the First Three Years of Childhood.* Berkeley: University of California Publications in Education 4, 1907.

❧

Nevins, Allan. *The Emergence of Lincoln: Douglas, Buchanan, and Party Chaos, 1857–1859*. Vol. 1. New York: Charles Scribner's Sons, 1950.

Carrie Adell Green Strahorn

Fifteen Thousand Miles by Stage: A Woman's Unique Experience during Thirty Years of Path Finding and Pioneering from the Missouri to the Pacific and from Alaska to Mexico. 1911. Reprint, with an introduction by Judith Austin, Lincoln: University of Nebraska Press, Bison Books, 1988.
❧

Edgerly, Lois Stiles, ed. *Women's Words, Women's Stories*. Gardiner, Maine: Tilbury House, 1994.

Martha Dunham Summerhayes

Vanished Arizona: Recollections of My Army. Philadelphia: Lippincott, 1908.
Vanished Arizona: Recollections of the Army Life of a New England Woman. 1911. Lincoln: University of Nebraska Press, Bison Books, 1979.
❧

Ball, Eve. *Indeh: An Apache Odyssey*. Norman: University of Oklahoma Press, 1988.
Cremony, John C. *Life among the Apache*. New York: Indian Head Books, 1991.
Lavender, David. *The Southwest*. Albuquerque: University of New Mexico Press, 1980.
Powell, Lawrence Clark. *Southwest Classics—The Creative Literature of the Arid Lands: Essays on the Books and Their Writers*. Tucson: University of Arizona Press, 1974.
Worcester, Donald E. *The Apaches: Eagles of the Southwest*. Norman: University of Oklahoma Press, 1979.

Rose Hartwick Thorpe

Ringing Ballads. Boston: D. Lothrop, 1887.
The White Lady of La Jolla. San Diego: Grandier, 1904.
The Poetical Works of Rose Hartwick Thorpe. New York: Neale Publishing, 1912.

❦

Gray, Janet, ed. *She Wields a Pen: American Women Poets of the Nineteenth Century.* Iowa City: University of Iowa Press, 1997.

James, George Wharton. *Rose Hartwick Thorpe and the Story of "Curfew Must Not Ring To–night."* Pasadena, Calif.: Radiant Life Press, 1916.

Willard, Frances E., and Mary A. Livermore, eds. *A Woman of the Century: Fourteen Hundred Seventy Biographical Sketches Accompanied by Portraits of Leading American Women in All Walks of Life.* Buffalo: Charles Wells Moulton, 1893.

Sarah Winnemucca Hopkins (So–mit–tone; Thocmetony)

"Letter from Sarah Winnemucca, an Educated Pah–Ute." In *A Century of Dishonor: A Sketch of the United States Government's Dealings with Some of the Indian Tribes,* comp. by H. H. [Helen Hunt Jackson]. New York: Harper and Brothers, 1881.

"The Pah–Utes." *Californian* 6 (September 1882): 252–56.

Life among the Piutes: Their Wrongs and Claims. Ed. Mary Mann. 1883. Reprint, Bishop, Calif.: Chalfant Press, 1969.

❦

Canfield, Gae Whitney. *Sarah Winnemucca of the Northern Paiutes.* Norman: University of Oklahoma Press, 1983.

Gray, Dorothy. *Women of the West.* Millbrae, Calif.: Les Femmes, 1976.

Knight, Denise D., ed. *Nineteenth–Century American Women Writers: A Bio–bibliographical Critical Sourcebook.* Westport, Conn.: Greenwood Press, 1997.

Mainiero, Lina, ed. *American Women Writers: A Critical Reference Guide from Colonial Times to the Present.* Vol. 2. New York: Ungar, 1979.

GENERAL SOURCES

Armitage, Susan H., and Elizabeth Jameson. *The Women's West.* Norman: University of Oklahoma Press, 1987.

———. *Writing the Range: Race, Class, and Culture in the Women's West.* Norman: University of Oklahoma Press, 1997.

Ball, Eve. *Indeh: An Apache Odyssey.* Norman: University of Oklahoma Press, 1988.

Beck, Warren A., and Ynez D. Haase. *Historical Atlas of the American West.* Norman: University of Oklahoma Press, 1989.

Carnes, Mark C., John A. Garraty, and Patrick Williams. *Mapping America's Past: A Historical Atlas.* New York: Henry Holt, 1996.

Cremony, John C. *Life among the Apache.* New York: Indian Head Books, 1991.

Egli, Ida Rae. *No Rooms of Their Own: Women Writers of Early California, 1849-1869.* Berkeley: Heyday Books, in cooperation with Rick Heide, 1997.

Fairbanks, Carol. *Prairie Women: Images in American and Canadian Fiction.* New Haven: Yale University Press, 1986.

Ferrell, Robert H., and Richard Natkiel. *Atlas of American History.* New York: Facts on File, 1993.

Goetzmann, W. H., and Glyndwr Williams. *The Atlas of North American Exploration: From the Norse Voyages to the Race to the Pole.* New York: Prentice Hall, 1992.

Gray, Janet. *She Wields a Pen: American Women Poets of the Nineteenth Century.* Iowa City: University of Iowa Press, 1997.

Hurt, R. Douglas. *The Ohio Frontier: Crucible of the Old Northwest, 1720-1830.* Bloomington: Indiana University Press, 1996.

Johnson, Paul. *A History of the American People.* New York: HarperCollins, 1997.

Knight, Denise D., ed. *Nineteenth-Century American Women Writers: A Bio-bibliographical Critical Sourcebook.* Westport, Conn.: Greenwood Press, 1997.

Lamar, Howard R., ed. The New Encyclopedia of the American West. New Haven: Yale University Press, 1998.

Lauter, Paul, ed. *The Heath Anthology of American Literature.* 2 vols. Lexington, Mass.: D. C. Heath, 1990.

Lavender, David. *The Great West.* New York: American Heritage Press, 1985.

———. *The Southwest.* Albuquerque: University of New Mexico Press, 1980.

Mainiero, Lina, ed. *American Women Writers: A Critical Reference Guide from Colonial Times to the Present.* Vol. 5. New York: Ungar, 1979.

Milner, Clyde A. II, Carol A. O'Connor, and Martha A. Sandweiss, eds. *The Oxford History of the American West.* New York: Oxford University Press, 1994.

Morgan, Ted. *A Shovel of Stars: The Making of the American West, 1800 to the Present.* New York: Simon and Schuster, 1995.

Morison, Samuel E. *The Oxford History of the American People.* New York: Oxford University Press, 1965.

Morris, Richard B., ed. *Encyclopedia of American History.* Bicentennial ed. New York: Harper and Row, 1953.

Moynihan, Ruth Barnes, Cynthia Russett, and Laurie Crumpacker, eds. *Second to None: A Documentary History of American Women.* Vol. 1, *From the Sixteenth Century to 1865.* Lincoln: University of Nebraska Press, 1993.

Nabokov, Peter, ed. *Native American Testimony: A Chronicle of Indian-White Relations from Prophecy to the Present, 1492-1992.* New York: Viking, 1991.

National Geographic Society. *Historical Atlas of the United States.* Washington, D.C.: National Geographic Society, 1988.

Patterson-Black, Sheryll, and Gene Patterson-Black. *Western Women in History and Literature.* Crawford, Nebr.: Cottonwood Press, 1978.

Powell, Lawrence C. *California Classics—The Creative Literature of the Golden State: Essays on the Books and Their Writers.* 1971. Reprint, Santa Barbara: Capra Press, 1982.

————. *Southwest Classics—The Creative Literature of the Arid Lands: Essays on the Books and Their Writers.* Tucson: University of Arizona Press, 1974.

Ruoff, A. LaVonne Brown. *Literatures of the American Indian.* New York: Chelsea House Publishers, 1991.

Showalter, Elaine. *Scribbling Women: Short Stories by Nineteenth-Century American Women.* London: Dent, 1997.

Stanton, Elizabeth Cady, Susan B. Anthony, and Matilda Joslyn Gage, eds. *History of Woman Suffrage.* 6 vols. 1881–1922. Reprint, New York: Arno Press, 1969.

Unruh, John D., Jr. *The Plains Across: The Overland Emigrants and the Trans-Mississippi West, 1840-1860.* Urbana: University of Illinois Press, 1993.

Waldman, Carl. *Atlas of the North American Indian.* Maps and illustrations by Molly Braun. New York: Facts on File, 1985.

Ward, Geoffrey C., narrator. *The West: An Illustrated History.* Based on a documentary film script by Geoffrey C. Ward and Dayton Duncan; with contributions by Dayton Duncan et al. Boston: Little, Brown, 1996.

Weber, David J. *The Spanish Frontier in North America.* New Haven: Yale University Press, 1992.

Western Literature Association. *A Literary History of the American West.* Fort Worth: Texas Christian University Press, 1987.

Western Writers of America. *The Women Who Made the West.* Garden City, N.Y.: Doubleday, 1980.

Wexler, Alan. *Atlas of Westward Expansion.* With maps and drawings by Molly Braun. New York: Facts on File, 1995.

White, Richard. *"It's Your Misfortune and None of My Own": A New History of the American West.* Norman: University of Oklahoma Press, 1991.

Who Was Who in America: A Companion Volume to "Who's Who in America." Chicago: A. N. Marquis, 1943.

Who Was Who in America: Historical Volume, 1607-1896. Chicago: A. N. Marquis, 1963.

Willard, Frances Elizabeth, and Mary A. Livermore, eds. *A Woman of the Century: Fourteen Hundred Seventy Biographical Sketches Accompanied by Portraits of Leading American Women in All Walks of Life.* Buffalo, N.Y.: Charles Wells Moulton, 1893.

Worcester, Donald E. *The Apaches: Eagles of the Southwest.* Norman: University of Oklahoma Press, 1979.

INDEX

ABOUT THE EDITOR

Susan Cummins Miller was born and raised in southern California. She received degrees in history, anthropology, and geology from the University of California, Riverside. After working as a field geologist with the U.S. Geological Survey and teaching at the College of San Mateo, California, she turned to writing full-time. She lives with her husband and two sons in Tucson, Arizona.